After Writing Culture

S. H ' (P.

D0265825

Who, what and how do we represent? These are pressing questions for those anthropologists who are now openly acknowledging that social anthropology can no longer fulfil its traditional aim of providing holistic, objective representations of the lives of members of 'exotic', other cultures. In *After Writing Culture* the contributors to this volume ask, therefore, what theoretical and practical role contemporary anthropology can play in an increasingly unpredictable and complex world.

Following the upheaval wrought by postmodernist theories, exemplified in social anthropology's 'writing culture' debate, *After Writing Culture* uses a series of ethnographic examples to show how anthropologists have been prompted to re-examine every aspect of the ways in which they now make representations: from the early stages of fieldwork through to the consumption of both their academic texts and their professional advice as consultants. What the individual chapters reveal is the new potential which anthropology is discovering and the ways in which this might be developed.

For those social scientists, both academics and practitioners, who might fear that postmodernism has eroded the objective foundations of their decision-making and practice, *After Writing Culture* details its creative potential. For example, the re-visioning of academic writing as conversation; the practical value of the 'good enough' model; the production of ethnography via flexibility and responsiveness in the field. In contrast with a traditional anthropology which provided a Western audience with objective information about the exotic 'Other', this book reveals a discipline in dialogue. Here both writer and reader can engage with fields as diverse as Japanese theme parks, UK dream workshops, gardens of Capability Brown and new settlers in Israel. The anthropological representations which go to make up this volume demonstrate not only the diversity of situated knowledge and social identities, but also the commonality which is the ability of human beings to enter into and engage with one another's social realities.

Allison James is Senior Lecturer in Applied Anthropology, **Jenny Hockey** is Lecturer in Social Policy and **Andrew Dawson** is Lecturer in Social Anthropology, all at the University of Hull.

SOAS

18 0575435 1

ASA Monographs 34

After Writing Culture

Epistemology and Praxis in Contemporary Anthropology

Edited by
Allison James, Jenny Hockey and
Andrew Dawson

London and New York

First published 1997
by Routledge
11 New Fetter Lane, London EC4P 4EE

Simultaneously published in the USA and Canada
by Routledge
29 West 35th Street, New York, NY 10001

© 1997 Association of Social Anthropologists, the collection as a whole; individual
chapters, the contributors.

Typeset in Times by Intype London Ltd

Printed and bound in Great Britain by Redwood Books, Trowbridge, Wiltshire

All rights reserved. No part of this book may be reprinted
or reproduced or utilised in any form or by any
electronic, mechanical, or other means, now known or
hereafter invented, including photocopying and
recording, or in any information storage or retrieval
system, without permission in writing from the
publishers.

British Library Cataloguing in Publication Data
A catalogue record for this book is available from the British Library

Library of Congress Cataloging in Publication Data
After writing culture: epistemology and praxis in contemporary anthropology /
   edited by Allison James, Jenny Hockey, and Andrew Dawson.
      p. cm. – (ASA monographs; 34)
Based on papers first presented to the Association of Social Anthropologists
Annual Conference 1995, held at Hull University.
Includes bibliographical references and indexes.
1. Ethnology – Philosophy. 2. Ethnology – Methodology. 3. Ethnology – Author-
ship. I. James, Allison. II. Hockey, Jennifer Lorna. III. Dawson, Andrew H. IV.
Association of Social Anthropologists. Conference (1995: University of Hull)
V. Series: ASA monographs; 34.
GN345.A33   1997
306–dc20   96–32469
                                                                          CIP

ISBN   0–415–15005–1
         0–415–15006–X (pbk)

SOAS LIBRARY

Contents

Figures

Contributors

Glenn Bowman is a social anthropologist lecturing in the interdisciplinary Programme in Image Studies at the University of Kent at Canterbury

Angela Cheater is Professor of Sociology and Social Anthropology at the University of Waikato

Andrew Dawson is Lecturer in Social Anthropology at the University of Hull

Iain R. Edgar is Lecturer in Social Anthropology at the University of Durham

Joy Hendry is Professor of Social Anthropology at Oxford Brookes University

Jenny Hockey is a social anthropologist lecturing in Social Policy at the University of Hull

Ngapare Hopa is Associate Professor of Maori Studies at the University of Auckland

Allison James is Senior Lecturer in Applied Anthropology at the University of Hull

Lisette Josephides is Professor of Anthropology at the University of Minnesota

John Knight is Research Fellow at the International Institute for Asian Studies, Leiden

Robert Layton is Professor of Social Anthropology at the University of Durham

Sharon Macdonald lectures in social anthropology at the University of Sheffield

Jane Nadel-Klein is Associate Professor of Anthropology at Trinity College, Hartford, Connecticut

Judith Okely is Professor of Social Anthropology at the University of Hull

Declan Quigley is Lecturer in Social Anthropology at Queen's University Belfast.

Nigel Rapport is Professor of Social Anthropology at the University of St Andrews

Bob Simpson is Lecturer in Social Anthropology at the University of Durham

Sandra Wallman is Professor of Social Anthropology at the University of Hull

Preface and acknowledgements

The chapters gathered together here were first presented to the Association of Social Anthropologists Annual Conference 1995, held at Hull University. Overlooking four inches of Easter snow, the comforts of an upstairs library at Ferens Hall gave us the opportunity to spend four days sharing our ideas and thoughts around the theme of representation. These were as diverse as they were roundly articulated and to all the participants at the conference, whether speaker or listener, we extend our thanks for the lively debates we shared and the humour with which differences of opinion were acknowledged and respected.

The highly successful plenary format permitted around eighty anthropologists to participate actively in a cumulative discussion of the fifteen papers, all but two of which are included in this present volume. We would like to thank both Mike Hitchcock and Italo Pardo for their contributions which we were not able to include. In addition, we would like to thank those who gave poster presentations: John Harries, Jon Mitchell, Justin Kenrick, Jane Nadel-Klein and Elizabeth Hallam. As befits the theme of the conference, the poster session permitted a different representative form for the presentation of fieldwork data and, as an innovation for an ASA conference, it proved both successful and enjoyable. Jane Nadel-Klein's poster presentation we have included in the volume, re-presented in a new form, in this way providing apt illustration of a major strand in the conference discussions about forms and modes of representation.

Chapter 1

Introduction
The road from Santa Fe

Allison James, Jenny Hockey and Andrew Dawson

The publication of Clifford and Marcus's edited collection, *Writing Culture: the Poetics and Politics of Ethnography* (1986), has come to be regarded as something of a watershed in anthropological thought. The outcome of a series of advanced seminars held in Santa Fe, New Mexico, its collective voice highlighted and responded positively to a crisis in anthropology that was inseparably epistemological and political. Eschewing the holistic persuasions of traditional anthropologists and recognising that their representations are fundamentally the products of asymmetrical power relations, it exhorted us to develop new forms of representation which could include the multiple voices of those being represented. Also rejecting its traditionally authoritative, realist and objectivist style it asked us to think of and explore anthropology itself as an institutionally, historically and politically situated writing genre. Together with its companion volume, *Anthropology as Cultural Critique* (Marcus and Fischer 1986), the collection instigated a wider debate about 'writing culture' which was celebrated as 'a new experimental moment in ethnographic writing' (ibid.).

Certainly, for some, these books heralded a new way forward and the implications for anthropological practice were embraced with enthusiasm (Rapport 1994: 5). However, for others, they constituted the inception of a reactionary and postmodern malaise: the perpetuation of a 'bourgeois, Western, individualistic ideology' (Sangren 1988: 423), the 'ultimate argument for armchair anthropology' and a recipe for 'navel gazing' (Jarvie 1988: 428). More cynically, Clifford, Marcus, Fischer and their cohorts were portrayed as 'scheming careerists' (cf. Fischer *et al.* 1988: 425) who, through the use of the millennial tones implicit in the phrase 'a new experimental moment' conferred on postmodern ethnography precisely the kind of authority they were seeking to destabilise (Sangren 1988: 408–10).

Rather than the books themselves it has been, if anything, the severity of the backlash which has given them their millennial significance. Indeed, as Woolgar observes wryly, 'we know that relativism brings out the religion in people. Reflexivity, it seems, brings out the venom' (1988: 430). As was noted at the time, the books represented a synthesis and extension of wider debates between modernists and postmodernists (Friedman 1988: 426) that had been already well rehearsed in other disciplines (McCarthy 1992: 638) and, indeed, in anthropology itself (McDonald 1988: 429). A decade later it is possible to see the 'Writing Culture' debate as a crystallisation of uncertainties about anthropology's subject matter (traditionally 'the other'), its method (traditionally, participant observation), its medium (traditionally, the monograph) and its intention (traditionally that of informing rather than practice).

In this volume the contributors eschew the antagonisms and pessimisms that the debate aroused and respond constructively to the challenge for ethnography which constitutes the heart of the matter. As Hughes-Freeland notes, rather than contending an 'empiricist theory of everything' or a 'hyper-postmodern end of everything' anthropologists will, as long as there is a road forward to be imagined, go down the middle of it (1995: 19). Thus, Hastrup's (1995) insistence that the theoretical 'crisis' in anthropology can be overcome through concrete experience is collectively demonstrated in the decidedly ethnographic focus of the majority of the chapters that follow. The richness and detail of the field material with which each author engages underlines the point that 'there is no anthropology to recapture because it was never at the point of vanishing' (Hastrup 1995: 10).

Central to the volume is an insistence on the inextricable relationship between epistemology, politics and practice which the 'Writing Culture' debate drew attention to. Here we explore this through questioning anthropology's representation of its own knowledge and its representational role in social, political and legal contexts. Collectively, the chapters ask who, what, how and why might we represent? In this sense the volume draws on the multiple meanings of the term 'representation': representation as interpretation, communication, visualisation, translation and advocacy. Brought together within the same continuum of concern – from the 'crisis of representation' through to a more recent and urgent insistence that the anthropological endeavour has a practical bent via the political act of representing others through advocacy (Harries-Jones 1991) – the theme of representation draws these contemporary anthropological activities and worlds into dialogue with one another. However, the volume does not present a mere larder of opportunity from which the reader might pick and choose according to whim or fancy; rather, we argue that both ends of this spectrum of choice have a great deal to say to one another and indeed, more strongly, that they should. A central organisational theme, therefore, is that theoretical debates about the possibilities and problems of representing other peoples' worlds are not just those of the Academy but can be both informed by and help inform the practice of anthropology and the practices of anthropologists. In turn the practising anthropologist – the development worker, the applied researcher or the consultant – is increasingly acknowledging the implicit politics of theorising which necessarily shape any kind of anthropology in action (Moore 1996).

Thus, as a framework for the papers that follow, this introduction sets out some key aspects of what, collectively, constitute an ongoing debate about representation through exploring in detail the different impacts that this questioning has had on forms and modes of representation within anthropological work of all kinds. We consider, for example, the ways in which different styles of representation reflect or help constitute particular theoretical stances towards the problem of representation itself. Furthermore, by way of offering a reframing of the questions to be asked about representation, we show that questions of praxis can be of practical concern to the pure as well as applied arms of contemporary social anthropology.

In brief, what this volume argues is that the 'Writing Culture' debate has alerted anthropologists to the need to pay closer attention to the epistemological grounds of their representations and, furthermore, has made them consider the practical import of that process of reflection, both for the anthropological endeavour and for those who are the subjects of any anthropological enquiry. What we show here is that these themes, reiterated in various guises throughout this volume, are themselves manifested within a series of more particular dilemmas of praxis that have been bequeathed to anthropology by the 'Writing Culture' debate. Thus, within this volume and in the most part through detailed ethnographic illustration, we examine issues ranging from the aftermath of modernist epistemologies of the subject and the possible existence of shared or universal external references which might make cultural 'translation' viable, through to questions of authorial style and the nature and status of models which may be deemed effective in an applied setting. In Moore's rendering, this process of interrogation problematises its own terms: 'whose knowledge; what sort of knowledge; what constitutes the social?' (1996: 1).

The chapters are diverse in their responses to such questioning, yet each addresses some of the core issues raised by the 'Writing Culture' debate for in practical, everyday terms, these dilemmas face every practising anthropologist. Although partially overlapping and often in necessary dialogue with each other, we suggest here that four discrete epistemological and practical challenges can nonetheless be identified, dilemmas which are variously addressed throughout the volume. They are as follows: (1) the humanism of representational practices; (2) the difficulty of uncovering whose representations are being represented and by whom; (3) the problem of the form that different representational practices can take; (4) the politics and ethics of making representations. All these problematics have emerged as practical issues in the epistemological fall-out from the 'Writing Culture' debate. This volume makes no attempt to foreclose the debate; rather it portrays some of the ways in which contemporary anthropology is actively and purposefully engaging with them.

THE HUMANISM OF REPRESENTATION

Despite its Durkheimian legacy, anthropology has in some respects never been quite comfortable with the idea of 'representation' as a way of describing how humans come to know and act in the world. As has been remarked (Bourdieu 1977), how people represent themselves or their 'world views' and what they do in the face of everyday contingencies are not always in harmony. Indeed, they may be quite at odds, rather than merely incompatible. For example, during the 1970s the influence of feminist perspectives within anthropology led to a recognition that ethnographers who found easy access to male informants might be misled into believing that the appealingly well-structured accounts of systems of social organisation they gained actually accounted for life as lived, and indeed life as lived by both men and women (Ardener 1975). Here, already, was a recognition of the potential multivocality of culture (see Rapport, Chapter 11 of this volume). Furthermore, as more effort was focused on explaining such inconsistencies between expressed thoughts and observed actions and on documenting more precisely the ways in which people come to 'believe in' a world view that is incongruous with their practice, so disquiet with the idea of 'systems of representation' increased. Moore and Myerhoff (1977), for example, highlighted the riskiness of ritual practices which, as representations of life-as-imagined, were ever vulnerable to the discovery of their arbitrariness. By the mid-1970s, therefore, the argument, baldly stated, was that to grant a determining role to representations as a system for structuring human thought and practice, rather than to acknowledge their negotiated status as the outcome of acts of meaning-making (Crick 1976), meant a failure to acknowledge the situated nature of representational processes.

It is of course precisely the situated nature of 'knowledge' or 'truth' that is central to the many discussions that banded together under the 'Writing Culture' rubric, though the emphasis on the contingent nature of meaning-making has shifted away from 'the other' to the anthropologists themselves as they undertake the task of representing. It is an unsurprising parallel. If the lives of the 'others' upon which anthropologists gaze are to be regarded as negotiated, even personalised worlds of becoming, rather than static worlds of being, then the 'professional' accounts or representations of those social worlds made by anthropol ogists – who, after all, are for the most part shareholders in humanity – must be similarly contextual, mediated and, in the end, partial. Thus the dilemma for anthropology raised by the 'Writing Culture' debate is that, if we acknowledge the situated nature of other peoples' 'realities' and social worlds, so we must finally reject any professional claim to being the purveyors of unmediated accounts or objective 'truths' (Tyler 1986).

Bowman (Chapter 3) contests the implications of such an approach, arguing that it throws out the baby of common humanity with the bathwater of modernism's project of imposing a universal regime of truth upon all humanity. Rather than a bemused concern with what might replace authority as a characteristic of academic products in a world where alterity rules, Bowman would have us recognise the commonality of a universal experience of contingent identity-making. Evidence for this view, he argues, is found within the fieldwork experience itself, where the 'difference' reified by a postmodern anthropology begins to dissolve as the ethnographer sets about amalgamating him or herself into another culture's conceptual space. Identity, in this view, remains fluid and contingent but the ability to create or perform an identity is fixed as a generalised human characteristic. Bowman, therefore, endorses the 'performative contradiction' of anthropology which makes 'claim to objective historical scholarship ... which is at odds with the implications of the anthropological practice of studying others by way of engagement' (Hastrup (1995: 4).

However, it would seem that a discipline that has grown up within a wider cultural climate of positivism cannot easily dispense with its claims to authority. For some, therefore, the present dilemma turns on whether or not, and in what form, to 'come out' with statements about the fictional, situated nature of our accounts. Can we argue persuasively for our accounts to be accepted if what we offer has to be acknowledged as the provisional product of our interaction, as individual anthropologists, with individual informants who are themselves interacting with and representing one another? Can we live with and within a discipline that sees each account as situated within the contexts of both the field encounter and the anthropologist's intellectual milieu?

In Josephides' view the answer to these questions is yes. In her account of three powerfully contrastive ethnographies (Chapter 2) she reveals the discipline's contemporary flexibility. It has, she argues, the potential (1) to reflect the metatheorising that already takes place among informants; (2) to claim authority by refusing a separation between ethnographer and informant; and (3) to focus on social action as the site of meaning-making within the field. What Josephides highlights is the need for ethnographic strategies that are shaped by the situations of informants, both locally and globally. In her view, therefore, theories about how to do fieldwork have to be constructed responsively in the field.

In contrast, Wallman (Chapter 15) argues that to abandon all authorial authority is to dismiss the practical role of anthropology and its appropriateness in the modern world. The act of representation, particularly for the jobbing anthropologist (Barnett and Blaikie 1994), involves making a good-enough model of the world, one which serves its intended purposes as, for example, is the case when working alongside medical specialists. The offer of an account that makes no claims to even a contingent authority might appear to reflect the integrity of its producer, but it is an account that cannot be evaluated, assessed or contested. One could add to Wallman's practical focus other political and ethical imperatives for maintaining the facticity frame. As Birth (1990) argues, it offers a standard of accountability against which the subjects of ethnographic writing can argue that the representation is a lie or a distortion. Both these points of view are a bulwark against anthropology, and its potentially counter-hegemonic message, being marginalised in the context of other more 'scientific' discourses (Sangren 1988).

A final and entirely different element in the dilemma raised by the 'humanism of representation' speaks to an older debate. Here the argument turns on the way in which forms of social theory that foreground representations as systems/modes of thought or social constructions of reality, ultimately ignore the materially grounded dimensions of individuals' everyday practices (Bourdieu 1977; Caws 1984; Stoller 1989; Ingold 1991; Richards 1993). The view of such authors, though variously expressed, is that a purely cognitivist vision of human agency underplays the individual's direct engagement with a social and material world and fails to account for the ways in which that engagement might actively contribute to or shape representational knowledge itself. As Lakoff and Johnson (1980) argue, systems of thought should be seen as experiential rather than either subjective or objective. In coining this phrase they are developing a view of representation-making as the generation of hypotheses that are tested through experience within the social and material environment, subsequently to be abandoned or developed as a result of their aptness or usefulness. Simpson (Chapter 4) provides an account of how separated parents actively seek to make sense of, or even reconcile, discrepancies between their own lived experiences of marriage and parenthood and the state's hegemonic models of 'the family', prompted by their everyday engagement with the social roles of 'husband', 'wife', 'father' and 'mother'.

In contrast with this emphasis on the embodied processes that produce representations, other chapters variously detail a knowing intervention by people in the political praxis of manipulating representations for explicit ends. Macdonald (Chapter 10), for example, provides an ethnography of expert museum staff, an elite which specialises in representation. Subject to external scrutiny in the form of mission statements and performance indicators, they reflect on their own acts of cultural translation and sense-making and it is to the politics of this process that Macdonald's chapter gives us access. Similarly Knight (Chapter 9) describes events that formed part of a Japanese village revival movement, a process of reinventing a rural past in order to promote municipal integration alongside tourism. Like Macdonald, Knight inserts his experiences into the text as field material in order to reveal the social and political processes that constitute acts of representation. In addition, both describe how they found them-selves – like it or not – appropriated by the very process of ethnographic representation that they were seeking to record. In comparative examples, Edgar (Chapter 5) documents the process by which members of a dream-work group facilitate a shared resolution to the problematic of their dreaming, by recounting and analysing one another's dreams, while Hendry's account of theme parks and gardens in Japan (Chapter 12) explores the appropriation of Western images for Japanese identity.

This emphasis on the negotiated character of representations, a quality that often emerges through participation in social and political events that have a quite evident material outcome, reminds us about the extent to which representation might be understood from a more materialist approach. Layton, for example, in his account of the politics of Aboriginal land claims (Chapter 8) bids us address the distinction between represen-tations that carry a direct reference to an external, locally situated material reality – a hole in a rock, a track, a river valley – and represen-tations that are self-referential, which carry meaning only to the extent that they make sense within the framework of a culturally specific knowl-edge-base. This might be a sacred site which marks the passage of a totemic creature. His intention is to examine the complexities for the Westerner of literally trying to 'see' the landscape which the Alawa understand themselves to inhabit. For Layton, therefore, some truths are more situated than others.

WHOSE REPRESENTATIONS ARE THEY?

If the battle against scientism (Okely 1975) may seem to have been finally won, or at least a truce to have been agreed, a second dilemma poses more of a problem. If anthropological representations are personal, non-replicable, difficult to verify, and if there are competing views within the anthropological world, then so too must the competing claims and dis-senting voices that constitute the social worlds of 'others' be taken account of. They also are multivocal. However, this recognition has impli-cations for ethnography's traditional claim to make representations of whole cultures in its writings. Forgoing holism threatens to strike at the heart of anthropological practice which, alongside a commitment to being comparative, has long been synonymous with the representation of 'whole cultures'. Indeed, it is this characteristic that, traditionally, has served to distinguish anthropology from its close cousin, sociology, a discipline which singles out particular attributes of social life that theorists understand to be fundamental to social formations.

Working within a discipline hereto committed to holistic accounts, Simpson's chapter, as noted, foregrounds the multivocality of conceptions of family. Using material from a very different locality, Cheater and Hopa (Chapter 13) similarly demonstrate the contested nature of the fundamental categorisations through which social identity is constituted in New Zealand. Rather than the relationship between the divorced individual and the state, which is Simpson's focus, Cheater and Hopa's ethnography delineates the relationship between indigenous Maori peoples and a Western colonialist power. Their detailed ethnographic account describes the twists and turns of an historical and political process of identity construction and contestation, which shows it to have profound material implications for land and fishing rights.

Thus, although collective understandings and representations were at one time anthropology's stock-in-trade, the 'Writing Culture' debate has faced us with the question as to whether we can offer a collective view only when a mass of individuals succeed in crowding into the same situation, whether within the field or within the discipline, like angels on a pin head. And if, as is usually the case, we are all differently positioned, can we be satisfied with relativity, assemblages and conversations in place of our more familiar and certain models or world views?

Such problematics make us more critical of our representational practices and force us to ask just who we are representing. If our texts comprise informants' accounts of their kinship system (see Cheater and Hopa, Chapter 13) or our own observations of ritual practice (see Edgar, Chapter 5), we must now consider who has generated the account – them or us – and for whom it has meaning. Despite our practical awareness that our material is bounded by local contexts – the individual, the moment and the place – that which we call 'culture' has in the past allowed us to transgress the limits of such immediacies. Traditionally, as Sperber says, 'what gets interpreted is often a collective representation attributed to the whole social group . . . and which need never be entertained, let alone expressed, by any one individual member of that group' (1994: 165). Rapport's chapter (Chapter 11) argues the case for subverting the discipline's representations of collectivity because they mask the individual nature of thought and experience. In place of collectivity, he offers an assemblage of thirty-one voices engaged in the continuous practice of making Mitzpe Ramon (a new-town in Israel) into home followed by at least fourteen ways of interpreting what is said by these voices. Multivocality, thus presented, and demonstrated in the form of the text, exemplifies an experimental approach to ethnography 'rooted in an appreciation of the fundamental perversity and unpredictability of human conduct' (Manning 1995: 250). Like Rapport, many of the authors within this volume are engaging with these dilemmas and asking whether it is still possible to cling to the talisman of 'holism' when it is now far from straightforward to decide which aspects of that which is seen and heard constitute 'collective' representations. Indeed, Quigley's account of the problem of the use of the category 'caste' in India (Chapter 7) reminds us that, deep-down, we may rarely feel convinced that our representations 'of what our informants are up to, or think they are up to' (Geertz 1975: 15) are 'true' to the original, let alone shared by any others. For Quigley, therefore, caste must be recognised for what it is: the lived experience of people. This is in contradistinction to the views of Dumont (1980) who takes issue with analytic categories such as caste which, for him, convey a spurious 'holism'. Thus, although acknowledging the danger of essentialism, Quigley would have us recognise that 'they' as well as 'us' also essentialise.

In further addressing the question 'Whose representations are they?' Edgar's focus (Chapter 5) on that most private of individual experiences, the dream, examines the meaning-making activities to which the inaccessible dream experience is subjected by the members of a specific cultural group, the participants at a dream 'workshop'. That the participants struggle to sense the meaning of the dream from the dreamer's recollections illustrates the conflict between the competing interpretive paradigms that are culturally available. Other chapters similarly focus on the ways in which the individual, situated in time and space, nonetheless interacts with broader cultural representations, transforming them into their own mental representations. Simpson, for example, describes the traumatic life-event narratives of divorced individuals as attempts to order, structure and make sense of experience which, in hegemonic terms, is disordered. Once divorce causes 'family' to be no longer contiguous with a single domestic site, individuals strive to re-cast or rework its elements – 'fatherhood', 'motherhood', 'love' and 'marriage' – in such a way as to repair a breach with hegemonic representations. What he points out is that the outcomes of these processes are often new and emergent representations, which may be made public at certain points and then become transformed into the mental representations of others.

To say that something is a collective or cultural representation is therefore to say that 'at a given level and from a given point of view' its instances can be interpreted by means of a common interpretation (Sperber 1994: 182). It is a way of picking out a common class of phenomena, however vague the criteria of choice may be. Some of the contributors would argue, therefore, that anthropology *can* continue to address the cultural, and persist with an exploration of the collective by examining that which exists above and beyond the mediated experience of the situated individual. Hendry (Chapter 12), for example, takes as her focus the 'cultures' of both Japan and the rest of the world as represented or appropriated in the form of Japanese parks, one of which is targeted at Japanese tourists and the other at foreign visitors. This view would see our ethnographies beginning life as an attempt to record the minutiae of our informants' everyday lives – material which subsequently becomes the 'stuff' within which we seek a pattern of common interpretations. This process, of course, parallels the ways our informants succeed in representing to themselves the unfolding events that go to make up their everyday experience. For example, we see in Nadel-Klein's chapter (Chapter 6) an attempt to find a commonality within a 'Scotland' that has been divided geographically, culturally and indeed ethnographically. Like Quigley, she would reclaim the centrality of holistic categories as core markers of identity. In the case of Scotland, she proposes that a focus on marginality and diversity, which characterises existing ethnographies of Scotland, in fact speaks to a country's desire for a national identity, expressed in a move from the periphery to the centre.

REPRESENTATIONAL FORMS

Though field material constitutes a description and therefore appears to offer something that corresponds fairly closely to the 'reality' evident in the field situation, ethnography requires us to interpret that which we observe. In so doing our language and our concepts become much more remote from what we are describing. As a result, it can become unclear as to how our representation relates to something we have witnessed, participated in or been told about, and, furthermore, from which local vantage point we have chosen to provide its grounding. Hendry acknowledges this explicitly in entitling her account of gardens, theme parks and the anthropologist in Japan: 'Who is representing whom?'

Through the discussions generated in the wake of the 'Writing Culture' debate, anthropologists have become or been made more aware that the making of any ethnography – the traditional medium through which anthropology has represented 'other peoples' worlds' – involves the use of literary devices, forms which we fear may lead us to distort or misrepresent those worlds. Thus, it is argued, we need to reconfigure our ethnographies in an attempt at evocation rather than referentiality (Tyler 1986). Perhaps, in the 1990s, we can provide some new answers to the question posed by Malinowski in 1922: 'What is this ethnographer's magic, by which he is able to evoke the real spirits of the natives, the true picture of tribal life?' (1978 [1922]: 6). Perhaps we can now embrace, rather than deny, the 'magical' elements of our craft. This should involve, for example, paying closer attention to the syntactic dimension of ethnography and indeed making strategic use of devices that serve to foreground the textuality of our products. Rapport, for example, in setting out field material and indeed interpretations in the form of lists that resemble the written dialogue of the playwright, makes strong theoretical claims for this novel representative form. He argues convincingly for the conversational nature of the interpretive process, which he sees as a dialogue, both open and incremental. Josephides similarly argues that styles of ethnographic writing go beyond the question of personal preference, training or skill and instead provide us with a means of connecting our epistemological standpoints with our mode of representation.

The making of anthropological representations can therefore be seen as the final outcome of a complex process of liaison between the informant and the researcher, each of whom is engaged in similar, though often separate attempts to generate interpretations which can encompass the multiplexity of everyday life. As Sperber (1994) argues, these representations are 'true-to-life' to the extent that they account for the original. They do not resemble it, however, as to do so would merely be to copy rather than to interpret. Wallman takes this perspective beyond the confines of the academy, bidding us to reflect on ways of working practically and indeed productively with notions of multivocality in the face of specific and often quite concrete social problems and issues. She argues that the models which we make to represent the cultural problems of one group of 'others' to another group of 'others' need to be effective rather than accurate representations to ease the task of those who, in applied contexts, are often driven to making decisions about vexed situations. In thus learning to live with the partiality of our accounts and to accept the limitations of the subjectivity of anthropological practice we are, in her view, enabled rather than disempowered from practising what we would preach.

This perspective raises questions about the forms we choose for our representations. The monograph, journal article or conference presentation are media which clearly do not offer a copy of the original, being a linear assemblage of words rather than a three-dimensional event or experience. Film, photograph or artefact involves visual images as well as language and might therefore appear to constitute a more 'faithful' representation. However, as Macdonald reveals through her ethnography of an official institution of representation – Britain's National Museum of Science and Industry – to choose and frame images and artefacts within the museum setting is also to engage in acts of translation and sense-making. Like anthropologists, museum staff find themselves required to represent rather than merely exhibit the objects that come under their care. Thus, although the significance of the 'Writing Culture' debate for anthropology has been seen primarily in terms of its impact for the anthropologist's craft as writer, this volume considers that representation involves more than inscription.

THE POLITICS OF REPRESENTATION

So far, as we have seen, much contemporary anthropology is concerned to explore ways in which the gaps between those who produce and those who use representations might be narrowed, for example, by making the multivocality of the anthropological voices chime more closely. However, important though these ideals and intentions are, the somewhat uncomfortable question remains as to whether such democratic representations are in the end possible, or even desirable. It is to these starker issues that this final section turns.

In the current climate of academic and institutional accountability, the sense-making that anthropology has long concerned itself with begins to take on a slightly different hue. Anthropologists are now accustomed to being asked to supply accounts from the field that may inform policy and its implementation. Applied anthropology has long suffered under the critical gaze of an academy for whom 'pure' research was, in Europe at least, the more respectable branch of the discipline (Grillo and Rew 1985). In the 1990s applied anthropology finds itself, ironically, in the eye of a political storm in which social science research is increasingly having to defend itself as being at least 'relevant' to contemporary social issues, if not always easy to apply directly.

While in some quarters the tightening of fiscal reins which this has implied has been a painful experience, invoking strong arguments for the protection of 'pure' research, elsewhere this shift in focus has been welcomed as a challenge, as many of the chapters in this volume amply demonstrate. Attention to the social and political consequences of our research – anthropology in practice – need not entail either a diminution of theorising or the compromising of academic standards. Indeed, it is rather the reverse. Collectively, the chapters in this volume reveal the necessary interplay between pure and applied research and the creative, symbiotic relationship to be struck between theory and practice. In this sense, the lessons about representation that form the legacy of the 'Writing Culture' debate are as central to contemporary anthropological praxis as they are to its theorising. They are not, as some have argued, simply part of an obscure and arcane debate of little relevance to getting the job done. In thus rendering transparent the processes through which ethnographies are made – that is, constructed as fictions or accounts, rather than objective truths – we become aware of our own humanity as meaning-makers. If the organisation of a text affects its meaning, the power to produce particularised meanings, ethnographic persuasions, becomes a political as well as simply textual problem of representation (Said 1978). The casting of spells or the imposition of metaphors carries power in material as well as fantasy worlds.

This interdependency is revealed in a number of ways. Faced with a now acclaimed subjectivity and, as we have seen, a new recognition and acceptance of the partiality of our accounts, we can no longer distance ourselves from responsibility for our texts. In Chapter 14, Okely charts the history of her own and other people's writings on Gypsy ethnicity. She shows that her questioning of an Indian origin of Gypsy ethnicity has, at different times, fed into the political arena constituted by, for example, the Commission for Racial Equality, and the criminal justice system, while contributing to the intellectual debates of gypsyologists. Like Macdonald's, Okely's texts have taken on a political life of their own.

These chapters argue, therefore, that, once we have committed to words on paper, or to visual representation through film, we may at one and the same time lose control yet be haunted by our representations of others. In the contemporary global context where texts and images not only proliferate but do so beyond the confines of the locality of their production, it behoves us to consider carefully, therefore, the political fall-out of our representational practices. These examples show that an interest in form and style, which might appear narrow, often takes on a political importance when research finds its way outside the academy; the complexities of a text are apt to become condensed into a media sound-bite with all subtlety lost, all complexity reduced and all contradiction dulled. It is clear, therefore, that the styling of representations is central to the ways in which our research can be used and be made useful.

A second, and more emotive consequence of this new consciousness about the practice of anthropological representation pertains to questions of advocacy. As anthropologists find themselves increasingly drawn into communicating visions of the world to non-anthropologists, on behalf of the powerless as well as the powerful, closer attention needs to be paid to the conversation-making that lies at the communicative heart of representational practices. In their own ways, the chapters contributed by Cheater and Hopa, Okely, Hendry, Knight and Layton each show that representations, once made, are open to re-representation, misrepresentation and appropriation.

CONCLUSION

This volume presents a range of different responses to the challenges raised by the 'Writing Culture' debate. As a collection, the chapters invite a re-examination of many aspects of our representational praxis, from questions of epistemology through to those of the political roles that anthropologists may take on. Thus, we now not only recognise the situated, 'fictional' nature of our accounts, but have also begun the task of putting those accounts forward effectively, as the basis for decision-making and the formation of policy.

The critics of the 'Writing Culture' debate have claimed a narrow focus on texts as the site of authority construction (Sangren 1988: 412). What this volume directs us towards is a consideration of the wider spheres within which texts come to be debated, criticised and used and their practical authority gains credence. In this sense, this volume not only calls for a re-examination, following Rabinow (1986) and Clifford (1988), of the practice of ethnography but bids us also to direct our gaze towards the social processes by which ethnography gains authority.

REFERENCES

Ardener, E. (1975) 'Belief and the Problem of Women', in S. Ardener (ed.), *Perceiving Women*, London: J. M. Dent.
Barnett, A. and P. Blaikie (1994) 'On Ignoring the Wider Pictures: AIDS Research and the Jobbing Social Scientist', in D. Booth (ed.), *Rethinking Social Development*, Harlow: Longman Scientific and Technical.
Birth, K. (1990) 'Reading and the Righting of Ethnographies', *American Ethnologist*, 17 (3): 549–57.
Bourdieu, P. (1977 [1972]) *Outline of a Theory of Practice*, Cambridge: Cambridge University Press.
Caws, P. (1984) 'Operational, Representational, and Explanatory Models', *American Anthropologist*, 76 (1): 1–10.
Clifford, J. (1988) Reply to Sangren, S. P. (1988) 'Rhetoric and the Authority of Ethnography: "Postmodernism" and the Social Reproduction of Texts', *Current Anthropology*, 29 (3): 425.
Clifford, J. and G. E. Marcus (eds) (1986) *Writing Culture: The Poetics and Politics of Ethnography*, Berkeley: University of California Press.
Crick, M. (1976) *Explorations in Language and Meaning: Towards a Semantic Anthropology*, London: Malaby Press.
Dumont, L. (1980 [1966]) *Homo Hierarchicus: The Caste System and its Implications*, Chicago: University of Chicago Press.
Fisher, M. M. J., G. E. Marcus and A. T. Tyler (1988) Reply to Sangren, S. P. (1988) 'Rhetoric and the Authority of Ethnography: "Postmodernism" and the Social Reproduction of Texts', *Current Anthropology*, 29 (3): 425–6.
Friedman, J. (1988) Reply to Sangren, S. P. (1988) 'Rhetoric and the Authority of Ethnography: "Postmodernism" and the Social Reproduction of Texts', *Current Anthropology*, 29 (3): 426–7.
Geertz, C. (1975) *The Interpretation of Cultures*, London: Hutchinson.
Grillo, R. and A. Rew (eds) (1985) *Social Anthropology and Development Policy*, London: Tavistock.
Harries-Jones, P. (ed.) (1991) *Making Knowledge Count*, Montreal: McGill-Queen's University Press.
Hastrup, K. (1995) *A Passage to Anthropology*, London: Routledge.
Hughes-Freeland, F. (1995) 'ASA Conference 1995: Anthropology and Representation, 27–30 March', *Anthropology Today*, 11 (5): 19–20.
Ingold, T. (1991) 'Against the Motion (1)', in *Human Worlds are Culturally Constructed*, Group for Debates in Anthropological Theory, Manchester: Dept. of Anthropology, University of Manchester.
Jackson, M. (1993) 'Knowledge of the Body', *Man*, XVIII: 327–45.
Jarvie, I. (1988) Reply to Sangren, S. P. (1988) 'Rhetoric and the Authority of

Ethnography: "Postmodernism" and the Social Reproduction of Texts', *Current Anthropology*, 29 (3): 427–8.

Lakoff, G. and M. Johnson (1980) *Metaphors We Live By*, Chicago: University of Chicago Press.

McCarthy, T. (1992) 'Doing the Right Thing in Cross-cultural Representation', *Ethics: An International Journal of Social, Political and Legal Philosophy*, 102: 635–49.

McDonald, M. (1988) Reply to Sangren, S. P. (1988) 'Rhetoric and the Authority of Ethnography: "Postmodernism" and the Social Reproduction of Texts', *Current Anthropology*, 29 (3): 429.

Malinowski, B. (1978 [1922]) *Argonauts of the Western Pacific*, London: Routledge & Kegan Paul.

Manning, P. K. (1995) 'The Challenge of Postmodernism', in J. Van Maanen (ed.), *Representation in Ethnography*, London: Sage.

Marcus, G. E. and M. M. J. Fischer (1986) *Anthropology as Cultural Critique: An Experimental Moment in the Human Sciences*, Chicago: University of Chicago Press.

Moore, H. (1996) *The Future of Anthropological Knowledge*, London: Routledge.

Moore, S. F. and B. Myerhoff (1977) *Secular Ritual*, Assen: Van Gorcum.

Okely, J. (1975) 'The Self and Scientism', *Journal of the Anthropology Society of Oxford*, 6 (3): 171–88.

Rabinow, P. (1986) 'Representations are Social Facts: Modernity and Postmodernity in Anthropology', in J. Clifford and G. E. Marcus (eds), *Writing Culture: The Poetics and Politics of Ethnography*, Berkeley: University of California Press.

Rapport, N. (1994) *The Prose and the Passion: Anthropology, Literature and the Writing of E. M. Forster*, Manchester: Manchester University Press.

Richards, P. (1993) 'Natural Symbols and Natural History: Chimpanzees, Elephants and Experiments in Mende Thought', in K. Milton (ed.), *Environmentalism: The View from Anthropology*, ASA Monographs 32, London: Routledge.

Said, E. W. (1978) *Orientalism: Western Conceptions of the Orient*, London: Routledge & Kegan Paul.

Sangren, S. P. (1988) 'Rhetoric and the Authority of Ethnography: "Postmodernism" and the Social Reproduction of Texts', *Current Anthropology*, 29 (3): 415–24.

Sperber, D. (1994) 'Interpreting and Explaining Cultural Representations', in G. Palsson (ed.), *Beyond Boundaries: Understanding Translation and Anthropological Discourse*, Oxford: Berg.

Stoller, P. (1989) *The Taste of Ethnographic Things*, Pennsylvania: Pennsylvania University Press.

Tyler, S. A. (1986) 'Post-modern Ethnography: From Document of the Occult to Occult Document', in J. Clifford and G. E. Marcus (eds), *Writing Culture: The Poetics and Politics of Ethnography*, Berkeley: University of California Press.

Woolgar, S. (1988) Reply to Sangren, S. P. (1988) 'Rhetoric and the Authority of Ethnography: "Postmodernism" and the Social Reproduction of Texts', *Current Anthropology*, 29 (3): 430–1.

Chapter 2

Representing the anthropologist's predicament

Lisette Josephides

I start from the premise that anthropological knowledge originates in the field encounter, where we extend our partial connections to the world. The phrase is of course Marilyn Strathern's (Strathern 1991). I want to extend her insights to a somewhat different field of enquiry, in order to examine how our identifications and complicities in the field determine (or at least strongly influence) the epistemologies that shape our monographs. Put simply, what is the relationship between the field encounter and our epistemological commitments?

I take three styles of ethnographic writing as the basis of my discussion. The first style (Tsing 1993) is an inspired interpretation that covers vast expanses of epistemologically and geographically discontinuous terrains, creating global connections and demonstrating simultaneously the theses of disempowering marginality and the empowerment of agency and self-definition. The second style (Seremetakis 1991) is a reflexive-authorial attitude that challenges theories by the application of ethnographic observations from which the ethnographer becomes progressively indistinguishable. A dream diary serves as an indicator of anthropological methodology, disclosing a cultural order which the ethnographer finally reclaims as her own. Here exegesis is spontaneous; meaning is already contained in the ritual act but needs to be co-created to be understood. The third style (Josephides n.d.) is an account of 'culture in action', which takes as its subject matter understanding 'culture' through the actions and talk of its participants. A local discourse of self and culture emerges, painting a picture of lived experience.

The impetus for this essay has two sources: a fascination with the peculiar way ethnographic encounters produce specific ethnographies that display the creativities of particular cultural contexts, and a curiosity about the differences in the creativity of our own co-inventions of field situations and relations. I 'deconstruct' the styles to glimpse what went into their making, not in order to reject them, but because I am fascinated with the persuasiveness of their approaches and their further implications. My intention is to carry their insights forward by asking several questions.

What pictures do they depict? What enables them to depict them in this way? And what are the necessary assumptions of their heuristics? These questions engage issues of representation by attending to the relationship between ethnographic methodology and epistemological concerns.

At the same time, I shall engage two different strategies of ethnographic writing, the self-reflexive/interpretive and the deconstructive (Visweswaran 1994: 78–9). The self-reflexive ethnographic approach is understood as one that questions its authority but does not abandon interpretation. While it assumes a shared horizon of knowledge between the reader and the ethnographer, the success of interpretation rests on a hermeneutically achieved unity between the ethnographer, as the subject of knowledge, and the studied people, as the objects of knowledge. This unity, moreover, is seen as the ethnographer's achievement. Before the understanding necessary for authentic interpretation is deemed possible, a certain degree of stability is required (for ethical and cognitive reasons) in the constantly negotiated positionings between the ethnographer and the local people. This understanding is described in terms of a breakthrough accomplished in the field, in episodes implicating the ethnographer's whole person, intellectually, psychologically, emotionally, cognitively. Thus it demonstrates a certain personal commitment for the ethnographer, which results in her transformation.

The identification with the reader, on the other hand, is assumed from the outset. The reader is expected, moreover, to understand the process of the hermeneutic circle (Ricoeur 1981) by means of which the ethnographer has achieved the necessary degree of identification with the people in the field. This collusion between the ethnographer and the reader excludes the people as subjects of knowledge, for understanding is always the ethnographer's achievement, which becomes objectified as self-consciousness. Interpretive ethnography is thus the achievement of different operations rooted in different kinds of identifications and relations of knowledge.

Deconstructive ethnography has a different project and strategy. It discourages identification with the reader by refusing to explain. In this sense it refuses collusion that excludes the object of knowledge, yet its very existence is an elicitation, an invitation to adopt an attitude towards the contents of the ethnography. Deconstructive ethnography may also set itself the task of deconstructing theories while presenting the ethnography without interpretation, except in terms of those now-fragmented theories (Tsing 1993). It finds its explanations and justification not so much in the hermeneutic circle of understanding as in the unpacking of the biases, assumptions and political attitudes behind those theories and perspectives (Visweswaran 1994; cf. Strathern 1981). Interpretation then becomes a global project seeking connections at the level of major historical configurations and political events, rather than the one-to-one empathetic understanding achieved by the ethnographer.

In what follows I shall present the three styles, then discuss the ethnographers' identifications and complicities. My subtitles attempt to encapsulate the ethnographic descriptions and the ethnographer's theoretical perspectives, thereby bringing together what each anthropologist did and what she perceived as enabling her to do it.

ANTHROPOLOGY AS COMMUNICATION IN BORDERLANDS: THE MERATUS OF BORNEO

Anna Tsing paints a picture of the Meratus Dayaks (South Kalimantan, Borneo) as living a culture of constant *bricolage*, stranger alike to both stability and totality. Part of her project is to explore how the Meratus are placed – or 'displaced', because they are placed as a problem – by broader policies and discourses in the context of the Indonesian state and 'civilisation' in general. This placing is not only external; the Meratus internalise and respond to it through various strategies of reinterpretation, challenge, mimickry and parody. For Tsing, this displacement is marginality, the space where state authority is most unreliable and the reinterpretation of its policies most extreme (Tsing 1993: 27). As the state displaces the Meratus, so do the Meratus misplace state rhetoric by copying it (ibid.: 280). This mutual misunderstanding is parallelled by mutual implication in each other's construction: while village politics contribute to making the state, villagers view as state institutions what state officials take for traditional ones (for example, the *adat* household organisation). Submission and autonomy are linked by Meratus local transformation of state policy into exotic ritual. The key elements that combine here are (mutual construction through) misunderstanding, marginality (through asymmetric relations) and connection. Given these interests, Tsing's ethnography 'transgresses' the conventions of separating between 'internal' cultural analysis and 'external' influences and dwells instead on the creativity of interconnections, situating local commentaries 'within wider negotiations of meaning and power at the same time as recognizing local stakes and specificities' (ibid.: 9). We should not expect, then, to find a description of a self-contained culture with underlying principles and structures that unify certain actions in specific contexts and time.

These concepts – misunderstanding, marginality, connection and their attendant social practices – are inextricably bound together. At times, 'misunderstanding' and 'transformation' become indistinguishable, as Meratus transform everything that comes from the outside into a form of contestation. Their cultural endeavours seem wholly taken up with this kind of processing. Prestige comes with external connections, yet what comes from the outside is either transformed into a form of contestation or it achieves local results for entirely serendipitous reasons.

As an example of this serendipity, Tsing recounts a local conflict around a young woman's two marriages. She was an unwilling bride to the first groom and refused to cohabit with him, but liked the second man whom she married after a token divorce fee had been sent to the first husband. As expected, the divorce was contested and several local leaders became involved in the conflict. There seemed to be stalemate, until a police section officer who had hiked over to adjudicate on a separate dispute happened to have a good stay in the homestead of one of the disputing local leaders. He was heard to mention that this leader's settlement was the only one that showed signs of development. The result was that one local point of view won because an official who knew nothing about anything had dined well. Tsing stresses that the story had no local resolution, because 'no local sense of cultural logic or justice was served' (ibid.: 151).

Yet why should Tsing assume the existence of a single and agreed upon 'local sense of cultural logic or justice' which conflict resolution must serve? In my own fieldwork among the Kewa of Papua New Guinea, local conflict management appears to serve local logic. But different resolutions would serve this logic equally well; it is not a monologic. In Tsing's example, prestige from the connection with the outside is presented as the deciding factor. Indeed, she argues that local leaders need state support to maintain their local prominence (ibid.: 111). But she cites no local opinions that suggest this. Her own voice is the only audible one in the construction of meaning on this occasion.

Though Tsing removes layers of 'difference' and replaces them with 'connection', she retains one kind of difference. This is travel, which also links with Meratus views concerning the relationship between the inside and the outside. Meratus do not perceive closed boundaries, but see instead open exchanges between the inside and the outside. Meratus shamanism has developed a notion of speaking subjects as 'those who can expand, not defend, their physical and social boundaries' (ibid.: 179). Despite the fact that this describes an opening to outside knowledge, ironically the neighbouring Banjar consider Meratus dangerous for their *localised* knowledge. Yet this localised knowledge is remarkable precisely for its open disposition, rather than for any specific content.

Tsing refers to this disposition as the ability to 'borrow power'. She describes one instance of bravado, in which Meratus men's submissive bantering with outsiders '[creates] an alliance with the powerful Other, which reaffirms the masculine sexuality of both parties' (ibid.: 199). This strategy becomes the empowerment of one sexuality over another, casting women as the sex over which men can have 'power'. Perhaps not all men are able to transform their humiliating experiences into sexual prowess at home, but they learn at least one lesson: that the assertion of a virile sexuality is linked to authority (ibid.: 199).

In another context women also can borrow power, without the mediation of humiliation. Uma Adang, a female shaman, gave more grandeur to her speeches by having Tsing record them and play them back to audiences. In another connection, Tsing discusses the empowerment of agency and self-definition in the face of disempowering marginality. Evidence for this is found in the self-empowerment of women who had had liaisons with foreign men. Instead of considering themselves victims used by men for their sexual gratification, the women see themselves as desired, free agents who make their own decisions to abandon relationships that interfere with their treasured autonomy and freedom.

Ironically, this activity of the Meratus appears, in the end, to create a certain stability in marginality. Rather than a shifting sand, a perception of disconnection, marginality becomes a perception of connection. *Bricolage* at the margins connects, it is creative play with any fragments one can grasp. Connections are themselves representations, of course. I shall return in the final section to the question of whether Meratus themselves represent to themselves these connections, or if they are Tsing's invention.

In the preceding paragraphs I tried to evoke the pictures that Tsing depicted. What enabled Tsing to depict the Meratus in this way? Her claim to speak from the realm of the diamond queen, the space of communication created by the ethnographer, and (some of the) local people gave her confidence in her authenticity as well as a position from which to speak. For Tsing, there is no neutral space, or the possibility of meeting in a space quite alien to one. Anthropology is communication in borderlands, where one situated commentator meets another. In this space, ethnography and theory merge when data are seen as derived from the living interactions and statements of people who have their own critical awareness. Here, atypical, eccentric informants offer metadiscourses on their culture and the wider world, since the metadiscourse of marginality is precisely their culture and lived experience. (Aside from the extraordinary, the eccentric and atypical, Tsing's other figures are shadowy.) This cultural experience of fragmentation becomes the ethnographer's theoretical perspective, as she engages bits and pieces of classic approaches with locally specific puzzles. 'Local' itself refers to acts of positioning, not to bounded communities. The ethnographer carries her own locality of critical awareness which she must engage in interaction with other local commentaries. This is how theory and ethnography merge analytically. Tsing and Uma Adang created a new event (space) for themselves from these bits and pieces, and this space made them see things, themselves and each other, quite differently. It was a new position.

Tsing gives us ethnography in vignettes. Fragmentation, even of theories, becomes an important part of her theoretical perspective: rather than succumb to the goal of grand theory building by pursuing the coherence of a single approach, her theoretical fragmentation mimics the fragmentation of people's experiences and their response to their marginality. But a shift of perspective could equally show the anthropologist simulating, perhaps inventing, fragmentation by her selective use of currently popular theories and switching between narrative styles. This suggests that what enabled Tsing's interpretation was already based on an interpretation of Meratus previous experience.

Tsing suggests that in entrusting their stories to her, Meratus were expecting her to interpret them to her own world. Interpretation was an activity in which they constantly engaged, not a nefarious one that gave the ethnographer power over them. When Tsing accepted Uma Adang's challenge to take her story of the world to the United States, she took on the responsibility to explain her themes. Thus, 'eccentric' Meratus are depicted as intellectualising about their cultural predicament. Uma Adang's story is a metadiscourse about culture and perceptions of the wider world, rather than just one of the discourses of her culture. But in another way it is one of Meratus cultural discourses. Tsing would not want to distinguish between a metadiscourse and a discourse, because the metadiscourse of a perception of connection also describes how people live their lives. There are no 'imponderabilia' in Tsing's ethnographic accounts, which show people dealing with their culture of marginality. In a later section I shall return to the question of whether people themselves make these connections.

IN AN AUTHENTIC VOICE: FUSING THE ETHNOGRAPHIC WITH THE BIOGRAPHICAL

Nadia Seremetakis's ethnography seems worlds apart from Tsing's. She constructed it in critical opposition to approaches by earlier Mediterraneanists, whose concerns with the binary sets of honour–shame, public–private and male–female presupposed identities formed in a shared social totality. Her point of departure is that 'female identity is constructed through the sign of death and alterity' (1991: 72), and thus 'to examine death in Inner Mani is to look at Maniat society through female eyes' (ibid.: 15, emphasis omitted). Her account of death rites differs from Hertz's in that she refuses to see them as accomplishing separation and reincorporation and thus restoring an assumed preexisting social stability. She justifies this difference by presenting her account as a description of the women's construction, what the women actually are *doing*.

The women of Inner Mani, Southern Greece, are marginalised both internally and externally, by the state (modernity) and by their gender. Though many old practices have fallen into disuse, women continue an age-old tradition of lamenting the dead, controlling attendant divinatory practices and exhuming the bones. The laments are powerful and dangerous performances which bring together women connected by shared substance with the dead person. The good death is a well-mourned one; a solitary singer indicates absence of past reciprocity. A chorus is needed for the antiphonic participation which acts as a mnemonic device that establishes the authority of the witness as guarantor (ibid.: 102). As the lament is passed from singer to singer, it becomes established as truth by the power of the pain that produces it and which it is capable of producing in others. The singing becomes an artefact or object, exchanged between women (ibid.: 118). Antiphony historicises the singer's discourse, making the lament the vocalisation of 'an entire social ensemble' (ibid.: 120). As a system of shared moral inference, the lament together with divination is a material force with a cultural power that makes it socially meaningful (ibid.: 230).

The description of how women's ritual action manages the spaces of inside and outside offers powerful insights into perceptions of self and other (cf. Kristeva 1991). In the separation of death, the estranged other becomes the foreign part of the self. '*Xenitia* (the outside, foreign space, death) is formed by detached parts of the self' (Seremetakis 1991: 216). We can get a better understanding of this formulation by considering how relations are made in life and remade at death. If, as in Maniat women's experience, the relations we construct with others are ones of shared substance, then through this sharing of substance the other is part of me and I am part of the other. When the other is gone into *xenitia* she/he still remains part of me, but an estranged me, a foreign part of the self. Thus foreign space itself – *xenitia* – can be construed as formed by detached parts of the self. It is these 'externalized parts, the exiled arte-facts of exteriority and "collective flesh," [that] demarcate this world from the other, this place from the space of estrangement, and in turn make *xenitia* an unending interiority' (ibid.).

Maniat women do not accomplish a separation at the first death rites. The dead person is not depersonalised at the lament, as at church funerals, but continues to be referred to by name as part of the community. At the time of exhumation the dry bones 'defamiliarise' the dead, but do not efface them. The material remains are reordered into a new symbolic-material relation (ibid.: 189). The symbolisation of death in this relation is not an allegory, but the foundation of historical consciousness (ibid.: 207), as the exteriority of death becomes interiorised into women's bodies (ibid.: 227). The labour of gathering into their bodies the undom-esticated exteriority of death makes each woman's body into a detached interior, replicating the cosmos as fragments of the whole (ibid.: 238). In this understanding, the cosmological does not preexist as a single totality, but must always await its formulation by the cultural coming together of the fragments that will bring it into being.

Making the cosmos into a gendered space of interiority (that is, bringing the outside into the inside) is labour that involves much pain and risk. In their corporeal mimesis of death in the mourning process, women transform their bodies into 'a text of disorder', by standing up to their full height, raising their fists at the sky, cursing and challenging God. The mind/body dualism expressed here is the opposite of philosophical concepts, where the mind is transcendent and the body circumscribed by material conditions linking it to the present. Instead, in the process of divination the mind moves into the future, as when a dream fixes a warning. Seremetakis cautions us not to neglect these powerful somatic aspects of the body by transforming it from a physical *soma* into a sign (*sema*) with only symbolic or metaphorical meaning.

In their work of exposing the finality of the social self, quite literally the bones of the society, women gain a 'cynical wisdom', an ironic stance which commentators have often mistaken for passivity. This fatalism imbues exhumers 'with a sense of futility that may be seen as acceptance of the male discourse of "common-sense"'. What women really exhibit is 'the ironic derealization of all social order' (ibid.: 223; emphasis omitted). Having constructed internal exile, the exhumer cannot feel permanence in this world. She has taken death, an event that 'discloses the invisible in the visible', and through linkages 'not accessible to the cognitive structures of every day social life' has represented the unrepresentable, that is the cosmological order.

How is Seremetakis able to represent the unrepresentable cosmological order, made visible only in its creation by Maniat women? Seremetakis refers to herself, in a complexly qualified way, as a 'native anthropologist' (1993: 2). Though kinship relations are great enablers – her recording and photography were not considered intrusive 'as long as they were perceived as an extension of kinship activity' – she was nonetheless 'objectified, classified, and subjected to a political reading by the Maniats' (1991: 10). Eventually shared substance, particularly food, displaced blood in what can be seen as a metaphor for the substitution of (male) relations of descent by relations of exchange. As an ethnographer, she could enter into the feminine space of death only by becoming a member of the chorus, a witness with contractual obligations who obeys local antiphonic rules for the production of truth (ibid.: 123). Pain is key: her obvious emotion when a particularly powerful lamenter drew tears from her eyes was taken as evidence of her commitment to this truth, at the deep level of unwilled feeling.

Though Seremetakis continues to use the third person in talking about the women, her voice speaks with the authority of someone who has experienced what she is describing. Her dream diary becomes an indicator of anthropological methodology, by tracing an involuntary drawing of her own consciousness into a physiological and cultural mimesis of women's cultural creations. At first she views her dreams as nightmares, until they are assigned a proper referent by Maniat women, who interpret them as warnings. Her own body, her unconscious and her consciousness became 'witnesses' that validated women's culturally creative power (ibid.: 232). It was not enough to see the women's world through their eyes; the ethnographer had to participate in its creation in order to experience what was being created.

Seremetakis distinguishes this ethnographic 'way of knowing' from scientific enquiry, leading her to a reflexivity which constructed a memory of a self quite different from the Western rationalised self. The dreaming disclosed her inheritance in a cultural order from which she had been estranged. Though itself involuntary and uncontrolled, the dream's interpretation was a conscious and deliberate designation of meaning; yet at the same time exegesis is spontaneous, 'and the dream sign operates like a collective voice inflected with shared meanings within the individual consciousness' (ibid.: 233). This voice spoke a language for which she had no translation, using symbols she did not control, 'signs that were both alien and within me; signs that spoke in reference to an internal Other I did not know' (ibid.: 236).

So interpretation is already in the act, one sees it by understanding the ritual. There is only one way to understand the ritual: actions, symbols, are not polysemic. Seremetakis ends on a true insider's note: 'All our lives, women of the Mediterranean have lived with a tradition of institutionalized male and civilizational discourses imposed from the outside that have fragmented and rendered irrational the experience of divination' (ibid.: 235). This identification gives Seremetakis her authentic voice and enables her to depict as she does. No critical space is left between description and interpretation; Seremetakis never questions her interpretation but presents it as the way things are. The voice of the ethnographer merges with the voice of those studied.

ETHNOGRAPHIC EXCESS: PORTRAITS IN ACTION

The portraits are of the Kewa people of Highland New Guinea, who live in societies traditionally described as egalitarian, structured by the big man system of prestige achievement and accompanying gender antagonism (Josephides 1985, LeRoy 1985). Here (Josephides n.d.) I concentrate on a different area of Kewa people's lives, the daily strategies by which they construct and make operational their 'culture'. I describe the Kewa, and allow them to describe themselves, in long and untidy narratives that bring together different kinds of materials: solicited self-accounts, my observations of the eliciting strategies in people's daily interactions, their fights, disputes and so on. These excessive accounts break up a continuous narrative, making untenable any single or generalising picture of 'Kewa culture'.

My approach provides a corrective to an earlier one that concentrated on the mystification of social action. Instead, I discuss how knowledge of the self and its social and moral context comes to be made explicit via the efficacy of social action. The portraits I present are not of persons in static situations, they are dynamic portraits in which strong individuals emerge who forcefully attempt to define themselves within certain contexts which they are also defining. They reveal situations in which results can never be predicted on the basis of norms or institutions, but are constantly negotiable. This is so because it always requires agency to bring things about, even to reactivate 'customs' (cf. Strathern 1988). Actual outcomes falsify the claim that the decisions of socio-political institutions constitute the final word that authenticates cultural practice, while daily strivings are prevarications or corrections. The two are, rather, different strategies for making claims about relations and the status of persons. My field materials enable me to show how individuals themselves subvert so many possible generalisations about social action and cultural institutions.

This picture of the Kewa people emerges from a writing strategy that does not censor excessive accounts. I do not craft stories as an architect who first models a structure in her head and then selects the blocks to build it. Ten years ago it was possible to keep a tight rein on my fieldnotes and use only as much as I needed to carry my points through, but now I can no longer subdue Kewa stories. What I can't subdue, of course, is my own internalised interpretation of my long years of association with the Kewa. When I returned to my fieldnotes they imposed on me a discourse which, like Seremetakis and her dreams, I felt I had little control over. With fieldwork, time and return are crucial factors. After such a long period of shared substances and emotions, I constantly carry my Kewa friends around with me, back to the field, to conferences, to classes. I reread my fieldnotes, their letters, I make constant connections when I read other writing, not only anthropological, which recalls a Kewa friend or event. In my own social relations and daily actions I constantly find parallells with Kewa situations. I become aware, in the middle of an event unfolding in my own professional life, that a critical analysis of a Kewa woman who apparently failed to attach her husband to her – therefore not strategising sufficiently cleverly with cultural norms – may apply to my situation, which nevertheless I view differently. I am forced to question why I view the situations differently. This 'reciprocal criticism' (Merleau-Ponty 1974: 119) is what gives authenticity to accounts arising out of the ethnographic encounter.

In 'The Production of Ethnography' I enclose these excessive stories within two different kinds of narrative. An introduction deproblematises the process of 'knowing the other' through a philosophical enquiry which instead problematises the self, and promotes anthropology as an extension of the everyday pursuit of self-construction. A concluding chapter reproblematises the other-knowing process by considering the ethnographic encounter, in which, after all, it originated. Partially by way of reproof, but more importantly as evidence, I reproduce in my account incidents of my own intransigence, my recalcitrant responses to field situations. They are relevant not only because they affected the story and how it was reported, but also because they show how independent of my feelings my descriptions often were, how powerfully certain narratives lodged themselves in my fieldnotes almost against my will and inclination, questioning assumptions about the authorship and ownership of ethnographic representation.

The strategy does more than present two sides of a picture. The introduction is also a maturer reflection, my intellectual reconstruction of the process of understanding. The conclusion describes what happened in the field, as part of lived experience.

Since I trace the process of coming to know through 'fractured understandings', perhaps I am guilty of recuperating failure as success: I point out 'the difficulties in our own epistemological assumptions and representational strategies' (Visweswaran 1994: 98), but don't, eventually, descry 'cognitive failure' when 'interpretation is unattainable' (ibid.). At this stage, it's not a question of interpretation; it's a question of personal transformation and the relations that make fieldwork possible.

IDENTIFICATIONS AND THEORY: SELF-REFLEXIVE/ INTERPRETIVE ETHNOGRAPHY AND DECONSTRUCTIVE ETHNOGRAPHY

I move to a consideration of these works from the perspective of interpretive ethnography and deconstructive ethnography. I think of the two approaches as espousing different identifications and complicities. Not that the ethnographers under consideration use one or the other approach exclusively, but there are noticeable emphases. First I want to introduce, briefly, a fourth ethnographer, whose strong and almost uncompromising views on the ethics and politics of representation make for stark contrasts with the more mixed approaches of the others.

Kamala Visweswaran, awarded the essay anachronistically (her sentiment but not precise words), has published her second book first. In a series of essays spanning some six years, she discusses her views on feminist ethnography and the impasses of representation. I am interested in her response to 'subject refusal', a form of non-cooperation with the ethnographer's enquiries. During fieldwork in India on the nationalist struggle for independence, Visweswaran was put in touch with a woman, M, who had been an activist. Her very designation – M – denotes Visweswaran's decision to reveal to the reader even less of M than M had revealed to her. In a first interview, M successfully evaded all the ethnographer's questions; in a second, she derailed her enquiries by speaking almost too much about 'irrelevant' issues. Visweswaran does not tell us the content of M's talk, which she clearly sees as a coded message. Instead, she contextualises M's refusal to speak of her involvement in the nationalist struggle as a 'critique of the nation' (1994: 67). Since the telling of individual stories necessitates telling of the collective itself, M's refusal is interpreted as a principled, and heartfelt, refusal to endorse the idea that individual lives should add to the creativity of a nation that has betrayed them.

In another essay, Visweswaran recounts her attempts to interview three women friends, again on their involvement in the nationalist struggle. Their answers are more forthcoming, but not always straightforward and in some cases deliberately misleading. Though this time the confusion is over two of the friends' marriages, the ethnographer easily finds that state betrayal is implicated in the women's unwillingness to speak. In a subtle way, one woman, Janaki, betrays the other to the ethnographer, and the ethnographer resorts to the archives in order, in the end, to tell us more of Janaki's story than Janaki ever told her. Two sets of betrayals are at work here, according to Visweswaran's own definitions: a betrayal of one of her subjects by another, and a betrayal of the subject by the ethnographer.

Betrayal and failure are Visweswaran's much-vaunted, deliberately provocative expressions. In her exchanges with M, Visweswaran herself provocatively '[recuperates] failure, as [a sort of] success', a strategy she critically attributes to feminist anthropologists. She transposes her own 'failure' to allow the subject to speak with a failure in the structure of knowledge and the methodology of enquiry.

As a result of these failures in communication, Visweswaran rejects dialogical ideas about being able to speak with people in the text of an ethnography. The subject's refusal is transformed into the ethnographer's textual refusal to invite the reader to participate in the interpretive experience. Instead, Visweswaran offers us her uncoding, an interpretation informed by historical contextualisation. She 'explains' the subject to us, but will not collude with the reader in an interpretation of the subject.

By means of two separate strategies, Tsing also refuses a collusion with the reader which would exclude the Meratus. First, she undermines the relevance of differences or 'exoticism' in the description of others. Her concern is to unravel and problematise layer after layer of obfuscating prejudice which defines the Western tradition of differentiation. (See, for instance, her discussion of the Tasaday hoax.) Her systematic construction of 'marginality' as a culture of (perhaps denied or deformed) connections is the concrete result of this critique. Second, she assigns to the Meratus a critical role in the ethnographic encounter (the invention of the new space) and in the theoretical framing of her ethnography (the merging of data with theory). Let me elaborate on the second point.

The approaches of self-reflexive interpretivism and deconstruction have fieldwork and writing components. In the text, the self-reflexive interpret-ivist brings to the reader an interpretation of the people which was the ethnographer's achievement in the field encounter. This is not Tsing's strategy; she does not represent the Meratus as the achievement of her own hermeneutic understanding, a triumph of human identification. (This is not to imply that one-to-one empathetic understanding is excluded as fieldwork methodology – Tsing's interactions with Uma Adang are ample evidence to the contrary; but I suggest that Tsing's work has different justifications, projects and strategies.) Her self-positioning is relevant here: she proceeds from analogy rather than empathy (or Ricoeur's hermeneutic). In particular, she draws attention to her own limitations as the lens responsible for reflecting back Meratus women's limitations. Nor does she present this creative analogy as always her own achievement. She describes how Tani, a woman who had had a liaison with a foreign man, befriended her, and redefined both of them as women with initiative and experience, rather than women lacking male protection. This rappro-chement was Tani's achievement, not Tsing's. Tani and other women with similar experiences told stories that alerted Tsing to the importance of seeking quite self-consciously for ways to construct cross-cultural relation-ships. (Tsing is careful to say that this is not culture-to-culture or woman-to-woman communication, but 'stories told by one situated commen-tator to another' (ibid.: 225).) These paths inevitably created new spaces and new positions from which to view.

Tsing refers to this neolocality as cross-cultural storytelling, or 'telling cultural differences'. The message that we must all take responsibility for a 'positioned imagination' would have been innocuous and unpromising without the additional suggestion that we should appreciate the pattern of other places (ibid.: 289). I take this to be Tsing's approach: to appreciate the pattern of another place by allowing its people full expression.

Co-inventiveness is foregrounded in the very naming of the Meratus, which Tsing and a Meratus scholar made up together (Tsing 1994: 286). Meratus also make their entry as scholars in the theoretical framing of Tsing's ethnographic enterprise. In a discussion of US minority scholars, Tsing adds Uma Adang's voice, thus bringing together the two groups as fighting analogous battles and facing analogous problems (ibid.). She brings Meratus community leaders directly to us as theorists 'involved in the active construction of a double consciousness' (ibid.: 289).

Vicente Rafael (1994: 299) notes that Tsing presents Uma Adang as a person who 'always already knows', whereas Tsing herself 'doesn't know, and knows she doesn't know'. This ignorance can also be seen as part of Tsing's deliberate political positioning. She makes an analytic choice in describing the Meratus in the way that she does, not as an autonomous 'traditional culture' but as a marginal one that illustrates the instability of social categories and provides a site from which to view that instability. She wants to deconstruct the local, but can only do it through another invention, the invention of emergence in an exchange relationship between the local and the global. 'Emergent' relations are not made up of local cultural categories. This exchange is symbolised in Tsing's own relationship with Uma Adang, which like all relations is realised in a co-construction, a neolocal space. For Rafael (1994: 300), the 'shared intimacies in the dark' may suggest a 'utopic fantasy of perfect communication across cultures'. An anthropologist has no choice than to retort that if communication across cultures is utopic, then we are living in a utopia.

Letting the people speak for themselves or allowing them agency as actors with their own theoretical perspectives still may not escape the suspicion that the ethnographer is using them for her own ends. Rafael, again, comments on an episode from *In the Realm of the Diamond Queen*, where Tsing undermines a male discourse with the voice of Uma Adang. The anecdote deserves to be told in full. In a heated exchange, non-Muslim Meratus men were debating with Muslim neighbours the relative merits of circumcision. Uma Adang piped up, irreverently deflating the men: 'As for me, I can't really tell the difference' (Tsing 1993: 293).

'A Meratus woman's voice is thus strategically deployed as a surrogate for a feminist anthropologist's, interrupting the masculinist monopoly of representations of alterity', comments Rafael (1994: 298). What does it mean to suggest that Tsing is using Uma Adang to make her own arguments? It suggests that it is not Uma Adang's intention to subvert 'the masculinist monopoly' created by the men. With a subtle and swift stroke, Rafael remystifies the 'difference' which Tsing was at pains to demystify: the difference between the local and the global, between the feminist anthropologist and the unmarked 'Meratus woman'. But what if Tsing is, by contrast, bringing Uma Adang directly to us, letting her speak in her own words and display her own strategic interventions?

Another strategy for bringing the Meratus close to the reader is Tsing's refusal to look for cultural difference 'in independent solutions to human existential problems' (1993: 151), by which I take her to mean that what defines 'the cultural' is not the degree of its exclusion of outside influence in reaching such solutions. This approach does not 'isolate the people represented from the world of readers in a dichotomy that overhomogen-izes both sides'. Thus she invokes a 'common world', but with 'diverse interpretive practices' (ibid.). When she explains the Meratus it is on the basis of her observation of their actions, not as a result of any special empathy.

Yet a question remains. Since Tsing does not wish to overhomogenise, we cannot assume that Uma Adang, Induan Hilling and the other 'eccen-trics' she brings to us are representative of the Meratus. If this is so, we cannot know if the 'Meratus' make the global connections which some eccentric personnages and the ethnographer delineate in their co-invented space. Tsing worries about anthropologists allowing nationalist politicians to frame their understanding of cultural meanings (1994: 288). But should local eccentrics be allowed to do so? Who can speak for the Meratus?

Tsing starts from the premise that parts of theories are ethically or politically wrong and therefore epistemologically unsound. Her point of departure is a global perspective, since prior considerations have con-vinced her that the local situation is inseparable from the global one. Thus there is a sense in which the explanations Tsing provides are not *ethnographic* explanations, or interpretations of the ethnography.

Seremetakis proceeds differently. She challenges theories by the more conventional method of attacking them with ethnographic observations. She is not reflexive in terms of questioning her own authority to interpret: identification replaces reflexivity. She follows a description of her brief apprenticeship by speaking *for* the women and from their perspective, painting a haunting picture of them scanning the horizon in search of a genealogy of shared substance in everything surrounding them, or for 'signs of the self in otherness' (1991: 217). Reading her text we get the uncanny feeling that we are looking through the woman's eyes as she looks into space. We get a double feeling, of looking at the woman looking and also looking through her eyes. If this is an 'archaeology of feeling', it is powerfully evocative.

Three of the texts I discuss in this chapter (Seremetakis, Tsing, Visweswaran) were part of the reading in one of my graduate seminars. Some students commented that though these ethnographic texts richly illustrated fascinating and even at times convincing theoretical points, they did not tell us enough about the people 'as a whole', or how they lived their everyday lives. Though descriptions are always partial, it would be a pity if they became even more confined and selective, especially as the more interesting task of ethnography is to describe the ways in which people create and recreate their lives and their cultures. Students articulated the dilemma by suggesting that there should be two books, since one was never sufficient. While they were engaged by the theoretical projects, they also longed for another account that would describe or evoke people's everyday realities.

My project was to provide this account. 'The Production of Ethnography' is about the relations needed to produce anthropological knowledge, but it also produces that knowledge itself. It attempts to show that while this knowledge originates in the field, it is both partial and excessive. Its partiality cautions me to acknowledge gaps and remain aware of the limits within which I can speak (cf. Strathern 1991). Its excessiveness forces me to abandon theoretical constraints, but leads to new theoretical formulations.

Tsing's fieldwork observations, despite the fact that she often refers to the actual outcome of events as serendipitous, are never excessive. They have a role to play, a point to make. I allow Kewa stories to unfold far beyond any ostensible point. Tsing's key informant, Uma Adang, addresses the reader through Tsing; she wants her stories taken to the powerful outside world. My storytellers just told their stories to me. Aside from their enjoyment of storytelling, they had two agendas. First, they didn't want someone else to represent them to me, but preferred to tell me their own stories, which would then become the basis of a personal, unmediated relationship with me. Second, telling stories was part of the process of eliciting responses to one's constructions of the self and reality.

If Kewa stories are addressed to me and to each other, do I betray them in my text by bringing them to the reader as the achievement of my understanding? There are two parts to my text, and each reveals a different identification. When I engage in philosophical questions of self and other, I use Kewa examples to demonstrate that Kewa social constructs as well as those of the ethnographic encounter can be understood by means of this enquiry. I am justifying my project and explaining my authenticity to the reader on the basis of what I hope are shared premises, and to this extent I identify with the reader.

But in the middle chapters, Kewa stories take over. Their legitimacy depends to some extent on my already established authority, but their persuasiveness resides in their power as stories. Here I bring the Kewa to the reader, and I bring to the reader's scrutiny my own exchanges and relationships. Undoubtedly sometimes I collude with the reader, in assuming that a picture is well painted and will be evocative. But then the excessiveness takes over, and I lose control of any defining process. My authority then shrinks to a wishful claim that I am presenting their accounts as accurately and authoritatively as possible.

What are the different projects of each ethnographer, and what kinds of complicities does each establish? One project is unassailable: a native anthropologist speaks about the senses. The other project is vulnerable, being political. Seremetakis always speaks authoritatively, fusing the ethnographic with the biographical in a reflexive anthropology of the senses (1993: 14) which reaches back into her own past, to recover a bodily memory implanted by the shared substance of commensality and the metaphorisation (transportation) of mythic meanings which 'create passageways between times and spaces' (ibid.: 6). She is unflinching, sure of herself, her descriptions are utterly convincing as descriptions of personal experience. A third project meticulously traces the negotiations, appropriations and resistances that enabled the ethnographer to do fieldwork at all, while at the same time documenting the observed process by which people's actions could lead to an understanding of 'culture'. Finally, the integrity of that documentation is presented as both the result and the enablement of those appropriations and resistances.

While Seremetakis is an assured spokesperson, Tsing speaks with diffidence, exposing her personal vulnerability and setting up Uma Adang as the knower who 'always already knows'. It is not sufficient to explain the difference by the observation that Seremetakis is a 'native anthropologist', a concept which she herself problematises. Visweswaran has a grandmother in India, but does not derive authority from this connection. Quite the contrary, she deliberately sabotages her authority, disempowering herself as a knower. She and Seremetakis use quite different methodologies and epistemologies.

While Visweswaran transforms the subject's refusal to speak into the author's refusal to allow the reader to participate in the interpretation, Tsing explains her ability to bring the Meratus to us in terms of the relations achieved in the field, as a result of concessions made on the part of both ethnographer and subject. Tsing speaks from this negotiated realm of the diamond queen, from the authority bestowed on her by Uma Adang, who asked, as a form of empowerment, for her stories to be taken to the powerful outside. This ethnographic detail shows how our ethnographic strategies are also shaped by the subjects' situations, their global as well as local perceptions, and their demands and expectations of us. There can be no blueprint for how to do fieldwork. It really depends on the local people, and for this reason we have to construct our theories of how to do fieldwork *in the field*. Probably Visweswaran would not tolerate the idea that the subject should make a concession. Yet without concessions there can be no communication, without communication no fieldwork, and without fieldwork no ethnography. Only the field encounter, creative, transformative, and authoritative, can offer legitimacy to ethnographic representation.

ACKNOWLEDGEMENTS

I am grateful to the graduate students who participated in my Anthropology and Feminism seminar at the University of Minnesota in the winter of 1995. For their insights, I thank Susie Bullington, Christy Garlough, Liz Hochberg, Solveig Moen, Jennie Robinson, Kathy Saunders, Twega Tshoombe and David Weinlick.

REFERENCES

Josephides, L. (1985) *The Production of Inequality*, London: Tavistock.
—— (n.d.) 'The Production of Ethnography', unpublished manuscript.
Kristeva, J. (1991) *Strangers to Ourselves*, New York: Columbia University Press.
LeRoy, J. (1985) *Fabricated World*, Vancouver: University of British Columbia Press.
Merleau-Ponty, M. (1974) 'From Mauss to Claude Lévi-Strauss', in J. O'Neill (ed.), *Phenomenology, Language & Sociology*, London: Heinemann.
Rafael, V. (1994) 'Of mimicry and marginality: comments on Anna Tsing's "From the Margins" ', *Cultural Anthropology* 9 (3): 228–301.
Ricoeur, P. (1981) *Hermeneutics and the Human Sciences* (ed. and trans. J. B. Thompson), Cambridge and Paris: Cambridge University Press, Editions de la Maison des Sciences de l'Homme.
Seremetakis, C. N. (1991) *The Last Word: Women, Death and Divination in Inner Mani*, Chicago: University of Chicago Press.
—— (1993) 'The Memory of the Senses: Historical Perception, Commensal Exchange and Modernity', *Visual Anthropology Review*, 9 (2): 2–18.
Strathern, M. (1981) 'Culture in a Netbag: The Manufacture of a Sub-discipline in Anthropology', *Man*, 16 (4): 665–88.
—— (1988) *The Gender of the Gift*, Berkeley: University of California Press.
—— (1991) *Partial Connections*, New York: Rowman & Littlefield.
Tsing, A. L. (1993) *In the Realm of the Diamond Queen*, Princeton: Princeton University Press.
—— (1994) 'From the Margins', *Cultural Anthropology*, 9 (3): 279–97.
Visweswaran, K. (1994) *Fictions of Feminist Ethnography*, Minneapolis: Minnesota University Press.

Chapter 3

Identifying versus identifying with 'the Other'

Reflections on the siting of the subject in anthropological discourse

Glenn Bowman

Edwin Ardener, in an essay entitled 'Social Anthropology and the Decline of Modernism' presented before the 1984 ASA conference (Ardener 1985, 1989), pointed out that anthropology was then traversing an 'epistemological break' opened by a growing awareness among practitioners in the field of the inappropriateness of modernist categories of 'self' and 'other' to their experiences of other peoples and other places. The symptoms of the crisis of confidence he noted there, as in much of the work he produced in the 1970s and 1980s (see Chapman 1989), have been elaborated throughout the past fifteen years in a wide range of writings by other anthropologists investigating the production of anthropological knowledge (see Fabian 1983; Asad 1986; Sperber 1985a; Appadurai 1992 and Thornton 1992). Pre-eminent among these symptoms are a questioning (1) of traditional anthropology's conception of the 'native' as 'fixed' in a time and a place which renders his or her practices and beliefs representative of the entirety of those of a distinct and holistically conceived 'people', (2) of how the anthropologist is 'located' in the cultural and social field of those he or she studies, and (3) of the way the anthropologist 'translates' the particularities of field experiences into a language of anthropological discourse.

All of these questions relate to how we, as academics and anthropologists, represent difference and alterity. That assertion is not, I imagine, contentious. More contentious, I expect, will be my argument that this crisis in how we represent the other is a consequence of how we conceive of subjectivity itself; not only the subjectivity of those we present as the objects of anthropological analysis but also, and more centrally, that of ourselves as those who look upon and interpret the lives of others. In this chapter I query the implications for the representation of other cultures of the concept of the subject which underwrites the anthropological endeavour. I argue that the anthropological subject – that person who objectifies the subjectivities of others – is a particular cultural construction of 'Western' thought[1] which has been rendered untenable by developments that are sloppily characterised in contemporary academic and popular discourse as 'postmodernist'. These developments are often seen to be aspects of contemporary global processes, in particular the elaboration of a global market of commodities and conceptions (Friedman 1992) and the concomitant erasure of clear lines of distinction between the space of ourselves and the space of the other (Foster 1991). Although I concur that such phenomena make the crisis of representation that afflicts our discipline all the more salient, I nonetheless contend that this crisis was already latent in the categories upon which our discipline was founded. It is not, in other words, that changes in the world have rendered the practices of our discipline unworkable, but that those changes have made the pretence of their functionality all the more visible in the contemporary situation. If anthropology does not 'work' in the contemporary world it is not because the world has changed. It is because anthropology, as a particular expression of an in-large-part European hegemonic project, has never functioned as a means of understanding other cultures. To clarify what I mean by this I will have to look more closely at the way we have thought about subjectivity and knowledge.

'Postmodernism' is, as I have claimed above, a sloppy term for understanding a wide and possibly interconnected range of phenomena afflicting contemporary culture and society. The term's lack of clarity is evident in the diversity of the phenomena it claims to label; these can be grouped, on the one hand, into aesthetic and cultural artefacts characterised by pastiche, intertextuality and an indiscriminate merger of 'high' and 'popular' stylistic registers and, on the other hand, into practices of philosophical reading and interpretation marked by an explicit disavowal of any claim to be discerning or representing reality *per se* (see Docherty 1993). Whether or not the future will reveal a common strand uniting this diversity remains to be seen; at present it seems best to distinguish between these two sets of phenomena and to draw from the interwoven congeries of postmodernist discourses those threads which can contribute to an understanding of how we, in the present day, read the world. One of the more salient contributions postmodern theorising can offer is Zygmunt Bauman's distinction between modernism as a commitment to describing – and legislating to effect universally – a vision of the future state of the world,[2] and postmodernism as a position from whence the modernist project of world transformation appears as an historically and culturally localisable programme that has no more claim to legitimacy than any other period's or culture's project of hegemonisation (see Bauman 1987, esp. 110–26).

Bauman's distinction between modernist 'legislators' and postmodernist 'interpreters' foregrounds the issue of who is in the position to define the real. Modernist thinkers defined themselves as members of an elite able to discern the lineaments of the future and to evaluate which tendencies in the present day would contribute to the realisation of that future and which would be retrograde and/or resistant to its coming into being. Postmodernists investigate that illusion of certainty through an attempt to comprehend what in the cultural repertoire of Western culture enabled such a confidence in prescience to emerge and to reign for so long. It is important for us as anthropologists – scholars deeply implicated in a tradition that has served to differentiate between those peoples involved in advancing civilisation and those stilled in the backwaters of 'primitive', 'pre-literate', 'traditional' or 'native' cultures (see Appadurai 1992: 35–8) – to investigate how our discipline bequeathed to us the high vantage point from whence we are allegedly able to look upon, site and evaluate the respective positions of persons of other cultures amidst the range of human societies.

An enquiry into the sources of modernist self-confidence cannot, of course, overlook the issue of sheer differential power; the West, from the period of the Conquistadors to that of twentieth-century colonialism, has proved able – through a combination of technology and strategy – to impose its visions of the past, the present and the future on other peoples (see Todorov 1984 and Asad 1983). Anthropology's early development in the cradle of colonialism has, as Ardener indicates, had a powerful influence on the way we have conceived (and – I will argue – continue to conceive) the character of the other as firmly affixed for the gaze of the anthropologist in a stable and unchanging cultural framework:

> Functionalist fieldwork was begun when the primitives themselves were politically and physically accessible. Classical fieldwork was done under peculiar conditions that led the synchronic approach to appear to be a perfect fit to the facts. The societies studied were unnaturally peaceful. They were held in a ring, in which conflicts were minimized under colonial rule. If the anthropologist entered, the place was stable.
> (Ardener 1989: 203)

The postcolonial period has shaken the confidence of modernist ideologues, including anthropologists, in so far as Western powers have been forced to loose their grip on the peoples of non-Western cultures they had previously held in thrall and Western intellectuals have consequently been forced to recognise that those others are also able to initiate moves in the arena of history. In that sense, the causes of the current crisis in modernist confidence do at least partially reside in the fact that the other has wrenched itself free from the artificial stasis of colonial domination and has developed the means of debating Western discourses on identity and culture.[3]

Force of arms and canniness of technique do not suffice, however, to explain the long, only now faltering, dominion of the West over the rest. That dominion, I would argue, had its enabling roots in the fourth century CE when an offshoot of Judaic diasporic theology, severed from its originary locale by the first- and second-century depredations of Israel by Roman imperial might, was grafted onto imperial ideology to create a union of state power and expansionist universal religion (see Frend 1984: 473–517 and 553–91 and Kee 1982). The Christian subject, forged in and against the multiculturalism of the Roman Empire, was a subject who not only knew the truth in an absolute sense but who also set that truth off against the world.

Christians were driven by a commitment to the world to come and, in pursuit of that world, were initially willing to cut themselves off from the social and cultural milieux in which they were raised so as to create communities modelled on their visions of a future world (see Meeks 1983). By the fourth century, when early Christian millenarianism was incorporated by Constantine and his successors into the will to dominion of the Roman imperial state, an ideology developed committed to the effacement of cultural difference in pursuit of the establishment of a divinely sanctioned this-worldly order prefiguring an other-worldly onto-logical fulfilment. The fifth-century disintegration of imperial power in the West left what remained of 'universal' political power in the hands of the church, and this – legitimated by the ideological programme Augus-tine set out in his *De Civitate Dei* (CE 413–26) – led to a compounding of worldly and other-worldly authority in the Western empire which was not matched in the Orthodox East where political power remained in the hands of the surviving state.[4]

The Christian (here presented as an 'ideal type') was one who knew the truth – not the truth of this world as is but the truth of what this world was intended by God to be. That truth was not yet realised but would be realised in an indeterminate future, and it was the work of the committed Christian to advance the advent of that realisation. A central element of facilitating the coming of the future perfect was the spreading – forcible where necessary – of the Word of God. Another, devolving from the first, was the separating out of 'good seed' from 'bad seed'. In practice this meant, first of all, the extirpation of 'paganism' and 'heresy' from Christian domains. Later, with the expansion of Western dominion over non-Christian cultures, the Christian project manifested itself in Crusades and missionisation. In all these instances alterity was either to be effaced or, where this proved problematic, quarantined. The other was an impediment to the coming of the 'New Jerusalem' and if it could not be convinced to abandon its non-Christian beliefs and practices (its culture) it had to be separated out like chaff so as not to corrupt or pollute the community of the saved.

Christianity, in its commitment to world transformation in the pursuit of the establishment of a future utopic state, was the first modernist project. When its image of the future came to be read by its Enlighten-ment inheritors as a false idol, it nonetheless passed on to the 'new' modernists the same subjectivity that had characterised its adherents. Enlightenment thinkers rejected the 'superstitions' of their Christian ancestors yet, while jettisoning the other-worldliness of Christianity and turning their gazes to the things of this world, retained the position of subjects who would know this world so that they might be better able to refashion it in the image of a 'real' world not yet born. The diversity of the projects grouped as 'Enlightenment' is great, but all of them depended on the discernment and classification of a 'real' (scientifically validated) order beneath the flux of contingency, deceitful appearances and cultural mislabellings (see Adorno and Horkheimer 1979, esp. 3–42). Mary Louise Pratt's stimulating examination of one of the early modernist projects – the eighteenth-century naturalist endeavour to know the order of nature – illustrates the character of Enlightenment understanding:

> natural history conceived of the world as a chaos out of which the scientist *produced* an order. It is not, then, simply a question of depicting the planet as it was. ... The eighteenth-century classificatory systems created the task of locating every species on the planet, extracting it from its particular, arbitrary surroundings (the chaos), and placing it in its appropriate spot in the system (the order – book, collection or garden) with its new written, secular European name. ... Natural history's naming is ... directly transformative. It extracts all the things of the world and redeploys them into a new knowledge formation whose value lies precisely in its difference from the chaotic original. Here the naming, the representing, and the claiming are all one; the naming brings the reality of order into being.
>
> (Pratt 1992: 30, 31, 33)

As she points out, this systematic bringing to consciousness of the real inherent order of nature was closely linked to 'an expanding search for commercially exploitable resources, markets and lands to colonize' (ibid.: 30). The disinterested pursuit of knowledge of the naturalist could not be disengaged from other, more explicitly materialist, projects of world transformation initiated at this time:

> The systematizing of nature ... models the extractive, transformative character of industrial capitalism, and the ordering mechanisms that were beginning to shape urban mass society in Europe under bourgeois hegemony. As an ideological construct, it makes a picture of the planet appropriated and redeployed from a unified, European perspective.
>
> (Ibid.: 36)

However, the avowed disengagement of the scholar from the actual processes of world transformation was vital to his (and very occasionally her) intellectual stature; the intellectual was not he (or she) who carried out the work of reworking the world, but the person who legislated for that labour. The scholar, by positing the real ordering principles of nature, history or whichever other global system came under his or her gaze, equated his or her knowledge with the will to power of the world itself; the latent yet unrealised truth he or she perceived was the same as the goal of natural, historical and human processes, and thus modernist knowledge mapped the yet-to-be-realised but inherent development of the world. The work of world transformation could be carried out by others in accordance with the plans the intellectual contrived; modernist knowledge was not part of the process of history but was a pre-cognisance of the goal of history.

The modernist subject – the intellectual – was, then, sited not within the world but in a place from whence he or she could look upon and assess the world from a detached vantage point. The task of the intellectual was, as Descartes (1596–1650) indicated, to think and, through that thinking, to bring order into a world which, without that thought, would be no more than chaos. This construction of the Enlightenment subject sited the intellectual as the locus in which reality finds its being, and thus effectively placed the intellectual on the throne which, with the collapse of Christian hegemony, had been vacated by the original transcendental subject – God. As Michel Henry argues, the modernist construction of the subject sites the intellectual (who is distinguished from the rest of humanity by his or her ability to think 'objectively', i.e. without the distorting influence of affect) as not only the legislator of but also the reason for the world:

> Man identified as the subject ... is granted an exorbitant privilege in that there is in the end no Being nor being except in relation to him, for him and through him, and this in so far as he constitutes the *a priori* condition of possibility for all experience and thus for all that is and can be, a least for us. It is inasmuch as he is identified as this subject that man appears as a super-being to whom everything that is has entrusted its Being, a Being that the subject henceforth has at his disposal and that he can make use of, not as he sees fit (in which case he might just as well not make use of it at all, or respect it, fear it, etc.), but rather as that which is in its principle subjugated to him by way of its ineluctable and unsurmountable ontological condition, as an ob-ject whose being is the Subject.
>
> (Henry 1991: 157–8)

Modernism then constitutes the world as a disordered material to be made over in accordance with images of its potential realisation generated by the thought of an intelligentsia. It furthermore valorises technology as the means by which that remaking is to be carried out. The place of the intellectual in the 'ivory tower' of academia – institutionalised by the modernist professionalisation of intellectual cogitation – is a location 'outside' of the world. From this vantage point the intellectual could gaze upon and legislate for the world without the danger of being implicated in its confusion.

The Enlightenment tradition which has given rise to our present-day conceptions of academic knowledge thus freed the thinker and legislator from the need to know the will of God and placed at the core of identity the ability to know in the abstract. Descartes's axiomatic assertion that the essence of being was thought – 'I think therefore I am' (Descartes 1968: 54) – left in abeyance the origins of and conditions for thought; the subject was constituted in thinking (those who could not 'think' were objects) and what the subject thought about was, in effect, defined *a priori* as 'truth'. By imaging thought as the ontological ground of being, the Enlightenment project rendered unthinkable the question of what cultural and material conditions made this will to truth possible; the thinker was positioned to look upon the world as the object of cogitation, but was unable to objectify his or her own subject position as an object to be analysed.[5] How 'thinkers' positioned themselves as those 'in the know' was a question this positioning rendered unthinkable; the priority of intellectual knowledge within an ideological system that needed intellectuals to validate its projects of world transformation was taken as self-evident. The cultural roots of modernism were thus outside of the frame of contemplation; Bauman (1987: 116) writes that 'no outside vantage point was available as a frame of reference for the perception of modernity itself. In a sense, modernity was ... self-referential and self-validating'.[6] What modernity – and the subject at the core of it – validated was a view of the world in which the thinker was separated from the world he or she thought while others, enmeshed in superstition and illusion, were objects to be analysed and legislated for. The place of intellectual knowledge was a place of power, but that concatenation of knowledge and power was rendered invisible by the detachment of the intellectual from the work of dominion.

Anthropology served modernity as a means of allocating places and roles to those who were coming under modernity's dominion but who were not, as yet, invested in its programmes. The anthropologist played an important part in imaging others as those who could, if they could be made to see the inadequacies of their ways, be brought into the progressive development of mankind. Whereas early anthropology was closely implicated in setting up categories of racial difference which distinguished the (white) human from sub-humans who were fit only to serve as matter to be manipulated, anthropology from the advent of functionalism until nearly the present day sought, in its attempts to discern the logic of social formations, to constitute an image of a dispersed yet potentially unifiable human nature which could, with modernisation, be realised. Asad, in his critique of Gellner (1970), indicates that as late as 1970 he was able to carry on a tradition of defining 'cultural translation' as

> a matter of determining implicit meanings – not the meanings the native speaker actually acknowledges in his speech, not even the meanings the native listener necessarily accepts, but those he is 'potentially capable of sharing' with scientific authority 'in some ideal situation'. . . . The fact that in that 'ideal situation' he would no longer be a Berber tribesman but something coming to resemble Professor Gellner does not appear to worry such cultural translators.
>
> (Asad 1986: 162)

Modern anthropology was concerned to discern a human nature that could, once it was understood, serve as a basis for understanding – and implicitly for dissolving – cultural difference. Its tendency to 'fix' the peoples of other cultures within social and cultural structures which entrapped them in the 'idioms of their beliefs' served to explain why they had to date played no role in the modernising process; the 'translation' of those beliefs into the idiom of modernist comprehension served as a prolegomenon to the destruction of those aspects of their cultures that prevented assimilation into the project of modernity. Anthropologists rarely dirtied their hands in that work of destruction, but they provided both the image of the other's potential assimilability and the knowledge of how that assimilation could be brought about and resistance to it overcome (see Asad 1983 and Kuper 1975: 123–49 and *passim*).

One of the symptoms for anthropologists of the epistemic break, Ardener hypothesised, is a thinking through of the way modernist anthropology structured the world it studied. Fabian's (1983) important enquiry into the way the other was displaced from the space of historical evolution, like Appadurai's examination of the way anthropological discourses present the peoples of other cultures as 'immobilized by their belonging to a place' (1992: 35), engages in a querying of the effects of the modernist distinction between those who can think (and carry out anthropological studies) and those who are thought for by their cultures. We can now, in a world in which rapid historical transformations and increased mobility between periphery and centre have made visible a plethora of other peoples not easily excluded from history, see the hubris of a world view which endowed thought (and thus being) only to those at the heart of modernism. Nonetheless, I would contend that anthropology – despite a wealth of approaches to the 'reinvention' of the discipline – remains ensnared in a conceptual trap which was constructed in the period of modernist hegemony. If the crisis of modernism has forced us to recognise that modernist constructions of knowledge and practice accord with the specific cultural codes of an historically specific society, we are nonetheless unwilling to rethink our self-defined distinction from persons of other cultures. If we cannot simply subordinate the other to our cultural projects we will redraw the borders of the modernist field and allow the other to occupy his or her cultural space while we remain ensconced in our own. Sperber (1985a: 62) succinctly states the logic of contemporary anthropology's remaking of the other as 'the Other':

> in pre-relativist anthropology, Westerners thought of themselves as superior to all other people. Relativism replaced this despicable hierarchical gap by a kind of cognitive apartheid. If we cannot be superior in the same world, let each people live in its own world.[7]

In today's anthropology the other still remains culturally 'in place' despite the evidence on the thoroughfares of any First World metropolis that his or her locale now overlaps spatially with our own. Today's reification of the same cultural difference that modernism was committed to dissolving is a negative development[8] and all contemporary anthropological attempts to 'reinvent' the discipline through hermeneutical understanding, reflexive writing and dialogical discourse are likely to be rendered ineffectual by the will radically to divide 'us' and 'them' which underwrites it.

Throughout the changes the modernist impulse has gone through over the past seventeen hundred years, it has retained a commitment to the unification of humankind under the aegis of an absolute knowledge. Those defined as 'human' were seen as having, beneath the historical accretions of idolatry, cultural primitivism and superstition, the potential for realising the truth and, once it was perceived, for subordinating themselves to its order. Modernism has always been potentially universalistic. The contemporary anthropological aversion to the hubris of Enlightenment modernism, which is evident in the celebration of radical alterity and cultural relativism, threatens to throw the idea of a common humanity out with the bathwater of modernism. This is more, I contend, than a reaction to the homogenisation implicit in modernism's project of subordinating all humanity to a universal regime of truth. The proclivity to assert cultural difference against modernism's programme of rendering all the world's subjects the same as an idealised Western subject is laudable, and the acknowledgement that people have a right to difference is not only laudable but also difficult in the contemporary world not to allow. However, the tendency, implicit in the new anthropologies, to characterise others as difference incarnate is regrettable. It is also, as Sperber (1985a: 62–3) affirms, counter-factual:

> The best evidence against relativism is, ultimately, the very activity of anthropologists, while the best evidence for relativism seems to be in the writings of anthropologists. How can that be? It seems that, in retracing their steps, anthropologists transform into unfathomable gaps the shallow and irregular boundaries that they had found not so

difficult to cross, thereby protecting their own sense of identity, and providing their philosophical and lay audience with just what they want to hear.

Sperber is, I believe, right to point to the ability of a fieldworker to integrate him- or herself into another culture's conceptual space as proof against ideas of radical cultural difference. His assertion that the anthropologist subsequently problematises that incorporation in order to protect his/her identity and provide a 'philosophical and lay audience with just what they want to hear' is more profound, however, than it sounds on a first reading; this is not a matter of an anthropological machismo but an investment of the anthropologist (and his or her audiences) in a conception of knowledge inherited from the modernist idea of truth elaborated above. As Sperber points out, there is a serious disjunction between the fieldworker's 'intuitive' experience of another culture and the way that experience is translated for an academic audience in anthropological texts presented in terms of 'a vague scientific project nursed in a compost of philosophical reminiscences' (1985b: 10). This project is the residual shadow of the modernism that nurtured the development of anthropology, and the reason the anthropologist retains allegiance to it is that it props up his or her investment in an intellectual subjectivity posited on the ability to know the truth about the world. It is not enough for the anthropologist to understand the logic of another culture; that logic must be elevated, through translation into a technical and universalising language, into something more authoritative and 'truthful' than anything an indigenous language could comprehend. Like the eighteenth-century naturalist, the anthropologist must dismember the world as experienced and reassemble it in accordance with a language that can account, in Sperber's terms, 'for the variability of human cultures' (ibid.) or which, in my own terms, can mark out the anthropologist as one who knows the truth behind phenomena.

Is there a way past this impasse? Is it possible for the anthropologist to resituate him- or herself in field and text in a site that does not simultaneously deny both his or her intuitive experience of being assimilated into another culture and the 'native's' ability to reason, innovate and adapt to change that makes itself so evident to the anthropologist in the field? I would argue that as long as the anthropologist retains an affiliation to the intellectual tradition that constitutes him or her as the subject who gazes upon the world as object and speaks its truth, he or she cannot escape those consequences. The unity of the Cartesian subject as 'the one who thinks the world' carries within it a radical, and nihilistically self-referential, alienation from that world; as Conrad observed in *Heart of Darkness*, his study of the modernist intellectual in the bush, Kurtz, the epitome of all that was progressive in European thought, 'had kicked himself loose of the earth . . . [and, in so doing] had kicked the very earth to pieces' (1925: 144). It is only through discarding that notion of the unified subject, whose distinguishing ability to ratiocinate has nothing to do with the world he or she thinks, that one can move beyond that profound, and profoundly destructive, alienation.

Freud's early twentieth-century enquiry into the grounding of consciousness in the unconscious posited the conscious, thinking subject not as an entity complete in itself but as one facet of a split subject which, on the one hand, represents itself to itself as an autonomous rational agent while, on the other hand, retaining in the unconscious the traces of its coming to conscious being as a subject. Lacan, who developed Freudian insights in his study of identity formation in the infant, contended that subjectivity is initiated in a moment of *méconnaissance* when the child, encountering an image of itself mirrored literally or linguistically, identifies with that exterior image embodying the self-control, bodily coherence and power to draw the attention of the carer that the child lacks. The infant, in this initial moment of identification, finds its 'ideal ego' in an image sited beyond the bounds of its body.

> This jubilant assumption of his specular image by the child at the *infans* stage, still sunk in his motor incapacity and nursling dependence, would seem to exhibit in an exemplary situation the symbolic matrix in which the *I* is precipitated in a primordial form, before it is objectified in the dialectic of identification with the other, and before language restores to it, in the universal, its function as subject.
>
> (Lacan 1977: 2)

This primary identification of the mirror phase provides, according to Lacan, 'the root of the secondary identifications' (ibid.). As the child moves into language and the web of social relations which progressively embraces it, it finds (both consciously and unconsciously) the images of selfhood to which it will aspire in the desires, speeches and rituals of those others with whom it comes into contact and on whom it depends. In Althusser's (1971) terms, identity arises through the interpellation of the self into the discourses of others.

The autonomous and self-generating place of identity of the thinking subject is, then, a *bricolage* of identifications – some recalled and others repressed – drawn from the social world in which it comes to consciousness. The self is then, in part, the not-self through which it constitutes itself, and, in recognising the penetration of the space of the autonomous subject with the constitutive presence of its other, the subject abrogates the right to judge the other as object from the place of the self as subject:

> It is the subject consisting of the 'I represent to myself' that is edged out of the problematic, which in other words can no longer claim to

reduce its whole being to its phenomenality, its 'consciousness', its 'I represent myself to myself', precisely because in its being there is a host of things that it is not representing to itself. . . . I do not represent to myself everything that I am, . . . my consciousness is not coextensive with my being, . . . there is an unconscious part of me, . . . I am not master of my own house.

(Henry 1991: 164)

The subject that imagines itself as set off from and assessing the significance of an objective world is, in fact, fundamentally and inescapably implicated in that world.

What, then, is the significance of this deconstruction of the subject for the work of the anthropologist? First, the dissolution of the autonomous position of the subject who knows allows us to turn attention to the issue of how that subject represents itself to itself as subject and whence comes the possibility of its seeing itself in those terms. This turning will reveal modernist subjectivity as an artefact produced within the specific history of Western ideologies by modes of pedagogy and situatings of authority which enabled and encouraged the modernist thinker to think itself in that particular way. The absolutist authority and autonomous being of the Cartesian ego is thereby dissolved back into the discourses of the societies from which it emerged and the subject can thus begin to think of its subjecthood as a social fact.

Second, an awareness of how the subject takes up its position in the anthropologist's own society provides a means of understanding the other not as one like ourselves in the sense of sharing a common identity but as one who, like ourselves, takes up its identity through identifications with subject positions offered it by the situations it encounters. The other then becomes like ourselves in so far as, like ourselves, he or she does not simply *have* an identity but *builds up* a repertoire of identities through identifications with subject positions set out in the discourses he or she encounters in negotiating his or her life. The anthropologist, who in carrying out fieldwork seeks to locate him- or herself as the site of address of discourses and practices of the people he or she studies, is legitimated in his or her feeling of achieving an intuitive understanding of another culture; he or she shares with those who are 'native' to the other cultural terrain the experience of learning to site him- or herself in the spaces of identification provided by that culture's *habitus*.[9] The other is not, then, fundamentally different from us – is not Other – but shares with us the need to construct its subjectivity out of the elements provided for it by its concourse with others in the social world; the difference between us and others lies in the specific characters and consequent configurations of the social facts we encounter. The anthropologist who attempts to 'see the world as the other sees it', works towards developing a new repertoire of identifications with others' spaces just as the 'native' develops means of recognising his or her self as addressed by other peoples' discourses when displaced from his or her home territory by any of the several delocalising powers in the contemporary world or encountering in his or her natal territory images and addresses originating elsewhere (see Ossman 1994).

In this sense 'culture' as a discrete entity which 'thinks' its subjects dissolves; culture is here reinterpreted as a set of potential sitings of those who take up identifications within the terrain it hegemonises. However, the taking up of identifications is a labile process, dependent not only on the vagaries of individual histories but also on the global situation in which that culture exists. 'Outside' influences 'coming in', like 'inside' persons 'going out', will introduce new articulations of identity into that space, and, as Friedman demonstrates with reference to Hawaii and the Congo, new formulations of identity by those who 'belong' to a particular culture will radically transform the character of that culture (Friedman 1992). My fieldwork in the Israeli-Occupied Territories and in former Yugoslavia has familiarised me with situations in which 'internal' developments and 'external' influences give rise to rapid and radical reformulations of identity (see Bowman 1993, 1994a, 1994b, forthcoming). These changes are limited by the sites of identification available to persons as well as by the traces left in their memories (conscious and unconscious) of previous interpellations, but they dissolve the idea of an essential culture that can be identified, while rendering laughable the idea of these 'natives' as people thought by their stable cultures and able only to suffer history rather than make it.

My earlier query about whether or not it is necessary to throw the baby of a common humanity out with the bathwater of modernism is here answered in the negative, in more senses than one. I contend that humanity does not, as modernism proposes, have a common essential (and yet-to-be-realised) identity. Instead humanity shares a common condition which is that of an absence of essential identity. Human beings, who constitute themselves semiotically rather than instinctually, identify themselves with subject positions (placements in relation to the actions or emotions of others) presented to them by discourses in language and other signifying systems (see Vološinov 1986 [1929] and Foucault 1978, 1985, 1986). Those identifications are motivated by the desire to find in the discourses of others the guarantors of identity human beings are unable to locate in selves which constantly adapt to changing contexts and situations. One of the more heady identifications in human history has been that of the person with access to an absolute and universal truth; modernism, which successively provided spaces for the cleric and the intellectual to attain that space of sovereign subjecthood, not only bequeathed that identity to the modernist subject but also, in doing so, presented that subject with the prerogative to identify all others. That he or she did so by making the others over in his or her own (deferred) image and with reference to his or her own desires has had a powerful and deleterious effect not only on the other so identified but also on the development of our ways of knowing the world and our selves. We, as anthropologists, already know that we come to know the other not through imposing distance but by striving in our fieldwork and in our subsequent analysis of that work to see the other's world (and ourselves as intruders in it) from the subject positions the other occupies. If we are to play a part in finding a way out of the impasse of modernism's epistemological failure, it can only be through discrediting the modernist imperative to 'identify' the other as object by attending to the processes of coming to knowledge (of other and self) through 'identifying with' the other as subject.

NOTES

1 I am not happy with the generalising category of 'Western' in so far as the borders it promises to delineate cannot be definitively mapped. I will nonetheless, for reasons set out below, use 'Western' as a shorthand means of marking out those communities that invested their identities in projects of inflicting a particular conception of 'truth' born out of a melding of Platonic philosophy, Judaic metaphysics and the *realpolitiks* of the collapsing Roman Empire not only on 'unenlightened' members of their own societies but also upon the rest of the world. This project of spiritual and political transformation transformed itself, after the collapse of the intellectual and political hegemony of the Christian project of missionisation, into the 'rationalist' agenda of modernisation and colonisation.

2 Ardener claimed that modernism 'consciously place(s) the label before the event. This development was, in modernism, parasitical on philosophies of historical progress, in which styles of the past in thought or taste received labels; the future received its labels in advance. The modern is thus a kind of appropriated future' (Ardener 1989: 200).

3 See *The Colonial Harem* (Alloula 1986) for a strong example of postcolonial redefinition of identity by the formerly colonised as well as, for an earlier illustration of the fact that the colonised were always – if not always successfully – engaged in a struggle over representation, *The Savage Hits Back* (Lips 1966).

4 This 'parting of the ways' (Brown 1982) was to have profound implications for subsequent developments in Christian ideologies and the systems of thought that devolved out of them (see Bowman 1991: 100–6). In light of this divergence I will henceforth, when discussing 'Christian' ideologies, be referring to Latin (both Catholic and Protestant) and not Orthodox Christianities.

5 Descartes, in Discourse Four of his *Discourse on the Method of Properly Conducting One's Reason and of Seeking the Truth in the Sciences* (1637), writes 'I . . . concluded that I was a substance, of which the whole essence or nature consists in thinking, and which, in order to exist, needs no place and depends on no material thing; so that this "I", that is to say, the mind, by which I am what I am, is entirely distinct from the body, and even that it is easier to know than the body, and moreover, that even if the body were not,

it would not cease to be all that it is' (Descartes 1968: 54). This positioning of the thinker in a place distinct from the objects it considers hindered those who subsequently attempted to think the conditions of thought. Thus Durkheim and Mauss, who were concerned with analysing the social ground of thought itself, carried out that analysis from a modernist position; in studying the conditions for the thinking of others who were unable to think 'objectively' (the primitive, the anomic, those constrained by the fetters of class and occupation) they retained their positions as subjects able to know the other while disavowing the necessity of analysing the site from which they thought that other.

6 Ardener states that 'the reason why modernism goes undefined [is that] it has for long been the water in which the ordinary intelligentsia, goldfish-like, has swum – and as everyone knows, "fish are the last to discover water" ' (Ardener 1985: 193).

7 This tendency, in contemporary anthropology, to retreat behind newly bulwarked borders of cultural difference must, I believe, be considered as analogous to and sharing a rationale with the current political tendency to celebrate and enforce exclusive nationalisms and ethnicities.

8 Its negativity is foregrounded by a new ethic of 'tolerance' to difference; tolerance is the benign version of the will to exclusion, and is prone – when the space of autonomous identity appears threatened by the presence of an other – to transform itself rapidly into xenophobia.

9 Sperber, in discussing how ethnographic interpretation can be presented, suggests that the process of rendering the conceptual framework of another culture intelligible involves a process not dissimilar to that by which a person comes to comprehend the significance of a novel subject position offered up for the taking; one sees analogies to sites one has already occupied and traverses the differences between those and the novel position through a creative distortion of earlier identifications (1985b: 25).

REFERENCES

Adorno, T. and M. Horkheimer (1979) *Dialectic of Enlightenment* (John Cumming, trans.), London: Verso.

Alloula, M. (1986) *The Colonial Harem* (Myrna Godzich and Wlad Godzich, trans.), Minneapolis: University of Minnesota Press.

Althusser, L. (1971) 'Ideology and Ideological State Apparatuses (notes towards an investigation)', in *Lenin and Philosophy and Other Essays* (Ben Brewster, trans.), London: Verso.

Appadurai, A. (1992) 'Putting Hierarchy in its Place', in G. Marcus (ed.), *Rereading Cultural Anthropology*, Durham: Duke University Press.

Ardener, E. (1985) 'Social Anthropology and the Decline of Modernism', in J. Overing (ed.), *Reason and Morality*, London: Tavistock.

—— (1989), 'Social Anthropology and the Decline of Modernism', in M. Chapman (ed.), *Edwin Ardener: The Voice of Prophecy and Other Essays*, Oxford: Basil Blackwell.

Asad, T. (ed.) (1983) *Anthropology and the Colonial Encounter*, London: Ithaca Press.

—— (1986) 'The Concept of Cultural Translation in British Social Anthropology', in J. Clifford and G. Marcus (eds), *Writing Culture: The Poetics and Politics of Ethnography*, Berkeley: University of California Press.

Bauman, Z. (1987) *Legislators and Interpreters: On Modernity, Post-Modernity and Intellectuals*, London: Polity Press.

Bellah, R. (1964) 'Religious Evolution', *American Sociological Review*, 29: 358–74.

Bowman, G. (1991) 'Christian Ideology and the Image of a Holy Land: The Place of Jerusalem Pilgrimage in the Various Christianities', in J. Eade and M. Sallnow (eds), *Contesting the Sacred: The Anthropology of Christian Pilgrimage*, London: Routledge.

—— (1993) 'Nationalising the Sacred: Shrines and Shifting Identities in the Israeli-Occupied Territories', *Man*, 28: 431–60.

—— (1994a) 'A Country of Words: Conceiving the Palestinian Nation from the Position of Exile', in E. Laclau (ed.), *The Making of Political Identities*, London: Verso.

—— (1994b) 'Xenophobia, Phantasy and the Nation: The Logic of Ethnic Violence in Former Yugoslavia', in V. Goddard, J. Llobera and C. Shore (eds), *The Anthropology of Europe: Identity and Boundaries in Conflict*, London: Berg.

—— (forthcoming) 'Constitutive Violence and Rhetorics of Identity: A Comparative Study of Nationalist Movements in the Israeli-Occupied Territories and Former Yugoslavia', in B. Kapferer (ed.), *Nationalism and Violence*, Oxford: Berg.

Brown, P. (1982) 'Eastern and Western Christendom in Late Antiquity: A Parting of the Ways', in *Society and the Holy in Late Antiquity*, London: Faber & Faber.

Chapman, M. (ed.), (1989) *Edwin Ardener: The Voice of Prophecy and Other Essays*, Oxford: Basil Blackwell.

Conrad, J. (1925) 'Heart of Darkness', in *Youth: A Narrative and Two Other Stories*, Edinburgh: John Grant.

Descartes, R. (1968) *Discourse on Method and the Meditations* (F. E. Sutcliffe, trans.), Harmondsworth: Penguin Books.

Docherty, T. (1993) 'Postmodernism: An Introduction', in T. Docherty (ed.), *Postmodernism: A Reader*, Hemel Hempstead: Harvester Wheatsheaf.

Dumont, L. (1982) 'A Modified View of our Origins: The Christian Beginnings of Modern Individualism', *Religion*, 12 (1): 1–27.

Fabian, J. (1983) *Time and the Other: How Anthropology Makes its Object*, New York: Columbia University Press.

Foster, R. (1991) 'Making National Cultures in the Global Ecumene', in B. Siegel (ed.), *Annual Review of Anthropology*, Palo Alto: Annual Reviews Inc.

Foucault, M. (1978) *The History of Sexuality* (Robert Hurley, trans.), New York: Random House.

—— (1985) *The Use of Pleasure* (Robert Hurley, trans.), New York: Random House.

—— (1986) *The Care of the Self* (Robert Hurley, trans.), New York: Random House.

Frend, W. H. C. (1984) *The Rise of Christianity*, London: Dartman, Longman & Todd.

Friedman, J. (1992) 'Narcissism, Roots and Postmodernity: The Constitution of Selfhood in the Global Crisis', in S. Lash and J. Friedman (eds), *Modernity and Identity,* Oxford: Basil Blackwell.

Gellner, E. (1970) 'Concepts and Society', in B. Wilson (ed.), *Rationality*, Oxford: Basil Blackwell.

Henry, M. (1991) 'The Critique of the Subject', in E. Cadava, P. Connor and J.-L. Nancy (eds), *Who Comes After the Subject?*, London: Routledge.

Herrin, J. (1987) *The Formation of Christendom*, Oxford: Basil Blackwell.

Kee, A. (1982) *Constantine versus Christ: The Triumph of Ideology*, London: SCM Press.

Kuper, A. (1975) *Anthropologists and Anthropology: The British School, 1922–1972*, Harmondsworth: Penguin Books.

Lacan, J. (1977) 'The Mirror Phase as Formative of the Function of the I', in *Ecrits: A Selection* (Alan Sheridan, trans.), London: Tavistock.

Lips, J. (1966) *The Savage Hits Back* (Vincent Benson, trans.), New Hyde Park, New York: University Books.

Meeks, W. (1983) *The First Urban Christians: The Social World of the Apostle Paul*, New Haven: Yale University Press.

Ossman, S. (1994) *Picturing Casablanca: Portraits of Power in a Modern City*, Berkeley: University of California Press.

Pratt, M. L. (1992) 'Science, Planetary Consciousness, Interiors', in *Imperial Eyes: Travel Writing and Transculturation*, London: Routledge.

Sperber, D. (1985a) 'Apparently Irrational Beliefs', in *On Anthropological Knowledge: Three Essays*, Cambridge: Cambridge University Press.

—— (1985b) 'Interpretive Ethnography and Theoretical Anthropology', in *On Anthropological Knowledge: Three Essays*, Cambridge: Cambridge University Press.

Thornton, R. (1992) 'The Rhetoric of Ethnographic Holism', in G. Marcus (ed.), *Rereading Cultural Anthropology*, Durham: Duke University Press.

Todorov, T. (1984) *The Conquest of America: The Question of the Other*, New York: Harper & Row.

Vološinov, V. N. (1986) [1929]) *Marxism and the Philosophy of Language* (Ladislav Matejka and I. R. Titunik, trans.), Cambridge, MA: Harvard University Press.

Weber, M. (1930) *The Protestant Ethic and the Spirit of Capitalism* (Talcott Parsons, trans.), London: Allen & Unwin.

Chapter 4

Representations and the re-presentation of *family*

An analysis of divorce narratives[1]

Bob Simpson

> Kinship does not consist in the objective ties of descent or consanguinity between individuals, it exists in human consciousness; it is an arbitrary system of representation.
>
> (Lévi-Strauss cited in Blackwood 1986)

In December 1992 the news finally broke that Charles and Diana, the Prince and Princess of Wales and future king and queen of England, were to separate. The *Daily Mirror* announced the 'end of a fairytale' and ran a twelve-page 'royal souvenir'. The tabloids poured forth on every conceivable angle, from the upset of the Queen and the fate of the 'little princes' to the astrologer who had predicted the separation in his charts. The royal family, iconic and nuclear, was evidently no different from many other families in Britain in the 1990s, the site of profound and deeply distressing contradictions between ideals and expectations on the one hand and actual experiences on the other.

Marital dissolution is the contemporary means to resolve the problem of incompatibility and failed expectations between husbands and wives. The rearrangement of roles, identities and relationships that follows such action signals a major transformation of domestic and kinship organisation in Britain over the last decade.[2] The primary reason for this is that divorce confounds normative patterns of social reproduction and transmission. As a consequence, the frequency with which couples resort to divorce has triggered its own particular crisis of representation regarding the *family*.[3] The crisis is evident in political and media rhetoric surrounding the *family* and among academic commentators who seek to construct textual representations of *family*. Indeed, a fundamental problem of studying *family* is that one is always dealing with representations of one kind or another and to write about *family* is to engage in the politics of description. Finally, for those who divorce there is always the question of who determines just what are to be considered appropriate, accurate or acceptable representations of domestic, interpersonal and intimate relationships?

The general theme for this essay is thus on *family* and the multiplicity of representations evident in British society at the present time. However, my particular ethnographic focus is upon the relationship between different levels of representation and in particular the relationship between dominant, hegemonic representations of *family* which have a wide currency and legitimacy and the reworking and re-presentation of these in the narratives of divorced men and women.

In their most general sense, acts of representation involve the making of 'part for whole' relationships. Cultural representations of *family*, for example, involve the reduction of evident diversity to a repertoire of highly selective and normative images of the kind Leach once suggested might be found on the back of a cereal packet (*Guardian* 29 January 1986). Acts of representation thus conceal and obscure diversity but rather more pertinently they conceal the broader issues of power and ideology through which a society regulates and orders its own physical and cultural reproduction.

Questions of legitimacy in relation to *family* forms have become of increasing importance in Britain as the discourse on familism has grown in its ubiquitousness. Throughout the 1980s familism was placed at the heart of the Thatcherite project and provided a rich fund of appealing and easily accessible metaphors – as Thatcher once remarked on the *family*, 'it is a nursery, a school, a hospital, a leisure centre, a place of refuge, a place of rest. It encompasses the whole of society' (Conservative Women's Conference 1988, cited in Franklin *et al.* 1991: 38). The reification of the *family* effectively drew attention away from the more ominous project of dismantling civic and public culture and letting the market reign. In her famous statement that 'there is no such thing as society. There are individual men and women and there are families' (cited in Strathern 1992: 144), Thatcher simultanously staked the outer limits of social concern and the locus of enterprise, choice and consumption. For many people in Britain the simple fact of the matter was that their own experience did not accord with the representations of *family* that figured repeatedly in the rhetoric. To be a single, homosexual or divorced parent, is to confound patterns of orderly physical and social reproduction in contemporary Western society. In other words, to go with the grain affirms the *family*, in its nuclear, heterosexual, co-resident, stable, monogamous form, as a natural, universal and self-evident structure, but to go against the grain highlights *family* as a problematic and potentially deviant artifice. The experience of those living in such arrangements was, and continues to be, one of marginalisation, with their alternatives to the normative images, values and expectations surrounding the *family* portrayed as pretence. The data that I draw upon reveal something of the response of those who find themselves portrayed in this way and shows how, through narrative, alternative representations of familial legitimacy are constructed.[4]

The generation of particular kinds of narrative in the context of the research interview is taken up in the second part of this chapter, which deals explicitly with divorce narratives. The narratives are analysed as emergent representations that are essentially in conflict with dominant representations of *family* in contemporary society. The narratives reveal evidence of values, attitudes and arrangements that exist within what might, *à la* Gramsci, be referred to as hegemonic familism. The particular sequence of representations and re-presentations I consider here is that of me telling you about a woman who told me about a marriage which ended five years before and, in particular, her experience of motherhood after divorce. This is supplemented by accounts provided by her ex-husband and his new partner. I am thus dealing with a story about power, gender, economics and choice but in its articulation it is a profoundly moral tale about *family* and its 'break-up' related in a series of extended informal conversations which loosely constituted 'research interviews'. The stories related in this context are, amongst other things, my informants' re-presentations of the past or, more accurately, a narrative representation of persons as they defined themselves and were defined through key social relationships in their shared past. But this is not just an exercise in making sense of individual self-representations through narrative. The exercise illuminates informants' attempts to re-present the *family* and its constituents in terms of an alternative socio-moral framework, that is, one in which the emergent pattern of kinship arrangements are plausible and justified despite their apparent deviance from hegemonic norms.

The final section of the chapter explores the full implications of such narratives for the emergence of new representations reflecting the diverse patterns of kinship and the proliferation of *family* forms in the present day. The chapter thus returns to the question of collective representation in that it illuminates the way in which individual attempts to narrate old patterns of kinship in the light of new and emergent ones might enter into the dominant system of representations of *family* in the present day. In working out who one is in relation to once and newly significant others the notion of *family* and *family* relations still provides a crucial, albeit radically transformed, store of metaphors and images.

FAMILY AND REPRESENTATIONS: DOMINANT, COLLECTIVE AND HEGEMONIC

Representation has lain at the heart of anthropological endeavour and will continue to do so precisely because of its centrality to human thought and human sociality. To represent carries the dual connotation of making present to the mind and the senses whilst standing for something that is not present. Acts of representation thus enable us to deal with absence as an imagined presence, a complex operation that is central to the distinctiveness of human thought both in individual and collective terms. Thus, as human beings we are continually and creatively condensing diverse experiences and emotions into complex distillations which are more easily given to intersubjective identification and understanding – we need only respond to the part rather than whole it represents. Representation in this sense is an aspect of what Foucault referred to as the 'principle of thrift' by which the proliferation of meaning is kept in check (1984: 118). Evidence of representation as a form of cultural condensation is all around, ranging from representation as reproduction, as in the case of scale models, through to symbols and metaphors that serve to capture the elusiveness of deity or nature. A representation thus carries with it characteristics of the ideal-type; or, as Derrida coined it, it is a 'locus of ideality' (1973: 50).

At the present time, *family* in Western culture might be seen as just such a 'locus of ideality'. From an early age children are socialised into deeply rooted expectations of a life-cycle in which romance, courtship, marriage, home-making, parenthood and the longer-term project of *'family life'* are, with minor variations, believed to follow on inexorably one from another (Mansfield and Collard 1988; Sarsby 1983). These patterns are encoded in domains of discourse such as those of the media, advertising, the welfare state, the legal system and the church, to say nothing of the rhetoric of politicians. In each of these domains are encountered powerful representations of what it is to be part of a 'normal family' in Britain in the 1990s.

Family is also linked implicitly and metonymically to that other most powerful of representations: the *home*. *Home* is thus assumed to be the privileged site in which love, safety, support, pleasure and intimacy associated with the *family* will be found. Located within the spatial context called *home* these are part of the self-evidential and therefore largely invisible functions that *family* is assumed to perform for its members. Concretised in powerful symbols and practices that inscribe relationships in space and time, the *family* conveys a powerful appeal of the 'natural' with the *home* being its 'natural' setting (Harris 1981).

To comprehend *family* as it is used in these contexts is to subscribe to an extremely powerful collective representation in the Durkheimian sense (1976 [1915]: 433–9) – *family* as collective representation thus 'correspond[s] to the way in which this very special being, society, considers the things of its own proper existence' (ibid.: 435) and, furthermore, carries considerable weight as an ethical and normative prescription. If we pursue this logic it is hardly surprising to find that at a time when *family* is allegedly fragmenting as a social institution, interest in the *family* as a discrete object of concern has arguably never been greater (cf. Strathern 1992). As Gubrium and Holstein suggest, *family* usage is not shrivelling into a private haven as Lasch would have it but is a rapidly expanding domain of application (Gubrium and Holstein 1990: 160). In short, when it comes to answering the question of who autonomous individuals are in relation to one another in contemporary society and how they might conduct their affairs, familial representations abound and the circumstances precipitated by divorce are a prime example.

Divorce is the major transformation in *family life* in the West today. It is the legally sanctioned ending of a legally recognised marriage and it has itself become a powerful representation in opposition to that of *family*. Whereas marriage is taken to constitute and consolidate *family*, divorce is its opposite and draws on the imagery of fission and fragmentation. This is seen, for example, in popular terms such as 'splitting up', '*family* breakdown' and 'broken *home*'. The term 'divorce' is thus itself taken as a sort of shorthand for the fundamental redefinition of primary kin relations in emotional and economic terms which occurs at divorce and the sadness, separation, loss, conflict, guilt and breakdown of trust which usually follow.

Out of such ruins, new representations of *family* emerge which it would be erroneous to characterise as either wholly collective or wholly individual. Rather, they are part of an increasingly fluid mix of representations of intimate and once-intimate relationships which serve to challenge hegemonic representations of *family*. Within this 'moving equilibrium' (Gramsci 1971) other voices can now be heard. For example, the different experience of men and women within a marriage, originally articulated by Bernard (1972) and increasingly realised and expressed as the metanarrative of *family life*, is replaced by a polyphony of lesser narratives or *petit recits*. Within this polyphony we find 'individuals negotiating their ways between competing centres of philosophical gravity and the shifting balances of their power, playing off one episteme against another as different existential strategies in different contexts' (Rapport, Chapter 11 of this volume). Where divorce is concerned, such 'epistemic pluralism' as Rapport (p. 181) coins it, is crucially expressive of disintegrative sociality rather than the integrative one suggested by many writers on the family.[5]

DIVORCE AND NARRATIVE

We dream in narrative, daydream in narrative, remember, anticipate, hope, despair, believe, doubt, plan, revise, criticise, construct, gossip, learn, hate and love by narrative.

(Hardy 1968: 5)

In any attempt to come to terms with a traumatic life-event, narrative plays a fundamental role as a means of both ordering past events and providing the *telos* for future events (MacIntyre 1981). As Arendt tells us, 'all sorrows can be borne if we can put them into a story' (Arendt 1958: 175). Where there is a problematic past or a breach in normative expectations, narrative provides a means of ordering, structuring and making sense of disordered experience (cf. Bruner 1990). The narratives with which this chapter is concerned are those generated in the wake of divorce. Such narratives are particularly revealing in that the breach they seek to repair concerns the fundamental and paradigmatic notions of *family* and its constituent elements such as 'fatherhood', 'motherhood', 'love' and 'marriage'. These notions are the very stuff of Euro-American kinship and constitute extremely powerful forces when it comes to shaping individual identity and conduct in contemporary society. The stories told about divorce and its aftermath are thus particularly revealing in that they concern the actions and assumptions that underpin Western notions of the *family*. It is in the examination of what happens when actions and expectations conflict with dominant representations that the *habitus* of domestic life can be glimpsed.

The particular need for men and women to narrate and thereby recast and rework these dominant and hegemonic representations is born out of the crises set in train by a radical transformation of domestic and familial relations. *Family* is no longer contiguous with a single domestic site in which both parents co-reside but is mapped onto multiple domestic spaces with single or multiple adult occupancy which are interconnected by the movement of children and resources.

DIVORCE NARRATIVES AS MORAL DISCOURSE

The conversations that were recorded in the course of the various research projects provide some extremely rich and moving accounts of how sense is made of the domestic, economic, social and emotional upheavals that divorce brings in its wake. However, in the original analysis of these data many of these aspects were overlooked in the necessary pursuit of answers to the questions for which particular research projects were commissioned.[6] The early phase of the research was, to use Geertz's phrase, 'experience distant' in its analysis, seeking to extract commonalities from a sample of men and women created as a result of having the shared characteristic of passing through the divorce courts in 1985. The present analysis is based on a re-examination of the assembled corpus of taped interviews in terms of 'experience near' concepts, that is, ones that are used 'naturally and effortlessly' by an informant to make sense of experience (Geertz 1983: 57).

An important feature to emerge from the analysis of divorce narratives in this regard is their role as performances in which the interviewee presents the interviewer with what is essentially a moral account justifying why they became divorced and why they have acted in the way that they have before, during and after divorce (cf. Riessman 1990, 1993 also Linde 1993). The failure of the companionate ideal of marriage and all that this entails for self, children and wider kin, is rarely something that can be passed off lightly. The interview thus provides the respondent with an opportunity to construct a self-representation in which they appear to be morally sound and coherent (cf. Goffman 1969: 241–4).

In this respect the interview might be likened to another form of representation that is never far from people's minds when they divorce, namely that of legal representation. Divorce causes the boundaries of public and private as they relate to *family* to be redrawn with somewhat greater permeability as the state, with its paramount concern for the 'welfare of the child', is apt to demand public scrutiny of private, that is, *family*, actions. The result may well be that a professional advocate is brought in to 'represent' the fragmented and often opposed interests of different members of the *family*. Divorce precipitates this wider concern precisely because it presages a dislocation of responsibility from the collective enterprise of *family* onto its constituent parts; it is no longer clear what the *family* is as its boundaries, roles and hierarchies have been drastically redrawn in ways that are unclear, conflicted and contradictory (Simpson 1994).

Those called in to represent the constituent parts of what was previously the *family* might include solicitors, social workers, guardian *ad litem*, the official solicitor and court welfare officers. These constitute the battery of professionals that one might encounter in the course of a conflicted divorce. They, like the research interviewer, each provide a context and a setting in which people are required, exhorted or merely invited to tell stories about themselves and their partners and the past that they once shared. Telling and hence fixing a story about the recent past is a necessary step in determining what happens next and the kinds of futures that the teller might anticipate.

It is interesting to note in this regard that in many of the interviews carried out the occasion of the interview was seen by the informant as an important chance to correct misrepresentations, assumed or actual, perpetrated by ex-partners, solicitors or the community at large. The opportunity to produce a self-representation unimpeded or criticised was clearly a welcome one, offering a means to expression, expiation and occasionally confession. Despite the fact that informants were aware that their self-centred tellings would not be conveyed beyond the research context they often commented on how valuable it had been simply to tell their story.

What seemed readily apparent in the accounts, especially of the men interviewed, was that the implicit, invisible and automatic aspects of *family life* were no longer there. This often amounted to a difficult realisation that *family life* in its non-nuclear form is a production that needs to be made, added to and pushed forward rather than simply unfolding within well-worn scripts. The narratives thus reveal evidence of individual attempts to recast dominant and hegemonic representations of *family* within an alternative socio-moral framework consistent with the radically altered context of action and experience. In the section that follows, this conflict and the search for resolution through narrative is explored in relation to motherhood as it appears in one woman's attempts to represent her own experience as a mother in the light of her experiences after divorce.

MOTHERHOOD AND REPRESENTATION

> In our personal myths home is the place where we are fully accepted, it is linked with the idea of a woman, mother.... Appeals to defend 'the privacy of the family' evoke powerful memories and dreams, and are thus able to strike chords in many hearts.
>
> (New and David 1985: 54)

In contemporary Western society, hegemonic representations of motherhood are arguably even more powerful than those of *family*, with the *mother* constituting the biological hub of the *family* and the embodiment of the 'nature' axis of Western kinship (cf. Schneider 1968, 1984). Consistent with this is a strong ideology which suggests that a *mother's* greatest contentment comes about through being with and doing for her *family*, that is, at the very least, her husband and children (Ribbens 1994). Motherhood is thus not only the state of being a female parent it is also a powerful cluster of expectations which occlude reflection on either the individual experience of the condition or the wider historical circumstances that shape this experience (Kaplan 1992).

In the section of narrative that follows,[7] Wendy, a working-class woman previously married to Neil, is reflecting on her relationship to her two children, Nichola and Sam, aged 11 and 13 (see Figure 4.1). The extract is taken from an interview with Wendy following a crisis which resulted in her son moving to live with his father. The difficulties that Wendy had experienced with her two children following the departure of her husband caused her to review fundamentally what it meant to be a *mother*. Her account reveals a repeated pattern in which there is a statement of things as they are, a counter-statement of how things were and an attempt to justify what she feels others might see as a moral discrepancy between the two positions. The transcripts are presented verbatim and reveal a soliloquy-like structure in which Wendy is talking to herself or, more

accurately, 'talking herself', as much as she is talking to me. Yet, even
from such a small piece of Wendy's story we might begin to read off
some of the assumptions about *family* and kin which make *family* such a
powerful representation in contemporary Western society.

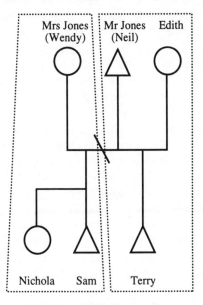

(oblique line represents divorce in 1985, dotted lines represent households in
1991

Figure 4.1 The Jones family

Wendy's story

The following section deals with a portion of conversation in which Wendy
has described the problem that she has in meeting the practical and
emotional demands of her adolescent daughter. Wendy sees herself as
caught in an invidious trap (cf. Newman 1991) in which she knows that
money is the key to running her household satisfactorily but, in order to
earn money, she has to be out of the house for long periods only to return
drained and exhausted with little energy available to be what she sees as
a 'good *mother*' to her daughter:

> she (Nichola) will come up and she'll say 'look mam I'm really fed up'
> and we'll sort it out from there ... but we're all right, I feel guilty
> now and again, but I find it's as if all my maternal instincts have gone,
> [laughs] because I think it's just been so hard, they've caused me so
> much grief, in some ways, I just don't want to know, I just want a quiet
> life now after all the hassle. It's a case of I love her and I'll do anything

for her and I wish I could do more. I wish I had money to spend on her and this sort of thing so she could do the things she wants [*pause*].

In this extract, Wendy is questioning the very premises upon which her idea of motherhood was previously built. Thus, on one level the relationship with Nichola works well – 'we're all right' she tells us. However, there are feelings of guilt and inadequacy continually rising to the surface, which prevents her open, direct and communicative relationship with Nichola being taken at face value. The feeling is that something that used to be there at the level of 'instinct' has gone and the extraordinariness of this conclusion causes her to laugh with incredulity – the idea of running out of instinct is an absurd notion. Being a *mother*, which used to be something that was automatic and pleasurable, has become something Wendy now finds intensely problematic and even painful. All she wants is 'a quiet life', which conflicts with the selflessness and sacrifice that is expected of working-class *mothers* living in Wendy's circumstances. The reason she gives for this withdrawal is the 'grief' that she suffered as a single parent who was far from prepared for the reaction that the dispatch of her husband would arouse in their children. She is left with a situation in which she does all the right things that a *mother* should do but, despite love, altruism and a profound desire to do more to make her daughter happy and contented, there is a discrepancy when measured against the sense of motherhood as previously experienced.

The same themes are reiterated with further nuances later on in the same interview. We are talking about the prospect of Nichola going to live with her father. Having raised this possibility I have just asked whether she found this a worrying prospect and below is given her reply *in extenso* (I have broken the discourse up as sentences for purposes of presentation and ease of comprehension):

No, because we're at the stage that if ever she wanted to go she could just go and I'd miss her and I'd be upset but I've got to the point where, maybe I'm wrong, but I look after me first and then, I take care of her and I look after her.

I think it's just all the hassle I had when they were here together, I went through so much. I've done a total about face. I was one of these people who absolutely loved children [*pause*] but now I haven't got time for them, I don't want to know.

I think, in their own way, my two have hurt me so much that I've gone totally selfish [*pause*] I've never been that way I've always been totally for children but I just seem to look after me first really.

I feel I did my best for them, they've had me while they were young and needed me most, and I'm still here if they need me but I'm looking after my own life. I do feel guilty about it I must admit but I can't seem to be any other way now. I suppose it's an awful thing to say really.

God if I knew then what I know now I would never've had children or got married. I might've had kids later on but I definitely would've had a bloody good career which is what I'm trying to get now.

but they have literally changed my attitude so much, it's hard to believe. I was one of these people who went ga-ga over babies. I don't want any more children, not interested. Towards the end of my marriage I was desperate to have another baby and I'm really glad that I didn't. That's the one thing I can thank him for really [*pause*].

it's looking after me time, you know, I've done my, sort of, bit. I've had my family, I've looked after them, they're both reasonably independent now. I mean she does everything for herself, so in a sense I'm not needed, so I tend to look after myself. She looks after me really.

I was in here sobbing my guts up and she heard me crying, she'd gone up to bed, she came down and was looking after me, she made me tea and some toast, I feel as if she's the mother and I'm the daughter.

The discourse spirals round as before, prompted this time by the question of Nichola's independence. Nichola is autonomous and can make up her own mind in opting to be with her father. If she were to make this choice Wendy would feel distress but it would be understandable and, although painful, would ultimately be manageable.

It is the ease with which Wendy envisages the possibility of her daughter's departure that prompts her to engage in a repetitive dialectic. In the emplotment which results she struggles to a position in which her feelings and stance are morally justified and comprehensible. As a mother she is not supposed to take lightly the prospect of her daughter's departure but her feelings contradict this assumption. Her sad but passive acceptance that her daughter may leave her is at odds with what she sees as the dominant expectations surrounding motherhood. This is revealed in phrases like 'maybe I'm wrong', 'I do feel guilty about it I must admit' and 'I suppose it's an awful thing to say really'.

This latter phrase is a particularly telling one because it reveals the extent to which Wendy is aware of the discrepancy between her feelings and actions – 'I can't seem to be any other way now', and the way she 'supposes' that these might be interpreted by others in general and me, as interviewer, in particular. She finds herself at odds with the dominant representation of motherhood as she perceives it in others and indeed as she herself once experienced it.

The extent of this transformation is made clear in a series of paired oppositions which contrast how she was then a devoted mother but now views things rather differently. She describes how she was the kind of person who willingly submitted to the unconditional and irrational pull of motherhood; she was one 'who absolutely loved children', was 'totally for children' and 'went ga-ga over babies'. Reference to 'one of these people' suggests how prominent this representation is in her assessment of her present situation. She 'was' one of these people but is no more. The reason for this is found in the contrast that she then goes on to draw with the present in which she puts her own needs before those of her children.

This is seen in a series of phrases such as 'but I look after me first', 'but now I haven't got time for them, I don't want to know', 'but I just seem to look after me first really' and finally, 'but I'm looking after my own life really'. Wendy drives this point home further by describing how, towards the end of the marriage, she was 'desperate' to have a third child.[8] Paradoxically, however, she finds herself acknowledging that her ex-husband was right to persuade her not to as she now feels that it would have been a mistake to respond simply to the impulse to produce babies.

The making of such statements is clearly painful for Wendy because of the extent to which it runs counter to what *mothers* should do and feel for their children. Significantly, each of these statements is followed by a justification as to how these honest but potentially deviant responses have come about. Wendy's reaction is primarily triggered by the behaviour of her children after the divorce and the extent to which they 'hurt' her. Incidentally, this also reveals an expectation of Wendy's that children, although supposed to act in certain ways, in this instance did not abide by the expected kin-script either.

Her secondary justification for her 'selfishness' makes explicit the implicit instrumentality of parenting and in so doing once again makes statements that border on maternal heresy. She points out 'I've done my, sort of, bit' with 'bit' referring to the package of expectations that anchor a *mother* within the *family* unit, that is, as the bearer and nurturer of children. In return for having carried out this task as the dutiful but now disillusioned *mother* she has arrived in what she describes as 'looking after me time', a period in which she is looking to her own needs rather than the needs of her children.

I would suggest that to see this process of justifying parental selfishness in terms of an exchange is not in itself problematic within the terms of *family* life conventionally construed and may indeed constitute an important part of the mechanism whereby parents and children establish their respective autonomy. What is problematic in this case is that the exchange is having to be made explicit prematurely, it has come too early for the children and therefore falls outside of the dominant expectations of the life-course and its key transitions as they relate to mother–child relations of dependency. The result is that the statement has to be justified and she seeks to do this by means of two illustrations, both of which in different ways show Wendy reflecting upon the life-course.

The first illustration begins, 'God, if I knew then what I know now', which is followed by a wholesale rejection of the project of *family* as she came to experience it. Her wish that she had avoided motherhood and marriage is tempered by the admission that she might have considered these later on but she would first have had to achieve a successful career on her own terms. Indeed, many of the difficulties of recent years have come about as a result of her struggle to earn a living from low-paid work, to improve her position in the job market through study and be a 'good mother' all at the same time. It is the bitterness of this experience that leads her to see quite explicitly that there was a life-course or script that she was following and to wish she had put together the sequence of life-course events in a rather different pattern.

Wendy's second reflection on the life-course contains an even more powerful re-presentation of herself as outside the fixities of the life-cycle as it once determined her outlook and expectations. Here Wendy is justifying her tendency to look after herself ahead of her children in terms of their independence and her redundancy – she is quite simply not needed anymore. What is intriguing about this section is that Wendy goes a good deal further than simply spelling out Nichola's independence and illustrates a critical inversion in the life-course. Wendy describes how she was upset and she was comforted by Nichola, leading her to feel 'as if she's the mother and I'm the daughter'.

Neil's story

Narratives such as Wendy's do not evolve in isolation but are enmeshed in those of significant others such as her ex-partner, her children, her parents and her friends who make up her changed and changing sense of *family*. Whilst the implications of this observation take us beyond the scope of this chapter, it is worthwhile reflecting briefly on Neil's story and in particular his assessment of Wendy as a *mother*.

In the interviews with Neil, Wendy's husband, there is far less evidence of an emergent narrative of opposition: no re-evaluation of role or shifting of the life-course. He remained a breadwinner and *father* throughout the divorce and indeed very soon re-established a new *family* with a new wife and a new baby in the profound hope that the formula that failed last time might yet work on this occasion. Throughout his interviews he expressed the simple but ardent desire 'to be a *family* again'.[9]

In the early interviews he expressed a degree of surprise that Wendy had felt things to be sufficiently dire to warrant taking divorce proceedings – 'if I'd been a wife-beater, or a gambler or anything like that but I'd done nothing!' Furthermore, Wendy's reasons for asking him to leave were, in his estimation, frivolous and seemingly to do with little more than her desire for a 'different lifestyle' which, in his opinion, could have been relatively easily modified had they been prepared to 'work at it'. The lifestyle to which she aspired was one in which his traditional idea of the *'family* man', solid, predictable, dependable and committed (but ultimately, in her view, oppressive and stultifying) had no part. In his narrative he is cast as the good man ejected from his *family* on the caprice of a cruel and selfish woman. Wendy's re-presented version of her life as he occasionally hears it from her and from the children, and sees it in her behaviour, simply becomes further evidence of her flawed motherhood – she allegedly 'lets the children run wild', 'she comes in at all hours', 'she's a bad manager of money' and generally does not look to the children's needs as a *mother* ought. The crowning evidence for him in this regard is the fact that their son chose to live with his *father* and not his *mother*! Neil's new partner also echoes these views in her accounts of recent events. Together, Neil and his new partner's accounts reveal considerable evidence of a meshing and reinforcing of narratives using Wendy, the 'inadequate *mother*', as a foil to bolster their aspiration to correspond with dominant representations of *family*.

TRANSFORMATION AND CONTRADICTION IN CONTEMPORARY *FAMILY LIFE*

Divorce narratives such as those of Wendy and Neil constitute private responses to tensions that originate in a broader pattern of historical change in the organisation of personal and domestic life in the West in general and Britain in particular. They reveal a major fault-line between the collective pull of kinship obligation and dependency on the one hand and the drive toward individuality, independence and self-determination on the other.[10] The tension is seen repeatedly in the accounts of women, like Wendy, who were quite clear about their own personal need to divorce their husbands but were far more equivocal about the implications of their actions for their children, whose personal needs and wishes they were all too aware they had overridden.[11] The key element here is that of choice under circumstances in which the making of choices now carries its own moral imperative. The capacity to choose is one of the primary devices whereby authentic individuality is asserted and publicly demonstrated. However, the growing assertion of choice in the field of familial relations over the past twenty years collides with a morality largely rooted in the renunciation of choice and a submergence in dependencies of one kind or another: *for better or for worse, in sickness and in health.*

Consideration of these tensions reveals important clues as to the ways that new and emergent representations are created to repair this fault-line in practice. These are woven out of, as well as in opposition to, the dominant representations of *family*. Thus, Wendy and Neil are not alone in the style and content of their narratives; their representions of self in relation to *family* are indeed representative of many people who were interviewed and no doubt countless more who weren't. They are illustrative of the crisis of representation of the *family* which gathers pace as *family* and *home* lose their concentricity and temporal stability in the lives of increasing numbers of children, women and men. *Mothers* and *fathers*, *husbands* and *wives*, *brothers* and *sisters* can no longer define themselves dyadically, or perhaps more accurately dialogically, in relation to one another and must seek new representations to capture emergent, novel and increasingly flexible configurations. For example, men and women who had once been intimates and who had succeeded in renegotiating an amicable relationship after divorce or separation would often describe their relationship as 'just like brother and sister'. In other words, a relationship of great closeness and familiarity but ultimately one in which sexual interests are wholly inappropriate and would ultimately be tinged with the horror of incest.

In divorce we are indeed witnessing what Strathern refers to as the first and second facts of modern English kinship writ large, namely 'the individuality of persons' and 'diversity' (1992: 22). In the case of Wendy, individuality and diversification is sought actively and with a sense of urgency; for Neil it is embraced with considerable reluctance and a hankering for the supposed certainties of traditional patriarchal arrangements. In either case they signal a move towards an ever more complex ordering of autonomous individuals in which there is continual reference back to the actual and imagined securities of *family* life at some point before divorce occurred.

Furthermore, the narratives reveal that the construction and deconstruction of representations of *family* is not just the preserve of the social commentator, politician or theologian but is also an activity of the informant (who might also be any of the aforementioned!). Indeed, the informant might be just as capable of weaving a Geertzian thick description (Geertz 1973) or incorporating the 'expert' discourses of law, psychology or the social sciences into a presentation of self in relation to new patterns of *family* and kinship (see Edgar, Chapter 5 of this volume). Emergent representations such as these gain ever greater currency in popular discourse and are increasingly reflected through film, television, advertising, chat shows, news reportage and popular magazines.

We are left with a disconcerting circularity or what Giddens has aptly referred to as the 'reflexivity of modernity' (1991: 14). In this instance 'we', the anthropological audience, might well be the natives, refashioning

our accounts of life-course and kinship, and the natives might well be us!
I conclude with a further reflexive turn in this representational loop,
namely the intriguing prospect that the textual representations of kinship
that I have described here might ultimately find their way back into the
milieu in which they were generated, thus becoming

> one small contribution to a vast and more or less continuous out-
> pouring of writings, technical and more popular, on the subject of
> marriage and intimate relationships . . . they serve routinely to organise
> and alter, the aspects of social life they report on or analyse.
>
> (Giddens 1991: 14)

ACKNOWLEDGEMENTS

Thanks go to Peter McCarthy and Janet Walker at the Relate Centre for
Family Studies, University of Newcastle, who were part of the original
research team and to Judy Corlyon, with whom the interviews were
carried out. Comments have been gratefully received from Mike Carrithers and Peter Collins of the University of Durham and Iain Edgar of
the University of Northumbria. Useful feedback was received when versions of this chapter were given in seminars in the Department of
Anthropology at Durham and at University College Stockton.

NOTES

1 Between 1985 and 1991 I worked at the University of Newcastle on a variety
   of projects concerned with divorce and separation. The projects followed a
   large sample of men, women and children over a five-year period following
   divorce. The research was ostensibly 'socio-legal' in that it examined the
   dissolution of a legally sanctioned conjugal relationship and the various structures that define and regulate relationships between family members
   thereafter. The assembled data provide a unique archive of quantitative and
   qualitative material concerning life after divorce. The research I am currently
   undertaking analyses the substantial corpus of interview data from a narratolo-
   gical perspective. The linking of accounts across time and between couples
   forms the basis of a more extensive ethnographic account of divorce and
   separation in England and Wales (for example see Simpson 1994).
2 The divorce rate increased sixfold in the period between 1960 and 1980 and
   went on to peak at over 160,000 divorces in 1985 (Office of Population,
   Censuses and Surveys 1990). Since then, the number of divorces has remained
   more or less at this level, giving Britain a divorce rate which in Europe is
   second only to Denmark (ibid. 1991). Just over half (55 per cent) of couples
   who divorced in 1990 had at least one child under the age of 16. Official
   statistics indicate that some 153,000 children under the age of 16 experienced
   their parents' divorce in 1990 (ibid. 1990). On present trends it has been
   estimated that by the turn of the century in England and Wales 3.7 million
   children will have experienced at least one parental divorce (Haskey 1988).
3 In writing about kinship intra-culturally as opposed to cross-culturally there

is the inevitable problem of how one represents in text key kinship terms. Family, for example, is simultaneously the language of the informant and the language of analysis. One strategy might be to ignore this rather obvious point and simply use family as an unproblematic notion throughout. Alternatively, one might go with the sociological propensity to bracket the word in inverted commas thus highlighting 'family' as a contested rather than essential concept. The usage I have adopted here is the standard anthropological one of placing indigenous terms in italics. Thus, *family* is used throughout to indicate that the term is part of native usage.

4 The role of the ethnographer should not be underestimated in the construction of representations of self and *family*. I was presenting myself to informants as a researcher with the legitimation of a university and a funding body. For ethical and practical reasons the words 'research' and 'university' necessarily had to be used not least because we were making contact with people at a time of maximal personal upheaval and sensitivity. Thus, regardless of the informality, friendliness and frequency of contact there was always a sense in which informants were treating my colleagues and I as kinds of expert or, at the very least, as people who were in the process of becoming experts. We were thus apt to become another 'expert' context, along with those of the counsellor, the doctor, the lawyer and the welfare officer, in which narratives of self-authentication could be rehearsed.

5 The idea of *family* as a transcendant and socially integrative entity has dominated American sociology and psychology of the *family*. This can be traced back to Burgess, described apparently without irony by Osmond as the 'true father of American family sociology' (1986: 113), who spoke of the *family* as 'a unity of interacting personalities' and as a form of 'super personality' (Burgess 1926, see also Berger and Kellner 1964). Reiss (1981) has likened *families* to small group cultures each with their own Kuhnian-type paradigms which occasionally shift. More recently, Llangellier and Petersen (1993), although adopting a critical perspective on the *family*, develop a narrative analysis which emphasises the integrative and controlling aspects of *family* narrative.

6 See, for example, Ogus *et al.* 1989; McCarthy and Simpson 1991; Family and Community Dispute Research Centre 1992; Simpson *et al.* 1995.

7 This interview is typical of the many I carried out in that it contains some of the most salient themes raised by women as single parents after divorce. For most, there was a desire to communicate their extraordinary struggle and hardship in terms of loneliness, finances, employment and children but there was also a certain exhilaration with a newly discovered potential for personal growth and autonomy. Small segments only of the interview are reproduced and discussed due to confines of space and time. The interviews that make up the data for the case discussed in this chapter alone run to over ten hours of taped conversation.

8 This was a strategy encountered frequently amongst informants who described having children during failing relationships, attempted reconciliations or in new relationships as a way of 'cementing' the relationship.

9 This rather odd usage, 'to be a *family* again', reveals something of the extent to which '*family*' is part of Neil's social identity and persona. It is a condition which, like many other men, he feels incomplete without. This is in contrast to Wendy, for whom completeness can seemingly only come through a profound reconfiguration and re-evaluation of *family*.

10 This may be as much to do with a particular working out of a much longer

tradition of English individualism (MacFarlane 1978; Strathern 1992: 13) as it is to do with the more recent rise of the enterprise culture, the penetrations of the market into the domestic sphere and the commoditisation of intimate relationships resulting in a 'post-modernist flexibility' (Harvey 1989) in the domain of kinship.

11 See Walkover (1992: 183) for an account of similar tensions experienced by couples over the decision to become parents.

REFERENCES

Arendt, H. (1958) *The Human Condition*, Chicago: University of Chicago Press.
Berger, B. and H. Kellner (1964) 'Marriage and the Construction of Reality: An Exercise in the Microsociology of Knowledge', *Diogenes*, 46: 1–23.
Bernard, J. (1972) *The Future of Marriage*, Harmondsworth: Penguin Books.
Blackwood, E. (1986) *Anthropology of Homosexual Behaviour*, New York: Haworth Press.
Bruner, J. (1990) *Acts of Meaning*, Cambridge, MA: Harvard University Press.
Burgess, E. (1926) 'The Family as a Unity of Interacting Personalities', *The Family*, 7 March, pp. 3–9.
David, M. (1985) 'Motherhood and Social Policy – A Matter of Education', *Critical Social Policy*, 12: 28–43.
—— (1986) 'Teaching Family Matters', *British Journal of the Sociology of Education*, 7 (1): 35–57.
Derrida, J. (1973) *Speech and Phenomena and Other Essays on Husserl's Theory of Signs*, Evanston: Northwestern University Press.
Durkheim, E. (1976 [1915]) *The Elementary Forms of Religious Life*, London: George, Allen & Unwin.
Family and Community Dispute Research Centre (1992) *A Longitudinal Study of the Impact of Different Dispute Resolution Processes on Post-divorce Relationships Between Parents and Children*, Report to the Ford Foundation (Fund for Research in Dispute Resolution).
Foucault, M. (1984) 'What is an Author', *The Foucault Reader* (ed. Paul Rabinow), Harmondsworth: Penguin.
Franklin, S., C. Levy and J. Stacey (eds) (1991) *Off-Centre: Feminism and Cultural Studies*, Hammersmith: Harper & Collins.
Geertz, C. (1973) *The Interpretation of Cultures*, New York: Basic Books.
—— (1983) *Local Knowledge: Further Essays in Interpretative Anthropology*, New York: Basic Books.
Giddens, A. (1991) *Modernity and Self-identity: Self and Society in the Late Modern Age*, Cambridge: Polity Press.
Goffman, E. (1969) *The Presentation of Self in Everyday Life*, Harmondsworth: Penguin.
Gramsci, A. (1971) *Selections from the Prison Notebooks*, London: Lawrence & Wishart.
Gubrium, J. F. and J. A. Holstein (1990) *What is Family?*, California: Mayfield Publishing Company.
Hardy, B. (1968) 'Towards a Poetics of Fiction: An Approach Through Narrative', *Novel*, 2: 5–14.
Harris, O. (1981) 'Households as Natural Units', in K. Young, C. Walkowitz and R. McCullagh (eds), *Of Marriage and the Market*, London: CSE Books.
Harvey, D. (1989) *The Condition of Post-modernity: An Enquiry into the Origins of Cultural Change*, Oxford: Basil Blackwell.

Haskey, J. (1988) 'Mid-1985 Based Population Projections of Marital Status', *Population Trends*, 52: 30–2.

Kaplan, E. A. (1992) *Motherhood and Representation: The Mother in Popular Culture and Melodrama*, London and New York: Routledge.

Lasch, C. (1977) *Haven in a Heartless World: The Family Beseiged*, New York: Basic Books.

Linde, C. (1993) *Life Stories: The Search for Coherence*, Oxford: Oxford University Press.

Llangellier, K. M. and E. E. Petersen (1993) 'Family Story-telling as a Strategy of Social Control', in D. K. Mumby (ed.), *Narrative and Social Control: Critical Perspectives*, Newbury Park: Sage.

McCarthy, P. and B. Simpson (1991) *Issues in Post-divorce Housing: Family Policy or Housing Policy?*, Aldershot: Avebury.

MacFarlane, A. (1978) *The Origins of English Individualism: Family, Property and Social Transition*, Oxford: Basil Blackwell.

MacIntyre, A. (1981) *After Virtue*, London: Duckworth.

Mansfield, P. and J. Collard (1988) *The Beginning of the Rest of your Life: A Portrait of Newly-wed Marriage*, Basingstoke: Macmillan.

New, C. and M. David (1985) *For the Children's Sake: Making Childcare More Than Women's Business*, Harmondsworth: Penguin.

Newman, J. (1991) 'Enterprising Women: Images of Success', in S. Franklin, C. Levy and J. Stacey (eds), *Off-centre: Feminism and cultural studies*, Hammersmith: Harper & Collins.

Office of Population, Censuses and Surveys (1990) *Marriage and Divorce Statistics*, London: HMSO.

—— (1991) *Social Trends*, London: HMSO.

Ogus, A., J. Walker, M. Jones-Lee, W. Cole, J. Corlyon, P. McCarthy, R. Simpson and S. Wray (1989) *Report to the Lord Chancellor's Department on the Costs and Effectiveness of Conciliation in England and Wales*, London: Lord Chancellor's Department.

Osmond, M. W. (1986) 'Radical-critical Theories', in M. B. Sussman and S. K. Steinmetz (eds), *Handbook of Marriage and the Family*, New York and London: Plenum Press.

Ribbens, J. (1994) *Mothers and their Children*, London: Sage.

Riess, D. (1981) *The Family's Construction of Reality*, Cambridge, MA: Harvard University Press.

Riessman, C. K. (1990) *Divorce Talk: Women and Men Make Sense of Personal Relationships*, New Brunswick and London: Rutgers University Press.

—— (1993) *Narrative Analysis*, London: Sage.

Sarsby, J. (1983) *Romantic Love and Society*, Harmondsworth: Penguin.

Schneider, D. M. (1968) *American Kinship: A Cultural Account*, Englewood Cliffs: Prentice-Hall.

—— (1984) *A Critique of the Study of Kinship*, Ann Arbor: University of Michigan Press.

Simpson, B. (1994) 'Bringing the Unclear Family into Focus: Divorce and Remarriage in Contemporary Britain', *Man*, (4) 29: 831–51.

Simpson, B., P. McCarthy and J. Walker (1995) *Being There: Fathers After Divorce*, Relate Centre for Family Studies, University of Newcastle, Working Paper No. 4.

Strathern, M. (1992) *After Nature*, Cambridge: Cambridge University Press.

Walkover, B. Cox (1992) 'The Family as an Overwrought Object of Desire', in G. C. Rosenwald and R. L. Ochberg (eds), *Storied Lives: The Cultural Politics of Self-understanding*, New Haven: Yale University Press.

Chapter 5

The tooth butterfly, or rendering a sensible account from the imaginative present

Iain R. Edgar

The continued enigma of the dream is well displayed in the famous story (Wu 1990: 153) of the Chinese sage who dreamt of a butterfly and, being of a speculative mind, considered the alternative explanation that perhaps he was being dreamt by the butterfly! This chapter considers how dreams are made to represent meanings and, accordingly, how such representation may offer insight into the nature of cultural representation itself and, furthermore, into the anthropological enterprise of writing embodied images down.

That dreamwork or dream interpretation is a cultural, rather than a solely psychological, activity is something few people other than interested anthropologists appear to understand. Jedrej and Shaw (1993), in their discussion of how dreams and social facts intersect and develop each other refer to Evans-Pritchard's classic study of Azande witchcraft in which he writes:

> The memory of dream images may influence subsequent behaviours and subsequent happenings may intrude upon the memory of dream images so that they conform to one another.
>
> (1937: 384)

Likewise, Herdt (1987: 82) has asserted

> that culture may actually change experience inside of dreams, or that the productions of dreaming do actually become absorbed and trans-formed into culture.

My own study (Edgar 1995) of cultural meaning-making and social action outcomes from dreamwork in groups showed how group members, through the medium of discussing their dreams, went on to make career and relationship decisions significantly based upon group discussion and process.

The complexity of this relationship between the experience of often bizarre mental imagery and their transformation into personal, group and cultural meaning is the focus of this chapter. It has two aims, first to show that the process of 'dreamwork' or dream interpretation is a sequence of representations of an original dream imagery into a satisfying narrative form, which, to quote Rapport (Chapter 11 of this volume), is embedded in an 'epistemic pluralism'. Second I intend to illustrate, through the presentation of an edited narrative of the interpretive discussion that took place in the dreamwork meetings, the emergence of a feminist-inspired empowerment paradigm of dream interpretation which both explicitly and implicitly rejected more traditional psychoanalytic interpretive paradigms. If humans are defined primarily through their ability to be 'self-interpreting animals' (Obeyesekere 1990: 275, quoting Heidegger), dreamwork provides an explicit and dynamic expression of this activity of interpretation and hence representation.[1]

THE CULTURAL CONSTRUCTION OF THE UNCONSCIOUS

I have recently demonstrated (Edgar 1994: 100–3 and 1995), as have others (Carrithers 1982; Charsley 1992), that the dream is both culturally formed, through a *bricolage* process, and understood symbolically in culturally specific terms. In that analysis I sought to show that arguably the remotest personal domain of all, that of the night dream, was susceptible to a culturally based enquiry. As the study progressed, however, I became more and more aware that the actual data of the dream are inaccessible, particularly to those in the group listening to the dreamwork account. Thus, issues of narration in the process of translation from image into a cultural discourse became paramount in the rendering of the image into a discursive form while the dream itself had to remain an 'unknown' or noumenon.[2] My focus in this chapter is on this culturally specific nature of dream interpretation as it took place among members of the dream group workshop.

Using Kracke's description of the dream as a 'highly condensed, visual or sensory, metaphorical form of thinking' (1987: 38), dream interpretation can be seen to consist of several stages. There is the recollection of the dream by the dreamer and the subsequent filtering of the original imagery into what Kracke (1987: 36) describes as 'language-centred thought processes'. This filtration of imagery into thought is an act of translation which can, in dream interpretation, begin the construction of meaning. Dream interpretation does this by relating the experienced visual imagery to the cognitive categories of the dreamer's culture. Such cognitive categories carry implicit ways of ordering and sequencing time and space, person and action that inevitably begin to define and delimit the possible readings of the text or narration. Thus, throughout the dream accounts I observed how often the narrator would struggle to translate his or her mental imagery into suitable words, by using such phrases as 'I sort of . . .' Holy describes this as a process of transformation of dream image into 'a cultural artefact in the sense of a culturally determined set of relevant signs' (1992: 88).

Analysing the process of narrating dream in a group context reveals the following interpretive process:

1 dream imagery;
2 dream narration;
3 psychodynamics of dream audience;
4 interpretive process;
5 relating of interpretation to future of self and group.

Thus, the representation of the dream cannot be regarded as the 'meaning of the dream'. Following Tedlock (1987) these dream reports were shaped inevitably by emic dream theory and took place within the context of the cultural and interpersonal dynamics of dream narration. Overall, then, the narrative of the dream in the group is significantly different from the original experience of the dream material. Even in its remembering the imagery is processed through the categories and forms of a culturally constructed existence. Association and embellishment, censorship, the desire for privacy and exhibition all influence the rendering of the tale of the dream. The dynamics of the dream audience, the degree of trust, prior friendship, shared values and length of time together combine in the 'narrating' and hence the 'narrative' itself (Genette 1988: 14). Thus, there is no final, original or definitive dream text; rather, the narrative is one of many possible renderings in a powerfully defining group and cultural context.

CASE STUDY

I will now present two examples of 'dreamwork'[3] from the three ten-week dreamwork groups of which I was the co-leader. These groups were of two to two and a half hours' duration and took place between September 1989 and June 1990. Recruitment to the group was by local advertising, word of mouth and through the membership networks of the local independent groupwork training agency where the sessions were held. The recruitment literature only suggested that potential group members should be interested in sharing their dreams. We did not interview or select members prior to the start of the first session of each of the three groups. The groups were held in that agency's premises. The room we used was distinctive in that it had no chairs, but only many large cushions. Group size was between six and twelve and included both men and women.

The group programme usually began with a structured round[4] in which members shared how they were feeling. This opening round provided the opportunity for members to begin to relax, join the group, shed preoccupations and share important current events in their lives. The participants would then give a short description of any dreams they had had and say if they wished to work on a particular dream or not. Then the group would choose two or three dreams to consider during the rest of the evening. The most common method of working with a dream was by suggestion, discussion, association and comparison. The group attempted to help the dreamer relate their dream imagery to their current daytime, conscious life. We regularly supplemented discussion with action techniques such as the use of gestalt exercises (particularly an emotional identification with different parts of the dream), psychodrama, artwork, meditation and visualisation. Every session was audio-taped for research purposes; members had access to the tapes, and I undertook follow-up individual interviews at the end of the group sequence.

Before presenting illustrations of the representational processes involved in the construction of meaning from narrated dream and fantasy imagery, gestalt theory and practice, as it relates to working with dream imagery, requires some comment. The gestalt perspective in the group was very important, gestalt techniques being regularly used in working with the dream imagery. Fitz Perls, the creator of gestalt theory, rejected the notion of an unconscious and focused on a concern with the person 'getting in touch with the here and now' and 'being in touch with their feelings'. Dreams in gestalt theory are 'the high road to integration', rather than Freud's 'high road to the unconscious' (Houston 1982: 44). Each part of the dream is seen as a part of the person that, potentially, they can get in touch with through dreamwork. Even an insignificant part of a dream is an opportunity to develop a further emotional integration of the various aspects of the self. Gestalt therapy is an action approach to re-experiencing the self in a more complete sense. Thus, in gestalt dream-work, the dreamer is advised to see each part of the dream as a part of him- or herself, and asked to identify emotionally with all or part of the dream imagery. Hence, they always speak of their dreams in the present tense – 'I am the . . .' – rather than as something 'out there' and imper-sonal. Stemming from humanistic psychology, this powerful technique has as its aim the intended arousal of neglected and avoided aspects, experiences and emotions. Often the body itself is seen as representing suppressed emotion and a gestalt therapist will often point out the difference between the spoken and unspoken expression of the self.

The evocative process between suggestion and insight that leads to a set of understandings about the dream by the dreamer can be seen in the ensuing discussion of the following dream:

> I stayed in bed one morning . . . it's only a snatch of a dream . . . its about my teeth . . . they are not a constant anxiety but I do have a fear of having my front teeth smashed . . . I do have crowns that I am

self-conscious of ... the dentist in the dream has put new teeth on ...
so I feel relief that I shall have teeth to cover the gaps ... then I look
in the mirror and I see they are my mother's teeth ... when I look in
the mirror I realise they are greyer ... this seems okay for a while till
I realise that the new teeth are much greyer which will show people
that the original teeth were crowns too.

The following is an edited version of the ensuing discussion.[5] D is the
dream narrator and Q, K, Z, J, A and U are group members:

D: I am thinking about being without teeth ... about being raw and
    exposed and about people knowing there is something false about
    you.
Q: Did she bite?
D: Its not about biting ... The dentist knew they were mother's teeth ...
    my relationship with my mother is okay but distant ... usually
    dreaming about teeth is about your own ageing ... typically teeth
    falling out is about ageing ... there's a lot about image and about
    being real ... I had a fear of breaking my teeth and it did happen ...
    I had a cycle accident and I lost my front teeth ... Lots of people
    visited and I was freaked about not having any teeth ... Why this
    fear about not having teeth? It must mean something about not
    taking care of myself and as it was an accident it was okay to have
    lost them.

The narrator then talks about the ugliness of having no teeth:

D: Something is rotting.
Q: Like being a toothless hag.
D: Yes ... I was glad to have my mother's teeth rather than being
    toothless ... it feels sad to have ended up with something not quite
    right ... I remember my mother taking her denture out of her mouth
    and cleaning it ... I didn't want my mother's teeth ... I want my
    own teeth undamaged ... there is something about pretence ... it
    was a double pretence ... as I had had the crowns first.
Q: What is being covered up?
D: [laughs] It's about not being truthful ... about pretending to be
    something that I'm not ... pretending to be more whole ... more
    perfect than I am.
Q: Putting on a good front.
D: That really fits in with work ... It's about the front ... about pre-
    tending to be together ... its about this job I am supposed to be
    doing ... I haven't been feeling together at all dealing with everyone
    else in emotional crisis.
Q: It's about being strong.

D: At work it's about me taking care of everyone else... and who takes care of me?

D talks about her feeling of pretending and of 'being strong' at work. There is nowhere at work for her to explore this... nowhere for her to get attention:

D: There is a limit to how long I can go on putting up the pretence... I have had a real battle getting the management to realise that workers needed their own support... I feel the management had not been supportive or understanding of these needs... sometimes I blame myself and think that I ought to be able to manage.

K: I feel D has had to wear it (the mask) for everyone else... like you are wearing the teeth... you are wearing it for everyone else in the workplace.

Z: You are the only one being 'shown up' [*like teeth*].

D: That is exactly like it is... I feel I am carrying it for the 'consumers' and in order to get the situation changed I have had to be very real about myself... and with people who I haven't felt responded sympathetically.

Q: You have to be mother?

D: Yes... I have to be mother to the whole fucking world... that's what it feels like... and yet I don't know how to stop.

J: The image of biting is coming across for me... that is the opposite of nurturing... softness.

A: Its like the nurturing I am really missing... I am also not being very caring about myself... but there is this sudden surge of anger... it is the resentment about giving out and not getting back... and the lack of response from other people.

D then talks about the dentist and her feeling that she is receiving second best concerning the teeth in the dream:

Q: Just like in the organisation.

D: They're not good enough... both the teeth and the work support are pretty shoddy... second best... shoddy... it fits but it's not very good.

D goes on to talk about not being happy in general at work and a member suggests the 'mother's' teeth are invasive in some way:

D: What I can pick up there is the invasive bit... about boundaries... I feel really overwhelmed and there is nowhere for me to go... a friend is staying with me and had made dramatic disclosures about their Y [*reference changed*]... also someone I know has been attacked [*reference changed*] this symbolised the last straw for me... so the invasiveness bit symbolised for me the awful side of

humanity ... it seems to be overwhelming and I am feeling overwhelmed by it.

Z: How can we resolve this within the time and prepare D for leaving
the group this evening?

D: As I think about it I feel angry about it and don't think it is good
enough ... I am angry ... it is quite hard for me to be angry ... I
feel it is difficult to confront ... to say I want and I deserve something better ... I feel he [*the dentist*] is doing his best but it is not
good enough.

D then speaks to the 'dentist' through a gestalt exercise:

D: I don't trust you enough to really give me some nice teeth I want
some really splendid teeth ... I can have the best crowns in the
world.

U: Are you going to ask him to do it or go somewhere else?

D: I don't trust him but it feels really threatening to go somewhere
else and to start all over again and to take this big risk ... and all
these dentists are men! My real dentist is very nice ... so it's about
not settling for things that aren't good enough.

In this grand discussion about the 'meaning' of the dream and of how
its imagery may relate to 'reality', there is a process of questioning and
suggestion and the gradual development of insight for the dreamer. That
this is not, however, purely a result of suggestion by group members is
shown at the beginning when the dreamer rejects the avenue of enquiry
suggested by the question, 'Did she bite?' The dreamer knows about the
'typical' connection of teeth with ageing but doesn't pursue that theme
in relation to her own ageing process. Rather, she connects the imposition
of the teeth with the loss of teeth in an accident and focuses instead on
the theme of the 'falsity' of the teeth. Then she talks about falsity and,
in response to a question about 'what is being covered up?' talks about
putting on a 'front' at work. The idea of a 'front' is suggested by a
member and the dreamer acknowledges how that really 'fits in with work'.
The next stage sees the dreamer sharing her perception that she is 'being
strong' for other people at work, particularly other workers. The 'teeth'
symbol now is explicitly connected with that of the 'mask' or 'persona'.
In response to the question 'you have to be mother?', the dreamer replies,
'Yes I have to be mother to the whole fucking world'. The dreamer here
is identifying with the 'motherness' of the teeth being inserted into her
mouth in the dream and recognises that that is how she feels in her work
setting. Following a suggestion that 'boundaries are being invaded' (i.e.
mother's false teeth in her mouth), the final level of interpretation reached
is that feelings of being overwhelmed by events in the world, the patriarchal world, are manifest. Feelings of anger are articulated and finally the

dreamer is facilitated to affirm her 'first-class' value and her right to have first-class teeth fitted.

This example illustrates very well the progression of insight through different levels. The image of the 'teeth' transforms to their being seen as representing the 'front' or 'persona' (originally the persona was a Jungian formulation). The word 'persona' then is expanded to refer to 'mothering', perhaps 'inappropriate mothering', and, finally, the identification with 'mothering' changes to a feminist articulation of anger at patriarchal abuse. Resolution is achieved through self-affirmation.

But any of these levels of insight, which expand referentially from the personal to the global, could be seen by the group as equating with 'meaning' for the dreamer, for at all stages 'sense' is being derived from the 'nonsense' of the dream. A series of themes, connected to life-events, has been derived from images: through reference to biographical data the physical context of the teeth as being in the 'front' of the mouth equates to being a 'social front' to others as well as being a functional piece of equipment for the mastication of food. But this understanding of the 'teeth' symbol relies on a public and culturally specific symbolism which evaluates the significance of teeth, and particularly the gendered nature of 'attractive' teeth, in certain ways. In Westernised culture teeth are perceived as being a very important part of our social front to the world, as evidenced by the amount of cosmetic dentistry (Nettleton 1992: 18–28). The 'mother' image in this dream is, by contrast, personally contextualised, but the dreamer states that 'her relationship with her mother is okay' and that possible avenue for exploration is not pursued. The 'mother' symbol is then connected instead with a social context, and her 'overwhelming' set of feelings of responsibility for others in her workplace. The cultural identification of care and responsibility for others with the 'mother' symbol is critically interpreted. It is not a fulfilling aspect of the dreamer's self, but rather an inappropriately acquired set of responses that she would like to divest herself of. Feeling like being a 'mother' to the 'whole fucking world' is a problem to her.

There is a translation here from personal mother to the 'archetypal' mother (Jung 1959: 81). As Jung states, all archetypes have a potentially positive and negative aspect and in this example a negative, or partly negative, rendering of that set of feelings and roles identifies this archetype for the dreamer. In this setting of the dream group the dreamer concludes with a feminist critique of herself, for coming to adopt such a 'false' persona and for identifying with such an inappropriate 'mother' role in relation to the world. However, her self-criticism is deflected, expanded and refocused into a generalised anger towards the abuse and rapacity of the male in this society. The conclusion is self-assertive, affirming her autonomous selfhood and her rights to the best. Thus it can be seen that the socially constructed transformative and evocative process of dream representation hinges on a series of transformations engendered through the interaction of the dreamer with the group: teeth = front = mothering = lack of self-care = anger at men = affirmation of self.

BINARY ANALYSIS: REPRESENTING THE DREAM REPORT

The next example is another 'tooth' dream:

> In church at choir practice there is the vicar and me and two other singers and I am waiting for it to start ... perhaps other people are still to come ... and I am clenching and unclenching my jaw ... like that and I am aware that there is a filling in a bottom molar and there is a filling in a top molar and they are touching ... and then I am aware that there is a piece of metal coming down ... [T starts crying a bit] and um it actually comes down and gets trapped in the bottom one and I am still clenching and unclenching my jaw ... and I am almost tempting fate doing it tighter every time to see if a hook of metal is going to trap into the bottom molar and I do this and sure enough I do it till they lock together and the only way I can open my jaw is by pulling out the bottom filling and I sort of go ... [makes noises] and the tooth underneath crumbles and the whole mouth feels full of bits ... and I am leaving the church and going into a small room and I look in the mirror ... and there is a huge filling in a load of bits and then a few hours later ... I have a sense of a few hours later ... there are still a few bits of tooth coming out and it feels just horrible and the tension is just horrible and I have this thing about metal in my mouth and I had an earlier dream about silver foil in my mouth and it is not the physical pain it is the tension ... waiting almost for a physical shock.

The dreamer is offered the opportunity 'to be the crumbly teeth'. She doesn't want to do this, and another member 'doubles'[6] and so acts as if she were the dreamer: T represents the dreamer. TT is the 'double' of the dreamer (T).

TT: I am falling out ... I am losing my grip and I am very insecure and wobbly and my contact with the living tissue ... stop me if this isn't right ... I am falling about into T's mouth ... and I have given up ... I am useless.

T: Thank you it is really helpful to see ... the thing I find really hard is the metal and the hardness of the tooth and the softness of the mouth and that really shakes me and sets my teeth on edge. Something shakes my whole being and it is the whole idea of eating chewing gum and a friend coming up and chewing onto the frame of *your* teeth and expecting it to be soft ... it is the hard/soft thing ... really horrible.

Y: There is no pain around this is there?

T: Not the physical pain it is the trauma ... same with the foil on the tooth ... its not the pain it is ... [*she becomes silent*].

X: Things seem insecure with your teeth falling out ... and any minute something is going to happen.

T: You are almost tensing your self for something to happen.

P: It is as if it is an alien body in the softness of your mouth that shouldn't be there ... it's like you are putting it to its final test ... to see what it is going to feel like and I am wondering where this hook is coming from.

T: It came out of the filling ... there is a hook in the top molar ... it sort of grew coming down and it was very small [*she demonstrates*].

Y: What made you cry?

T: When I was talking about the metal in the tooth. [*T is still shuddering and upset*].

P: Do you want to look at these two sides of yourself ... the hard and the soft?

T: I recognise I have both sides in me ... over the last few months I have come to terms with the darker side of me and recognising it ... giving it more space like the soft side ... saying 'we love one another don't we?' ... I have been angry and voiced more difficult things than usual ... is this the soft/hard thing? ... yes ... as the soft is the more accommodating side and the hard side says no ... actually that has pissed me off for many years ... I was afraid to express feelings that weren't positive and it is new to feel that that is alright and that I can relate to the hard and the soft ... the accommodating and the not accommodating sides.

I: That is rational but what about the horror of the metal in the teeth ... can you associate the picture with anything else outside?

T: I made a connection yesterday ... the night before the dream I had an experience of some boys barring the way whilst I was cycling and one of them grabbed my bum ... and today I made this connection and I was happily cycling along and I saw these four boys and I went headlong into the situation ... and afterwards I was quite shaken ... I had to get down off the bike and I felt quite vulnerable ... and that has shaken me and then I had the dream that night.

F: You said you should have foreseen it.

T: I was talking about it and I felt I wasn't to blame and I was really angry about it [*crying still a bit*] why should I have to look out all the time ... why can't I just feel open?

A member then suggests that she is making a connection between the 'fault' in her tooth dream and the real-life threatening incident. The dreamer says she is not sure if the two are related.

T: I'm not sure if the dream is related to this incident.

Here the dreamer voices her concern that the possibly interpretive connection is illusory. A discussion followed about whether T feels possibly guilty. T doesn't affirm this hypothesis and the dialogue continues:

Q: [*Talks about how as a nurse*] you feel responsible for their sexual harassment.

T: [*Talks about why feeling so*] vulnerable when they are only thirteen year olds ... when I am really shaken it is my teeth that shake with fear, hence the connection between the fear of boys and the tooth dream?

I: So the teeth are 'on guard' like a portcullis.

Then the dreamer, deciding to 'work' on this feminist-inspired interpretive avenue, elects to act out her feelings and speak to the harassing boys and uses a cushion to express her feelings in a cathartic way. Other members 'double' for her:

F: [*Shouts at the boys (role-playing 'being T')*] Fuck off go away leave me alone ... get your filthy paws off my bum.

T: [*Says they will carry on*] 'daring' [*(to invade her space) and (in tears)*] I don't feel strong enough ... I still feel too small and vulnerable.

T: [*coming out of the drama by now*] I feel when you two are speaking that it is penetratingly real and I want to speak at them like that but I don't have the strength to say ... but it feels very real and if I put it in my mouth it will ... I will crumble. [*Another member asks T*] Can you tell those boys quietly what you feel?

T: [*Does so.*]

P: [*Becomes the boys saying (as boys)*] We had a good laugh ... you looked really cute coming along there.

T: I am not here to look cute for you ... I am just here to live my life ... I should be able to do what I want.

P: I didn't mean you any harm ... it was a good laugh.

T: But you intruded.

The discussion continues with the expression of anger towards such kids and then a discussion of how women can protect themselves from such verbal and physical harassment.

In this example the group develops an embryonic structuralist analysis consisting of oppositions linked by analogy and homology, and I shall use binary analysis as a way of structuring and making intelligible the interpretive flow of the above discussion. The appropriateness of such an approach lies in its resonance with the way that the narrator and the group began to structure their own explanations and associations with the narrated dream imagery. In so far as I am defining and contextualising this group-articulated perspective I am mingling both an emic and an etic perspective.

Several interpretive processes occur in the group. In the first sequence the group facilitates a connection with the imagery of the dream in a subjective way. The imagery is thought to refer to the duality or set of opposites within the personality of the dreamer. The key opposition is that of hard/soft. Within the discussion of the dream imagery, the opposition between the hard teeth and soft tissue is developed; and between the 'natural' tooth and the 'unnatural' metal filling. The opposition between the soft mouth and hard tooth is developed by an invitation from a group member for the dreamer to look at that opposition as a reference to the two sides of herself, the soft and the hard sides. The dreamer takes up this suggestion in terms of the tension between her loving, caring and nurturing side and her assertive side, the side that is able to deal with conflict and can voice difficult feelings:

> the soft is the more accommodating side and the hard side says no! . . . I was afraid to express feelings that weren't positive . . . I can relate to the hard and the soft . . . the accommodating and the not accommodating sides.

The dreamer then re-expresses this opposition in terms of 'accommodating' and 'not accommodating'. At this point the dreamer declares a possible connection between the dream imagery of that night and the harassing experience of the day before. At first she declares that this connection may not really be related to the imagery, there being no clear 'hook' for the projection. However, shortly after, she identifies the connection in terms of her feeling that her teeth shake with fear, and, for her, this establishes the connection between 'teeth' and the frightening experience of the day before. With this information the group leaves the previous interpretive format, a more gestalt mode, and takes a more social and political, even feminist stance in relation to reclaiming physical space for all people and particularly women. The 'crumbling teeth' at one point becomes a metaphor for her current non-assertive and 'crumbling self' and is turned, in the ensuing role-play, into an assertive voice which claims her rights and exposes her criticism of the boys. Further oppositions have by then emerged: male/female; danger/safety. The opposition between inside/outside becomes an analogy at two levels: between that of the accommodating self/the non-accommodating self and also the feminist/non-feminist self; passivity and assertiveness are also polarised. However, the opposition inside/outside also resonates with the possibilities of a subjective/objective[7] interpretive reference for the dream itself. Overall, in the dynamics of the group discussion in which the dream is repossessed and represented, a system of binary classification emerges through their articulation:

- Soft mouth: hard metal
- Natural: unnatural
- Soft nature: hard nature
- Accommodating disposition: non-accommodating disposition
- Inside: outside
- Crumbling: hard
- Female: male
- Feminist: non-feminist
- Internal referents: external referents
- Psyche: world

Linked by homology and analogy (Needham 1979: 66), this set of oppositions is evident in the text. Yet change in attitude and the affirmation of the self are literally being enacted in this dramatic representation of a crumbling mouth and a harassing incident. The soft, passive and non-assertive accommodating self is changed into an assertive self. In the individual interview with this member, after the group, she agreed that the group had affected her life. She said, 'Oh yes, particularly in my reaction to conflict . . . it has underlined my avoidance of conflict . . . and made me value confronting conflict.'

CONCLUSION

Both these examples of dreamwork illustrate the representational processes involved in rendering a visual experience meaningful through the dynamics of narration, group process and the metaphorical playing with meaning that became the hallmark of this group's interpretive style. The use of binary oppositions in the last example demonstrates the system of epistemological dualism embedded in Western cognition itself.

Further, in both examples from the dreamwork group is evidence of a broadly feminist perspective on the dreamwork process, and it is clear that the dream image is developed and transformed by the group to 'mean' whatever the dreamer and the group want it to.

I would argue, therefore, that these examples illustrate clearly the cultural reworking of dream and visual imagery within and through the group process. Meaning is created, the self is represented and invented in new, and often disturbing, garments. Consciousness becomes its imagery and opens up new fields of potential mental and affective connectedness. Such new fields, encompassing both the narrator's mind and the consciousness of the group, are not, however, limitless. Meaning is not evoked from outside its context. Interpretive possibilities are those already dormant within modern society's repertoire of potential meaning for material objects and cultural processes. A tooth, whilst capable in these groups of becoming a lived metaphor evoking, symbolising and representing a gendered personal identity and relationship, remains a tooth firmly within the terms normally understood in society. The interpretive and representational processes recorded then are culturally contextualised and pertinent to our modern or postmodern society, not any society (see Layton, Chapter 8 of this volume).

In this chapter I have aimed to show how a feminist-inspired perspective evoked a particular cultural reality for group members; a feminist sense arising from a surreal nonsense. Such a processual analysis of the generation of a social text can be transferred also to the production of the ethnographic text itself, as Josephides (Chapter 2 of this volume) does. The question arising then for the anthropological venture of representing the 'other' is how far the final written or visual text is the outcome of a similar, though usually unrecorded, negotiation of meaning through interaction and dialogue with significant others both within and without the original fieldwork context. Also, if the repertoire of possible meanings is culturally specific, how sensitive to these meanings can an anthropology be that is not 'at home'? Finally, the question can be asked whether an intended anthropological study of the 'visible' contents of the unconscious raises any separate and different representational issues. I would argue, at this point, that such a 'psychoethnography' (Obeyesekere 1990: xix) is necessarily limited to the observation and understanding of public narratives whose referents are culturally formulated and imaginatively reinterpreted by both participants and anthropologist.

NOTES

1 My use of ethnographic examples in the form of group dialogue is intended to illustrate the creative flow of emerging signification.
2 Even the original imaginative experience of the dream image is, arguably, filtered through language and personal and cultural association into a narrative formulation, and often a story.
3 I am using dreamwork in the sense popularised by the dreamwork movement: to refer to the work of non-professionally trained people to understand their dream imagery, often in a group context and in the belief that dreams embody potentially important but implicit meanings for the dreamer.
4 A 'round' refers to a groupwork technique in which each person in turn has the opportunity to speak without being either interrupted while speaking or subsequently having their contribution immediately discussed.
5 Method of transcription: whenever I quote verbatim from the text of the dreamwork groups I rarely use punctuation so as to try and show the actual flow of the spoken word. I indicate pauses by the speaker by the use of three dots. I retain the use of question, exclamation and quotation marks.
6 'Doubling' is the action in psychodrama when one of the group, not the protagonist or director, goes behind the protagonist and imaginatively speaks as they feel the protagonist is 'really' feeling and thinking.

7 The 'subjective' and 'objective' interpretive opposition refers to the continual question in dream interpretation whether to understand a dream image with reference to 'real-life' external referents or to an aspect of the inner psyche.

REFERENCES

Carrithers, M. (1982) 'Hell-fire and Urinal Stones: An Essay on Buddhist Purity and Authority', in G. Krishna (ed.), *Contributions to South Asian Studies*, vol. 2, Delhi: Oxford University Press.

Charsley, S. (1992) 'Dreams in African Churches', in M. Jedrej and R. Shaw (eds), *Dreaming, Religion and Society in Africa*, Leiden: Brill.

Edgar, I. (1994) 'Dream Imagery Becomes Social Experience: The Cultural Elucidation of Dream Interpretation', in A. Deluz and S. Heald (eds), *Anthropology and Psychoanalysis: An Encounter Through Culture*, London: Routledge.

—— (1995) *Dreamwork, Anthropology and the Caring Professions: A Cultural Approach to Dreamwork*, Avebury: Aldershot.

Evans-Pritchard, E. (1937) *Witchcraft, Oracles and Magic among the Azande*, Oxford: Clarendon Press.

Genette, G. (1988) *Narrative Discourse Revisited*, New York: Cornell University Press.

Herdt, G. (1987) 'Selfhood and Discourse in Sambia Dream Sharing', in B. Tedlock (ed.), *Dreaming: Anthropological and Psychological Interpretations*, Cambridge: Cambridge University Press.

Holy, L. (1992) 'Berti Dream Interpretation', in M. Jedrej and R. Shaw (eds), *Dreaming, Religion and Society in Africa*, Leiden: Brill.

Houston, G. (1982) *The Red Book of Gestalt*, London: The Rochester Foundation.

Jedrej, M. and R. Shaw (1993) 'Introduction', in M. Jedrej and R. Shaw (eds), *Dreaming, Religion and Society in Africa*, Leiden: Brill.

Jung, C. (1959) 'Psychological Aspects of the Mother Archetype', in *The Collected Works of C. G. Jung*, vol. 9, part 1, London: Routledge & Kegan Paul.

Kracke, W. (1987) 'Myths in Dreams, Thought in Images: An Amazonian Contribution to the Psychoanalytic Theory of Primary Process', in B. Tedlock (ed.), *Dreaming: Anthropological and Psychological Interpretations*, Cambridge: Cambridge University Press.

Needham, R. (1979) *Symbolic Classification*, Santa Monica: Goodyear Publishing Co. Inc.

Nettleton, S. (1992) *Dentistry, Pain and Power*, Buckingham: Open University Press.

Obeyesekere, G. (1990) *The Work of Culture*, Chicago: University of Chicago Press.

Perls, F. (1969) *Gestalt Therapy Verbatim*, Lafayette, CA: Real People Press.

Tedlock, B. (1987) 'Dreaming and Dream Research', in B. Tedlock (ed.), *Dreaming: Anthropological and Psychological Interpretations*, Cambridge: Cambridge University Press.

Wu, K. (1990) *The Butterfly as Companion*, Albany, NY: State University of New York Press.

Chapter 6

Crossing a representational divide
From west to east in Scottish ethnography

Jane Nadel-Klein

PROLOGUE

As with Europeanist ethnography, the field of study for the anthropology
of Scotland is not self-evident. That, in brief, is what the issue of representation is all about. The whole discipline, and its many regional
incarnations, has broadened its understanding of what constitutes its
subject matter. A necessary part of studying any people now includes our
personal and disciplinary relationship to them. Herzfeld's seminal argument in *Anthropology Through the Looking Glass* (1987b) invited
Europeanists to consider the question of how anthropological theory has
been built in relation to our ethnographic practices, suggesting that our
choice of field sites replicates assumptions we make about familiarity and
otherness. In this chapter I want to consider how ethnographers have
represented Scotland and, in particular, how the conventional division of
Scotland into 'ye hielands and ye lowlands' has conditioned our perspective. This division – so famed in song, story and tourist guidebook – has
become reified in our accounts through a disproportionate attention to
the north and west of the country, that is, the Highlands and Islands. And
it has been reinforced, not through conscious intent, but through the *de
facto* absence of a discourse that links and engages the various ethnographies of Scottish communities into a larger discussion. This division is
thus strangely parallel to the popular tourist vision embodied in a recent
travel brochure:

> For many people, the North of Scotland epitomizes their image of the
> country as a whole. Mountains, heather, kilts & whisky are just some of
> the ingredients that contribute to the magnetic charm of the Highlands.
> ('Golf Vacations in Scotland')

The missing discussion might thus be called the 'anthropology of Scotland'. It is not often that one hears such a reference.[1] Perhaps this is
simply because less work has been done there than in some other European regions. Yet something more complex and subtle is involved here

concerning the issue of how anthropologists have represented Scotland not only to others, but also to themselves. I was made acutely aware of the possibility that 'Scotland' could imply a significantly incomplete representation recently when an English colleague, upon learning that I did research in Scotland, enquired about where in the *Highlands* I worked. Apparently, a Lowland field site was inconceivable.

It is not only anthropologists who bear the weight of this representational problem. In the case of Scotland – a country that has been characterised by all sorts of regional constructions about what it means to be Scottish – representation is central to identity debates at local, regional and national levels. The anthropology of Scotland requires the exploration of these contending positions about 'Scottishness' and its domains.

Anthropologists are normally not shy about declaring area specialties: at the annual meetings of the American Anthropological Association, networks of ethnographers organise gatherings under such rubrics as 'British and Irish ethnography', 'Hungarianist Research Group', or 'Eastern Europe'. Mediterraneanist discourse has a long history and has generated considerable debate, not only over whether the honour/shame complex truly characterises the Mediterranean, but over the utility of the culture-area concept itself (Boissevain 1979; Brandes 1987; Davis 1977; Gilmore 1982, 1987; Goddard *et al.* 1994; Herzfeld 1987a, 1987b; Peristiany 1965; de Pina Cabral 1989). And now the anthropology of the nascent European Union is emerging (Boissevain 1994; Shore and Black 1995; Wilson and Smith 1993). If we can speak in these various ways of the anthropology of Europe (Cole 1977; Goddard *et al.* 1994), why not, indeed, the anthropology of Scotland?

Practically and theoretically speaking, an 'anthropology' is above all a heuristic device, a broad – in this case, regional – framework that enables comparison and connection, perhaps most fruitfully within the region itself. To speak about agricultural marginalisation in Scotland, for example, one would wish to be able to compare the experiences of, say, Hebridean crofters and northeast Lowland farmers. To have 'an anthropology' presumes some consensus on what is included – or at least what to argue about. For instance, to speak about an anthropology of Scotland there must be a degree of self-conscious dialogue among ethnographers; a proposing, a questioning, and a criticising of such an undertaking, an engagement with pan-Scottish institutional structures and problems, a discourse of Scottishness that goes beyond issues of cultural or political nationalism, and an active cross-referencing and engagement of Scottish work.

I would argue that such an anthropology has yet to be fully articulated, despite the comment made by Condry in his 'Report on Scottish Ethnography' regarding the Social Science Research Council's belief that

'Scotland was a field of particular relevance for social anthropology since it contained many small-scale isolated communities which would be best studied by the detailed techniques of the anthropological method' (Condry 1983: i). (This rather antiquated view of what anthropologists do best may itself be part of the problem, if that is how projects are funded.) This failure of coherence in Scottish anthropology is due, in some degree, to our own localised – and regionalised – ethnographic practices in researching and writing about Scotland.[2] Of course, ethnographers have come a long way from the days when functionalist, 'bounded' or ahistor-ical community studies were standard practice. Critics of this approach have made it impossible now for anyone successfully to describe any locality either as isolated or as 'traditional' (Bell and Newby 1971; Brody 1974; Ennew 1980). And, indeed, ethnographers working in Scotland today, such as Parman (1990) in the Western Isles, Cohen (1987) in Shetland or Neville (1994) in the Borders have taken great care to contex-tualise the social processes they describe and analyse in regional and even global terms. What is still missing, however, is a discourse that links our various ethnographic productions across that Scottish symbolic gulf known as the Highland/Lowland divide.

Such a discourse could begin by asking questions such as: To what extent and in what ways is 'Scotland' a meaningful space and symbol for contemporary ethnographic studies? How do Highland and Lowland identities mutually construct each other across the divide as significant cultural spaces? Does 'Scotland' mean different things in the late twen-tieth century for Highlanders than it does for Lowlanders? Aside from the obvious salience of political nationalism for Scottish voters (whether favourably inclined or otherwise), how is Scotland imaginatively con-structed by those who live within it (Anderson 1983)? How has the 'tartan kitsch' (Nairn 1977) iconography, endlessly reproduced by the Scottish tourist industry, been received in Scottish homes and conversations? How do local identities respond to regional, national and European issues? These and related questions become all the more relevant when placed in the context of current debates over the cultural future of the European Union (Parman 1993; Shore 1993; Wilson 1993), as well as the emergence of what Stolcke (1995: 4) calls 'cultural fundamentalism' in discourses relating to the inclusion and exclusion of immigrants. It is clearly neces-sary to explore the dynamics animating relationships among the multiply embedded and interdigitating identities of peoples who are now being asked to contemplate a renewed and redefined 'Europeanness' (S. Mac-donald 1993; M. McDonald 1993).

The issue of a Scottish anthropology is *not* settled, I would argue, by dismissing 'Scotland' itself as an 'unsociological generality' (Cohen 1978: 130). For one thing, all explanation in the social science requires a certain measure of abstraction. That, after all, is what distinguishes knowledge from everyday practice. The question is which generalities are more or less helpful than others. In this I follow Quigley (Chapter 7 of this volume), who also argues against throwing out infants with effluents; that is, of discarding concepts (in his case, the contentious category of caste) wholesale because they have been subject to misuse, misinterpretation or essentialising. Certainly I would agree that there is a danger in reifying any civic entity as a cultural collectivity or in seeing fixed and imper-meable boundaries where none exist. But 'Scotland' appears to be a pretty meaningful concept to many of the people who live north of the River Tweed, not to mention the millions of their relatives living all across the globe. A burgeoning tourist industry is cashing in precisely on the appeal of this concept. Nor is this confined to marketing Scot-Land itself. There is no shortage of attempts to replicate little versions of the homeland in Highland games and Scottish fairs all across North America. For this reason, 'Scotland' as an intersection of many representations, is an object worthy of anthropological regard.

Moreover, as Cheater and Hopa point out (Chapter 13 of this volume), there is an ethical dimension to the representational debates in which we engage: ethnographers have a responsibility to acknowledge their subjects' own self-representations in a 'real world of contested representations of identity as a political process', whether or not we choose to see these as 'folk models' (p. 220; see also Holy and Stuchlik 1981; Shore and Black 1995). That Scotland's meanings are fluid, multiple, variable, contested and strategic does not mean that we can ignore them altogether and retreat into localism. In any case, representational dangers lurk there as well. As Knight (1994: 215) argues,

> It is certainly the case that the nation, by virtue of the institutional power of the state, is a key source of essentialized representations in society. This should not, however, be allowed to obscure the fact that such representations are found at other social levels too.

We cannot observe 'Scotland' directly. Any anthropological analysis is subject to a version of Heisenberg's uncertainty principle, namely that the identity we are exploring alters by virtue of our intervention, however delicate. To this we may add a further factor, that no identity ever stands still. Because of this, we must at least (1) endeavour to see as many of its aspects as possible, from as many positions as possible; and (2) represent Scotland as a set of articulating arguments, rather than as independent assertions. Thus, in the terms Rapport has set forth in this volume, this effort should substantially improve and expand our conversational abili-ties with those whom we study, as well as amongst ourselves. Additionally, this should enhance the interest and relevance of 'Scottish studies' for Europeanists, as well as for a broader anthropological audience. For it is only in so doing that we de-parochialise the position of Scottish work regarding its tendency to elaborate the construction of identity on a purely local basis and bring it to the forefront of debates about identity construction.

This should be not taken as a call either to engage in an ethnographic 'saturation bombing' of all potential field research sites between Gretna Green and John O'Groats, or to launch a project of defining national character. We can occasionally step back, however, and think about how representations of various Scottish communities might be linked together, and – specifically here – about how the prevailing 'Highland tilt' to Scottish research has conditioned our perspectives. Are we, as scholars, entirely free from perceiving Scotland as 'the west and the rest'? As Sharon Macdonald has suggested, for many people a cognitive map of Scotland would show the Highlands greatly enlarged to dwarf the Lowlands (1995, personal communication).

A SCOTLAND OF REGIONS

For the most part, ethnographic work in Scotland has been highly regionalised. By that I mean two things: first, that by far the greater part of ethnographic work has been done in the Highlands and Western Isles and, to a lesser extent, in the Shetlands (see Condry 1983); second, that work on both sides of the Highland Line has tended to be rather regionally self-referential. In suggesting that we more explicitly address the relevance of Scotland as a whole to local identities, I am not trying to essentialise or objectify that territory between the Border and the Shetlands, but to consider (1) how our various regional and community discourses might more productively respond to one another; and (2) how our own acquiescence in the Highland/Lowland divide has conditioned what we write and how we see our ethnographic horizons. Moreover, we might wish to consider the consequences of a localist discourse which effectively isolates, however unintentionally, each community such that its struggles for social and cultural survival appear independent of those of others who experience the same bureaucratic, legal, religious and educational systems, as well as historical references. This must certainly have implications for how ethnographers construct Scotland itself as a region, as regions, or as a nation.

We might approach the problematic of a 'Scottish' anthropology, then, by asking precisely what, if any, regional traditions exist within ethnographic writing about Scotland. I take seriously Fardon's point that, with a 'relational view of locality', we see that 'ethnographies are also reworked versions, inversions, and revisions of previous accounts... images of places which need to be understood as multiply determined' (Fardon 1990: 22). As Fardon has noted, interest in particular problems, such as lineage organisation or ideologies of honour and shame, is what draws us to our field sites. What themes have drawn ethnographers to Scotland? What themes, by contrast, have been left out of Scotland's construction as an anthropological subject?

CROSSING THE HIGHLAND LINE

While it is safe to say that much scholarship about Scottish politics, the Scottish economy, Scottish literature and the arts has a distinctly urban and Lowland orientation; the anthropology of Scotland has been very heavily concentrated in and on those areas north and west of the so-called Highland Line. Condry's comprehensive review of Scottish ethnography clearly indicates the consistent popularity of Highlands and Islands field sites (Condry 1983), a popularity which does not appear to have waned in the dozen years following his account.

The Highland 'Line' embodies the notion that society and culture in Scotland have historically been sundered along an axis that basically corresponds to the geological formation known as the Highland Boundary Fault. One of three roughly parallel faults that trisect Scotland from southwest to northeast, the Highland Fault has come to stand for a schism in Scottish society.

North and west of the Fault, the land rises steeply in bleakly corrugated hills. (Envision the paradigmatic image of John Buchan's hero of 'The Thirty Nine Steps' striding across the moors.) The climate is harsh – cold and wet. Settlements are dispersed through the narrow valleys known as glens, or clustered along the deeply indented coasts. Cultivation is difficult and most of the land is given over to rough pasture, vast sporting estates and, along the coasts, fisheries and salmon farming. One is generally reminded here of the postcard with twin images juxtaposed against one another, depicting 'Summer in the Highlands of Scotland' and 'Winter in the Highlands of Scotland'. Each side shows the same wet sheep.

Historically, the Highlands were the scene of the notorious Clearances of the late eighteenth and nineteenth centuries. This was the process – really a grim late gesture of the pan-European movement of 'enclosure' – whereby a society organised around kinship and subsistence farming was forcibly thrust into the world of capitalist agriculture. By all accounts it was a brutal process of eviction and emigration (Prebble 1963; Smout 1969). While historians debate the economic and social rationale of the Clearances, their legacy has been one of continuing concentration and the export of wealth by landowners, and thus of a continually depressed economy for most Highland communities. Not surprisingly, most scholarship of recent years refers to the Highlands as a 'peripheral' or 'marginal' area.

The Line demarcates the historical, linguistic and social constructs famed in song, story and political rhetoric as the Highlands and the

Lowlands. In the history of Scotland, especially in its more popular versions, there has been much attention paid to the epic battles and singular romantic tragedies (and farces) of Highland life: Flora MacDonald rescuing Bonnie Prince Charlie from the disaster at Culloden; the Clearances and the great migrations out of the glens. Not to mention the blue-painted Mel Gibson as 'Braveheart'.

The Highland Line has a powerful resonance not only within Scotland, but everywhere that Scotland is imagined as a place of rough, wild and mountainous splendour. It is also a crucial selling point for the tourist industry, which has depended heavily upon the 'invented tradition' of kilt and caber, clan legacy and quaint natives living isolated lives (Trevor-Roper 1983). (Most recently, this image of the eccentric aborigine has been played up in a British television series based upon the phlegmatic – and to some, offensive – character of Hamish McBeth, unambitious Highland policeman extraordinaire, based on the novels by M. C. Beaton.) Despite the obvious fact that in modern times, communication, travel and kinship across this 'Line' are necessarily commonplace, it may be seen as Scotland's equator, dividing the known from the unknown, the developed from the un- or the underdeveloped, the domesticated from the feral, the mundane from the sublime.[3]

Chapman makes an intriguing suggestion that may help to explain the historical origins of the regional bias in Scottish ethnography. He notes that when anthropology came to be defined in the 1920s as 'the study of primitive people who did not have history' (1992: 4), Celtic peoples became the province of 'folklorists, linguists and archaeologists' and thus 'For two generations, therefore, Celtic studies and social anthropology almost completely stopped meeting' (ibid.: 5; also see Urry 1984). However, the 1970s saw the rise of new interest in European peoples and hence in the Celts (Chapman 1992: 5), albeit in a less antiquarian and more cultural survivalist mode. But 'Celt' is not a gloss for 'Scot'. As Chapman earlier noted in *The Gaelic Vision in Scottish Culture*, 'When Scottish identity is sought, it is often by the invocation of Highland ways and Highland virtues that it is found' (1978: 9), thus leaving out the vast majority of Scots for whom 'Celtic' identity is rather far removed.

The Highlands has been theorised as a region marked by underdevelopment, a perspective embodied as social fact in the creation of the Highlands and Islands Development Board in 1965, and by dependency (Carter 1975). Its occupants have been assimilated into that socio-cultural and political economic construct known as the Celtic Fringe (Hechter 1975). They are known for geographic remoteness (Ardener 1987) and for strongly marked and marginalised communal identities. Chief among these identities, as far as anthropologists have been concerned, have been those of the Celt and the crofter.

The crofter is a species of Highlander. Drawing upon accounts by

Parman (1990) and Ennew (1980), one can say that crofting is a way of life emblematic of the Highlands and Islands. A croft is a small-holding, the tenancy arrangements of which are protected by legislation dating back to the land reforms of the 1880s, though this legislation has been substantially modified since. Crofters combine small-scale, semi-subsistence farming and sheep raising with any other source of income they can lay their hands on, including fishing, tourist hospitality and the weaving of Harris tweed (Mewett 1977). Crofters typically are economically marginal. No one works a croft with the expectation of 'making it' in Scottish society. In some respects, and for some individuals, crofting has come to stand for resistance to modernity and urban values, a rejection of both contemporary materialism and bureaucratic control over daily life (Parman 1990).

It is almost entirely within the crofting regions of the west and northwest that the remaining speakers of Scotland's Celtic language – Gaelic – are to be found (Dorian 1981). Parman (1990) provides a critical account of crofting and its symbolic association with the idea of the 'Celt', a cultural icon strongly associated with life in the Hebrides and with notions of a wild, rebellious past. Indeed, as Ennew noted in her prologue to *The Western Isles Today*, there is a 'tendency to mythologise the islands, to use them to conceptualise notions of Community, peasantry and pre-industrial history' (Ennew 1980: xiii). The Celt has become a somewhat ambiguous, partly mythical figure who has captivated the romantic imagination of folklorists, songwriters and tourists alike for many years.

One highly significant contrast point between Highland and Lowland has been and continues to be differences in language. Gaelic, the indigenous language officially suppressed after 1745, remains a conspicuous symbolic presence in the Highlands, though not a language actually spoken today by many people (Armstrong 1986; Dorian 1981), despite attempts to revive it.[4] As Chapman notes, the Highlands and Lowlands are conceptually divided

> by the polarization of metaphorical dualities along an axis between the two societies as represented by their languages. Such a simplicity is of course thoroughly subverted both by bilingualism and by the dispersion throughout Scotland of its Gaelic speakers.
>
> (Chapman 1978: 198)

In representational terms, the significance of this is not merely that of *different* languages, but the emphasis upon Gaelic as an *exotic* language that stands for a kind of cultural secrecy or mystery. I would add the observation that English-speaking Scotland is itself extremely diverse linguistically, not only in terms of what, say, an American can perceive, but most pivotally in terms of how communities define themselves by reference to distinctive dialects and vocabularies. The short trip from Fife to Angus or Aberdeen takes the traveller from one linguistic challenge to another. Lowland Scots is far more difficult for foreigners to understand than is the English spoken in the Highlands. Highlanders, in fact, are often complimented for the 'purity' of their English speech.[5]

Another intensively researched, though less popularised 'identity' has been that of the Norse-inflected Shetlands. Works by Byron (1986), Byron and McFarlane (1980), Cohen (1978, 1982, 1987) and McFarlane (1981) have recorded the distinctive issues faced by residents of these islands: the challenge of offshore oil development; insider–incomer relations; Shetlanders' problematic connections to the mainland, or 'da sooth', as the Whalsay Islanders say it (Cohen 1987); organisation of the fisheries; and the general difficulty of economic survival in an unforgiving climate.

It sometimes seems as though the Lowlands have been left out of Scotland's ethnographic equation. In the discussion that follows, I want to follow up on Chapman's thesis and consider what it might mean to discern Scotland's identity through the Lowland vision in Scottish anthropology. If, as Chapman says, 'the Scottish Gaels ... have long filled the role of "noble savage" for the first industrial nation' (1978: 192), what niche has been left for the unromantic, insufficiently 'remote' Lowlanders? (See Ardener 1987.)

Is it in fact the case that Scotland is being constructed as an object represented by only some of its parts? With the Highlands coming to stand for 'Scotland' in so much of the ethnographic as well as popular literature, it sometimes appears that the Lowlands of Scotland can be seen as the residual category: that which is outside the Highlands. How have anthropologists viewed Lowland communities and identities? Do any overarching themes parallel those of the Highland concerns with distinct language and culture? Or have the Lowlands merged into that slippery category Jackson (1987) refers to as 'at home', where we do 'auto-ethnography'?

It is possible, then, that the Lowlands have been overlooked because they appear to be too familiar, not really 'Scotland' but 'north Britain' (Parman 1993). Auto-ethnography still retains the aura of being a new and slightly uncomfortable concept, even though anthropologists have been working in their own or closely related cultures for quite some time. (It is, of course, not always clear what degree of 'nativeness' is required to justify the auto-ethnographic rubric. If I, as a native of Connecticut, USA, study Scotland, surely I am not working 'at home', unless western Europe and North America are seen as sharing a single 'culture'.) Jackson goes so far as to say that 'the basic difference between sociologists and anthropologists is a love of and a distaste for modern society' which anthropologists 'try to escape' (Jackson 1987: 8). Perhaps, then, the Lowlands are too modern. But modernity itself has come under scrutiny of late, problematised and deconstructed under the postmodern gaze, to the point where it no longer looks as homogeneous or as homogenising as it once did. A close examination of life in the Lowlands reveals considerable diversity of form, experience and practice in social life.

LOWLAND ETHNOGRAPHY

East and south of the Highland Line one finds a generally gentler topography, a greater concentration on arable farming, a shrinking dairy industry, and a much larger and more densely settled population. The Lowlands are often depicted as a region of sober industry, great intellectual achievement, urban decay, and – very significantly – a history of invidious cooperation with English interests, in short, a region whose culture has been heavily anglicised.[6] Chapman implies that the Lowlands may even sometimes be seen, from the Highland point of view, as a mere northern extension of England (1978: 15–16).

Urban Scotland is Lowland Scotland. All of Scotland's cities (Glasgow, Edinburgh, Dundee and Aberdeen) are to be found there. However, the converse is not the case. Not all of Lowland Scotland is urban. Perhaps the most significant difference between Highlands and Lowlands in determining the shape of economic development has been not just the presence of cities, but the dispersed presence of nucleated towns in the Lowlands known historically as Royal Burghs or Burghs of Barony that continue to exercise considerable hegemony over a wide hinterland. These settlements emerged as centres of commerce and industry in the eleventh and twelfth centuries, when they were given charters defining and consolidating their rights to monopolise trade. These burghs have had a powerful organising effect on the economic and political lives of smaller settlements, particularly fishing and farming villages, that became their effective satellites (Millman 1975; Mitchison 1978; Nadel 1984; Smout 1969).

Despite the diversity of Lowland settlements and occupations, scholarly research by anthropologists there is a much scarcer product.[7] It was not until 1963, with the publication of Littlejohn's *Westrigg*, that we had our first detailed ethnographic survey of a dispersed agricultural Border parish. But it was not until the threat and the promise of North Sea oil emerged in the 1970s that ethnographers began sustained work in the Lowlands, and almost all of that has been centred on coastal areas. Still, very little has been done on communities inland, the prominent exception being Neville's recent work on Protestantism and civic ritual in the market towns of the Borders. She points out that the annual ceremonies known as Common Ridings celebrate not only local identity but also Scottishness by commemorating the Battle of Flodden, a battle heroically lost to the English in 1513 (Neville 1994).

The Lowlands generally have drawn the interest of those – including myself – who have been primarily interested in fishing communities and/

or the impact of North Sea oil (see Postel-Coster and Helmerin 1973; Baks and Postel-Coster 1977; Byron and Chalmers 1993; Knipe 1984; Moore 1982; Nadel 1983, 1984, 1986; Nadel-Klein 1988, 1991; Turner 1981). To some extent, fishing communities have drawn such attention because they seem to stand apart from the 'everydayness' of Scottish commerce. They are conspicuously not 'middle class' or suburban, despite the economic and lifestyle aspirations of many of their current residents. They are, I daresay, the perfect Lowland analogue to the crofter, providing the ethnographer with a little corner of exoticism close to – but not exactly – 'hame'.

As one might anticipate, there are some similarities between Highland and Lowland localities in terms of how their inhabitants experience Scottish modernity and inequalities of power. Many of these eastern coastal communities today are also, like their Highland and northern counterparts, struggling with issues of identity and 'belonging' (Cohen 1982). This can be seen through the recent upsurge of interest in 'heritage'. Fishing villages, for example, are still widely regarded by other Scots as backward, dubious or, at best, quaint. Ironically, this is precisely what makes them so marketable to an international heritage industry. This reified version of 'tradition' is being commodified today for tourist consumption. The Scottish Tourist Board has established a 'Fishing Heritage Trail' for visitors to follow, and it now seems as though every other fishing village from Eyemouth to Wick has its own museum or heritage project underway (Nadel-Klein 1993). Some may deplore this phenomenon as yet another instance of the triumph of commercialism, as the objectification of villagers for eager tourists, yet it is much more than this. Such projects provide an arena where identity can be celebrated, debated and constructed. The arena comes at a price, of course. The construction of identity now becomes a partly public process, and all kinds of outsiders, including tourists, ethnographers and museum professionals, are invited to weigh in, particularly when 'authenticity' is at stake. Not surprisingly, the discussion can be rancorous. I have heard fishermen in one town rail against academics as 'them toffee-nosed buggers from the University' who dare to tell the local community how its own past should be represented in museum displays.

As in the Highlands, language forms a dynamic element in the discourses of boundary-making. In every fishing community I have visited, from Nairn on the Moray Firth to Ferryden on the east coast, local people stress the distinctiveness and even the peculiarity of their speech. Along the Moray Firth coast, people are proud of their northern dialect, which they call the Doric, and which they use alternately with a more standard broad Scots. Testifying to its vitality, they point to local poets like Peter Buchan or Isobel Harrison, who publish in the vernacular. They also insist on their local distinctiveness. 'D'ye ken what we mean by a "gow"?'

an old man asked me in Buckie. 'In the Broch [Fraserburgh] they call it a "pule". That's a seagull, ye ken.'

Local people often claim that their speech is virtually impossible for outsiders to understand (and in fact, when I did – more or less – understand them, they seemed almost disappointed). In the Fife village of Pittenweem, a fisherman rattled off a quick phrase to show me how strange local vowels were; and in Ferryden, in Angus, two elderly ladies laughed delightedly at my bafflement as they corrected my errant course by saying what sounded like 'y'r oop the wrong dreel'. Even when they drew it out as 'you're up the wrong drill', I didn't get it until they explained that a drill was the row between potatoes or raspberries and that they were simply telling me I was going the wrong way. In each case, dialect was used very deliberately and self-consciously to do two things; to put me in my place as an outsider and to make the local place seem interesting by exhibiting something unique and wonderful.[8]

CONCLUSION

Surveying the literature on Scottish communities, what appears to link the various ethnographies and ethnographers of Scotland is a concern with identity and boundary-making in the context of marginality and marginalisation. This is more than a preoccupation with coasts, difficult though that is to avoid in such a sea-bound country. The edges of society engage our interest as challenges to the apparently overwhelming homogenisation and hegemony of Western modernity. And Scotland has many such liminal spaces, not all of them rural. From the nationalist perspective, Scotland itself is a periphery seeking to be a centre. Yet from the urban and industrial perspective, Scotland has lost much of its former centrality to the economy of the UK. Indeed, it may be difficult to tell where, if anywhere, the centre of Scotland lies[9] – or, for that matter, whether it even makes sense to talk about 'a centre' at all. In some ways, in fact, the Borders, Western Isles, Northern Isles, northeast Lowland farms and east-central Lowland fishing villages all effectively constitute a whole in the way the threads of a tapestry weave a picture. Without the edges, the centre unravels and becomes the margin. If the notion of a 'centre' has any validity, it must be seen not as a real and specific space, but as the intersection of various nodes and modes of power (see Gupta and Ferguson 1992). The notion of a centre, like the notion of the margin, is a relational concept.

Let me play with some (perverse?) inversions here. One might consider that, viewed from the ethnographer's perspective, the Lowlands would seem to exemplify what Ardener means when he says that there are 'areas so "remote" anthropologically that there was nothing written on them. Yet, when reached, they seemed totally exposed to the outer world:

they were continually in contact with it' (Ardener 1987: 42). Of course, Ardener was referring to Western Scotland as the 'area in which canonical levels of remoteness are to be found' (ibid.: 43). And equally, of course, the Lowlands are seemingly very well 'known', at least to other disciplines such as economics, history, politics and sociology.[10] Have we, though, marginalised the *Lowlands* by a kind of inverse Occidentalising, whereby the Highlands are the mysterious, Oriental 'other' (and thus fair game for anthropologists), while the Lowlands are the presumably known, familiar, 'Western' (and thus to be safely ignored) 'self' (Carrier 1992; Nadel-Klein 1995)?

ACKNOWLEDGEMENTS

For their help in thinking through some of the issues presented in this chapter I thank Dona Lee Davis and Bradley S. Klein.

NOTES

1 For a few years in the 1970s and 1980s, the Edinburgh-based Association for Scottish Ethnography attempted to fill this gap, but it now appears to be defunct.

2 A significant exception to this is Malcolm Chapman, whose work on *The Gaelic Vision in Scottish Culture* (1978) and *The Celts: The Construction of a Myth* (1992) are both synthetic and stimulating.

3 Smout says that this set of oppositions dates back to the fourteenth century, when Highland chiefs began threatening Lowland settlements 'in a sudden renaissance of Gaelic power and confidence in its mountainous stronghold' (Smout 1969: 40).

4 The population of Gaelic speakers is estimated at under 80,000, or 1.6 per cent of the Scottish population, largely concentrated in the Western Isles (Clement 1984: 318).

5 The widespread conflation of Scotland with the Highlands is hard to escape. This was brought home to me in teaching a course on 'Peoples of Europe'. I opened the section on Scotland with a general lecture on Scottish geography, history and regional differentiation. I discussed my own work on east-coast fisherpeople. Then I assigned Susan Parman's *Scottish Crofters* as the main text. Though Parman unambiguously locates her discussion of crofters in the specific socio-legal and geographic environment of the Hebrides, students began to refer to 'crofters' as a gloss for 'Scots'. In other words, they conflated the two categories unproblematically and unthinkingly. I might have dismissed this as a purely trivial, if irritating indication that the students didn't listen in class and did not read carefully, if it were not for a parallel phenomenon I have noticed in other classes. There, students writing about peoples in New Guinea, Australia or sub-Saharan Africa frequently refer to them as 'Indians'. Intrigued by this confusion, I asked the class what an 'Indian' was and found that students had conflated the terms 'Indian' and 'indigenous'. (Few of them considered India in their reflections.) But their ability to do so could only be accounted for in terms of their own images of both Indians and indigenes as peoples who live in wild, exotic places. This led me to speculate that Scots in

general also occupy a similar semantic space, as people who live in a wild, exotic place and who do not need to be distinguished from the subset of Hebridean crofters.

6 The pacific image thus conjured up contrasts with the picture conveyed of social turbulence in many eighteenth-century Lowland communities by Christopher Whatley (1990).

7 Other Lowland ethnographic research includes that of Charsley on Glasgow (1986); an unpublished Ph.D. dissertation by Diane Meily (1984) on a Fife fishing village; the work by Farnham Rehfisch on Scottish travellers (1975); doubtless there is much I have missed and I apologise to those inadvertently omitted.

8 It seems worth noting here the comment in *Language in the British Isles* that, relative to the English, the Scots display 'a more persistent dialect-loyalty' (Aitken 1984).

9 Though the Scots say it's at the hill of Schiehallion.

10 I am indebted to Sharon Macdonald (personal communication) for the reminder of how sociology has been concerned much more heavily with urban and Lowland issues.

REFERENCES

Aitken, A. J. (1984) 'Scottish Accents and Dialects', in Peter Trudgill (ed.), *Language in the British Isles*, Cambridge: Cambridge University Press.

Anderson, B. (1983) *Imagined Communities*, London: Verso.

Ardener, E. (1987) ' "Remote Areas": Some Theoretical Considerations', in Anthony Jackson (ed.), *Anthropology at Home*, Association of Social Anthropologists Monograph No. 25, London: Tavistock.

Armstrong, K. (1986) 'The Changing Roles of Women in a Scottish Fishing Village.' Paper presented at the Annual Meeting of the American Anthropological Association.

Baks, C. and E. Postel-Coster (1977) 'Fishing Communities on the Scottish East Coast: Traditions in a Modern Setting', in M. Estellie Smith (ed.), *Those Who Live From the Sea*, St Paul: West.

Bell, C. and H. Newby (1971) *Community Studies*, New York: Praeger.

Boissevain, J. (1979) 'Towards a Social Anthropology of the Mediterranean', *Current Anthropology*, 20 (1): 81–93.

—— (1994) 'Towards an Anthropology of European Communities?' in V. Goddard, J. Llobera and C. Shore (eds), *The Anthropology of Europe: Identities and Boundaries in Conflict*, Oxford: Berg.

Brandes, S. (1987) 'Reflections on Honor and Shame in the Mediterranean', in David Gilmore (ed.), *Honor and Shame and the Unity of the Mediterranean*, American Anthropological Association Special Publication No. 22.

Brody, H. (1974) *Inishkillane*, New York: Schocken Books.

Bryden, J. (1979) 'Core–Periphery Problems – The Scottish Case', in D. Seers, B. Schaffer and M.-L. Kiljunen (eds), *Underdeveloped Europe: Studies in Core–Periphery Relations*, Atlantic Highlands, NJ: Humanities Press.

Byron, R. (1986) *Sea Change: A Shetland Society, 1970–1979*, St John's, Newfoundland: ISER Books.

Byron, R. and D. Chalmers (1993) 'The Fisherwomen of Fife: History, Identity and Social Change', *Ethnologia Europaea*, 23: 97–110.

Byron, R. and G. McFarlane (1980) *Social Change in Dunrossness: A Shetland*

Study, North Sea Panel Occasional Paper No. 1, Social Science Research Council.

Carrier, J. (1992) 'Occidentalism: The World Turned Upside-Down', *American Ethnologist,* 19 (2): 195–212.

Carter, I. (1974) 'The Highlands of Scotland as an Underdeveloped Region', in E. de Kadt and G. Williams (eds), *Sociology and Development,* London: Tavistock.

—— (1975) 'A Socialist Strategy for the Highlands', in Gordon Brown (ed.), *The Red Paper on Scotland,* Edinburgh: EUSPB.

Chapman, M. (1978) *The Gaelic Vision in Scottish Culture,* London: Croom Helm.

—— (1992) *The Celts: The Construction of a Myth,* New York: St Martin's Press.

Charsley, S. R. (1986) ' "Glasgow's Miles Better": The Symbolism of Community and Identity in the City', in Anthony P. Cohen (ed.), *Symbolising Boundaries,* Manchester: Manchester University Press.

Clement, R. D. (1984), 'Gaelic', in Peter Trudgill (ed.), *Language in the British Isles,* Cambridge: Cambridge University Press.

Cohen, A. P. (1978) 'Oil and the Cultural Account', *Scottish Journal of Sociology,* 3 (1): 129–41.

—— (1982) *Belonging,* Manchester: Manchester University Press.

—— (1987) *Whalsay,* Manchester: Manchester University Press.

Cole, J. (1977) 'Anthropology Comes Part-Way Home: Community Studies in Europe', *Annual Review of Anthropology,* 6: 349–78.

Condry, E. (1983) *Scottish Ethnography (A Report to the Special Science Research Council on the Present State and Future Prospects of Social Anthropological Research Relating to Scotland),* London: Social Science Research Council.

Davis, J. (1977) *People of the Mediterranean: An Essay in Comparative Social Anthropology,* London: Routledge & Kegan Paul.

de Pina Cabral, J. (1989) 'The Mediterranean as a Category of Regional Comparison: A Critical View', *Current Anthropology,* 30 (3): 399–406.

Dorian, N. (1981) *Language Death,* Philadelphia: University of Pennsylvania Press.

Ennew, J. (1980) *The Western Isles Today,* Cambridge: Cambridge University Press.

Fardon, R. (1990) 'Localizing Strategies: The Regionalization of Ethnographic Accounts', in Richard Fardon (ed.), *Localizing Strategies: Regional Traditions of Ethnographic Writing,* Edinburgh: Scottish Academic Press.

Gilmore, D. (1982) 'Anthropology of the Mediterranean Area', *Annual Review of Anthropology,* 11: 175–205.

Gilmore, D. (ed.) (1987) *Honor and Shame and the Unity of the Mediterranean,* Washington, DC: American Anthropological Association.

Goddard, V., J. Llobera and C. Shore (eds) (1994) *The Anthropology of Europe: Identities and Boundaries in Conflict,* Oxford: Berg.

Gupta, A. and J. Ferguson (1992) 'Beyond "Culture": Space, Identity, and the Politics of Difference', *Cultural Anthropology,* 7 (1): 6–23.

Hechter, M. (1975) *Internal Colonialism: The Celtic Fringe in British National Development, 1536–1966,* London: Routledge & Kegan Paul.

Herzfeld, M. (1987a) ' "As in Your Own House": Hospitality Ethnography, and the Stereotype of Mediterranean Society', in David Gilmore (ed.), *Honor and Shame and the Unity of the Mediterranean,* American Anthropological Association Special Publication No. 22.

—— (1987b) *Anthropology Through the Looking Glass: Critical Ethnography in the Margins of Europe,* Cambridge: Cambridge University Press.

Holy, L. and M. Stuchlik (1981) 'The Structure of Folk Models', in Ladislav Holy and Milan Stuchlik (eds), *The Structure of Folk Models*, London: Academic Press.

Jackson, A. (1987) 'Reflections on Ethnography at Home and the ASA', in Anthony Jackson (ed.), *Anthropology at Home*, Association of Social Anthropologists Monograph No. 25, London: Tavistock.

Knight, J. (1994) 'Questioning Local Boundaries: A Critique of the "Anthropology of Locality"', *Ethnos*, 59: 3–4 (213–31).

Knipe, E. (1984) *Gamrie*, Lanham, MD: University Press of America.

Littlejohn, J. (1963) *Westrigg: The Sociology of a Cheviot Border Parish*, London: Routledge & Kegan Paul.

McDonald, M. (1993) 'The Construction of Difference: An Anthropological Approach to Stereotypes', in Sharon Macdonald (ed.), *Inside European Identities: Ethnography in Western Europe*, Providence: Berg.

Macdonald, S. (1993) 'Identity Complexes in Western Europe: Social Anthropological Perspectives', in Sharon Macdonald (ed.), *Inside European Identities*, Providence: Berg.

McFarlane, G. (1981) 'Shetlanders and Incomers: Change, Conflict and Emphasis in Social Perspectives', in Ladislav Holy and Milan Stuchlik (eds), *The Structure of Folk Models*, Association of Social Anthropologists Monograph No. 20, New York: Academic Press.

Meily, D. E. (1984) 'Scottish Entrepreneurs Across Three Generations: The Fishing Town of Pittenweem.' Unpublished Ph. D. dissertation, Rutgers University.

Mewett, P. (1977) 'Occupational Pluralism in Crofting: The Influence of Non-Croft Work on the Patterns of Crofting Agriculture in the Isle of Lewis since about 1859', *Scottish Journal of Sociology*, 2 (1): 31–50.

—— (1986) 'Boundaries and Discourse in a Lewis Crofting Community', in Anthony P. Cohen (ed.), *Symbolising Boundaries*, Manchester: Manchester University Press.

Millman, R. N. (1975) *The Making of the Scottish Landscape*, London: Batsford.

Mitchison, R. (1978) *Life in Scotland*, London: Batsford.

Moore, R. (1982) *The Social Impact of Oil: The Case of Peterhead*, London: Routledge & Kegan Paul.

Nadel, J. H. (1983) 'Houston's Little Sisters: A Cross-cultural Perspective on Offshore Oil', *Human Organization*, 42 (2): 167–72.

—— (1984) 'Stigma and Separation: Pariah Status and Community Persistence in a Scottish Fishing Village', *Ethnology*, 23 (2): 101–15.

—— (1986) 'Burning with the Fire of God: Calvinism and Community in a Scottish Fishing Village', *Ethnology*, 25 (1): 49–60.

Nadel-Klein, J. (1988) 'A Fisher Laddie Needs a Fisher Lassie: Endogamy and Work in a Scottish Fishing Village', in Jane Nadel-Klein and Dona Lee Davis (eds), *To Work and to Weep: Women in Fishing Economics*, Institute of Social and Economic Research, St Johns, Newfoundland: Memorial University of Newfoundland.

—— (1991) 'Reweaving the Fringe: Localism, Tradition, and Representation in British Ethnography', *American Ethnologist*, 18: 500–17.

—— (1993) 'Hopping Down the Heritage Trail.' Paper delivered at the 1993 meetings of the American Anthropological Association.

—— (1995) 'Occidentalism as a Cottage Industry: Representing the Autochthonous "Other" in British and Irish Rural Studies', in James Carrier (ed.), *Occidentalism: Images of the West*, Oxford: Oxford University Press.

Nairn, T. (1977) *The Break-Up of Britain*, London: New Left Books.

Neville, G. K. (1994) *The Mother Town*, Oxford: Oxford University Press.

Parman, S. (1990) *Scottish Crofters: A Historical Ethnography of a Celtic Village*, Fort Worth: Holt, Rinehart & Winston.

—— (1993) 'The Future of European Boundaries: A Case Study', in Thomas Wilson and M. Estellie Smith (eds), *Cultural Change and the New Europe: Perspectives on the European Community*, Boulder: Westview.

Peristiany, J. C. (ed.) (1965) *Honor and Shame*, London: Weidenfeld & Nicolson.

Postel-Coster, E. and J. J. Helmerin (1973) 'Fishing Communities in the Scottish East Coast', Leiden.

Prebble, J. (1963) *The Highland Clearances*, Harmondsworth: Penguin.

Rehfisch, F. (1975) 'Scottish Travellers or Tinkers', in Farnham Rehfisch (ed.), *Gypsies, Tinkers and Other Travellers*, London: Academic Press.

Shore, C. (1993) 'Inventing the "People's Europe": Critical Approaches to European Community "Cultural Policy"', *Man*, 28 (4): 779–800.

Shore, C. and A. Black (1995) 'Citizens' Europe and the Construction of European Identity', in Victoria Goddard *et al.* (eds), *The Anthropology of Europe: Identities, Boundaries and Conflict*, Oxford: Berg.

Smout, T. C. (1969) *A History of the Scottish People 1560–1830*, London: Fontana/Collins.

Stolcke, V. (1995), 'Talking Culture: New Boundaries, New Rhetoric of Exclusion in Europe', *Current Anthropology*, 36 (1): 1–24.

Trevor-Roper, H. (1983) 'The Invention of Tradition: The Highland Tradition of Scotland', in Eric Hobsbawm and Terence Ranger (eds), *The Invention of Tradition*, Cambridge: Cambridge University Press.

Turner, R. (1981) 'Gala Day as an Expression of Community', in Anthony Jackson (ed.), *Way of Life and Identity*, North Sea Oil Occasional Paper No. 4, Social Science Research Council.

Urry, J. (1984) 'Englishmen, Celts and Iberians: The Ethnographic Survey of the United Kingdom, 1892–1899', in George Stocking (ed.), *Functionalism Historicized: Essays on British Social Anthropology*, Madison: University of Wisconsin Press.

Whatley, C. (1990) 'How Tame were the Scottish Lowlanders during the Eighteenth Century?', in T. M. Devine (ed.), *Conflict and Stability in Scottish Society 1700–1850*, Edinburgh: John Donald.

Wilson, T. (1993) 'An Anthropology of the European Community', in Thomas Wilson and M. Estellie Smith (eds), *Cultural Change and the New Europe*, Boulder: Westview.

Wilson, T. and M. Estellie Smith (eds) (1993) *Cultural Change and the New Europe*, Boulder: Westview.

Chapter 7

Deconstructing colonial fictions?

Some conjuring tricks in the recent sociology of India

Declan Quigley

The theme of the argument to be developed here can be divined easily from the titles of some of the works that form the ethnographic and theoretical backdrop: *Imagining India* and 'Orientalist Constructions of India' (Inden 1990, 1986); 'The Invention of Caste' and 'Castes of Mind' (Dirks 1989, 1992), 'Inventing Village Tradition' (Mayer 1993). At a substantive level, the claim being made in these and a number of other works is that some of the most cherished concepts used by anthropologists and sociologists to depict institutions in India are at best so problematic as to be virtually useless, and at worst simply figments of the imagination. I will focus here on the construct that has come in for most criticism – caste.[1]

What is at issue is not only of interest to anthropologists specialising in the region. The inspiration for much of what is being said here comes from debates around questions that are of general concern – Orientalism, the invention of tradition, the politics of representation and, underlying all of these, questions about relativism which have always divided anthropologists and which seem destined to haunt the subject for the foreseeable future. There is, however, a particular South Asianist twist to these debates which derives largely from a peculiar intellectual involution in the anthropology of Hinduism over the last thirty years or so.

To set the scene, however, let me first recall the main themes of Said's *Orientalism*, which provides inspiration for much of the material to be discussed here. There is a central dilemma in Said's argument which can be summarised in a question that he raises without answering, though it is, he says, 'the main intellectual issue raised by Orientalism' (Said 1985: 45):

Can one divide human reality, as indeed human reality seems to be genuinely divided, into clearly different cultures, histories, traditions, societies, even races, and survive the consequences humanly? I mean to ask whether there is any way of avoiding the hostility expressed by the division, say, of men into 'us' (Westerners) and 'they' (Orientals).

The question is echoed in one form or another by a number of the contributors to books in the genre of *Writing Culture* (Clifford and Marcus 1986) and *Recapturing Anthropology* (Fox 1991b): how to talk about others without underlining their otherness in a way that could be construed as either derogatory or somehow exerting power over them. Said is not alone in appearing to want it both ways: the differences are genuine; yet to comment on them is unforgivable.[2]

As is well known, the central theme of Said's argument is that in so far as the West has represented the East, more often than not it has *mis*represented it, and *systematically* misrepresented it. This misrepresentation has been as much a political act as an intellectual one: the portrayal of the Orient as a place that was (and remains) either mysterious or hostile, in any case generally irrational, was (and remains) a way in which the West could assert both its own rationality and the justness of its own political institutions. Among other failings that Orientalists are accused of is the tendency to resurrect (or invent) a glorious past when the 'true' Islam or Orient manifested itself and by the standards of which modern Orientals can be seen to be grossly deficient. Said ties this kind of false revivalism to the privileging of textual scholarship over the kind of knowledge that can be gained from direct knowledge of other peoples (Said 1985: 92). For Said, Orientalist theory did not (and does not) derive from objective knowledge, but from disciplines such as philology which set out to discover an 'essential' Orient as it could be found in long-forgotten languages or texts.

The difficulty with this argument is that while it appears at first sight to be straightforward and compelling, in fact it contains a number of very tricky overlapping questions. These could be summarised as follows:

1 Is there such a thing as the 'true' Orient, as opposed to the Orient (or Orients) which Said claims that outsiders have manufactured?
2 Is it possible to have an understanding of 'others' without imposing on them a framework that they themselves would not accept?
3 Is it necessarily illegitimate to define others in ways in which they would not define themselves?
4 Is the representation of others always a political act and, if so, what are the consequences of this for scholarly research, or is scholarship always something of a sham?
5 Is representation, in other words, always *mis*representation?

According to Said, 'Orientalism is a style of thought based upon an ontological and epistemological distinction made between "the Orient" and (most of the time) "the Occident"' (Said 1985: 2). 'Anyone who teaches, writes about, or researches the Orient – and this applies whether the person is an anthropologist, sociologist, historian, or philologist – either in its specific or its general aspects, is an Orientalist and what he or she does is Orientalism' (ibid.). Whether or not this includes Said himself is a question he does not consider.

The indiscriminate 'Occidentalism' of Said's claim is breathtakingly ironic as others have noted (see, for example, Rocher 1993). The damned include poets, novelists, philosophers, political theorists, economists and imperial administrators (as well as anthropologists of course) – all of whom, Said says, 'have accepted the basic distinction between East and West as the starting point for elaborate theories, epics, novels, social descriptions, and political accounts concerning the Orient, its people, customs, "mind", destiny and so on' (Said 1985: 2–3). What is more, it is not only naive novelists and political theorists who get taken to task alongside the imperialists; so too do some of the heroes of more contemporary anti-imperialism – Marx in particular. As far as Said is concerned, Marx is as much of an Orientalist as Victor Hugo or Lord Cromer, England's representative in Egypt from 1882 to 1907, who once remarked: 'I content myself with noting the fact that somehow or other the Oriental generally acts, speaks, and thinks in a manner exactly opposite to the European' (Cromer 1908: vol. 2, 164; quoted in Said 1985: 39).

Said's thesis continually oscillates between being a *moral* critique and a critique of intellectual practices and it contains a number of cross-cutting strands. One is that a 'real' Orient (as opposed to a linguistic Orient, a Freudian Orient, a Darwinian Orient, a racist Orient and so on), something other than the fabrications of Westerners, did exist: 'At most, the "real" Orient provoked a writer to his vision; it very rarely guided it' (Said 1985: 22). The Orient which has been presented to the West, he says, 'is not the Orient as it is, but the Orient as it has been Orientalized' (ibid.: 104). On the other hand, towards the end of the book, he questions the whole concept of the Orient 'as it is': 'It is not the thesis of this book to suggest that there is such a thing as a real or true Orient (Islam, Arab, or whatever). . . . On the contrary, I have been arguing that "the Orient" is itself a constituted entity' (ibid.: 322).

This leads Said to the conclusion that the underlying question is whether there can be a true representation of anything or whether, because all representations are caught up in the linguistic, cultural and political constraints of the observer, they are always necessarily distorted.

We must be prepared to accept the fact that a representation is *eo ipso* implicated, intertwined, embedded, interwoven with a great many other things beside the 'truth', which is itself a representation. What this must lead us to methodologically is to view representations (or misrepresentations – the distinction is at best only a matter of degree) as inhabiting a common field of play defined . . . not by some inherent subject matter alone, but by some common history, tradition, universe of discourse.

(Ibid.: 272)

This classically relativist position inevitably leads one to ask whether it is possible to say anything about anything which is not a misrepresentation? Said raises the question without attempting to answer it. One irony of his position, of course, is that if he were to be consistent, he would have to concede that his anti-Orientalist thesis is equally just another representation or misrepresentation and therefore not to be taken as any more 'truthful' (all such words henceforth being put in inverted commas) than the pictures provided by nineteenth-century administrator-imperialists or philologists or whoever. In fact, Said does seem to be vaguely aware that this is the logical outcome of his argument because he makes little attempt to answer the more abstract question of whether a representation can ever escape from being a misrepresentation.

He does, however, very briefly confront the question of whether an alternative to Orientalism in the narrower sense is possible. 'Is this book', he asks, 'an argument only *against* something, and not *for* something positive?' (ibid.: 325). But by the time he asks the question there are only three pages left in the book and his answer, couched in terms of humanistic scholarship, provides no clear guidelines as to *how* one might proceed without falling into the same old Orientalist traps. There is, however, an implicit prescription in his statement (with which I completely agree) that 'interesting work is most likely to be produced by scholars whose allegiance is to a discipline defined intellectually and not to a "field" like Orientalism defined either canonically, imperially, or geographically' (ibid.: 326). What is more, he notes that 'there are many individual scholars working in fields such as Islamic history, religion, civilization, sociology and anthropology whose production is deeply valuable as scholarship' (ibid.).

Regrettably, Said does not balance his account by showing what exactly these scholars have achieved, what it is they have demonstrated that is not a misrepresentation, or how they did it when so many others failed. Instead, after pointing out that some ideologically untainted scholarship is not only desirable, but actually possible, he quickly reverts (after one page) to his main theme of Orientalist-bashing. While apparently advocating some kind of vaguely defined humanistic scholarship as a recipe for escaping from the pitfalls of Orientalism, Said seems uneasy about how far scholarship should be allowed to go and at times even seems to suggest that humanism and sustained study of other people are incompatible. He concludes the book by saying, 'Perhaps too we should remember that the study of man in society is based on concrete human history and experiences, not on donnish abstractions, or on obscure laws or arbitrary systems' (ibid.: 327–8).

There are obvious problems in this, however, the most banal being the indispensability of abstractions in providing any kind of intellectual order. To label the ordering process itself as donnish, obscure or arbitrary is to confuse the issue by stigmatising any and all forms of enquiry. And, of course, the very concept of Orientalism which Said pushes on us so persuasively is itself a masterpiece of abstraction, not least because it ignores a huge body of work which, Said himself admits, avoids the common Orientalist pitfalls and constitutes valuable scholarship. There is a rather alarming selectivity here: we are offered neither evidence to illuminate the true nature of that which has been distorted nor guidance about what would count as acceptable evidence. These are curious omissions indeed given that one cannot come to any conclusions on the strength of Said's case without them.

If Said is not strong either on epistemology or on alerting us to some more positive methods of enquiry, his moral critique is nevertheless very effective. What modern Orientalists have done, he argues, is to bolster the historical division between Christendom and Islam, the latter being 'the very epitome of an outsider agent against which the whole of European civilization from the Middle Ages on was founded' (ibid.: 70). The underlying failure of Western Orientalism is that it does not live up to the standards of acceptable scholarship which it self-righteously claims are the hallmark of modern Western civilization and denigrates other cultures for failing to embrace. In the end, Said claims, this avowedly liberal, enlightened scholarship succumbs to precisely the same stereotypes as popular racism.

More than any other region, perhaps, India has become increasingly opaque to non-specialists in spite of the huge amount of material that is available. Dumont's *Homo Hierarchicus* cannot be held solely responsible for this opacity though it has undoubtedly been the most influential villain. A theory which claims as one of its main virtues that it is contradicted by the facts is not guaranteed to make much sense to non-specialists. Yet it possessed unparalleled appeal for a generation of South Asianist anthropologists and some still cling to the theory's basic premises in spite of the clear demonstration that these inevitably lead to unsustainable conclusions. This is an intellectual puzzle worthy of a Ph.D. thesis in its own right: i.e. why is it that Dumont's nonsensical theory exerted such influence for so long? My concern here, however, is more with the debris that has ensued from the piecemeal demolition of *Homo Hierarchicus*.

Over the last twenty years, the dismantling of Dumont's theory of caste has tended to push students of the subject in one of three directions. A minority has sought to provide an alternative theory of caste – and there are various possibilities on offer, though only one of these, as I have argued elsewhere, considers the full range of facts.[3] Since I have a vested interest in this camp and since by far the greater volume of paper has been produced by those moving in the other two directions, I will concentrate on the latter here.

On the one hand, some have sought refuge in area studies, dressed up as 'a return to the facts', as opposed to the high-flown theorising of Dumont or indeed anyone who would attempt to put forward any model of any institution in India. Though impossible to quantify, this probably accounts for the majority of anthropologists working on India today for whom the central point of reference is India, not anthropology, and not only India, but postcolonial India. For those of us who do research on neighbouring Nepal and Pakistan, let alone anyone else who sees the heart of anthropology to be comparison, this parochialism, both geographical and historical, is particularly striking.

On the other hand there is a kind of vacuous theorising, for the most part admonishing our intellectual ancestors (and poor Dumont is again usually one of the main targets) for their Orientalism, essentialism, and so on, and advising us to avoid these sins in the future. As with Said, however, what we *should* be doing is generally rather less clearly articulated by these authors, the most influential of whom is Ronald Inden.

What Said claims for the Arab or Muslim Orient, that this was the 'other' against which the West conspiratorially defined itself, Inden claims for India: 'Without the dark rock of Indian tradition under its feet, European rationality would not have seemed so bright and light' (Inden 1990: 32). Inden argues cogently that we should not think of Indology as being marginal to the way in which the human sciences were constructed in the nineteenth and twentieth centuries – and particularly how they were constructed in the image of the natural sciences. Like Said, he places much emphasis on the role of comparative philology which, he claims, was right at the heart of the way in which images of the Orient were constructed. Also like Said, Inden asserts that the problem of Orientalism is not simply a question of how one represents the East, but of how one represents other cultures in general. Indeed, for Inden the problem is nothing less than the status of the human sciences.

Inden's favourite term of abuse is 'essentialism', which he uses to castigate other social theorists in much the same way that some people use 'functionalism' or 'positivism' as a term of abuse. The problem with Orientalism, he says, 'is not just one of bias or of bad motives and, hence, confined to itself. The problem lies, in my view, with the way in which the human sciences have displaced human agency on to essences in the first place' (ibid.: 264). The obvious essential quality attributed to Indians is caste but this is only one among others which pepper the literature: fatalism, addiction to ritual, divine kingship, the 'Indian mind', and so on. Defining populations in terms of such unchanging essences, Inden contends, prevents one from considering people as agents, thinking and acting, capable of forcing change or making rational decisions. A large part of the problem, he insists, is in the reifying nature of much sociological vocabulary and unless we tackle this we are unlikely to make much progress. He himself makes a number of suggestions, but with the single exception of the proposal that the concept 'polity' is often more appropriate than the word 'society', the other changes require awkward neologisms which seem to me to be more likely to cause confusion than clarity.

The way in which Indians were made to appear irrational, Inden claims, was a direct result of the way in which populations were classified in successive censuses, beginning in 1872. The late nineteenth and early twentieth centuries saw a profusion of publications based on these censuses with the usual title of 'The Tribes and Castes of . . . [such and such a place]'. 'Here in these tomes of alphabetized empiricism', as he scornfully puts it, 'is to be found . . . the hegemonic discourse on caste of the Anglo-French imperial formation' (ibid.: 58). In Inden's hands, and of course he is not alone, 'empiricism' is another term of abuse, much like 'essentialism'. What Inden is scornful of here is the attempt to force populations into administrative pigeonholes, even when it was clear that these categories were repeatedly challenged by Indians themselves.

The name that is most closely associated with the Indian censuses is undoubtedly that of Herbert Risley, the Commissioner of the 1901 census, author of *The Tribes and Castes of Bengal* (1891), which became a model for later studies, and *The People of India* (1908), where he attempted to summarise the main findings of the census material. The criterion chosen by Risley for ordering the 'tribes and castes' of India was 'social precedence as recognized by native public opinion' (1908: 111) but, as was apparent to all, this generated enormous dispute since the question of who preceded whom was rarely, if ever, entirely clear. Risley himself declared, with reference to the census question asking for someone's caste, tribe or race, that: 'no column in the Census schedule displays a more bewildering variety of entries, or gives so much trouble to the enumerating and testing staff and to the central offices which compile the results' (ibid.: 109).

Inden's quite justifiable complaint is that Risley's anthropological successors persisted in their efforts to classify castes along an unambiguous hierarchical scale in spite of the fact that this had generated endless petitions and polemical literature. What they should have done, he argues, was to question the nature of the order they sought to impose and to ask whether castes really existed in the way the British colonial administrators had imagined. The question is, of course, entirely legitimate, and I myself have argued strongly against seeing castes as arranged along a hierarchical ladder with Brāhmaṇs at the top and Untouchables at the bottom. Indeed, I would even go so far as to say that if one begins with this kind of assumption (as does virtually every anthropologist looking at India, whether pro- or anti-Dumont) one could not *possibly* understand how castes are ordered in relation to each other.[4] An obvious question arises, however: if such a fundamental assumption about caste is to be abandoned, what is left?

Inden is quite correct that to part with such a cherished element of the traditional understanding of caste is too much to contemplate for most anthropologists specialising in South Asia. As a result they generally prefer to adopt theories which only explain some of the facts while claiming that the facts which are not explained (or are downright contradictory) are not that important; or to claim that the theoretical premises transcend what is actually observed out there (and cannot therefore be contradicted at all by observation). Inden's own preferred solution, adopted by a number of others since, is to attempt to pull the discussion of social organisation in India away from caste altogether. (Given that he is jointly responsible for the *Encyclopaedia Britannica* entry on caste, it is of more than passing interest that he now claims to have been misguided in his earlier incarnation in having paid so much attention to this subject in his previous work.)

In *Imagining India*, Inden therefore advocates concentrating on kingship and polities more generally rather than on caste, purity and pollution. One reason for this is that it has commonly been argued that addiction to caste and its associated ritual is a cause of political weakness and instability. Inden claims that historically the causation was the other way around. He also puts the development of caste organisation at a much later date than is conventional, and concludes that it was the weakness and collapse of Hindu kingdoms in the medieval period that produced caste. This is a very interesting hypothesis which is worthy of sustained investigation. Unfortunately Inden does not explore it in any depth himself, and it has one obvious drawback in that it does not account for the much earlier preoccupation with *varṇa* and *jāti* – the two (quite different) concepts which are most often translated as 'caste'.

In any case, Inden argues, reports of political instability in India's history have been much exaggerated and this should also lead us to look away from caste. The last third of his book is spent looking at one particular medieval case where he can both develop this argument and use his agent-centred theory of Indian history while deploying his various neologisms. While Inden's deconstruction and the exposure of the essentialism of Risley *et al.* are convincing, his reconstruction of medieval Indian history is anything but. The particular example which Inden chooses, 'the polity of the imperial Rashtrakutas', is as good an illustration of political instability as any because it was a kingdom that was subject to interminable internal dissension and disintegrated after the relatively short space of a few hundred years (see Basham 1975).

Perhaps the central weakness with the construction of Inden's argument (and here we are back to a general tendency with much of the cognate literature) is to be found in his assertion that the object of *Imagining*

India is to produce 'a history of intellectual practices' (Inden 1990: 99) rather than an historical sociology. When, for example, he quotes James Mill's (1858) *The History of British India*, he is able to depict poignantly the colonial legacy just as Said does by employing the words of Lord Cromer and others. According to Mill, 'there is an universal agreement respecting the meanness, the absurdity, the folly, of the endless cere-monies, in which the practical part of the Hindu religion consists' (quoted in Inden 1990: 92). Few today would dispute that this kind of judgement merely demonstrates the meanness, absurdity and folly of certain Western interpretations of other societies. But Inden's claim strikes much deeper than this because for him it is the very use of labels such as caste and Hinduism which inevitably leads the interpreter, however involuntarily, to the kind of racist, essentialist stereotypes that nineteenth-century imperialist scholars and administrators used unashamedly. It is for this reason that some new approach, and the neologisms that go with it, become inevitable.

If Inden does not quite advocate the abolition of the word 'caste', others do. Baechler (1988: 16), for example, argues that the concept causes so much confusion that we should return to the indigenous concepts of *varṇa* and *jāti*. But since these terms are equally contested, this is hardly a solution. Robert Levy, in a remarkable ethnography of ritual practices in a Hindu city-kingdom in Nepal, adopts a slightly different theoretical tack. He eschews the use of such generalising concepts as 'caste', 'sub-caste' and '*jāti*' in order to avoid what he sees as forcing the manifold relations between lineages into 'a procrustean bed of generalizing analytic terms' (Levy 1990: 74). On this argument, however, his own very useful analytic concept of 'archaic city', which he uses to make productive parallels with the pioneering work of Fustel de Coulanges and Paul Wheatley, would also have to be thrown out.[5]

In any case, Levy still has to find some kind of label for the various groups whose institutions and rituals he discusses so thoroughly. His replacement of the concept 'caste' by discussion of what he calls 'macro-status levels' hardly advances matters because the underlying problem remains: why are there groups who do not intermarry or interdine or perform rituals together and whose members may have a variety of other differentiating markers: access to education, clothing, jewellery, even dom-estic architecture?[6]

A somewhat different argument is found in the work of Nicholas Dirks and finds echoes in the writings of two recent authors on the so-called *jajmānī* system.[7] Dirks's concern is less with the colonial *representation* of caste than with the idea that it was not in fact a traditional form of social organisation at all but one which was manufactured by the demands of colonial government (Dirks 1989: 43). Echoing Inden and Said (whose

Orientalism he regards as 'tremendously important' (ibid.: 48)), Dirks argues that

> The academic study of India has ... unwittingly furthered a colonial project. . . . Caste continues to be the central social fact for South Asia and ... [t]he regnant importance of scholars such as Dumont (1980) and Heesterman (1985) suggests that the ghost of colonial sociology still haunts us: anthropologists still write about the need for a soci- ology of India and historians still borrow what they need to know about Indian society from Weber and Dumont before proceeding to do social history.[8] Anthropologists of India have themselves remained so firmly wedded to a Dumontian position (even in dissent) that India has become marginalised as the land of caste.
>
> (Ibid.: 43–4)

The basic sentiment here is undoubtedly true, though some of Dumont's detractors could hardly be accused of being wedded to his position. As soon as Dumont (1957) had proposed his sociology of India, advocating a marriage of the ethnographic findings of village studies with the reflec- tions of Brāhmaṇ scholars in ancient Sanskrit texts, F. G. Bailey denounced the enterprise as a form of 'culturology': 'There can be no "Indian" sociology,' Bailey argued, 'except in a "vague geographic sense", any more than there are distinctively Indian principles in chemistry or biology' (Bailey 1959: 99). Bailey was, of course, right even if Dumont's notion of a distinctively Indian sociology (manifested in such alleged complexes as the hierarchical disjunction of status and power) has regret- tably prevailed.[9]

On the other hand, 'the regnant importance of scholars such as Dumont', as Dirks rather snidely puts it, has less to do with their furthering some colonialist agenda, wittingly or unwittingly, than with the fact that there is a genuine sociological problem to be explained. Why *have* there been reports for centuries, in a great variety of South Asian localities, of groups that are simultaneously bound together and rigidly separated from each other, the whole seemingly underscored by con- tinuous ritual and pervasive concepts of purity and pollution? These ingredients are not the creation of Dumont (though the cake he bakes with them is) and their apparent 'otherness' from the experience of most European commentators surely does merit explanation. It is too facile to suggest that commentator after commentator, generation after generation, invented this otherness: whether or not they were justified in being horri- fied by what they perceived as excesses in ritualism and inequality, or by practices such as *sati* and female infanticide, they were also genuinely puzzled, and neither this sense of puzzlement nor the need to find adequate answers appears to have diminished right up to the present day.[10]

There is one central element of Dirks's argument with which I fully agree. First set out in his impressive (1987) historical monograph, it is nicely summarised in a later article:

until the emergence of British colonial rule in southern India the crown was not so hollow as it has generally been made out to be in Indian history, anthropology, and comparative sociology in general. Kings were not inferior to Brahmans; the political domain was not encompassed by a religious domain ... Indian society, indeed caste itself, was shaped by political struggles and processes.

(Dirks 1989: 44–5)

More problematic is the conclusion Dirks draws from this appraisal:

Paradoxically, colonialism seems to have created much of what is now accepted as Indian 'tradition', including an autonomous caste structure with the Brahman clearly and unambiguously at the head, village based systems of exchange, isolated ceremonial residues of the old regime state, and fetishistic competition for ritual goods that no longer played a vital role in the political system ... caste – now disembodied from its former political contexts – lived on.

(Ibid.: 45)

There is a nice irony in this observation because the idea that colonialism actually did create 'an autonomous caste structure with the Brahman clearly and unambiguously at its head' has been shown, most convincingly by Raheja (1988a, 1988b), to be simply one contemporary representation among others – as it always has been.[11] The Brāhman's status on the ground is, of the essence, extremely ambiguous and this is for very straightforward reasons. There are thousands of Brāhman castes, some supplying priests, some not, but all continually disputing each other's status. Of those that supply priests, the ritual functions they perform cover a wide range, from the most auspicious – which border on renunciation – to the least auspicious – absorbing the impurities of the dead whose obsequies they preside over. To say that *the* Brāhman stands at the head of *the* structure immediately begs the questions: 'which Brāhman?' and 'which structure?'.

Paradoxically, while decrying Dumont (and those who dissent from him) for portraying modern formations as traditional, Dirks seems to go along with Dumont in claiming that, thanks to colonialism, caste does indeed become 'disembodied from its former political contexts'. There are two mistakes here. One concerns the classic distinction between kings and kingship. The other derives from the failure to consider comparative material from places where caste has not undergone the colonial experience: the case of neighbouring Nepal (the last surviving Hindu kingdom) is the obvious example.

There is no doubt that the colonial elevation of the Brāhmaṇ to a position of unambiguous superiority at the 'top' of the caste hierarchy derived from a classificatory sleight of hand which is contradicted by ethnographic and textual evidence from every corner of Hindu South Asia. It is much more accurate and revealing to represent caste systems not as ladders or league tables, but as clusters of lineages ranged around a centre, both real and ideological, which is typically represented as royal, towards which every group is pushing, and which all aspire to occupy, though of course they cannot all do so. In fact, of course, no *group* can occupy the centre if one takes the idea of a centre literally, i.e. as a point, and the king really only occupies it at particular ritual moments when the world is made to stand still.

A number of recent authors have shown for India, Sri Lanka and Nepal that the disappearance of traditional kings has not entailed the disappearance of the underlying structure of kingship since dominant castes continue to play the kingly, centralising role with all its attendant pomp and ceremony, replicating (as they always have done) what Geertz (1980) has aptly called the 'exemplary centre'.[12] Those who have the means still 'hold court' by being attended to by specialists from a variety of castes. And it does not take too much readjustment of the (Risley/ Dumontian) way in which ethnographies have normally represented castes as ordered in vertical hierarchies to see that throughout South Asia dominant castes (and indeed households of any means from any caste) have always emulated the royal function. The principle of replicating the royal function is clearly also the foundation of the unfortunately named *jajmānī* system, as indeed it is of the even more misleadingly labelled phenomenon of Sanskritisation, and of certain rituals where priestly castes are patronised – most explicitly, perhaps, wedding ceremonies, where the bride and groom are modelled on queen and king.

What is more, *contra* Dirks, there is no evidence whatsoever to suggest that colonialism is responsible for the generation of the pollution concepts and the ritual practices that are associated with caste organisation – the rules and restrictions revolving around food, marriage and contact of other kinds so extensively documented in the ethnographic literature.[13] The concern with such notions was there long before the colonial period and has always been at the heart of caste quite independently of outside representations of the phenomenon. It was not colonisers, for example, who inculcated ideas relating to untouchability – that certain lineages should, by virtue of the functions they perform, be separated from society proper both literally and symbolically.[14] It was not colonisers who introduced the practice of hypergamy whereby those of lower status seek to improve themselves through marriage alliances with families of higher status, whether of a reputable lineage of the same caste or of another caste altogether.[15] It was not colonisers who dreamed up the idea of the 'poisonous gift', passed from patron to officiant in the course of a ritual as a means of expunging the accumulated inauspiciousness of social life.[16]

A strong argument can be made that Hindu preoccupations with purity and pollution do not derive fundamentally from Brahmanic teachings even if they are strongly reinforced by them. I would argue further that the apparent all-pervasiveness of pollution concepts and the ritual that accompanies them derive from the conflicting demands of the decentralising forces of kinship on the one hand and the centralising forces of kingship on the other. Historically this is set against a relatively unstable political climate where differentially powerful kinship groupings attempt to assert and defend their integrity *vis-à-vis* each other in a situation where this integrity is forever in danger of being compromised, both from within because of internal competition for resources and from without because of the dangers posed by other hostile and potentially predatory polities. The result is that neither kinship nor kingship is able to assert itself definitively over the other and political and ritual space must therefore be found for each of these competing principles of organisation.

Had the Portuguese never coined the word '*casta*', it is unlikely that this would have caused the British to order the populations of India in any significantly different way. It is regrettable that the word 'caste' has stuck both in academic and popular consciousness and is by now immovable. Were we free to describe the social formations which we normally refer to as caste-organised communities without actually using the word 'caste', we could do this with relatively few difficulties by referring to the tensions that are set in place by the opposing demands of kinship and kingship respectively. This would also have an immediate positive consequence. The comparative applications of the sociology of Hinduism would automatically become opened up instead of being blocked as they have been for so long by the insistence that India is unique because of its 'classic' ideology of purity and impurity, its 'unique' insistence on the superiority of Brāhmaṇs, and its 'peculiar' institution of untouchability.

How then should one represent the order of castes in any locality? My own preference would be for abandoning linear, ladder-like hierarchies altogether. These obscure the fact that Brāhmaṇ and Untouchable castes often have more in common with each other than with other castes and, in this sense, are not 'poles apart' as conventional models suggest. Second, such linear representations cannot cope with the disputes over relative status that are referred to by Risley and reported in virtually every ethnography. To resolve these disputes arbitrarily, as most anthropologists, and before them census administrators, have tried to do, by squeezing castes into an artificial vertical line where each caste must be unambiguously higher or lower than every other caste is simply to violate ethnographic reality.

The disputes and the fuzziness about status form an integral element of the structure of caste-organised societies. It is not as if each caste has a certain amount of points like a football league team. Each household in each caste orientates itself to the centre by attempting to patronise households from as many other castes as possible. If, then, a Potter and a Barber, for example, both assert superiority of status over each other, this makes perfect sense, for each can claim to patronise certain other castes in their emulation of the (royal or dominant caste) centre and each can claim to exclude the other from its rituals and from its range of acceptable marriage partners. The fuzziness of their status positions relative to each other is precisely because they are normally asserting their status claims in relation to the dominant caste(s) and not to other non-dominant castes like themselves.

The model of caste systems I would prefer would be based around a dominant centre comprising landholding lineages which ideally would have at *its* centre a king, and in the relatively recent past did so in many cases. The advantages of such a model are several but the most important of these is simply that it is *possible* to represent caste in a way which allows for the ambiguous relations between different groups and which shows the structurally similar positions of castes that perform analogous priestly functions – as Barbers and certain Brāhmans are often reported to do. A simplified and idealised model is given as Figure 7.1.

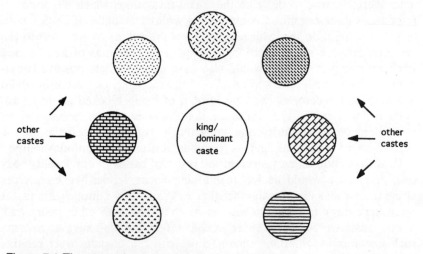

Figure 7.1 The general structure of caste systems

To those who object to models or ideal types of any kind in principle, there is little one can say. The model is meant simply to orient the analysis of caste away from perpendicular hierarchies, not to deny that reality is much more complex.[17] One factor to be considered, for example, is that castes vary enormously in size and the larger they are, the more likely they are to be differentiated internally into more or less exclusive sub-groups whose lineages prefer, where possible, to marry only with each other. Another is that Untouchables may be regarded, both literally and symbolically, as simultaneously in the community and outside it and there may be others in the locality, such as wandering ascetics, members of independent sects, and those who belong to other ethnic groups, who enjoy a status of a differently ambiguous nature. This is only the beginning of the complications: the underlying structure of caste depicted in Figure 7.1 is subject to endless variation, but there is, for all that, *an* underlying pattern.

When generalised in the manner of Said, the anti-Orientalist argument is not only powerful, it effectively inhibits Western anthropologists from saying anything about anyone for fear of equating otherness with inferiority. While there is no doubt that the concept of caste is particularly prone to being hijacked by essentialists, often unwittingly, this does not mean that it can simply be conjured away. Nor does it mean that one cannot make certain straightforward claims about caste organisation which allow one to begin to construct a theory of how the institution works. It is clear, for example, that caste is a product of the fertile plains, not of the mountain, forest or desert, nor indeed of the modern bureaucratic state – even if it has managed to find a new niche there in the Indian case. It is also apparent that caste cannot in general be explained in terms of race or occupation, as many have sought to do. There are some correlations with both of these, which is why certain people constructed theories in terms of them in the first place, but there are also so many exceptions that some other kind of explanation must be sought.

As for whether the concept of caste is ours or theirs, it is, in an important sense, neither. The concept of caste with which anthropologists are dealing is not one that is in general use in any Western culture. Many anthropologists and sociologists, let alone the general public, have only the foggiest idea of what caste organisation is all about. We can explain what such concepts mean in ordinary, everyday English, French or German but we could equally well explain them using Hindi or Nepali or any other South Asian language.

The dominant message of the deconstructionist literature in anthropology is that we should renounce our old essentialist habits and move on. But curiously the same literature delights in wallowing morbidly in the intellectual practices of our forerunners, insinuating that their ghosts may well prove impossible to escape from. Various methods of exorcism have been proposed, the most common being reflexive awareness, but the remedies seem to have limited effectiveness. Are we, then, to be left commenting only on the positions from which we look, and no longer on what we look at? Some, like Rabinow (1991), seem to lean in this direction. Or should we retreat into nativist anthropology as others have suggested? If so, what implications does this have for the comparative perspective, so assiduously cultivated? Paradoxically, the authors I have been considering seem to agree implicitly that we are now stuck with that too.

The 'relativism underlying the postmodernist critique', as Fox (1991a: 6) calls it, seems to have led to the theoretical impasse and self-censorship that I alluded to in opening with Said: social divisions are real enough, but we are now forbidden from commenting on them in any way that could be construed as essentialist. And which cannot? Ironically, this 'deconstruction' has led to a bizarre kind of regression which can be illustrated by returning one last time to the debate over the nature (or insubstantiability) of caste.

The village studies that characterised the post-Independence period in India were an attempt to correct the distorted view that had been con-cocted by the marriage of administrative pigeonholing with fanciful abstraction from ancient religious texts. This undoubtedly represented an advance in so far as it placed a premium on observation over speculation, but it tended to produce a rather blinkered form of village-study empiri-cism. Dumont's theory of caste was an attempt to transcend this blinkered vision and in this respect it too represented a genuine advance by insisting on the search for underlying structures and by linking this search to more general problems in comparative sociology. Of the two currently prevailing tendencies, however, neither is likely to supply the kind of stimulation provided by *Homo Hierarchicus* for over a quarter of a century. On the one side, there are those who find evidence of Orientalism everywhere they look; on the other, we see a new particularism, in large measure the result of the increasing influence of historical studies. Both tendencies are more stifling of theory than anything produced by either the old village studies or the wilder speculation of their colonial prede-cessors.

Perhaps absence of theory is now the point: this certainly seemed to be the dominant message coming from the last conference on caste I attended.[18] And yet, when all the anti-Orientalist and anti-essentialist huffing and puffing is done, there seems to be a residual realism, an acknowledgement that the particular divisions into what have conven-tionally been called 'castes' do not seem to be in any imminent danger of disappearing (in the present or in the past) even if the word 'caste' is itself increasingly problematic for both political and analytical reasons and can be dispensed with through a little terminological conjuring. I have no hesitation in adding to the chorus that Dumont's representations of India, of Hinduism and of caste amounted to gross misrepresentations. But his misrepresentations had, nevertheless, certain virtues.

NOTES

1 Much of the discussion here could be directed in similar fashion at recent critiques of the *jajmānī* system which certain authors have tended to regard, like caste, as a kind of fiction.

2 In an excellent review article of recent Middle Eastern ethnography which appeared just as the final draft of this chapter was going to the editors, Charles Lindholm comes to a very similar conclusion: 'Unfortunately, Said's rhetoric of opposition, though emotionally powerful, had nothing to offer in the way of a model useful for positive analysis' (Lindholm 1995: 808).

3 See Quigley (1993, 1994).

4 The reasons for this are explored in detail in Quigley (1993).

5 I have examined aspects of Levy's *Mesocosm* in more detail in Quigley (1995).

6 One might add that the term 'macrostatus levels' also implies the 'caste equals a form of social stratification' kind of reductionist approach to which Dumont rightly objected so strongly (Dumont 1980: 247–66). Dumont's opposition to seeing caste as a form of stratification and the structuralist method he advocated are the two features of *Homo Hierarchicus* that represented very significant advances in the understanding of caste. Unfortunately both remain rather poorly understood.

7 See Fuller (1989) and Mayer (1993).

8 Heesterman is a Sanskritist whose work on the ambiguities surrounding priest-hood has been of particular influence.

9 I have argued elsewhere (1993) that the equation of caste with either India or Hinduism with which Dumont began is itself profoundly misleading.

10 A good non-academic illustration of this is Rettie (1994). M. Searle-Chatterjee and U. Sharma (1994) provide a range of current perspectives as well as a number of useful bibliographies.

11 See also Burghart (1978) and Das (1977).

12 On the relevance of kingship in modern South Asia, see Galey (1989), Raheja (1988a, 1988b), Yalman (1989), Fuller (1992), Toffin (1993), and chs 1 and 10 of Gellner and Quigley (eds) (1995).

13 Selwyn (1980) provides a very useful account of interactions and prohibitions revolving around food which preoccupy all of the castes in a Central Indian village.

14 For some illustrations of practices relating to untouchability, see Deliège (1992, 1995), Hutton (1963: 167–94), Moffatt (1979), and Gellner (1995).

15 Parry's (1979) account of hypergamy is particularly clear.

16 See Raheja (1988a), Parry (1994: ch. 4).

17 See Quigley (1993: ch. 7) for alternative representations of this model.

18 The proceedings of this conference, held at the School of Oriental and African Studies, London, in July 1993 were published as C. J. Fuller (ed.) (1996).

REFERENCES

Baechler, J. (1988) *La Solution Indienne: Essai sur les origines du régime des castes*, Paris: Presses Universitaires de France.

Bailey, F. G. (1959) 'For a Sociology of India?' *Contributions to Indian Sociology*, 3: 88–101.

Basham, A. L. (1975) 'Medieval Hindu India', in A. L. Basham (ed.), *A Cultural History of India*, Oxford: Clarendon Press.

Breckenridge, C. A. and P. van der Veer (eds), *Orientalism and the Postcolonial*

Predicament: Perspectives on South Asia, Philadelphia: University of Pennsylvania Press.

Burghart, R. (1978) 'Hierarchical Models of the Hindu Social System', *Man* (ns), 13: 519–36.

Clifford, J. and G. E. Marcus (eds) (1986) *Writing Culture: The Poetics and Politics of Ethnography*, Berkeley, University of California Press.

Cromer, Lord (Evelyn Baring) (1908) *Modern Egypt*, New York: Macmillan.

Das, V. (1977) *Structure and Cognition: Aspects of Hindu Caste and Ritual*, Delhi: Oxford University Press.

Deliège, R. (1992) 'Replication and Consensus: Untouchability, Caste and Ideology in India', *Man* (ns), 27: 155–73.

—— (1995) *Les Intouchables en Inde: Des castes d'exclus*, Paris: Editions Imago.

Dirks, N. B. (1987) *The Hollow Crown: Ethnohistory of an Indian Kingdom*, Cambridge: Cambridge University Press.

—— (1989) 'The Invention of Caste: Civil Society in Colonial India', *Social Analysis*, 25: 42–52.

—— (1992) 'Castes of Mind', *Representations*, 37: 56–78.

Dumont, L. (1957) 'For a Sociology of India', *Contributions to Indian Sociology*, 1: 7–22.

—— (1980 [1966]) *Homo Hierarchicus: The Caste System and its Implications*, Chicago: University of Chicago Press.

Fox, R. G. (1991a) 'Introduction: Working in the Present', in R. G. Fox (ed.), *Recapturing Anthropology: Working in the Present*, Santa Fe: School of American Research Press.

Fox, R. G. (ed.) (1991b) *Recapturing Anthropology: Working in the Present*, Santa Fe: School of American Research Press.

Fuller, C. J. (1989) 'Misconceiving the Grain Heap: A Critique of the Concept of the Indian Jajmani System', in J. Parry and M. Bloch (eds), *Money and the Morality of Exchange*, Cambridge: Cambridge University Press.

—— (1992) *The Camphor Flame: Popular Hinduism and Society in India*, Princeton: Princeton University Press.

Fuller, C. J. (ed.) (1996) *Caste Today*, Delhi: Oxford University Press.

Galey, J.-Cl. (1989) 'Reconsidering Kingship in India: An Ethnological Perspective', *History and Anthropology*, 4: 123–87, volume reprinted in 1990 as J.-Cl. Galey (ed.) *Kingship and the Kings*, Chur: Harwood Academic Publishers.

Geertz, C. (1980) *Negara: The Theatre State in Nineteenth-Century Bali*, Princeton, Princeton University Press.

Gellner, D. N. (1995) 'Low Castes in Lalitpur', in D. N. Gellner and D. Quigley (eds), *Contested Hierarchies: A Collaborative Ethnography of Caste among the Newars of the Kathmandu Valley, Nepal*, Oxford: Clarendon Press.

Gellner, D. N. and D. Quigley (eds) (1995) *Contested Hierarchies: A Collaborative Ethnography of Caste among the Newars of the Kathmandu Valley, Nepal*, Oxford: Clarendon Press.

Hutton, J. H. (1963 [1946]) *Caste in India: Its Nature, Function and Origins*, Bombay: Oxford University Press.

Inden, R. (1986) 'Orientalist Constructions of India', *Modern Asian Studies*, 20 (3): 401–46.

—— (1990) *Imagining India*, Oxford: Basil Blackwell.

Levy, R. (1990) (with the collaboration of K. R. Rājopādhyāya) *Mesocosm: Hinduism and the Organization of a Traditional Newar City in Nepal*, Berkeley: University of California Press.

Lindholm, C. (1995) 'The New Middle Eastern Ethnography', *Journal of the Royal Anthropological Institute*, 1 (4): 805–20.

Mayer, P. (1993) 'Inventing Village Tradition: The Late 19th Century Origins of the North Indian "Jajmani System"', *Modern Asian Studies*, 27 (2): 357–95.

Moffatt, M. (1979) *An Untouchable Community in South India: Structure and Consensus*, Princeton, NJ: Princeton University Press.

Parry, J. P. (1979) *Caste and Kinship in Kangra*, London: Routledge & Kegan Paul.

—— (1994) *Death in Banaras*, Cambridge: Cambridge University Press.

Quigley, D. (1993) *The Interpretation of Caste*, Oxford: Clarendon Press.

—— (1994) 'Is a Theory of Caste Still Possible?' in M. Searle-Chatterjee and U. Sharma (eds), *Contextualising Caste: Post-Dumontian Approaches, Sociological Review* Monograph Series, Oxford: Basil Blackwell.

—— (1995) 'Conclusion: Caste Organization and the Ancient City', in D. N. Gellner and D. Quigley (eds), *Contested Hierarchies: A Collaborative Ethnography of Caste among the Newars of the Kathmandu Valley, Nepal*, Oxford: Clarendon Press.

Rabinow, P. (1991) 'For Hire: Resolutely Late Modern', in R. G. Fox (ed.), *Recapturing Anthropology: Working in the Present*, Santa Fe: School of American Research Press.

Raheja, G. G. (1988a) *The Poison in the Gift: Ritual, Prestation, and the Dominant Caste in a North Indian Village*, Chicago: University of Chicago Press.

—— (1988b) 'India: Caste, Kingship and Dominance Reconsidered', *Annual Review of Anthropology*, 17: 497–522.

Rettie, J. (1994) 'India's Oppressed Millions Awake', *The Guardian*, 5 March, p. 12.

Risley, H. H. (1891) *The Tribes and Castes of Bengal*, 4 vols, Calcutta: Bengal Secretariat Press.

—— (1908) *The People of India*, London: W. Thacker.

Rocher, R. (1993) 'British Orientalism in the Eighteenth Century: The Dialectics of Knowledge and Government', in C. A. Breckenridge and P. van der Veer (eds), *Orientalism and the Postcolonial Predicament: Perspectives on South Asia*, Philadelphia: University of Pennsylvania Press.

Said, E. W. (1985 [1978]) *Orientalism*, Harmondsworth: Penguin.

Searle-Chatterjee, M. and U. Sharma (eds) (1994) *Contextualising Caste: Post-Dumontian Approaches, Sociological Review* Monograph Series, Oxford: Basil Blackwell.

Selwyn, T. (1980) 'The Order of Men and the Order of Things: An Examination of Food Transactions in an Indian Village', *International Journal of the Sociology of Law*, 8: 297–317.

Toffin, G. (1993) *Le Palais et le Temple: La Fonction Royale dans la Vallée du Népal*, Paris: Centre National de Recherche Scientifique.

Yalman, N. (1989) 'On Royalty, Caste and Temples in Sri Lanka and South India', *Social Analysis*, 25: 142–9.

Chapter 8

Representing and translating people's place in the landscape of northern Australia

Robert Layton

INTRODUCTION

Anthropology and indigenous discourse

According to the traditions of the Alawa people of northern Australia, ancestral beings who had both human and animal attributes shaped the landscape. As they travelled these beings devised the dramas which living people perform today. The routes taken by ancestral beings across the landscape and the sites they created during their travels map the shaping of the land. They also provide a framework for the allocation of spiritual responsibilities to people within delimited areas known in the anthropological literature (following Stanner 1965) as *estates*. Each local group holds the responsibility to re-enact episodes in the dramas that the ancestors first performed within its area of land. Such obligations are passed from one generation to the next, so that the responsibilities of living people can be specified in terms of those formerly discharged by their parents and grandparents. Alawa legends and kinship terminology can therefore also be interpreted as providing, amongst other things, a representation of relationships between people and the land. Aboriginal communities recognise that normal processes of maturation and death, demographic accidents which deplete or enlarge groups and the pressures of colonial settlement necessitate repeated renegotiation of people's responsibilities and even their position within a kinship system, but the ancestral framework within which these negotiations are conducted is considered to be unchanging. While the former are acknowledged to be an arena for indigenous political contestation the latter is not, even though any individual's claims to knowledge of the ancestral order are subject to political assessment.

A map of the routes taken by ancestral beings and the distribution of clan estates shows a clear correlation between Alawa and Western representations of the landscape. Ancestors tend to travel along creeks, while the margins of estates frequently lie on watersheds. This invites a translation of Alawa traditions in ecological terms. Yet anthropological translations of the indigenous ontology have never been entirely satisfactory, because they cannot render practices such as increase rites at sacred sites, also predicated upon legend, as rational. 'Sacred sites' are places where ancestors were born, camped or entered the ground. Their creative power remains within the rock or ground and can be released by striking or rubbing the site. In the course of this chapter I will argue that both Alawa and Western discourses encompass *representations* of the landscape and ask how adequately the indigenous representations can be translated into those embodied in Western discourse. I will argue that there is a difference between what can be achieved during the face-to-face discourse of fieldwork and the derived discourse of ethnographic texts.

Land rights

Anthropology is not the only Western tradition that has attempted to translate Australian indigenous culture. A legal translation of indigenous discourse is embodied in the Northern Territory's Land Rights Act of 1976. The ability of claimants to match the legal criteria during hearings is tested according to methods and criteria of proof that are alien not only to the claimants, but also to anthropologists (Bern and Labalestier 1985; Hiatt 1984; Layton 1983, 1995). In the course of a land claim, the anthropologist as 'expert witness' (see Okely, Chapter 14 of this volume) must juggle with alternative representations (indigenous and Western) and different translations of indigenous representations (anthropological and legal), in a way which makes the relativity of each representation apparent.

The Alawa have made two successful land claims under the terms of land-rights legislation in the Northern Territory of Australia. Unlike Maori rights defined in the Treaty of Waitangi, or the more recent Mabo legislation in Australia, the Australian Northern Territory Land Rights Act of 1976 does not acknowledge that legal title existed prior to colonisation. Rather, it is the Federal Government which surrenders its freehold over unalienated land to successful claimants (as in the Maori case, no claim can be lodged to land which has already been alienated to others). Like the Maori, claimants under the Northern Territory Land Rights Act must demonstrate that they belong to local descent groups, show the location of sites on the land for which such groups are responsible, and demonstrate that they have continued to perform their responsibilities despite the depredations of colonialism. Land claims can be challenged by government agencies and both private corporations and individuals who assert competing interests in the land (see Cheater and Hopa, Chapter 13 of this volume).

This chapter takes material collected in the course of preparing the Hodgson Downs and Cox River land claims to Alawa country as a case study (see Figure 8.1), in order to explore the extent to which points of contact can be found between Alawa and Western discourse on people's place in the landscape. I shall argue that discourse, in the sense defined by Foucault (1972), is the linguistic equivalent of artistic style, as discussed by Gombrich (1960). The French postmodernist Jacques Derrida argued that the impossibility of exact translation between languages demonstrates there is no transcendental meaning which exists outside of language. Since we can only know the world in terms of its meaning for us, knowledge is an artefact of language and as arbitrary as language itself (Derrida 1976: 49–50). Derrida considers that written and spoken language are subject to the same constraints. His claim underlies many of the arguments advanced in the 'Writing Culture' debate and it will be critically evaluated in the course of this chapter.

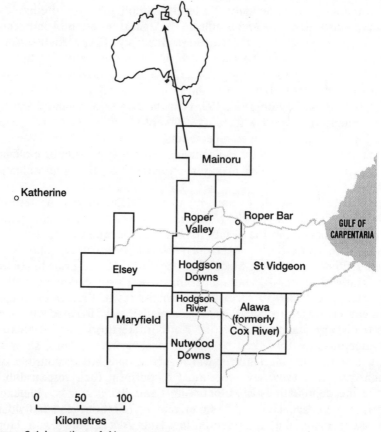

Figure 8.1 Location of Alawa country

VISUAL STYLE AND VERBAL DISCOURSE

Representation in art

Saussure considered that speech was the primary expression of language, and writing a secondary representation. By redefining writing as 'any form that leaves a trace or inscription' (Derrida 1976: 46–8), Derrida was able to render speech as a form of writing and thereby obscure the possibility of ostensive reference. All forms of language become self-referential, defining the meaning of words by situating them in opposition to other words. Rapport, in Chapter 11 of this volume, uses 'reference' in Derrida's sense. I argue, to the contrary, that representations point in two directions. They point outwards, by means of ostensive reference to a world of experience which we and the artist can both perceive, such as the topography of northern England. They also point inwards, by means of structural meaning, signification or self-reference to an intersubjective world defined by the artist's or cartographer's culture. I suggest that our capacity to perceive the world, while never total or unmotivated, is always more fine-grained than any particular representation of it we may construct.

In his book, *Art and Illusion* (1960), Gombrich argued that representational styles are intended to convey certain types and quantities of information. A J. M. W. Turner painting of the River Greta contains very different sorts of information to a topographic map of the same location but, as Gombrich argued, both can be regarded as 'correct'.

> To say of a drawing that it is a correct view of Tivoli ... means that those who understand the notation will derive *no false information* from the drawing – whether it gives the contour in a few lines or picks out 'every blade of grass'.
>
> (Gombrich 1960: 78; original emphasis)

Turner's location can be identified by matching his painting with the appearance of the same location today; the topographic map can be tested by using it to navigate to the junction of the Tees and Greta. An appreciation of the success of the style can be gained from considering what purpose it was intended to achieve. Turner had been commissioned to illustrate a history of Yorkshire, and was attracted to the River Greta, not only because Cotman painted it eleven years earlier, but because Sir Walter Scott had composed a poem extolling the wildness of the trees and rushing water (Hill 1984: 68–9). No one could find their way from Barnard Castle to the Greta using Turner's painting but, equally, no one could appreciate the grandeur of the scene from a topographic map. Any visual style demands a compromise between representational detail and clarity of expression. Turner's painting foregoes details of the foliage to evoke a sense of distance; the topographic map renders woodland in terms of a standardised and repeated 'tree' motif without regard for variations in form or distribution.

Referential (ostensive) and structural meaning

In contrast to Derrida's position, Gombrich's argument rests therefore on the premise that artistic styles can be evaluated with reference to objects that exist outside the artistic tradition. Can the same argument be made of linguistic discourse? The philosopher Quine imagines an anthropologist or linguist arriving in an unfamiliar community and seeking to understand its language. Quine argued that a distinction can be made between words that refer to objects and those that do not. Words like 'rabbit', which refer to objects, can be learned through 'ostension', that is, by pointing to one of the class of objects to which they refer (Quine 1960: 17) but many words such as 'bachelor' are only partly explicated by ostension. 'Collateral information' is required to provide a full understanding of the status of bachelor. Causal theories belong to the cultural structure and a sentence such as 'neutrinos lack mass' (or, one might add, 'sacred sites contain creative energy') lie at the opposite pole to 'rabbit' (ibid.: 76). Experience is never adequate to determine which of many possible theories is accurate: 'alternatives emerge: experiences call for changing a theory, but do not indicate just where and how' (ibid.: 64).

Puttnam suggested that the problem with Quine's distinction between *observation* and *theoretical* sentences was that a term like *bosorkanyok* might equally well mean 'ugly old woman with wart on nose', or 'witch'. The latter is embedded within a theory of being, the former apparently is not (Puttnam 1995). I suggest that terms such as '*bosorkanyok*' can be elucidated in phrases which show the causal connections postulated between ostensive referents, such as 'a "bosorkanyok" makes people ill by travelling at night as a white light and eating their organs'. However, if representations are underdetermined by experience, we can only make an imperfect match with causal constructs in our own culture. As Puttnam notes, it is the translation of indigenous theoretical sentences, unlike 'observation sentences', that will inevitably be incomplete (ibid.).

DISCOURSE AS VERBAL REPRESENTATION

Gombrich showed that style is a necessary dimension of any art tradition. The same is true in language. Gombrich's conception of style corresponds in many of its aspects to Foucault's conception of 'discourse', as the following passages from their work indicate.

Gombrich (1960)

The historian knows that the information pictures were expected to provide differed widely in different periods (p. 59).

It makes no sense to look at a motif unless one has learned how to classify and locate it within the network of schematic forms (p. 63).

A 'correct' painting is not a faithful record of a visual experience but the faithful construction of a relational model (p. 78).

The amount of information reaching us from the visible world is incalculably large, and the artist's medium is inevitably restricted and granular (p. 182).

We cannot hold two conflicting readings of an ambiguous figure simultaneously in our minds (p. 198) ... we are blind to the other possible interpretations (p. 210).

Habits are necessary to life, the postulate of an unbiased eye demands the impossible (p. 251).

The revision Gombrich advocates in the history of visual representation parallels the revision which has been demanded in the history of science (p. 271).

Foucault (1972)

A history of the referent is possible, but Foucault wishes to study how things are talked about within the terms set by a particular discourse (p. 48).

The book and the *oeuvre* must not be treated as totalities; each book relates to others written in the same tradition (p. 24).

A discourse is not a mere intersection of words and things, but a practice which systematically forms the objects of which it speaks (p. 49).

The 'positivity' of a discourse specifies the objects with which it deals, the types of enunciation and concepts it manipulates and the strategies it employs. These establish the possibilities of use and appropriation offered by the discourse (p. 183).

The rules of a discourse determine what positions the subject can take towards the object of discourse: as direct questioner, observer, decipherer, etc., and defines which statements are deemed valid, marginal or irrelevant (p. 62).

The principal difference between Gombrich and Foucault is that Gombrich has a more modernist stance toward the perceived world. He *is* interested in how a postulated natural world is represented whereas Foucault tends to put this question to one side, not because it is impossible to investigate – 'such a history of the referent is no doubt possible' (Foucault 1972: 47) – but because he wishes to confine his analysis to the internal relations of a discourse (ibid.: 45). This chapter will argue, however, that anthropological understanding of another culture's representations depends on identifying the objects to which those representations refer. Only then can we search our own cultural repertoire for corresponding representations and attempt to translate indigenous discourse into a familiar one.

Like different art styles, each discourse focuses on certain qualities of experience and disregards others. The causal premises that underwrite a discourse make certain interpretations unquestionable, but also enable other interpretations to be put in question, that is, to be posed and assessed. Like the historian or anthropologist of art, the student of exotic discourses can ask in what ways an unfamiliar discourse provides apparently familiar representations and in what ways it depicts qualities of the world to which our own discourse is blind.

Thus, while I agree with Rapport (Chapter 11 of this volume), that 'human beings act toward things on the basis of the meanings that the things have for them', I question whether it can be said that 'there is no objective truth about the world, [because] the world can be interpreted equally well in vastly different and deeply incompatible ways' (Rapport p. 182). Agreement *may* be reached on the truth that certain objects exist. The difficulty is that our judgements of the rationality of each other's discourses about those objects will always be couched within the causal hypotheses embedded in our own discourse. Our representations, albeit of the same objects, are being pulled in different directions by their embeddedness in different systems of signification. When we fail to match their representations to an object whose existence we concede, the traditional anthropological strategies have been either to dismiss their discourse as irrational (as in Evans-Pritchard's analysis of Azande witchcraft (Evans-Pritchard 1976)), or (as in Durkheim's analysis of religion (Durkheim 1915), to assert that the real object is not the one posited by indigenous discourse. Quine (1960: 69) regards such appeals to 'primitive mysticism' as a last resort. I argue that a preferable strategy is to suspend our judgement and allow sufficient cognitive 'space' for conflicting ontologies to coexist.

The first attempt by an indigenous community in the Northern Territory of Australia to obtain legal recognition of its traditional title to land failed because the judge ruled that Australian law did not embody a definition of ownership corresponding to that which the community claimed (see Layton 1985). When the Federal Government responded by introducing the Northern Territory Land Rights legislation, it created such a 'space' by writing into the legislation a translation of indigenous representations. A culturally relative concept of collective responsibility for sites was recognised, which defined traditional Aboriginal ownership as stemming from 'common spiritual affiliations to a site on the land, being affiliations that place the group under a primary spiritual responsibility for that site and the land' (Aboriginal Land Rights (Northern Territory) Act 1976, section 3, paragraph 3).

TRANSLATING INDIGENOUS REPRESENTATIONS

A review of the history of Australian anthropology shows that the trans-lations that have been proposed for indigenous discourse depend substantially on which objects are taken to be the referents of that dis-course. At the turn of the century, Baldwin Spencer and F. J. Gillen carried out fieldwork in central and northern Australia during the early colonial period, some twenty years after the earliest cattle stations had been set up on land along the route of the overland telegraph line between Darwin and Adelaide. Spencer and Gillen's work had two prin-cipal themes: kinship terminology and ceremony. Many of the communities with whom they worked were still living in their traditional country, and Spencer and Gillen were able to sketch out the links between kinship and ceremony which were established by locating their referents in the landscape. They wrote of neighbours of the Alawa, that

> Each totemic group of individuals originated as the offspring of one ancestral, eponymous creature who walked about the country making ranges, creeks, waterholes and other natural features. Wherever he performed sacred ceremonies, there he left behind him spirit indi-viduals, who emanated from his body.
>
> (Spencer and Gillen 1904: 170)

Spencer and Gillen found that ceremonies celebrate the activities of ancestral heroes at sites on the land: 'the one we witnessed was connected with a snake totem called Putjatta, and was associated with a place known as Liaritji' (ibid.: 222). They record the word *mingaringi* (miniringgi) as the term for 'headman' among coastal tribes, and found the role to be transmitted patrilineally (ibid.: 23–4).

In his preface to Spencer and Gillen's *The Native Tribes of Central Australia* (1899), J. G. Frazer picked up what he considered to be the support their ethnography provided for his theories of cognitive evolution. He interpreted the topographic features that are subjected to increase rites as the primary object of Aboriginal religious discourse and argued that Spencer and Gillen's work pointed to the belief in spiritual concep-tion, in which the unborn baby is animated by the spirit of an ancestral being, as the most probable source of totemism. He wanted to elucidate the principle of causation that allegedly enabled a ritual striking or painting of rocks to increase the numbers of a totemic species, and concluded that Spencer and Gillen's findings supported Hegel's theory that an Age of Magic had preceded the Age of Religion (see Ackerman 1987: 154). Durkheim, on the other hand, found a demonstration of his theory of the sociological origin of religion in the work of Spencer and Gillen. The social group was seen as the object to which rites referred. Ceremonies, Spencer and Gillen observed in 1896–7, were interpreted as a symbolic expression of the interdependence of society and the individual. 'The essential thing', Durkheim wrote, 'is that men are assembled, that sentiments are felt in common' (1915: 386). The social collectivity was taken to be the referent of religion. Since Durkheim, unlike Frazer, claimed to have found a real function for Aboriginal religion, rather than an illusory one, his approach provided the dominant paradigm for the functionalist anthropologists who followed.

Spencer was among the advocates for the creation of special settlements on reserves to protect Aboriginal people from exploitation by colonists and to train them for assimilation into the dominant community (Rowley 1970: 248, 256). When anthropologists set out to explore the internal structuring of Durkheim's units of elementary human social organisation, they seized upon the 'genealogical method' because individuals were ideal referents upon which to anchor social constructs. Radcliffe-Brown's research in the north of Western Australia was carried out in an area severely disrupted by pastoral settlement. Much of his information was collected at an isolation hospital for victims of venereal disease, where he obtained genealogies and statements of marriage rules, but did not observe daily life in his informants' own country (Kuper 1983: 44–5). Although some groups such as the Alawa and Gurinji remained on cattle stations, subsequent ethnography was generally conducted on the church missions and government settlements to which most Aboriginal people in the Northern Territory had been removed. Warner's detailed research among the Yolngu (his 'Murngin') of northeast Arnhem Land was conducted primarily at Millingimbi mission between 1926 and 1929 (Warner 1937). Warner noted the significance of sacred sites in the legends and ritual he studied. He regarded nature and social organisation as the two 'referents' of Murngin ceremony (Warner 1958 [1937]: 400) but his analysis of religion is essentially a development of Durkheim's theory and much of his fieldwork was devoted to showing how the structure of the kinship system related to the give and take of daily interaction between kin (see also Meggitt 1962; Hiatt 1965).

Thus, it was not until Aboriginal people themselves began to leave the artificially large and sedentary settlements created by the colonists and to return to their traditional countries that it became feasible for anthropologists to study the relationship between world view, people and the land. The ethnography that follows examines this relationship in detail.

THE ALAWA CULTURAL LANDSCAPE

The Alawa live in the Northern Territory of Australia. Although traditionally hunters and gatherers, the Alawa have been subject to a century of colonisation by pastoralists who brought a cattle-ranching economy to the region. Alawa people have nonetheless maintained a continuous presence on their traditional territory, despite massacres inflicted during the early colonial period. The Maori situation described by Cheater and Hopa (Chapter 13 of this volume), in which Maori identity no longer has a rural base, differs markedly from that of many indigenous communities in the Northern Territory of Australia. Traditional hunting and gathering practices remain important and the Alawa have been so successful in retaining their traditional system of land tenure that, thanks to the Cox River and Hodgson Downs land claims on two former pastoral leases, much of their traditional country is now Aboriginal freehold. Roper Kriol is the usual medium of daily conversation, although many middle-aged and older people are fluent in Alawa.

SUBSISTENCE: MAPPING ONTO ECOLOGY

The environment

Hodgson Downs is situated in the Gulf Country of the Northern Territory, within what Western ecological discourse calls the monsoon climatic zone, and is dominated by open savannah woodland vegetation. Grassland covers the river flood plains. Lagoons and their banks are the richest in useful species, followed by the woodland, which grows on sandy soil and gravel ridge country. Fewer useful species are found in cliff country. Water is not only intrinsically important for human survival; permanent natural reservoirs of water also support the majority of subsistence resources. In the following account of the Alawa environment I draw on the instruction of senior Alawa, received during preparation of the Cox River and Hodgson Downs land claims.

Alawa orient themselves within their environment according to two principles, the position of the sun and the direction of river flow. The following lists give Alawa terms in the left-hand column and their Kriol equivalents on the right.

ngunagadi	sunrise side (East)
lurunggadi	sunset side (West)

Since the prevailing direction of river flow is from south to north, the Alawa directional terms upstream and downstream tend to correspond, fortuitously, to the terms south and north.

werdi	upstream
lenjeri	downstream

A detailed terminology for describing the landscape exists in the Alawa language. Country, in the material sense of *soil* or *ground* is *bangara*. Among the ecological zones identified by the Alawa are:

urai or *wuran*	black soil
mangguru	open plain
lirrimunja	gravel ridge country
namurlmiyn	round hill (*namurl* = large rock)
ngayiwurr	cliff country

The general distribution of these ecological zones is represented in Figure 8.2.

Country can also be referred to according to the dominant species in the woodland. *Mandiwaja* is scrubby wattle country, such as grows on sandstone hills or rock outcrops (the 'object' which the Alawa call *Mandiwaja* is translated by Wightman *et al.* (1991) as *Cassytha filiformis*, a twisting vine which grows over other plants). *Anawun* or lancewood country (lancewood = *Acacia shirleyi*) is found on steep hillsides. *Bijinlan* is white-gum country, *Wamba* is the sand-hill gum tree (I have not been able to obtain equivalent names in Western botanical discourse for *Bijinlan* and *Wamba*).

Propositions about where to forage can be made and tested within Alawa discourse. *Mandiwaja* country is good for hunting emu. *Wiyaragu*, smoke-tree/yellow-jack country, is good for hunting plains kangaroo (*Wiyaragu* = *Eucalyptus pruinosa*). The dense foliage of *Anawun* (lancewood) prevents other plants from growing underneath and the sharp ends of its broken branches are fatal to the tyres of four-wheel drive vehicles. *Anawun* is not a rich habitat for foraging. Povinelli (1993) provides good comparative examples of discourse about the probability of successful foraging on the Cox Peninsula.

The idea that Western science can learn from indigenous ecological knowledge is now well established (e.g. Williams and Baines 1993; Baker *et al.* 1993; Richards 1993). But Alawa ecological knowledge is founded on a different set of causal premises from ours. The landscape is seen as the product of sentient forces, and even the most practical inferences have different implications from those they might hold for us (cf. Povinelli 1993; Wilkins 1993). Is a creature, for instance, behaving as if it were just a game animal, or as the embodiment of an ancestral being? Discourse on the actions of the ancestral heroes is rather like an indigenous geomorphology, revealing the causal structure underlying mere ground or soil.

ANCESTORS AND ECOLOGY

In the words of one Alawa man, 'When the world was put up, the dreamings made the places'. As the heroic beings who combined the attributes of humans and animals camped and travelled across the country,

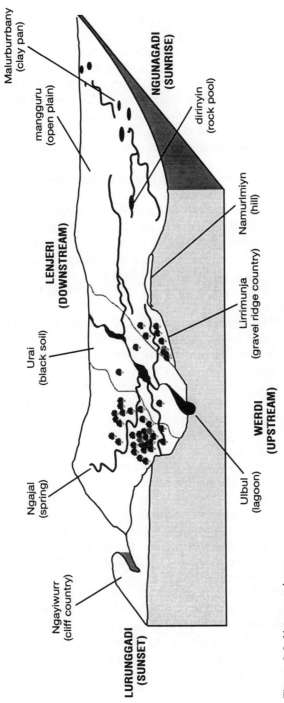

Figure 8.2 Alawa ecology

their bodies, artefacts and actions became places imbued with their presence. If the routes of ancestral beings are plotted on a topographic map it becomes clear that they generally follow (because they moulded) rivers, creeks or valleys during their travel. Often ancestors released springs or dug wells in their search for water. When an ancestral being crosses dry rocky country (s)he does not normally stop. References to the landscape are profoundly embedded in Alawa discourse about the ancestors, but translation is sometimes more difficult than is the case with topography and natural species because they express the Alawa theory of landscape formation.

Yargala, the Plains Kangaroo, travelled down the route of Lilirrganyan Creek to the point where it runs into swampy ground and merges with the main Hodgson River. On the only occasion he threatened to leave the creek he was chased back by the Bush Turkey, who had her nest on a neighbouring hill. Yargala was hunted by two dogs. He was also ill, and coughed up spit which became red ochre at Danggalaraba, downstream from Lilirrganyan. The ochre is regularly used by Alawa for painting barks and other artefacts. On reaching Iwujan, Yargala became so sick that he had to crawl the remainder of the way to Minyerri, where he met up with the Guyal Goanna. Yargala addressed Goanna as *Gugu* ('Granny' mother's mother) and asked her to find him a wife. Goanna only offered him an elderly woman. Yargala was so cross that he spat out his Bad Cold Sickness, which remains embedded in the rock platform next to the lagoon at Minyerri. After travelling a short distance up the Hodgson River, he turned east and followed creeks which drain into the Hodgson River across Windiri Plain. Reaching the head of these creeks, he stood up on the watershed and looked down on the plains and clay pans that occupy the eastern side of Hodgson Downs, speaking Mara for the first time, before travelling down Dirinyinji (Mason Gorge) Creek.

Wadabir, the Black Goanna, travelled up the Hodgson River, creating many of the permanent lagoons between her birthplace and Minyerri, site of the Station homestead and the Alawa community. The same pattern can be seen in the routes of other ancestral beings. The Mungamunga ('Wild Women') travelled up the Hodgson River, taking a route slightly to the west of the Goanna. One pair of Warradbunggu (Pythons) came down Awulngu (Paisley) Creek, which drains the southeastern corner of Hodgson Downs, stopped on the Hodgson River at Muwalanlan (Cork Hole), then turned up Midiri (Kempsey) Creek. A second pair of pythons travelled across the low-lying clay pans in the northeast corner of Hodgson Downs. These pythons are known, respectively, as the 'Top' and 'Bottom' Warradbunggu.

KINSHIP WITH THE LAND

People and country

Rights to, and responsibilities for looking after the land are held by groups of living people. The areas of land held by such groups are frequently referred to in the anthropological literature as 'estates' (following Stanner 1965). Alawa refer to them as 'countries'; but the Alawa word for a 'country' in this sense (*ninda*) is not the word used to signify country in the topographic sense (*bangara*). Countries (estates) are essentially clusters of sites rather than bounded areas of land. The groups holding these estates are associated with four semi-moieties. The Murungun and Mambali semi-moieties together comprise one unnamed moiety, while the other consists of the Budal and Guyal semi-moieties.

Major rivers are divided into blocs belonging to countries of alternating semi-moieties. Each extends back along tributary creeks. On rivers and creeks, estate boundaries are typically precisely defined and a sacred tree, rock or water hole will be known to mark the 'last place' in a given estate. Away from major water courses, boundaries are less well defined but tend to correspond to watersheds. The focus of countries is, however, on central points rather than margins, in contrast with the Western notion of bounded areas. It is the tracks taken by the heroic beings that determine the foci of estates. Each ancestral hero belongs to a particular semi-moiety. Yargala (Plains Kangaroo) is Budal, Wadabir (Black, or Water Goanna) and Jambirina (Bush Turkey) are Guyal.

Inheritance of rights and responsibilities

Membership of semi-moieties, like Maori *Iwi*, is transmitted from father to child. Marriage is forbidden between Budal and Guyal, constituting, as they do, an unnamed patri-moiety. Marriage is likewise forbidden between Murungun and Mambali. The preferred marriage pattern is for Budal to marry Mambali in one generation and Murungun in the next. The other three semi-moieties should observe a similar alternation. The subsection system specifies the marriages that should be fulfilled to maintain such a pattern. Every individual should therefore have close relatives in all four semi-moieties. Those who inherit membership of the group responsible for a country through their fathers are termed *miniringgi*. Those who inherit membership through their mothers are termed *junggaiyi*, while those who inherit membership through their mother's mothers are termed *darlnyin*. Each individual will belong to three such groups, each holding a different country, and (s)he will perform a different role in each group.

The ancestral tracks described in myth map this kinship onto the landscape. Alawa kinship terminology has the same structure as the sub-section system. Each patriline corresponds to a semi-moiety, but takes four rather than the two generations of the subsection system to complete a patri-cycle. The performance of ceremonies is key to asserting one's position within Alawa society. Alawa themselves state this clearly. 'Ceremony holds the country' (Dawson Daniels, a Mara man). 'As soon as you lose ceremony, you're finished' (Philip Watson).

There is an inescapable political interdependence between people of different clans and opposite moieties. Those who stand in the relationship of *miniringgi* to a ceremony ask for it to be performed, but it is the *junggaiyi* and *darlnyin* who agree on timing. Participation of *junggaiyi* in a ceremony is essential. Nor are they mere assistants. 'If I say I want a [ceremony]', said a Mambali man, now deceased, 'them blokes got to do the work'. The *junggaiyi* prepare the ceremonial danceground and equipment, they decorate the *miniringgi* and sing the songs. *Junggaiyi* can express their domination over *miniringgi* during ceremonies by teasing them and criticising their performance. As the late Silas Roberts said during the ceremony performed at Hodgson Downs in 1979, 'he (the *junggaiyi*) is allowed to do that because he's master of ceremonies'. Gudabi said, 'No one can argue with the *junggaiyi*, because he's a winner.' *Miniringgi* cannot approach important sacred sites, in case the ancestral power emanating from them makes them ill. *Junggaiyi* care for sacred sites. If a *junggaiyi* found the tracks (footprints) of a *miniringgi* going to a closed site, he would fine him. If a branch has fallen off a sacred tree, the *miniringgi* are required to pay a fine to the *junggaiyi* (see Layton 1985).

Conception filiation

Each adult has a personal name which is the name of a site to which he is *miniringgi*. Thus, Sandy Mambuji (now deceased), was named after the rock in Minyerri Lagoon where the Goanna was killed. Hatrick Buranjina is named after one of the lagoons at which the Goanna stopped on her journey to Minyerri. It is Hatrick's right to decide who will bear the name when he dies. Stephen Roberts's father (a Budal man) had two hunting dogs whom he named after the dogs that pursued Yargala, the Plains Kangaroo.

Animating spirits of unborn children were left at certain points in the landscape by the ancestral heroes. Each child is said to have been 'soaked in the water' in which its spirit lay prior to conception. A child's animating spirit is usually found by one or other of its parents, generally in an estate of the semi-moiety to which its father is *miniringgi*. Less frequently, it is an estate of the other semi-moiety belonging to the same unnamed moiety.

Conception affiliation, therefore, provides a means of mapping contingencies onto an otherwise apparently inflexible system of social affiliation and is a crucial element of Alawa discourse on people's place in the landscape. Characteristically, the animating spirit uses an item of plant or animal food collected by its parents to reach the mother's womb. Since the parents must be camping on an estate to find a baby there, conception affiliation is likely to reflect residence patterns. During the periods of social upheaval created by colonialism and work in the pastoral industry described below, conception affiliation provided a means for children born far from their parents' estates to be integrated into the community where the parents had taken up residence.

If the animating spirit is not found in the estate which is its father's by patrilineal descent, the baby has the potential rights of *miniringgi*-ship in both its father's estate and its estate of conception, although these can only be ratified by the *junggaiyi*. If the 'boss (*junggaiyi*) of that water' consents, then the child of Alawa parents 'soaked' in Mara country can become *miniringgi* to a Mara estate and the child of a Murungun man 'soaked' in a Mambali estate can become *miniringgi* to Mambali.

Wrong marriages

There are two principal forms of 'wrong marriage'. In the first, people marry into the correct patri-moiety but the 'wrong' semi-moiety within that moiety, i.e. their mother's and mother's brother's semi-moiety. In practice, this marriage choice is tolerated, and occurs relatively frequently (in about 25 per cent of cases in a sample drawn from genealogies compiled for the Cox River/Alawa land claim). Although such a marriage reduces the scope of Ego's social network, it does not infringe the basic distinction between *miniringgi* and *junggaiyi* roles. It simply means father and son will be *junggaiyi* towards the same semi-moiety, rather than different semi-moieties in the same patri-moiety.

Far more serious are intra-moiety marriages, i.e. between Guyal and Budal, or Mambali and Murungun. Such marriages are termed 'marrying one's granny', and because Ego's father and mother come from the same patri-moiety, Ego is potentially both *miniringgi* and *junggaiyi* to the same ceremonial complexes. Since the two roles are absolutely opposed (*junggaiyi* must perform duties forbidden to *miniringgi*), one individual cannot discharge both and a decision has to be made as to which will be chosen before the individual can take on ceremonial status. Here, again, Alawa discourse provides alternative propositions. Conventionally, children of wrong marriages are assigned the semi-moiety and subsection status they would have received had their mother married correctly. If the father's family are powerful, however, they can insist that the children 'follow the father'. Whichever course of action is taken, one group will lose potential members. In the first case, the mother's group retains the children as *junggaiyi*, but the father's group loses them as *miniringgi*. In the second, the mother's group loses *junggaiyi*. The outcome of any case will be a matter for negotiation (see Bern 1979), and powerful arguments can be mounted on either side. The matter cannot be resolved without determining which estate the children are to be associated with, whether as *miniringgi* or *junggaiyi*. It is the *junggaiyi* of the appropriate estates who must decide.

Alawa discourse on people and the land thus enables a fine-grained debate on how rights and responsibilities might be allocated. Although it embodies a normative model which shows how people's affiliation ought to be determined, Alawa acknowledge that circumstances may diverge from the model and recognise alternative ways of dealing with such discrepancies. Social anthropology, in general, recognises the validity of such debate. While it was questioned during the first application of the Northern Territory Land Rights Act at the Ranger Uranium Environmental Enquiry (see Layton 1985: 156–7), it has also, in principle, been conceded during land claims under the Act. In the case of traditional ecological knowledge, cross-cultural dialogue is possible because it is assumed that both indigenous and Western discourses represent objects external to both. In the case of social affiliation, individual humans are taken as common points of reference (the genealogical method) as is the land, but anthropological orthodoxy regards social relationships between people as entirely culturally constructed and therefore determinable only by those who are competent participants in the culture. We can suspend disbelief because we accept that our own ideas of kinship are culturally constructed. The critical step with regard to land claims, however, was the demonstration that succession was governed by principles rather than opportunism; a point successfully argued by anthropological witnesses at the Ranger Enquiry (Peterson *et al.* 1977).

SACRED SITES

There is a third aspect of Alawa representation, however, which does not coincide with any Western representation of the landscape. This is the phenomenon of sacred sites. There are a number of places created by ancestral beings where their creative power can be released by rubbing or striking the rock. One such case is that of Wadabir's eggs, left at Galal-galal-arrganya. Yargala's spit, left at Minyerri, is protected by boulders to ensure that it is not accidentally struck, releasing an epidemic of colds. While preparing for the Hodgson Downs claim, Ross Howie, the lawyer who was to represent the claimants, asked a number of people why it was important to perform ceremonies. A general reason given for commemorating the ancestors' travels is to renew the fertility they created. Ceremonies are performed 'to keep the country alive' or, as Bandiyan put it, 'Ceremony keeps the country alive, it's our life.' Since Hodgson Downs lies at the very heartland of pastoral colonisation in the Northern Territory, it is a remarkable fact that it remains a centre for cults that celebrate people's traditional attachment to the land. This is precisely the other reason people gave for performing ceremonies. Ashwood Farrell expressed it modestly, 'the ceremony looks after the country, so we don't want to lose our country'. August Sandy put it more forthrightly: if ceremonies were not held, 'someone like you mob might shoot us and drive us off our land'.

While indigenous ideology holds that sites were created by the ancestral beings during a past time, it is still possible to perceive previously unidentified sites in the landscape. During preparation of the Cox River land claim we visited a well-known site on the Arnold River at which the pythons had left their eggs. As we travelled toward the preceding site on the pythons' track, one of the senior men I was accompanying discovered a similar collection of spherical boulders in a hollow on the river bank some miles downstream. Knowing that the pythons had journeyed upriver it was immediately apparent to him that this was another site on the same track (see Layton 1993: 117). When preparing the Hodgson Downs claim a similar event occurred. We had been taken to a site where a group of ancestors first performed a ceremony that entails the erecting of wooden poles. During the return journey, along a track that followed the direction of their route, the party stopped to cut trees for use in a forthcoming mortuary rite. Walking across a rock platform, we encountered two weathered holes in the rock which looked like the post holes left after a ceremony. It was clear that the same ancestors had stopped here.

A fascinating aspect of the Northern Territory Land Rights Act is its recognition that Aboriginal rights to land could not be translated into Western proprietary concepts, and its consequent embodiment of a definition in terms of responsibility for sacred sites. It is, however, implicit in the Act that the sites that are the object of 'traditional ownership', and the knowledge associated with them, are predetermined by a body of tradition. The case of conflicting readings of Coronation Hill is an example where disagreement within the indigenous community was taken by White Australian opponents of land rights to discredit Aboriginal claims as fictions (Keen 1992; Merlan 1991; cf. Weiner 1995).

However, the recognition of previously unknown sacred sites is not the opportunistic act it may seem to someone whose representations regard such sites as illusory. Tony Tjamiwa, one of the senior custodians of Uluṟu in central Australia, commented while I was working on the renomination of the Uluṟu National Park for the World Heritage List on the pleasure he derived from teaching tourists to recognise sacred sites around the

Rock. People who have spent their whole lives in the country, he said, can recognise a place belonging to the law when they see one, but tourists have to be taken and have it pointed out. 'What's that thing?' they ask. And then, he continued, you can see the elation in their faces as they start to understand. Another incident that occurred during preparation for the Hodgson Downs claim exemplifies Tjamiwa's point. August Sandy, a senior Budal man, knew of a site within the claim area that had been created when the Barramundi and Native Cat jumped to a rocky escarpment from country further east. He had been shown the site as a young man, when he was mustering cattle. August also knew the traditional owners were those who held the Barramundi and Native Cat sites to the east. When the owners were approached it was clear that these men had never visited the place. A helicopter trip was arranged which would put August, the owners and an anthropologist down on the top of the remote escarpment. As we approached, the owners could immediately tell where the site was, pointing excitedly to the two rock pools on the edge of the cliff. Such experiences provoke an intriguing sense that Alawa representations of the landscape are sensitive to features to which Western representations are blind.

CONCLUSIONS

The style of Alawa representations of the landscape, and people's proper place within it, brings into focus a number of 'objects' to which 'objects' of Western discourse correspond. The kinds of proposition that can be framed within Alawa ontology and subjected to critical assessment sometimes correspond closely to ones familiar to us but, at other times, strike us as decidedly exotic. The question, 'where are game animals and food plants likely to be found?' is one over which Alawa and Westerners can engage in fruitful dialogue. Both we and they regard the everyday behaviour of prey as independent of human conceptions of it and we therefore both accept that hunting experience will put our representations of those 'objects' to the test. On the matter of people's affiliation to the country, we recognise the people themselves and places within the landscape to which they belong as 'objects' to which Alawa discourse makes reference, but regard Alawa discourse on social affiliation as an autonomous sphere of cultural construction. Discourse on the question, 'what is a sacred site?' is harder to translate. Alawa discourse represents the landscape as the embodiment of animate agencies, whereas we represent it as the product of blind forces. Like Evans-Pritchard on Nuer ecology, we can represent the Alawa landscape as an ecological space that shapes Alawa conceptions of social space (Evans-Pritchard 1940), but with regard to Alawa discourse on sacred sites we are tempted, again like Evans-Pritchard, to conclude that 'They reason excellently in the idiom of their beliefs, but they cannot reason outside, or against, their beliefs because they have no other idiom in which to express their thought' (Evans-Pritchard 1976: 159). However, as Ahern (1982) demonstrated, Evans-Pritchard was equally bound by his own constitutive rules. Foucault's analysis of discourse demonstrates how Western representations have themselves changed over time, bringing new questions into focus and rendering others irrelevant or uninteresting. Identifying the referents of discourse makes possible some measure of cross-cultural translation (cf. Kohn 1995). If the criterion for complete translation is that we render even the causal theories of the other cultures familiar, then complete translation of Alawa representations is impossible.

When we identify 'objects' of Alawa discourse in the landscape and in people we can compare Alawa representations with our own, as we might compare the contrasting artistic styles of Ordnance Survey maps and J. M. W. Turner's paintings, or two Foucaultian discourses. We can ask what aspects of the referents are brought into focus, and which are rendered invisible, in either discourse. But causal theories are part of signification and, although manifest in Alawa discourse, they are no more wholly determined by experience than are our theories. Causal hypotheses are always provisional, and rest on premises that cannot be examined from within the theory. It is a measure of the political autonomy acceded to Aboriginal culture by the dominant community that, in the Northern Territory Land Rights Act, indigenous rationality has been given a degree of 'space' to coexist with that of the dominant community.

ACKNOWLEDGEMENTS

The Northern Land Council, Darwin, has given me permission to use material collected while employed by them to work on the two land claims. All material was checked for publication with the Alawa in the course of preparing the anthropologists' reports on the claims. Barry Gower and Jim Good directed me to the writing of Quine and Puttnam, and Nigel Rapport urged me to read Derrida more closely. All have helped to improve this chapter.

REFERENCES

Ahern, E. M. (1982) 'Rules in Oracles and Games', *Man*, 17: 302–12.
Ackerman, R. (1987) *J. G. Frazer, his Life and Work*, Cambridge: Cambridge University Press.
Baker L. S., S. Woenne-Green and the Muṭitjulu Community (1993) 'Aṇangu Knowledge of Vertebrates and the Environment', in J. Read, J. Kerle and S. Morton (eds), *Uḻuru Fauna: The Distribution and Abundance of Vertebrate Fauna of Uḻuru (Ayers Rock–Mount Olga) National Park, NT*, Canberra: Australian National Parks and Wildlife Service.

Bern, J. (1979) 'Politics in the Conduct of a Secret Male Ceremony', *Journal of Anthropological Research*, 35: 47–60.

Bern, J. and J. Labalestier (1985) 'Rival Constructions of Traditional Aboriginal Ownership in the Limmen Bight Land Claim', *Oceania*, 56: 56–76.

Derrida, J. (1976) *Of Grammatology*, (G. C. Spivak, trans.), Baltimore: Johns Hopkins University Press.

Durkheim, E. (1915) *The Elementary Forms of the Religious Life*, London: Unwin (French edition 1912).

Evans-Pritchard, E. (1940) *The Nuer*, Oxford: Clarendon Press.

—— (1976 [1937]) *Witchcraft, Oracles and Magic Among the Azande*, Oxford: Clarendon Press.

Foucault, M. (1972) *The Archaeology of Knowledge*, London: Tavistock.

Gombrich, E. (1960) *Art and Illusion*, London: Phaidon.

Hiatt, L. R. (1965) *Kinship and Conflict: A Study of an Aboriginal Community in Northern Arnhem Land*, Canberra: Australian National University Press.

Hiatt, L. R. (ed.) (1984) *Aboriginal Landowners*, Sydney: Oceania Monographs No. 27.

Hill, D. (1984) *In Turner's Footsteps Through the Hills and Dales of Northern England*, London: Murray.

Keen, I. (1992) 'Advocacy and Objectivity in the Coronation Hill Debate', *Anthropology Today*, 8: 6–9.

—— (1994) *Knowledge and Secrecy in an Aboriginal Religion*, Oxford: Oxford University Press.

Kohn, T. (1995) 'She Came Out of the Field and Into my Home', in A. P. Cohen and N. Rapport (eds), *Questions of Consciousness*, London: Routledge.

Kuper, A. (1983) *Anthropology and Anthropologists, the Modern British School*, London: Routledge.

Layton, R. (1983) 'Pitjantjatjara Processes and the Structure of the Land Rights Act' in N. Peterson and M. Langton (eds), *Aborigines, Land and Land Rights*, Canberra: Australian Institute of Aboriginal Studies.

—— (1985) 'Anthropology and Aboriginal Land Rights in Northern Australia', in R. Grillo and A. Rew (eds), *Social Anthropology and Development Policy*, London: Tavistock.

—— (1993) *Australian Rock Art, a New Synthesis*, Cambridge: Cambridge University Press.

—— (1995) 'Relating to the Land in the Western Desert', in E. Hirsch and M. O'Hanlon (eds), *The Anthropology of Landscape*, Oxford: Oxford University Press.

Meggitt, M. J. (1962) *Desert People*, Sydney: Angus & Robertson.

Merlan, F. (1991) 'The Limits of Cultural Constructionism: The Case of Coronation Hill', *Oceania*, 61: 341–52.

Morphy, H. (1984) *Journey to the Crocodile's Nest*, Canberra: Aboriginal Studies Press.

—— (1991) *Ancestral Connections: Art and the Yolngu System of Knowledge*, Chicago: University of Chicago Press.

Peterson, N., I. Keen and B. Sansom (1977) 'Succession to Land: Primary and Secondary Rights to Aboriginal Estates'. Unpublished submission to the Ranger Uranium Environmental Enquiry.

Peterson, N. and J. Long (1986) *Aboriginal Territorial Organisation*, Oceania Monograph No. 30, Sydney: Oceania Publications.

Povinelli, E. A. (1993) ' "Might be Something": The Language of Indeterminacy in Australian Aboriginal Land Use', *Man*, 28: 679–704.

Puttnam, H. (1995) *Pragmatism, an Open Question*, Oxford: Basil Blackwell.

Quine, W. V. O. (1960) *Word and Object*, Cambridge, MA: MIT Press.

Richards, P. (1993) 'Natural Symbols and Natural History: Chimpanzees, Elephants and Experiments in Mende Thought', in K. Milton (ed.), *Environmentalism: The View from Anthropology*, London: Tavistock.

Rose, D. B. (1993) *Dingo Makes us Human*, Cambridge: Cambridge University Press.

Rowley, C. D. (1970) *The Destruction of Aboriginal Society*, Canberra: Australian National University Press.

Spencer, B. and F. J. Gillen (1899) *The Native Tribes of Central Australia*, London, Macmillan.

—— (1904) *The Northern Tribes of Central Australia*, London: Macmillan.

Stanner, W. E. H. (1965) 'Aboriginal Territorial Organisation: Estate, Range, Domain and Regime', *Oceania*, 36: 1–26.

Warner, W. L. (1958 [1937]) *A Black Civilisation*, New York: Harper.

Weiner, J. (1995) 'Anthropologists, Historians and the Secret of Social Knowledge', *Anthropology Today*, 11 (5): 3–7.

Wightman, G. M., D. M. Jackson and L. V. L. Williams (1991) *Alawa Ethnobotany: Aboriginal Plant Use from Minyerri, Northern Australia*, Darwin: Conservation Commission of the Northern Territory.

Wilkins, D. P. (1993) 'Linguistic Evidence in Support of a Holistic Approach to Traditional Ecological Knowledge', in N. Williams and G. Baines (eds), *Traditional Ecological Knowledge: Wisdom for Sustainable Development*, Canberra: Aboriginal Studies Press.

Williams, N. and G. Baines (eds) (1993) *Traditional Ecological Knowledge: Wisdom for Sustainable Development*, Canberra: Aboriginal Studies Press.

Chapter 9

Echoing the past in rural Japan

John Knight

INTRODUCTION

This chapter is about the anthropological study of much-studied places. My sudden participation in a newly established festival in the Japanese upland municipality of Hongū (recalled in detail below) occasions an examination of a state-led rural revitalisation campaign as an institutionalised form of representation management. My active presence in the Echo Festival has led me to reflect on the way in which my own anthropological practice became locally subsumed and institutionally directed to an internally specified purpose. What follows is an attempt to explore, with respect to contemporary upland Japan, a particular local manifestation of what Giddens calls 'institutional reflexivity' (1991). In order to present an outline of this local theatre of self-representation, I identify the earlier scholarship carried out, and the uses to which it is put.

Anthropologists working in rural Japan often encounter written folklore and active folklorists in their field. Ben-Ari found that an account of the rite in a commuter village he studied had already been published by a folklorist in the region (Ben-Ari 1991: 92). Martinez recalls the particular problem she encountered at the beginning of her fieldwork in the diving village of Kuzaki:

> [A]ll my questions were answered with 'Read this article please, it will tell you all you need to know' or 'You know, a very learned professor from X university asked me exactly the same thing last year and I had to tell him that I didn't know, I just do it.'
>
> (Martinez 1990: 105)

The southern Kii Peninsula, where I have carried out anthropological fieldwork, is also a much-studied and written about place. It is nationally famous for the Kumano pilgrimage, which began in the early eleventh century, although more recently it has been hailed as a repository of indigenous stone-age culture.[1] As one of the remotest places in the Kansai area, Japanese folklorists too have long been interested in the southern part of the peninsula. Some well-known Japanese cultural anthropologists have also conducted research in the area, before going on to carry out fieldwork abroad later on.[2] A further body of literature is that emanating from regional writers (schoolteachers, journalists, etc.) mostly outside the university. A visitor to the bookshops in either of the two coastal towns would discover special shelves of such local publications.

Martinez describes a situation where local knowledge has become textualized, where field research comes to resemble library research. Here my concern is with a less obvious local legacy of such earlier studies. Informants may defer to past scholarly publications on some matters, but the process of knowledge management in contemporary rural Japan may equally mean that local people become more active and assertive. Moreover, I shall suggest that the legacy of past scholarly studies must be seen in conjunction with the strategic management of knowledge practised in Japanese rural municipalities. Local government is a sponsor of the observation, documentation and dissemination of knowledge of local tradition and history. This is a process in which outside researchers can, as we shall see, find themselves conscripted.

THE ECHO FESTIVAL

Today, on the third Sunday in November, the 'Echo Festival' (*kodama matsuri*) is being held in the mountain village town of Hongū. The courtyard and environs of the twenty year old Mountain Village Development Centre have been prepared with tents and (flags-of-the-world) bunting. By 10 a.m. a crowd has gathered of some two thousand people, mostly locals but also day-trippers from other parts of the peninsula and tourists from the city staying at the local spa resorts.

One of the main features of the festival is the team marathon which circles the town. There are lots of other different attractions. Included in the range of stalls set out are those selling local home-made produce such as jams, pickles and bread, and others selling ready-to-eat hot food such as fried noodles and steaks. Elsewhere are stalls displaying farm produce, woodcrafts, stamps and antiques. Among the other attractions are a mini-zoo with wild boar, deer, monkeys, rabbits, ponies and parrots; diverse join-in activities such as rice-pounding, rope-climbing, woodwork, (sedge) hat-making and (straw) sandal-making; there is also an exhibition of farm and forestry machines and, inside the centre itself, of orchid flowers. In the foyer of the centre is a permanent display of stuffed forest animals (serow, weasel, fox), traditional farming and forestry tools (old ploughs, sickles, axes, saws) and items of traditional clothing (sedge hats, sandals) – the beginnings of what is hoped will eventually evolve into a local museum with its own separate building. Later on in the day, a live performance by a local drum troupe will take place.

One corner of the courtyard seems to be attracting particular interest from the festival crowds, the children and the television cameras there to cover the event. In 'John's corner' (*jon san no kōna*) is a foreign anthropologist sitting at a table in front of a large notice-board bearing a picture of a wolf. Here wolf stories are being told by passers-by (mostly old men), written down, and then stuck on the notice-board.

The Echo Festival, established in 1985, is a new event, organised and supervised by the town office. The basic idea of the festival is that the citizens put on the attractions themselves. Each local group, workplace and association – the firemen, the post office, the Forestry Cooperative, the Youth Group, the Women's Association, etc. – is called on to do something for the festival. There are many local 'festivals' but these are mostly *village* festivals; the Echo Festival is an occasion when the population of the *town* as a whole can congregate and mix, and when citizens can appreciate each other's 'cultural activities' (*bunka katsudō*). The festival is about enjoyment, with citizens entertaining citizens, but also about instruction, citizens teaching citizens. There is a forestry corner where people can get tips and advice on timber growing and plantation care for the family forests. And there are folkcraft displays where the 'teachers' are old people who still remember the traditional local crafts and who, on this day, have the chance to pass on their knowledge to the young.

My participation in the festival was due to a last-minute idea by K, my friend and chief informant. K is a forest landowner (*yamanushi*, 'mountain owner') in his fifties who, ten years ago, built a guesthouse in one of the central spa villages. It was his initiative to arrange, with the town office, for me to have my own corner. I had carried out fieldwork in Hongū between 1987 and 1989, during which time I had focused on the theme of rural depopulation, particularly its local social effects. Five years on, I was back in Hongū on a five-week return-trip, this time to investigate local ideas about the forest. I developed a stock reply to the inevitable, recurring question of what I was doing back in Hongu. Last time I had investigated 'village matters' (*sato no koto*); this time I wanted to learn about 'mountain forest matters' (*yama no koto*). K was particularly delighted about my now well-developed interest in forestry. As a forester from an upland village, *he* was the one to help me out.

I started to move around interviewing people about the forests, and soon discovered a rich lore about its animal and spiritual inhabitants. One animal, in particular, kept recurring: the wolf. The Japanese wolf (*nihon ōkami*) is officially said to have become extinct at the beginning of the century – the body of the last Japanese wolf is to be found in the Natural History Museum in London – yet there have been many claimed wolf sightings, wolf encounters or the discoveries of wolf traces since, and some people hold that wolves are still out there in the mountains somewhere. K had family wolf stories of his own – how his grandfather had been followed along a forest path by a wolf – and he developed an intense interest in what I was doing. We soon started to go around together talking to people known to have wolf stories to tell.

Then, as my stay was drawing to a close, came the idea for a corner at the festival. K was adamant. It would be an excellent opportunity to collect more wolf stories, and besides, as it would be my last day there (I was scheduled to return to Britain the next day), it would give people a chance to say goodbye to me. I would not have to worry about it at all; he, K, would organise the whole thing and be there alongside me. A little reluctantly, I agreed.

As K and I collected the stories at the festival, it struck me that this was the first time I had ever collected data involuntarily. I was interested in wolf lore, but I was not interested in collecting 'testimonies' (*mokugekiolan*) as such, which I associated with the salvage-type researches of Japanese folklorists, and I was uneasy at the thought of doing it as a public spectacle. The whole thing was the idea of K and the town office organisers, and I was doing it because I was asked to. I played my part, duly listening to and collecting the stories, finding some of them interesting (there was much repetition). A Wakayama television film crew were covering the festival as a whole, and while collecting the stories I was duly interviewed – about wolves, village traditions and my relationship to Hongū. All along I was conscious of my *performative* role as a quasi-folklorist and that this gathering of 'testimonies' (accounts by those who experienced something – in this case wolf encounters – first-hand) and folktales was *not* my style of research.

K was quite knowledgeable himself and was an experienced informant, having been interviewed by visiting folklorists and other academics many times in the past (and mentioned by name in their books). He took charge of 'John's Corner'. He knew the procedure, ensuring that all those with wolf stories wrote down their name, age and village. After a while, K, unsatisfied both with the quantity and quality of the testimonies we had so far collected, decided to do something about it. It was important to cover at least the top part of the notice-board to attract attention, so that people would stop to read it. So, determined to make the thing a success, K started to circulate among the crowds in the courtyard, pulling out landowners and forest labourers he knew (in some cases almost forcibly). For the most part, those brought over seemed happy to co-operate and give us their stories, but others struggled. As one old forester, pen in hand, was trying to think of something, K, first encouragingly and then a little impatiently, listed some of the stories we had already heard from others. Had not the old man heard of such-and-such a story – for example, the wolf coming at night to drink out of the family urine bucket (placed outside the house), the family finding the bucket empty next morning – when he was young, from a parent or grandparent, or from somebody else in his village? The encouragement largely proved successful; others, who remained doubtful, were directed by K to the notice-board, in the hope that they would find enough inspiration from it to give us a story.

K's hands-on tactics seemed to work: most of those he brought over managed to write something down before moving on, and by the end of the morning we had twenty-six 'witness' (*mokugekisha*) testimonies. 'My mother says that when she was young the wolf came at night to drink the urine from outside the house.' 'I was out collecting mushrooms from the mixed forest near X, and as I was descending into a valley I saw on the hillside right in front of my eyes what I thought at first was a dog running past really fast. About forty years ago now.' 'When I was working in the mountains over in X – in 1944 or 1945 – one night I walked with a friend from Y to Z and we heard the nightsparrow [a legendary bird associated with the wolf].'

The festival scene brings together a number of different themes, including (1) social hierarchy (K the forest landowner using his power to accumulate testimonies), (2) the divide between upland villages (with their preponderance of forester families) and the increasingly concentrated settlements downstream, (3) the display of citizen proficiencies, and (4) the transmission of the traditional past.

My own participation in the festival, I would suggest, fits in with the main theme: the process whereby traditional, folkloric knowledge of the older villagers is documented and then displayed in public, serving to educate younger citizens about the traditional heritage of the town they live in. The unlikely feature of the event was that this transmission of knowledge was apparently being organised and orchestrated by a young foreign scholar.

RURAL REVITALISATION

The mountain village area of Hongū, located on the Kii Peninsula in central Japan, has lost over half of its population during the past thirty years through outmigration to the cities. The postwar Japanese state has attempted to support and revive depopulated areas like Hongū through the use of subsidies of one kind or another and to attract Japanese capital away from urban centres into the area.

In the 1950s local government units were amalgamated in the name of administrative rationalisation. Hongū comprised some fifty village settlements which made up five old districts prior to the amalgamation. Amalgamation encountered some opposition locally, and one of the old districts split as a result. In an effort to integrate the new localities socially, many rural municipalities have, since the 1970s, launched community-building programmes, known variously as *machizukuri* (lit. 'town-making') and *komyunitizukuri* ('community-making'), involving the establishment of new municipal facilities, the enhancement of municipal infrastructure and the development of new municipal symbols, festivals and the launching of municipal awareness campaigns. Municipal festivals, events and symbols (logo-flag, song, flower, tree, bird, etc.) are the common means employed to promote identification with the municipality among citizens. Municipal governments actively attempt to overcome what they see as village parochialism in the course of promoting solidarity among the municipal citizenry.

There is a preoccupation with projecting local identity to the outside, through the production and sale of locally distinctive goods. Japanese rural revitalisation represents a competition between rural municipalities for distinction in the eyes of the urban population. Such rural products become the 'face' of the municipality to the world beyond (Hiramatsu 1988: 1).

Rural municipalities simultaneously look inwards to promote social integration and outwards to the wider national (market) space to secure their economic future. In both cases, the past occupies a key place: it forms the traditional heritage of the new municipal community and the basis of the nostalgic appeal of locality to urban Japanese in tourism and the sale of food products.

From village lore to town tradition

The past is an object of great concern in present-day rural municipalities. As in Japan more widely, the scale and pace of postwar Westernisation – in the areas of work, dress, food and lifestyle more widely – has been acutely felt in rural areas. In the elderly population of Hongū, much of this past remains: older women wearing the *monpe* pantaloons, eating *okayu san* (rice gruel) rather than rice, the transplanting of rice seedlings by hand, etc. The large-scale outmigratory depopulation in the postwar decades, by removing the younger generations *en masse*, only reinforces this impression of old, traditional communities. But this same trend has, in an important sense, fractured local continuity.

Before, when the three-generational co-residential stem family was the norm, knowledge and traditional lore could be transmitted down the family line. One aspect of this was the *kafū*, the ways of the family, transmitted from mother to the inmarrying wife of the son. Another was evening storytelling by grandparents.

> Dependent upon its own resources for entertainment, the family turned to its elderly members for stories to while away the long winter evenings. The grandfather, born in the house in which he then lived all his

life, was required to recall the tales he had heard as a child from
his own grandparents...

(Adams 1967: 107)

In the migrant villages of the present-day, however, such traditional
knowledge is no longer directly passed on to the younger generations.
Even if younger people do actually reside locally, they tend to do so, if
married, apart from parents, in separate houses. The traditional past is
scarcely less cut off from the younger generations than the remote upland
villages are from the city. In accentuating spatial marginalisation, rural
depopulation threatens a radical discontinuation of local tradition.

Local governments have responded to this situation by stepping into
the breach to become custodians of the traditional past. One aspect of
this role is the passing on of oral tales and knowledge to the next
generation in written form. In the 1980s, most municipalities of the Kii
Peninsula, like Japanese municipalities more widely, have (through their
Education Sections) produced books on local customs, traditions, folklore
and history. Totsugawa mura, to the north of Hongū, has produced folktale volumes specifically for young children with large print and simplified
use of Chinese characters (TMKI 1989). The idea behind this is to enable
the younger ones to learn about the lore of their home village or *furusato*.
The mayor of Totsugawa praises another book on 'old tales',
(*mukashibanashi*), produced by the Education Section of the municipal
government in the following way:

> Hidden within old tales, our traditional culture, is the wisdom and
> way of life of our ancestors. But these old tales are rapidly being lost
> to us, and if we do not gather them together now, we will not have
> another chance. . . . It is extremely important that now, in the various
> fields of education, at home, at school and in society, these precious
> old tales can now be listened to [by children], or used [by them] to
> write new compositions.

(TMKI 1989: i)

When queried, municipal officials are explicit about the surrogate grand-
parental role of such texts. While a generation ago there was a
grandparent storyteller, today this is less and less the case. Hence the
importance of parents reading these tales to their children.

There are two folklore collections on Hongū, both published in the
1980s. One was produced by a group of scholars from the Kinki Folklore
Scholars Society (KMG 1985). The other was produced by the Wakayama
Prefecture Folktale Society (WKMK 1981), an amateur group which has
produced folklore publications for municipalities throughout the prefecture.

Kumano Hongū no Minwa (Folktales of Kumano Hongū) (WKMK

1981) is a large 200-page book based on a three-day field trip in July 1980 by a fifteen-member 'reporting team' or *tanpōdan* (all the members of which were resident in the prefecture). In this time the team, breaking down into five groups of three, visited twenty separate village settlements and met just over seventy elderly 'narrators' (*katarite*). Altogether the groups collected with their tape recorders 146 pieces of 'small talk' (*sekenbanashi*) 85 legends (*densetsu*), 15 old tales (*mukashibanashi*), 70 reports on traditional customs (*seikatsudan*), and 22 songs (*uta*) – 338 pieces of information overall. For each item of folklore, the name and village of the 'narrator'-informant are given, plus the name of the person who recorded it. At the back of the volume, the names of the members of the 'reporting team' are reproduced (showing that it had only one woman member), along with the names, village affiliations and dates of birth of the seventy 'narrators' (ten of whom were women).

The largest section of the book (some fifty pages), that on *sekenbanashi*, consists of sayings about and short accounts of the spirits and animals that inhabit the mountain forest. Many *sekenbanashi* refer to strange incidents that occurred in the mountains: such as when the narrator or a family member, neighbour or other acquaintance was tricked by an animal (such as the raccoon-dog), or again when a mythical animal (the *tsuchinoko* serpent) was spotted. The main forest animals featured are the fox, raccoon-dog, wild boar, wolf and snake, and the tales are of animal trickery, animal spirit possession, mysterious or nocturnal encounters with dangerous animals or monsters and so on.[3]

New communities too need traditional pasts. In the 1980s a citizen's charter was established in Hongū in which was enshrined the goal of 'looking to a prosperous future, while valuing our nature, history and traditions'. A similar sentiment is often expressed by the Hongū mayor. While in his speeches and news-sheet messages, the mayor invariably refers to the future (for example, the building of the town for the twenty-first century), there are also references to the ancestral past.

> From our distant ancestors, we have inherited the great nature of our furusato [home village], and these forebears, enduring great hardship, built our history, culture and tradition. I believe that it is our responsibility again to pass on an even better furusato to our descendants.

If the citizens of the new community are still descendants, they also continue to be villagers – only now in a traditional, *ancestral* sense. Thus, while the basic village disposition to treat all non-villagers as outsiders must be opposed, other features of the village can be reclaimed as tradition. It is in this respect that the official enthusiasm for folklore in the 1980s can be best understood. Through the folkloristic appropriation of the legends, remembered customs and old beliefs of its constituent villages, the modern rural municipality acquires a traditional past and a deeper history. There is a place for village particularity in the new rural communities providing it is detached from any sentiments of village exclusivity. Once fiercely separate villages are now textually listed and serialised as so many items of folklore which together become the traditional past of the municipal community.

In the bimonthly Hongū town news-sheet, two full-time municipal archivists write a regular feature on town folklore and history.[4] Items such as the association of a particular rock with giant snakes, the spiritual character of a strangely shaped camphor tree, or the danger associated with a particular stretch of river due to water-goblins (*kappa*) were hitherto known only to nearby local villagers, and only older ones at that. What the news-sheet does is to help convert village lore into town tradition, such that the disappearing beliefs of the old come to be preserved as a common heritage shared by the younger generation.

Outside appeal

Folklore, tradition and history are of growing importance in present-day Japan. Japan is said to be experiencing a 'nostalgia boom' in areas such as the arts, entertainment, the mass media, publishing, tourism and politics (Kelly 1986; Robertson 1991, 1995; Ivy 1995). For Ivy, 'Japanese of all generations' are seeking a 'recognition of continuity' in response to the instability of capitalist modernity (Ivy 1995: 10). Rural Japan often provides the focus for this national concern with revitalising tradition. Villages are represented as the repositories of a national tradition – of social solidarity and harmony – lost in the cities.

Folklore is also used as a resource to make rural areas more appealing to urban Japanese. One particularly famous place in the annals of Japanese folklore – the area of Tōno whose customs were documented by Yanagita Kunio – has, since the 1970s, used its folkloric fame to make itself into a large theme park to attract tourists (Ivy 1995: ch. 4; Kanzaki 1988: 108–20; see also Hendry, Chapter 12 of this volume). But less well-known rural areas throughout Japan, as surviving village (*furusato*) repositories of otherwise disappearing folk customs, have been similarly engaged in projecting a traditional image to the wider nation by building folk museums and holding festivals.

The 1980s saw a trend whereby many urban Japanese formed affiliations with rural municipalities, represented as their 'second home village' (*dai ni furusato*), and became honorary villagers. Although for the most part these associations known as *furusatokai* are vehicles for a trade in foodstuffs, they have, as the *furusato* idiom suggests, a pointed affective component. In the Hongu *furusatokai* formed in 1984, in addition to the quarterly food parcels sent to urban 'members', is a specially prepared news-sheet containing 'home village' news (e.g. bumper harvests, flood damage), profiles and interviews with local people (particularly the food producers), and regular features on local dialect and folklore.[5]

Similarly, history and folklore are prominent in tourist pamphlets. In his analysis of a commuter village's public ceremony popular with tourists, Ben-Ari stresses the references to the Tokugawa period (1603–1867) (Ben-Ari 1991: 94). Antiquarianism in Hongu typically centres on medieval times, and the eleventh and twelfth centuries (the late Heian period) in particular. Tourist visitors to Hongū can read about the medieval pilgrimage lore, tales of miraculous cures that occurred at the local hot springs, or legends of hidden villages settled by the defeated side in the twelfth-century Genpei wars. Folklore may also be the source of local symbols used in tourism and the inspiration for tourist events such as the hunting expeditions for legendary creatures said to inhabit the mountains.[6]

The revival of festivals is a further aspect of this strategic use of the past in the present. This trend, found throughout Japan, is promoted by the central government which, in 1992, passed legislation making state funds available to local municipalities for the purpose of reviving traditional festivals in connection with tourist promotion (Shioji 1994: 33–4). In Hongū old, discontinued festivals have been revived, existing festivals embellished, and new ones established.[7] Again there is a twofold logic at work here: in addition to making Hongū more appealing to the outside, festivals are a means of promoting municipal integration.

Publicity management

Japanese local governments have a thirst for publicity. It is common for newspapers, radio and television to be contacted in advance in order to secure coverage of local events. Often a local archive is kept of media appearances or mentions of the municipality. In Hongū, town-office staff commonly refer to the importance of 'PR' in rural revitalisation, and this tends to mean publicity. The more publicity a place like Hongū receives, the greater will its 'name-recognition' or *chimeido* be – a marketing term commonly used in local government circles. Localities try to project themselves as so many 'brands': the greater the name recognition, the more likely it is that they will be visited or that their special local goods will be purchased. Most municipal governments strive to attain such public recognition and sometimes this is through rather blatant publicity-seeking means. I recall participating in an expedition to catch the mythical serpent, the *tsuchinoko*. Of the hundred or so people gathered, around half were from the mass media (television crews, newspaper and magazine reporters, etc.)!

There is an intense competition for media exposure among Japanese municipalities. Event-making is therefore a very important activity. Ideally, events should be telegenic, spectacular, attract crowds and involve unusual activities, unusual dress and outsiders. The presence of television cameras represents a recognition of an event's importance and may add an extra excitement to the proceedings. From the municipal government's point of view, the degree of media exposure may well be a measure of the success of a local event.

The increasing importance attached to publicity-seeking is reflected in the growth of the Tourist Section in the Hongū town office, which has virtually become a PR department. When an enquiry comes in from a television producer about making a programme on such-and-such a topic, the staff consult an informal list of local people knowledgeable about different things. Given his knowledge of forestry, his passion for rural revitalisation and his articulateness on television, K is often contacted, and has appeared on television countless times. Outside observers, such as the anthropologist, may also find themselves conscripted into media appearances.[8]

While television and other forms of media coverage are first and foremost about publicity in the world beyond, it is also something enjoyed locally. Thus, whenever a television programme featuring Hongū is scheduled to be shown, the town office will daily remind citizens over its public address system for a week beforehand to watch it. Such programmes are invariably taped and an informal video archive exists.

THE ECHO DESIGN

The Echo Festival was a product of a specific municipal image-building initiative in the mid-1980s. Under the direction of the town office, in 1984 a committee was formed made up of fifteen eminent Hongū citizens for the purpose of drawing up a long-term plan for the town's development into the twenty-first century. K was the committee chairman; among the committee members were other forest landowners, tourist guesthouse proprietors and town councillors. An urban development consultancy firm advised the committee on its tasks: to consider the basic objectives of Hongū's development, the means by which they are to be realised and the sort of image the town needs to project. The process aimed to combine expert advice (on place promotion) with democratic consultation and popular participation. The committee held 'hearings' at which representatives of a wide range of local groups and associations (Women's Association, Youth Group, Guesthouse Proprietors' Association, etc.) were invited to offer their views and opinions, and questionnaire surveys of the citizenry were carried out. As the emphasis placed on the *citizen* character of the committee suggests, community-building and strategic planning should emanate from the citizens. With the guidance of municipal officials and professional consultants, the committee members were invited to deliberate on the shape and appearance of the local community in the years ahead, and to re-package it symbolically.

Eventually, over a year after it was formed, the citizen committee produced its 150-page 'long-term comprehensive report'. Making liberal use of box-and-arrow diagrams, the first part of the report presents the 'vision' for the future, a key principle of which is the preparation of the local population – the main 'resource' (*shigen*) for the future – to meet the challenge of economic trends such as the growth in tourism and the interest in folk arts and crafts. The second, larger, part makes suggestions for improvement in the areas of education, health, welfare, employment and road-building. A recurring theme is that of motivating local people to strive to improve things by participating more in local society ('community-making'), as well as encouraging them to develop themselves fully (through adult education, sports, arts and so on).

The report adopts a set of keywords, key concepts and catchphrases. Henceforth 'echo' (*kodama*) would be Hongū's 'keyword'. Hongū would be 'Echo Town' (*Kodama no machi*) and would hold an annual 'Echo Festival'. It would also be Hongū's 'brand' (*burando*): the establishment of a '*kodama* brand' identity is a key to the local appeal to the outside and therefore economic success in areas such as tourism.

The word *kodama* has a ready local association: the echo that comes back on shouting into the mountains. Indeed, another word for echo, *yamabiko*, includes in it the character for 'mountain'.[9] In addition to this, the committee selected the term because it is written with the two Chinese characters for 'tree' and 'spirit' respectively.

> 'Echo' represents both the distinctive local resource of Hongū and its use in local revitalisation (the spreading out of the echo waves).... 'Tree', as the character suggests, indicates the rich resource of the forests, and expresses the warm feeling of timber.... On the other hand, 'spirit' expresses the atmosphere of Hongū, its historical culture based on the religion of Kumano [the old name of the region], its spiritual culture, its festivals and traditional observances, in other words, the invisible human and other resources.

In the report, *kodama* is used both as a noun and as a verb. Hongu is 'Echo Town' (*kodama no machi*), and its development is likened to the outward spread of the soundwaves of an echo – 'town-making that echoes' (*kodama suru machizukuri*) – a sort of ripple effect. The report illustrates this point with a concept diagram showing the concentric soundwaves of the echo. The message is clear: the task ahead, as the twenty-first century approaches, is 'to widen the echo of Hongū' (*Hongū no kodama o hirogeru*).

The mountain echo is a natural multiplication of a human act: by shouting into the mountains – projecting one's voice across space – the sound is extended through time. This metaphor of development is similar in type to that of 'activation' (*kasseika*, a term originally taken from chemistry (see Steffenssen n.d.), widely used in Japanese rural revival: here the task of leaders is to start a (chemical-like) process, making what is dormant into something active.

In both cases, human acts lead to disproportionate returns. If only citizens make an initial effort – band together to sell farm produce at roadside stalls to visitors, or undertake collective litter-collecting, to give two recent examples – they will stimulate a response in others, and in this way an inordinate social effect will result from a small initial effort. It should be added that the committee's report also placed a strong emphasis on leadership and 'leader-making' (*riidazukuri*): young people should be encouraged to develop leadership qualities in order to 'activate' the potential of rural society. Here ideas of innovative leadership, whereby individuals are encouraged to develop new ideas and convince others of their worth are seen as complementing the communal traditions of village solidarity and cooperation. 'Village awakening' (*mura okoshi*) is premised on the idea that, for the Japanese village to deal with the difficult present-day circumstances, there needs to be a 'stimulus' (*shigeki*) in the form of young local leaders to wake it up.

The Echo Festival, then, was one of the first concrete results of this exercise in long-term planning. It would provide a stimulus to local people to undertake 'cultural activities'; by displaying or performing them publicly, other citizens too would be encouraged to take up such pastimes.

CONCLUSION

The festival in which I was caught up forms part of a wider strategy of community-building, one that involves the input not only of municipal officials, but also of a range of outsiders – tourists (amateur and professional), folklorists, television crews and professional consultants.

My unease at my role in the Echo Festival had to do with my awareness of the existing local institutionalisation of a tradition of study-folklore. This did not take the form of local practitioners (apart from the two municipal archivists) or the hiring of outside experts (but see the rise of public archaeology in Japan (Barnes 1993: 36). It had more to do with the local familiarity with outside researchers and in particular with folkloric traditions of salvage research. It was this instituted tradition of observation and documentation during the Echo Festival that generated my feeling of a loss of autonomy.

A second 'echo' should be recognised. For Japanese rural municipalities, the nation beyond is also the means to an echo effect. The attentions of outside scholars are put to local purpose, making local lore into textualised municipal tradition. Through this external – and titled – recognition, such scholars confer an importance on local lore. Just as by shouting into the mountain interior one's voice comes back from another place, so through the textual take-up of local lore by academics and scholars from outside, the local past comes to be experienced anew, as emanating from another (national) place.

Folklore is often related to nationalism, and the demand for locally sited national tradition (Herzfeld 1982; Kirshenblatt-Gimblett 1992: 41–4). The ostensive purpose of folklore is to conserve local traditions, customs and lore, although in the process of national documentation and exposure, transformation may well take place. The reason for national (or at any rate outside) intervention is precisely that of salvage: lest a discontinued local tradition be lost altogether. National intervention in the form of folkloric documentation therefore is itself often an expression of local decline; ideally, the new national exposure received by local tradition will, by virtue of an enhanced sense of importance, result in local conservation.

But the local disposition to folklore I deal with here is rather different. Although there most definitely is a strong national interest in local custom – characterised as the true repository of national tradition – the initiative to observe and document here is endogenous. It is not a case of national concern and local indifference to local tradition, or simply of a national exhortation to conserve. For, along with the belief that the national amplification of local tradition can enhance its value, there exists a strong, well-diffused awareness in places like Hongū of the imperative of appealing to the wider nation as a regional repository of a vanishing tradition. It is an example of a locality asserting its national self-importance in the context of a multiplicity of similar, competing claims from other rural municipalities.

To recognise the importance of outside forces of representation is not, however, to accept a one-way, nation-to-village determination. In a place like Hongū, the scale and regularity of outside representation is such (mass media, tourist agencies, academics) that no single source can be deemed to have a hegemonic power of representation. Rather, the uptake of outside representations is active and selective in character because the locality has its own representational interests.

This situation of representational pluralism with respect to the village has certain implications. The fact that there already exists a history of local self-reflection and image/identity (re-)formulation, something that has intensified in the past two decades, creates a specific sort of context for the placement of anthropological practice. In Japanese rural municipalities, the anthropologist is dealing with a social context in which culture is an object of design and elaboration, and where there is a routine and strategic projection by the local state of communal representations both to local citizenry and to the wider nation.

This placement is, of course, further mediated by the individual relationships struck up between anthropologist and informants. In my relationship with K – a man who straddled upland and lowland, forestry and tourism, tradition and community-building – I had in fact found an important nodal point in this complex representational process. This was not a point of observation outside of this process, but a niche internal to it. In playing the folklorist at K's behest, I too found myself contributing to the echo of the village past in the municipal present.

NOTES

1 One of the most prominent Japanese intellectuals, the philosopher Umehara Takeshi, characterises the Kumano area as one of only three remaining sites where the legacy of Jomon culture can be experienced (Umehara 1990: 38–44).
2 The Africanists Yoneyama Toshinao and Ichikawa from Kyoto University for example.
3 *Mukashibanashi* do not refer to historical time but to the vague distant past. They also tend to be rather fantastical, such as the vengeance tale in which a young wife killed by her mother-in-law returns as a snake to take revenge. No great credence is attached to them as indications of what actually happened. *Densetsu* (legends) also refer to long ago but are believed to be past actuality, even though to outsiders they verge on the incredible. According to this typology, what K and I were collecting in the Echo Festival were *sekenbanashi*. It should be pointed out that the officially extinct status of the wolf is not something universally accepted on the Kii Peninsula. Therefore over half (fourteen) of the testimonies we collected contradicted this official view that the Japanese wolf became extinct in 1905. As claims to have encountered a supposedly non-existent animal, they cannot be accorded the status of objective observation or natural history, and increasingly resemble the category of claimed observations or encounters with trickster animals, spirits, demons and ghosts.
4 Some recent items include the story of how the local hot springs were discovered thanks to a crow guide; the practice of abandoning smallpox sufferers in remote mountains; snake legends associated with particular local places; floods and other disasters from earlier times; and rainmaking shrines.
5 The folklore feature consists of legends associated with particular local places, such as the place of two *sakaki* trees where a village daughter was cured of smallpox by a benevolent monk; traditional customs such as bear-hunting; or tales of the various sorts of demon said to inhabit the mountains. The cumulative impression created is of an enchanted, exotic village world saturated with a mysterious past. The man who compiles this news-sheet mostly draws on the 1981 volume on Hongū folklore mentioned above.
6 In the 1980s the municipality of Kiwa cho became the *tsuchinoko* town. The *tsuchinoko* is a strange, rotund serpent-like creature said to spit poison. Although generally believed to be mythical, the Kiwa authorities claim that it exists in the area. The municipality's Tourism Section arranges local hunting expeditions for the creature, attracting tourist visitors from outside and considerable media attention; visitors are sold ceramic models of the creature, *manju* beancakes in the shape of the creature, and towls, lampshades and keyrings all with the *tsuchinoko* image.
7 A recently established annual festival in Hongū features palanquin-racing: the

palanquin was the box in which noble women travelled, carried on the shoulders of male bearers; in the festival, teams of five – four male bearers and a woman passenger (in medieval dress) – race around a set course.

8 I have appeared on Japanese television at least five times, radio once, and print five or six times – usually at the behest of the town office. I was aware – and accepted – that my own presence in a remote mountainous area could serve to attract publicity. (Also, as I myself had drawn on the local media as a source of data, I felt some obligation to give something back.) Even though I would often sing the praises of Hongū as a place of natural beauty, tradition, etc., I am unconvinced that this media exposure did have much material effect.

9 *Yamabiko* was the title of a local news-sheet in the 1960s.

REFERENCES

Adams, R. J. (1967) 'Folktale Telling and Storytellers in Japan', *Asian Folklore Studies*, 26 (1): 99–118.

Barnes, G. (1993) *China, Korea and Japan: The Rise of Civilization in East Asia*, London: Thames & Hudson.

Ben-Ari, E. (1991) 'Posing, Posturing and Photographic Presences: A Rite of Passage in a Japanese Commuter Village', *Man*, 26 (1): 87–104.

Friedman, J. (1992) 'The Past in the Future: History and the Politics of Identity', *American Anthropologist*, 94 (4): 837–59.

Giddens, A. (1991) *Modernity and Self-Identity*, Oxford: Polity Press.

Herzfeld, M. (1982) *Ours Once More: Folklore, Ideology, and the Making of Modern Greece*, Austin: University of Texas Press.

Hiramatsu, M. (1988) 'Umi o Koe, Sekai no Kakuchi de Chi'ikizukuri ga Kasseika shiteiru', *Yasuda*, 69: 1–7.

Ivy, M. (1995) *Discourses of the Vanishing: Modernity, Phantasm, Japan*, Chicago: University of Chicago Press.

KMG (Kinki Minzoku Gakkai) (ed.) (1985) *Kumano no Minzoku: Wakayama Ken Hongū Chō* (The Folk Customs of Kumano. Hongū Town, Wakayama Prefecture), Shiga: Kinki Minzoku Gakkai.

Kanzaki, N. (1988) *Chi'iki Okoshi no Fōkuroa (The Folklore of Regional Revival)*, Tokyo: Gyōsei.

Kelly, W. (1986) 'Rationalization and Nostalgia: Cultural Dynamics of New Middle-class Japan,' *American Ethnologist*, 13 (4): 603–18.

Kirshenblatt-Gimblett, B. (1992) 'Mistaken Dichotomies', in Robert Barron and Nicholas Spitzer (eds), *Public Folklore*, Washington: Smithsonian Institution Press.

Martinez, D. P. (1990) 'Tourism and the Ama: The Search for a Real Japan', in Eyal Ben-Ari, Brian Moeran and James Valentine (eds), *Unwrapping Japan*, Manchester: Manchester University Press.

Robertson, J. (1991) *Native and Newcomer: Making and Remaking a Japanese City*, Berkeley: University of California Press.

—— (1995) 'Hegemonic Nostalgia, Tourism, and Nation-making in Japan', in Tadao Umesao, Harumi Befu and Shuzo Ishimori (eds), *Japanese Civilization in the Modern World IX: Tourism*, Osaka: Senri Ethnological Series No. 38.

Shioji, Y. (1994) 'The Road to the Past, Present and Future: A Case Study of Heritage Tourism in Contemporary Japan'. Unpublished MA Thesis, Roehampton Institute, London.

Steffenssen, S. K. (n.d.) 'Wanted: "The Era of Localities" – Fifteen Years of National Discourse in Japan'. Unpublished manuscript.

TMKI (Totsugawa Mura Kyoiku Iinkai) (ed.) (1989) *Totsugawa Go no mukashi-banashi (Old Tales of Totsugawa Village)*, Tokyo: Dai'ippoki Shuppan.

Umehara, T. (1990) *Nihon no genkyō, Kumano (Kumano, the Heart of Japan)*, Tokyo: Shinchōsha.

WKMK (Wakayama Ken Minwa no Kai) (ed.) (1981) *Kumano Hongū no minwa (The Folktales of Kumano Hongū)*, Gobō: WKMK.

Chapter 10

The Museum as mirror
Ethnographic reflections

Sharon Macdonald

INTRODUCTION

Museums, like anthropology, have experienced a version of the so-called
'crisis of representation'.[1] Questions have been raised about the legitimacy
of established styles and conventions of exhibition, about authority and
authorisation, about silences and marginalisation, and about accountability and audience. As in anthropology, these are contested matters.
And as in anthropology, they take place within a politicised context in
which practice is being increasingly subject to scrutiny and formalisation
through such cultural devices as 'performance indicators', 'public accountability', 'formative and summative evaluation', 'peer review', 'managerial
restructuring' and 'mission statements'.

My intention here is to explore some of the political and theoretical
implications of different representational practices in anthropology
through reflections drawn from an ethnography which I carried out in
Britain's National Museum of Science and Industry (the Science
Museum), London, between 1988 and 1990.[2] I am concerned both with
the particular representational dilemmas that such a powerful official
institution of representation may create for ethnography, and with the
way in which museum curators' own practices and contexts of representation may shed light on those of anthropology. A museum, I suggest, is
well suited for providing such illumination, for not only is it part of a
familiar Western cultural framework, it also offers parallels and overlaps
with ethnography's own institutional context, politics and practices. That
is, it mirrors and collides with aspects of the ethnographic endeavour
itself.

Writing about 'anthropology at home', Marilyn Strathern suggests that
particular problems are raised by trying to carry out anthropology in the
context that produced anthropology itself. She terms this 'auto-anthropology' (1987). The problem arises from the fact that we share concepts
with the subjects of our research and, therefore, the specificity and
context-dependency of these concepts is not thrown into relief.[3] This

means that we lack the 'routine reflexivity' (ibid.: 28) that more culturally distant fieldwork generates. This is not to say that anthropology close to home is impossible or not proper anthropology but that we have to work harder to introduce the kinds of 'contrivance' (ibid.) that highlight speci-ficity and relativity. If this is a particular challenge to close-to-home anthropology, however, it also offers particular promise. For the very fact of shared concepts means that in exploring the semantic constellations and implications of our subjects' knowledge and practice, we simul-taneously explore our own. This makes ethnographers of the closely reflective context particularly well placed to turn anthropology to the kind of 'cultural critique' – 'the job of reflecting back on ourselves' (Marcus and Fischer 1986: 111) – in which Marcus and Fischer, among others, feel it should be engaged. This is a job that culturally distant ethnography, for all its potential 'routine reflexivity', often neglects (ibid.).

In this chapter I discuss political and theoretical problems of represen-tation primarily through descriptions of museum curators' accounts of my presence as an ethnographer in the museum and of responses to some of my early attempts at writing about my fieldwork. Tackling the issues in this way enables me to illustrate shortcomings as I see them in some of the emphases of the 'Writing Culture' school (Clifford and Marcus 1986). Dilemmas of ethnographic representation, I argue, permeate every stage of the ethnographic process and are certainly not confined between book covers (cf. Spencer 1989).[4] Throughout this process, those we seek to write about intervene, in varying ways and to greater or lesser extents, in the shaping and reshaping of what will be written – and rewritten (and published or left unpublished). Indeed, it is this dialogic nature of the ethnographic *process* that is one of the most important aspects of, and reasons for doing, ethnography. The ethnographer is thoroughly part of this process not only as author but also as 'a sign open to interpretation' (Herzfeld 1983: 158; Hastrup 1987: 100), and this needs to be recognised not merely out of reflexive correctness but because those interpretations both reflect on substantive features of the case we are exploring, and on the context(s) of our own endeavour.[5] Moreover, this whole process – including the interpretation of the content and form of our writing – itself takes place within a political context: that is, a context in which attempts to define, impose or stabilise meanings have consequences.

POLITICS IN PROCESS

At the time that I carried out my fieldwork, events in the Science Museum were highly politically laden. Many national museums were undergoing major changes – charging for entry, marketing themselves, divesting them-selves of research staff – and these were often severely criticised in the press (see Macdonald and Silverstone 1990). Another national museum had already decided against hosting the study because of staff sensitivities at a time of institutional restructuring. That the Science Museum agreed to be 'guinea pig' (as it was referred to in the Museum) was due in part to the fact that the research, in being funded under the ESRC's 'Public Understanding of Science' programme, meshed neatly with the Museum's newly formulated mission statement to promote the 'Public Understanding of Science'.

The focus of the study was the making of a major (£1.2 million, 750 square metres) long-term exhibition about food: *Food for Thought: The Sainsbury Gallery*. Because this exhibition was the first to be wholly produced since the appointment of a new Director of the Museum, and because it was being heralded widely in the Museum and in the press as symptomatic of a new direction for national museums, my account of it would inevitably provide potential ammunition in the battles over the proper role, strategies and objectives of museums – though for which side nobody (including me) was yet sure.

It took me some time to realise this. Because most of those to whom I was introduced in my early days in the Museum seemed to welcome the study, I was deceived into believing that its status was, therefore, somehow unproblematic. What was happening, however, was that different individuals, groups and factions of museum staff were investing the embryonic study with their own interpretations, hopes and expectations. As a scribe in their midst, I was there to be won over. The willingness of many museum staff to talk to me, with some spontaneously offering themselves for interview, was not, then, surprising. Initially, however, I took it as a sign of openness and even of a disinterestedly 'scientific' attitude towards research. I had yet to lose my innocence.

Although I was initially naive about the immediate political implications of my position in the Museum, my 'gatekeeper' there was not,[6] though at the time I thought his sensitivities overwrought. Occasionally, I even suspected that he was not wholly supportive of the research, though the acts which I interpreted as sabotage were, I realise in retrospect, attempts to protect it. For example, he made a consistent and concerted attempt to define the politics out of the study – or at least to persuade me that if it was to be included then it should be in heavily veiled form. He defended a decision that I should not attend a particularly sensitive meeting on the grounds that I was interested 'in actions not perceptions' and the meeting would only be revealing of the latter; he also supported a request that I should not tape-record another set of meetings on the grounds that my interests were in the general issues raised and not in specific encounters. At some meetings in the Museum he would comment loudly that I must be sure to take note of what participants were wearing, thus, I presumed, deflecting attention from that to which my gaze was actually directed. (Though, in fact, he later told me, he was trying to alert me to the casual dress of some museum staff, which he interpreted as their presenting themselves as academics – something which I wholly failed to pick up.)

Over time I became increasingly aware of marked differences among Museum staff views over recent changes in the Museum and directions that the Museum should take; and aware of the very real problems for Museum staff, many of whom feared for their jobs within a climate of constant managerial restructuring and 'rationalisation'. I became more self-conscious about what I could and should write down. On one occasion, when somebody gave a politically delicate and personally compromising account of processes involved in the making of another exhibition, I did not take notes, so conspicuous did my writing feel. A curator next to me noticed that my pen was still: 'I would have thought you would have been scribbling that down frantically' he remarked. And so I should have been, had it not been for my feeling that the indigenous view would have been that I should not. It was difficult, then, to maintain the position of 'total inscription' (impossible though such a thing is, of course, in any case). The act of writing was itself conspicuous, an act imbued with the meaning that something meaningful was going on.

I also came into contact with staff who were suspicious of the research I was doing, some of whom saw it as analogous to an earlier consultancy exercise which was believed to have led to redundancies. The very label of my research – 'Public Understanding of Science' – carried connotations which suggested as much, 'Public Understanding of Science' being used in the Museum as a shorthand to refer to changes underway which shifted the institutional emphasis more towards catering for visitors, and less towards caring for artefacts, than had previously been the case. Yet while the 'Public Understanding of Science' label carried connotations of which I was initially unaware, other labels with which I was associated, notably 'academic', carried very different ones. As in my gatekeeper's comment on dress, above, 'academics' were implicitly opposed to 'managers': they were regarded not only as relatively scruffy (an image to which I conformed) but also as inherently on the side of scholarship and of a kind of disdain for the trifling material immediacies with which 'managers' were supposedly obsessed. Overall, then, there was uncertainty as to quite what my position might be, and the fieldwork process entailed not only my negotiation between different groups but their negotiation, and attempts to influence, what I saw and what I might write. I, and my activities, might be referred to in terms that seemed familiar, but in the Museum they carried a specific semantic load of which I only became aware over time.

ON DIGGING AND FLYING

During fieldwork I was given many references and some advice on how to write my account. There were here two rather different perspectives which came from those with alternative views on the way that museum exhibitions should look. On the one hand was a desire that I should not write in jargon and that my account should be as transparent and comprehensible as possible. This call came, by and large, from those museum staff who also contend that museum exhibitions should cater for as wide a lay-audience as possible and that the text of museum exhibitions should be easily comprehensible. On the other hand, there were those who themselves rather revelled in academic arguments and literary devices. They looked forward, or such was my perception, to an account that would – by mirroring their own practices – play a game in which they were privileged readers. For example, one particular piece of advice that I was given was to couch my arguments in obscure metaphors: Queen Elizabeth I's court might be too obvious but surely I could find some half-forgotten Roman emperor that only the literati – or the aspiring literati – would have the patience to look up.

These two perspectives were about much more than my ethnography. This was but a manifestation of a ramifying set of differences between museum staff. The perspectives should be seen as ideal types rather than an absolute division of individuals, however, for in practice some individuals were ambivalent or shifted their positions (though I have also found that, on reading drafts of this chapter, most museum staff are adept at identifying just who is of which type). Even if all individuals do not fit it absolutely and there are some grey areas, the division can be seen as a central line of fission in the Museum and, as such, one of the motive forces of action and events. The two sides represent competing classificatory systems, mapping out the semantic space that is the Museum through their conceptual clashes. The terms that I use to describe these types take their inspiration from a comment by Clifford Geertz about ethnography, published around the same time as my fieldwork and referring to responses to ethnography's crisis of representation. These responses, he suggests, have been polarised into an attitude of 'digging in ("Don't think about ethnography, just do it")' and 'flying off ("Don't do ethnography, just think about it")' (1988: 139). Based on these, I use the names Diggers and Flyers.

The Diggers in my museum story are the pragmatists; those who rather distrust metaphor, complex argument and 'big words'. Exhibition-making is not so much a matter of creativity and self-expression as a process to be managed, a matter of relative efficiency or inefficiency. For Diggers, a relatively non-specialised readership, or audience, is both the main motive for creating the exhibition and the main legitimation for its success or otherwise. The exhibition at the heart of this ethnographic study was dominated largely (though by no means entirely) by a Digger ethos, though there is also a tendency within exhibitions as they progress to transform themselves from a relatively flying off position to a more entrenchedly dug in one.

Flyers, by contrast, love intellectual argument and ideas *per se*. Many of them regard the Museum and its politics as a game – a game in which they may participate but only while simultaneously standing back and observing themselves doing so. This is not to say that Flyers are necessarily cool quiet types: on the contrary many of them are passionate argumentative people, aware that this is a game in which the stakes can be high. These stakes include 'power', 'status', 'intellectual freedom' and 'academic credibility'. When exhibition-making, Flyers place great store by research, and perhaps quite sophisticated notions of what the exhibition is to achieve. They may, for example, try to find ways of introducing different 'voices' and 'reflexive dimensions' into their exhibitions. In general, Flyers are not nearly so concerned about what Diggers emphatically call 'the Public'. Indeed, it is usual for Flyers to object to such a 'monolithic' concept and to argue that the audience with which the Museum deals is a good deal more sophisticated/complex/educated/intelligent than Diggers realise.

So how did Diggers and Flyers regard an ethnography of the Museum? As I have mentioned, there were different expectations about the style of writing that would be employed: transparent (the Diggers) or couched in literary allusion (the Flyers). There were also differences in the ways that Diggers and Flyers behaved towards me. On the whole, Diggers left me to get on with my peculiar task. They sometimes expressed puzzlement about what on earth I would 'discover' or how I would manage to process the data I had collected. For the most part, however, it seemed to me that they saw the research rather as a management consultancy exercise. I was there to observe how they 'made decisions'. Central to the outcome of any decisions were 'practical constraints' which Diggers emphasised could not, and should not, be underestimated. A detailed account of the exhibition-making process must inevitably show these up clearly; and hopefully it would vindicate the good sense and effective management of Diggers by showing them battling as successfully as possible against intransigent external forces. Common sense is a key Digger ideal and organising principle.

Flyers have a rather different vision. As regards their interactions with me in the Museum they were reluctant to see themselves as objects of the ethnography. They were themselves onlookers and the knowledge which they were imparting could not possibly have the status of 'data': it had already been configured into something rather like ethnography, or so they assumed. For this reason, Flyers sometimes did not want me to record conversations with them or even to take notes: ours was a discussion between observers, not observer and observed. Although Flyers saw their own individual talks with me as observer to observer, they were in general quite keen to have an ethnographer as audience or witness in their interactions with the rest of the Museum. Of importance here is the fact that Flyers, even though they may hold high office in the Museum, tend to define themselves as separate from the rest of the Museum: they see themselves as a misunderstood minority. What they wanted was for me to see their intellectual calibre and to see them, perhaps wryly and wittily, highlighting 'the nonsense' (as one put it) of museum managerialism. Like the Diggers they hoped for a kind of vindication, though not so much in the world of museum management and evaluation as in the academic domain.

What Flyers seemed to expect of the resulting ethnography was that at the least it should be clever and full of subtle *doubles entendres* and allusions, and at the most that it should present the Museum in a thoroughly new and exotic light. One curator circulated a short piece called 'The Museum People: An Interactive Approach', heavily influenced by Colin Turnbull's *The Mountain People*, which was an amusing exotic version of the sort of account that she imagined I might write. Flyers seemed to want to be made strange. In part this was simply an expectation of what anthropologists do. But there was more to it than this, I think. First, such exoticising would be to play the sort of game that Flyers are attracted towards: making-strange would, of itself perhaps, deny the serious concrete business of common sense that Diggers wished to uphold. In this respect (as in many others), Flyers are not unlike relativising ethnographers for whom there is no such thing as 'common sense' – it is 'a cultural system' (Geertz 1983: ch. 4) By showing up the present Museum system in all its peculiarities as culturally specific and relativised, the system is deprived of some of its authority. One Flyer, for example, used to repeat to me that the Museum was 'Lululand' or 'Bozoland'. He contrasted it with 'the real world' of 'big business' and 'the City' where such things as 'accountability' mattered. He himself preferred 'Lululand', he claimed, not because he was deceived into believing it to be the real world but because it amused him. For Flyers, then, an ethnographic account exoticising the Museum – showing it up as 'Lululand' – would concur with their own perception of the Museum as somehow not part of 'the real world'. The ethnographer would be able to demonstrate that behind its rhetoric the Museum was, in fact, a thoroughly non-rational and possibly 'primitive culture'.

Another perception of an ethnography – one which could be coupled with either Digger or Flyer ideas – was that it would specifically highlight the individual, idiosyncratic and human features of exhibition-making. In its harshest form what seemed to be expected was 'the dirt': a tale of bitchiness, errors and individual profiteering. More mildly it was an expectation of an account in which chance and random events, personal interrelationships and the very individually specific features of 'creativity' would be the central operators. While such factors certainly do play a part, such an expectation in the Museum was often characteristic of a malaise with all attempts to restructure the museum or find more effective and efficient ways of organising and training people. The ethnography, by suggesting that unplanned, chance and individualistic factors were the real motive forces behind the ensuing shape of the exhibition would throw doubt on the whole enterprise of trying to change the Museum.

Diggers and Flyers did not have quite equal status in the Museum during the period of my fieldwork. Although more senior posts were held by Flyer-types, the dominant rhetoric was closer to that of the Diggers. This had been brought in by a new Director who wanted to put the Public to the forefront and to abolish what he called a 'dinosaur' mentality. The Director often spoke Digger language in his attempt to sweep away what he saw as certain conservative forces in the Museum, the dominant cultural mode for changing institutions in the late 1980s being a discourse of efficiency and management. However, he was also attracted to a Flyer-type academic credibility and it seemed to me that the swings and vacillations which many Museum staff perceived him to be making could be seen as attempts to reconcile elements of these competing systems.

These various perceptions of the ethnography were not particularly challenged by the way in which I carried it out. Sitting around taking notes or tape-recording, drinking coffee and generally tagging along and asking questions, were innocuous enough to be interpreted in any way. The *saying* or describing of the ethnography, however, was potentially more formative, and I found myself adapting my descriptions as time went on and in relation to my audience. At first, I used generally to emphasise that the project was funded under a 'Public Understanding of Science' programme, thus focusing, I imagined, on its worthiness and use-value. However, I soon dropped my rather garbled additional muttering about 'conceptions and constructions of science' as the exhibition team themselves had already configured the research into management consultancy format and would rescue me by saying that I was there to look at 'the way we make decisions'. Although I was never quite happy with this characterisation – worrying that it would set up rather concrete expectations of useful results – it was one which I sometimes found myself adopting.

At other times, particularly with Flyers, I would make the most of my enigmatic role, occasionally making cryptic comments about such things as totemism or shamanism. As the research progressed I came to put the definition of myself as an anthropologist more to the fore. There was much amusement in the Museum over the idea that the Food exhibition team were my 'tribe' and, having adduced that talking in such terms was not considered grossly offensive, I felt some relief in divesting myself to some small extent at least of the practical policy-making mantle in which the research had been bedecked in its early stages.

THE POLITICS OF PARALLEL CONTEXT WRITING

The different visions of what I would produce created a dilemma for writing up. Was I to produce the kind of account that Diggers might wish or that which Flyers would prefer? And what would be the consequences of the selection? It was abundantly clear that whatever I wrote would be rapidly circulated and avidly read within the Museum and that it would be appropriated into the ongoing debates and diverse agendas.[7]

Perhaps not surprisingly, the first piece of writing about the fieldwork was a disappointment to both Diggers and Flyers – and politically it went down like a lead weight.[8] A grand analysis of the shifts in modes of display in museums, locating recent changes within a broader political context, it was both too couched in literariness for Diggers and insufficiently arcane for Flyers. Fortunately, friends of both Digger and Flyer type in the Museum set about trying to retrieve something of the embarrassing situation. Diggers told me that a relatively descriptive section about the exhibition itself 'seemed much more sensible than the rest'. A Flyer, by contrast, remarked that towards the end of the paper, when it had begun to delve into some of Susan Stewart's ideas about objects and the nature of the collection, it had 'begun to get interesting'. Embedded as I was in the Museum's culture at the time, and more enduringly in the not dissimilar University culture, I also tried to make excuses for what felt at the time potentially disastrous. I emphasised that the paper had been written for a specific audience, and an extremely peculiar one at that, the readership of *Cultural Studies*. It was not the sort of thing I might normally write. This 'target audience' argument was very much one with which Diggers would have sympathy, even if they might think the choice of audience perverse (especially for a first paper after fieldwork). I also implied that the paper was not as 'academic' as some would be (an argument to appeal to Flyers); and that I would be writing different things for different purposes and audiences (trying to please everybody), some would be more matter of fact and others would be more 'anthropological', looking at the Museum as a strange and alien culture.

Writing, then, was problematic both because it inevitably entered the fray of existing competing agendas; but also because the *form* of the writing ('anthropological' and 'academic' or 'matter-of-fact' and 'descriptive') could itself be seen to support the perspective of one or other faction within the Museum. Ethnographers in many other, often far from parallel, contexts have, of course, experienced similar sets of understandings over the form and consequences of their work: the expectation that they will act as advocates or policy creators for example (see, for example, Okely, Chapter 14, and Knight, Chapter 9 of this volume). An overlapping and closely reflective context such as a museum, however, has a number of more specific overlaps which yield particular theoretical as well as political problems.

One objection to the first research paper was its rather liberal reference to the 'crises' facing museums. The description of museums being in crisis was widespread both within the Museum and in contemporary media reports and I regarded the use of the term in the paper to be an ethnographic description of this widespread perception. Several Museum readers, however, understood it as my own evaluative term and argued that the paper, in sharing a term with the media, was therefore 'journalism'. 'Journalism' was itself opposed to 'research'; and it was impressed upon me that if what I wrote was to be *seen* as 'research' then it was imperative that it did not *look* in any way like journalism. Moreover, I was told that I risked jeopardising the whole precarious status of research within the Museum if I produced work which did not look like 'proper research'. The problem was not seen to lie in the accuracy or truth of my account, nor its academic referencing, but in what Museum staff perceived to be too close a resemblance to other cultural forms of representation (journalism); and to the fact that it was regarded as neither sufficiently useful and prescriptive, nor sufficiently obscure and scholarly.

The problem, then, was one of very similar classifications in the Museum culture but not complete identity. Our visions of research were similar but not precisely the same. Here misunderstandings of quite a subtle order could occur. One, for example, involved the use of inverted commas. The draft of the article was heavily sprinkled with them. This is something that I often find myself doing: it is part of a distancing which I find necessary for analysis. Terms in inverted commas are terms which, were it not the case that my subjects share the same mother-tongue as myself, would be in a foreign language. However, inverted commas in other forms of writing – especially journalism – have a rather different sense. They signal the pejorative or ironic. And this was how they were interpreted by some readers in the Museum. 'Management', thus, became something which I was implying was only 'so-called management', 'mission statements' and 'performance indicators' objects of ridicule. In the parallel context, then, significance could be attributed to the ethnographer's actions at a very fine level indeed: in this case that of the diacritics used in writing.

It is important to note that we are dealing here with degrees of overlap and what Michael Herzfeld has called a 'relativity of innocence' (1987: 181) rather than identity. It is very easy in a close-to-home context to think ourselves knowing where in fact we are neophytes, as the example of my own initial naivety about the effects and classifications of my presence as ethnographer in the Museum illustrates. Overlapping though the Museum's visions of research may be, they are not always precisely our own. However, as with the inverted commas, the differences are sometimes of a rather subtle order – they are the sort that catch you unawares.

Ethnography's problem here also concerns the critical space for inter-pretation. Conceptual compatibility easily renders cultural specificities and context-dependencies invisible. The task appears like translating our own language back into itself. However, in practice – in the throng of a shifting, negotiated empirical context – there are constantly gaps emerging through which we can glimpse the meaningful categories and patterns at work (Ardener 1982). If auto-anthropological fieldwork reflects back on ethnography, the images it provides are often blurred at the margins, and there are cracks in some surfaces (cf. Fernandez 1980: 36). Close attention to these, exploration of those chance everyday misunderstandings that ethnography continually throws up, and mapping of the shifting patterns and allegiances around definitions, is all part of the process by which we can distinguish the meaningful and the culturally or contextually specific. Precisely because museum curators and interpreters (as they are now frequently called, significantly enough) have opinions upon, and practices associated with, questions that are central also to ethnography – questions such as the relationship between knowledge and ownership, of what constitutes a valid or authentic account, or of the part that we accord the readers in our texts – offers a context in which we can observe the very active and even contested construction and reconstruction of 'ethno-graphic' concepts.

At the same time the reflective, close-to-home, context also effaces the comforting distinction between the 'being there' and the 'being here' of ethnographic research (Geertz 1988). Subjects of the ethnography expect to read what is written about them and they are likely to be forthcoming in voicing their views of it. Any text is thoroughly 'worldly' (Frankenberg 1993: 54; after Said 1983) – an event capable of affecting the status and career of individuals. Indeed, some types of text indigenous to the Museum make this particularly likely. The management consultancy report, for example, is a document intended to have immediate and concrete effects. This was brought home to me particularly forcefully after I wrote up an account of the making of the *Food* exhibition and presented it to the Museum in report format. A member of the Museum's staff was instructed by the higher management to make changes to the exhibition in line with the recommendations that it was assumed I would have made. Yet the report contained little that could be immediately 'operationalised' in this way. Again, the disjuncture between our expectations of a report was of a subtle order.

The life of writing in overlapping ethnography does not necessarily stop at the point at which it re-enters the fieldwork context, however. In the present world of social research, dissemination beyond academia, and policy relevance within arenas like the museum and leisure industries, have become part of the means by which our research is legitimated and its performance assessed. Just as in the Museum, 'users' have assumed an increased status in the legitimation of our practice and products. This means that the power of the subjects of the research to define it – as 'irrelevant', 'superficial' or 'errant nonsense' perhaps – is a power with potentially very real effects in the world of contemporary ethnographic research. Our subjects may become not just readers but referees of our work. And an institution like a national museum is capable of speaking with an indubitably authoritative voice. Indeed, I was told on one occasion in the Museum, in a more helpfully friendly way than the words might imply, 'Remember, we do have some clout. We could say "Oh yes, she was here for a while but she did not really understand what was going on." We are probably more powerful than you are.' Doubtless.

PARALLEL PROBLEMS

Yet the difficulty of writing about the Museum is not only a matter of dealing with 'a powerful institution' (or 'studying up') but is also one of negotiating a way through rather different agendas and expectations – and different politicised perspectives on representation itself. Here, I have tried to describe this through my experience of representing the Museum and their representations of what I was doing. This, however, is only one realisation of an ongoing debate within the Museum about its own representational roles and styles – a debate that became increasingly heated and polarised during the 1980s. Many dilemmas perceived by museum staff arose from the difficulty of reconciling different demands over, for example, scholarship versus populism, acting as a showcase for national science and industry or informing the public of the best of science and technology. All of these problems were exaggerated by the multiple, and often contradictory, demands made upon the Museum. On the one hand, its future funding looked like it would be related to the number of visitors it managed to attract, on the other it was being called upon to fulfil an educational role; the extent of its vast collections in storage was questioned, as were their selectivity and silences; its nationalism was being challenged at the same time as it was being called upon to exhibit Britain; visitor numbers were being mooted as a key performance indicator at the same time that visitors began to be charged an entrance fee; research outputs were being monitored while curatorial and research budgets and personnel were cut. These multiple demands, it seemed to me, created a sense of threat which fuelled a polarisation between digging and flying. Diggers held out for the possibility of creating exhibitions that would not manifest the intellectual arrogance of the past (described as 'PhD theses pasted onto panels' by one); Flyers feared being swamped by philistinism ('We've reached a point where exhibitions are managed in the same department as the toilets'). Each was unwilling to give ground to the other because so much had become entwined in each and every issue.

Digging and flying are familiar alternatives to ethnographers. Are we to dig in to description or fly off into interpretation? Are our ethnographies to be factual, 'experience-near' and common-sensically written? Or, are we to write the sort of exoticised, 'experience-distant', reflexive, literary and dense accounts that the Flyers desire? What the Museum shows us is that these questions cannot be disentangled from their political context and implications. Our academic colleagues and research review exercises might demand high flying, our funding bodies and fieldwork hosts that we be down to earth. In anthropology's 'Writing Culture' debates, such politics have been only semi-present. We have considered the implications of particular styles for authority and silencing; but – with the exception of some feminist critiques (e.g. Mascia-Lees et al. 1989; Callaway 1992) – have been more reticent about the political contests over writing in the academy and policy arena.

The notions of representation held in an ethnographic context such as a national museum are, then, disconcertingly close to home. They cannot be safely described into alterity because they are part of our own discourse and of a largely, though not wholly shared world of contested representational semantics. In what we write, we participate – however much we might wish it were otherwise – in a meaning-ridden battle over representation and its uses in which the very format and styles of our chosen modes of representation are liable to consequential interpretation. By writing, we inevitably write ourselves in to a particular, and politicised, context. The challenge is to disrupt easy positioning and to highlight the semantics and politics of representational practices themselves.

ACKNOWLEDGEMENTS

I wish to express my sincere thanks to staff in the Science Museum, especially those with whom I was most closely entangled, for both hosting the research and, in many cases, commenting on versions of this and other pieces of writing. I also offer thanks to the following for commenting on drafts or presentations of versions of this chapter: Michael Beaney, Georgina Born, Michael Herzfeld, Michael Hitchcock, Eric Hirsch, Janet Rachel, Roger Silverstone, colleagues in the Department of Sociology and Social Anthropology at Keele University, colleagues working on the 'Public Understanding of Science' programme, the audience at the 'Anthropology and Representation' conference, and the editors of this volume. While acknowledgements are not, of course, an innocent textual convention, those thanked should not be held to be in agreement with my arguments here.

NOTES

1 On museums, see, for example, Karp and Lavine (1991), Karp *et al.* (1992), Macdonald and Fyfe (1996), and also Clifford (1988). For a general overview of the 'crisis' in anthropology see Marcus and Fischer (1986), and for various further discussion, Nencel and Pels (1991), Rosaldo (1993) and Hastrup (1995).
2 The research was carried out under the auspices of the Economic and Social Research Council's 'Public Understanding of Science' programme and directed by Roger Silverstone, then at Brunel University.
3 For further related discussion see Crick (1982), Ardener (1987), Hastrup (1987), Traweek (1989: prologue), Strathern (1992), Rapport (1993), Rappaport (1994), Harvey (1996, esp. chs 1 and 2).
4 Edwin Ardener's analysis of levels of structuring in 'event-specification' has partly shaped my thinking on this matter (1989). The dilemma that he identifies – that 'structures of text' can ignore other levels of structuring – clearly has parallels with the 'forgetting' of process that we too often see in the 'textual turn'.
5 For various relevant further discussion see Okely (1975), Karp and Kendall (1982), Fardon (1990), Okely and Callaway (1992), Hastrup and Hervik (1994).
6 The 'gatekeeper' was the member of the Museum staff who had liaised with the University and had been particularly instrumental in persuading the Museum to host the research. He was responsible in the early days of the research for introducing me to Museum staff.
7 For further examples and discussion of the implications of subjects of research reading – and reacting to and acting upon – anthropological writing, see McDonald (1987, 1989), Bretell (1993) and Born (1995).
8 A revised version of this paper, which was jointly written with the director of the research project, Roger Silverstone, is published in *Cultural Studies* 1990 under the title 'Rewriting the Museums' Fictions: Taxonomies, Stories and Readers'.

REFERENCES

Ardener, E. (1982) 'Social Anthropology, Language and Reality', in D. Parkin (ed.), *Semantic Anthropology*, London: Academic Press.
—— (1987) 'Remote Areas: Some Theoretical Considerations', in A.
Jackson (ed.), *Anthropology at Home*, London: Tavistock.
—— (1989) 'The Construction of History: "Vestiges of Creation"', in E. Tonkin, M. McDonald and M. Chapman (eds), *History and Ethnicity*, London: Routledge.
Born, G. (1995) *Rationalizing Culture*, Berkeley: University of California Press.
Bretell, C. (ed.) (1993) *When They Read What We Write*, London: Bergin & Garvey.

Callaway, H. (1992) 'Ethnography and Experience: Gender Implications in Field-work and Text', in J. Okely and H. Callaway (eds), *Anthropology and Autobiography*, London: Routledge.

Clifford, J. (1988) *The Predicament of Culture: Twentieth Century Ethnography, Literature and Art*, Cambridge, MA: Harvard University Press.

Clifford, J. and G. E. Marcus (eds) (1986) *Writing Culture: The Poetics and Politics of Ethnography*, Berkeley: University of California Press.

Crick, M. (1982) 'Anthropological Field Research, Meaning Creation and Knowl-edge Construction', in D. Parkin (ed.), *Semantic Anthropology*, London: Academic Press.

Fardon, R. (ed.) (1990) *Localizing Strategies: Regional Traditions of Ethnographic Writing*, Edinburgh: Scottish Academic Press, and Washington: Smithsonian Institution Press.

Fernandez, J. (1980) 'Reflections on Looking into Mirrors', *Semiotica*, 30: 27–39.

Frankenberg, R. (1993) 'Who Tells the Tale? Texts and the Problem of Gener-ational and Social Identity in a Tuscan Rural Commune?', in S. Macdonald (ed.), *Inside European Identities*, Oxford: Berg.

Geertz, C. (1983) 'Common Sense as a Cultural System', in *Local Knowledge: Further Essays in Interpretive Anthropology*, New York: Basic Books.

—— (1988) *Works and Lives: The Anthropologist as Author*, Cambridge: Polity Press.

Harvey, P. (1996) *Hybrids of Modernity: Anthropology, the Nation State and the Universal Exhibition*, London: Routledge.

Hastrup, K. (1987) 'Fieldwork among Friends: Ethnographic Exchange within the Northern Civilisation', in A. Jackson (ed.), *Anthropology at Home*, London: Tavistock.

—— (1995) *A Passage to Anthropology: Between Experience and Theory*, London: Routledge.

Hastrup, K. and P. Hervik (eds) (1994) *Social Experience and Anthropological Knowledge*, London: Routledge.

Herzfeld, M. (1983) 'Looking Both Ways: The Ethnographer in the Text', *Semiotica*, 46 (2/4): 151–66.

—— (1987) *Anthropology Through the Looking-Glass: Critical Ethnography in the Margins of Europe*, Cambridge: Cambridge University Press.

Karp, I. and M. B. Kendall (1982) 'Reflexivity in Field Work', in P. F. Secord (ed.), *Explaining Social Behaviour*, London and Los Angeles: Sage.

Karp, I., C. M. Kreamer and S. D. Lavine (eds) (1992) *Museums and Communities: The Politics of Public Culture*, Washington, DC and London: Smithsonian Insti-tution Press.

Karp, I. and S. D. Lavine (eds) (1991) *Exhibiting Cultures: The Poetics and Politics of Museum Display*, Washington, DC and London: Smithsonian Institution Press.

McDonald, M. (1987) 'The Politics of Fieldwork in Brittany', in A. Jackson (ed.), *Anthropology at Home*, London: Tavistock.

—— (1989) *We are not French!* London: Routledge.

Macdonald, S. and G. Fyfe (eds) (1996) *Theorizing Museums*, Oxford: Basil Blackwell.

Macdonald, S. and R. Silverstone (1990) 'Rewriting the Museums' Fictions: Taxo-nomies, Stories and Readers', *Cultural Studies*, 4 (2): 176–91.

Marcus, G. E. and M. J. Fischer (1986) *Anthropology as Cultural Critique: An Experimental Moment in the Human Sciences*, Chicago: University of Chicago Press.

Mascia-Lees, F. P. Sharpe and C. Cohen (1989) 'The Postmodernist Turn in Anthropology: Cautions from a Feminist Perspective', *Signs*, 15 (1): 7–33.

Nencel, L. and P. Pels (eds) (1991) *Constructing Knowledge: Authority and Critique in Social Science*, London: Sage.

Okely, J. (1975) 'The Self and Scientism', *Journal of the Anthropological Society of Oxford*, 6: 171–88.

Okely, J. and H. Callaway (eds) (1992) *Anthropology and Autobiography*, London: Routledge.

Rappaport, R. A. (1994) 'Disorders of our Own: A Conclusion', in S. Forman (ed.), *Diagnosing America: Anthropology and Public Engagement*, Michigan: University of Michigan Press.

Rapport, N. (1993) *Diverse World Views in an English Village*, Edinburgh: Edinburgh University Press.

Rosaldo, R. (1993 [1989]) *Culture and Truth: The Remaking of Social Analysis*, London: Routledge.

Said, E. (1983) *The World, the Text and the Critic*, London: Vintage.

Spencer, J. (1989) 'Anthropology as a Kind of Writing', *Man*, 24: 145–64.

Stewart, S. (1984) *On Longing: Narratives of the Miniature, the Gigantic, the Souvenir, the Collection*, Baltimore and London: Johns Hopkins University Press.

Strathern, M. (1987) 'The Limits of Auto-anthropology', in A. Jackson (ed.), *Anthropology at Home*, London: Tavistock.

—— (1992) *After Nature*, Cambridge: Cambridge University Press.

Traweek, S. (1989) *Beamtimes and Lifetimes: The World of High Energy Physicists*, Cambridge, MA: Harvard University Press.

Chapter 11

Edifying anthropology

Culture as conversation; representation as conversation

Nigel Rapport

Conversation, understood widely enough, is the form of human transactions in general.

(Alasdair MacIntyre, *After Virtue*)

THREE BEGINNINGS

From Clifford Geertz, from Jane Austen and from Michael Oakeshott,
we receive depictions of cultural process – the construction, exchange
and interpretation of cultural forms – as *conversation*. Their convergence
on this image appeals to me; also the way that their depictions can be
found to converse one with another, pointing up an image of cultural
process at once complex, multiple and counterpoised. I begin, then, with
their conversation.

Clifford Geertz tells us of the endemic interpretation of experience
which culture members undertake so as to make meaning and sense out
of what happens (and what they cause to happen) to their fellows and
themselves. 'The actual living through of events', is never mere sentience,
but always sentience interpreted: 'all experience is construed experience'
(Geertz 1973: 405). However, this is not to 'give way' to psychologism,
because human experience and its interpretation are things human beings
undertake – 'like anything else' – in the social world, in public: an
'outdoor psychology' locates thought firmly 'out in the world' (Geertz
1983: 153). Thinking, therefore, is no mysterious process which takes place
in a secret grotto in the head. Rather, thinking is a public activity, and
inherently social in its origins, functions, forms and applications. Outdoor
activities (ploughing and peddling) are as good examples of it as are closet
experiences (wishing and regretting). For thinking consists of trafficking in
a community's available symbolic forms – rituals, tools, words, idols, water
holes, gestures, markings, images, sounds. It is these symbolic forms –
derived from a cultural tradition, guaranteed by a social status quo – that
enable (that carry, that embody) meanings, and no thinking is possibly
undertaken without them: thinking is symbol, use is social action. In

short, experience and its thinking-through take place in the same public world: their natural habitat alike is the house-yard, the market place, the town square. What characterises both of them is the public exchange of shared systems of symbols. Indeed, it is 'under the guidance' of these symbols that any thinking about culture must be understood, while social life may be characterised as a conversation of symbols: an ongoing exchange of cultural forms in which life is both lived as experience and interpreted as significance.

If, for Geertz, human perceiving, cognizing, remembering, reasoning, intending, imagining, judging, feeling and acting are determined by the symbolic forms in whose terms they are expressed and so 'take place', then for Jane Austen, the conversation of forms permits of more subtle appreciation (cf. Handler and Segal 1990). In contrast to an over-determining depiction of normative behaviour in which cultural conventionality inexorably translates as social sharing, homogeneity, consistency and communication, Austen's view of language-games and the (symbolic) forms of (social) life is that they are always subject to creative interpretation: to an independent manipulation and re-rendering by an individual: to what Handler and Segal call (1990: 87) 'alter-cultural action'. (She plays Ayer to Geertz's Wittgenstein.) For Austen, symbol system and *habitus* are not so much guarantees of meaning, legitimacy and the reproduction of established order as communicative resources and counterbalances to the pragmatics of different individuals' 'serious social play' (ibid.: 16). For the heroines of Austen's writings, and their partners, rather than rules to be taken literally or normatively, conventional etiquette and propriety are matters for metacommunicative comment and analysis – and thereby displacement – in the personal construction of order. Hence, in the patterning and structuration of early nineteenth-century English society (however seemingly axiomatic and unambiguous), Austen depicts no singular, unitary, integrated or bounded socio-cultural system. Rather, she encourages her readers to appreciate the malleability and the mutability of social reality, and the creative potential of alter-cultural individual world-making. Thus, not only are her heroines conversant with what they may variously create out of the symbolic norms of the day, but between their creations there is not so much common denomination as conversation (deliberation, negotiation, confrontation). Readers find interaction and inter-referencing between multiple realities, represented textually by a narratory dialogics without closure and without end, in which no one voice maps, overpowers or mediates the others. Social life, Austen evinces, is a diversity of stories which must be told together.

For Michael Oakeshott, conversation is what human cultures accomplish and what human societies inherit. Conversation is a meeting of voices speaking in different idiom or mode. Science, poetry, practical activity, history – Geertz's symbol systems – are such modes of speech, different universes of discourse (Wittgensteinian forms of life). It is the very diversity, the manifold of different voices speaking in different idioms or modes, that 'makes' conversation. The voices do not compose a hierarchy, and the conversation does not amount to an argument; the diverse voices may differ without disagreeing, and they may appear to be saying the same thing without agreeing. Hence, conversation is not an enquiry, contest, exegesis or debate; it does not set out to persuade, refute or inform. Conversation has no truth to discover, no proposition to prove, no conclusion to seek; reason is neither sovereign nor primary, and there is no accumulating enquiry or body of information to safeguard. Instead, as 'thoughts of different species take wing and play round one another' – responding to and provoking one another's movement, obliquely interrelating without assimilating – so their individual thinkers engage in the 'unrehearsed intellectual adventure' of social life (Oakeshott 1962: 198). Going on in public and inside themselves, the conversation ultimately contextualises every human activity and utterance . . .

What I wish to do here is to take seriously such conversing depictions of the conversation of social life: to treat them as a recipe for the anthropological representation of social life. Representation may be fatally prone to reduction, in as much as concepts replace complex processes of interpretation and singular texts stand for plural exchanges. However, if bringing together in one text the distinct, diverse and incompatible voices and epistemes of a social milieu in such a way as to point up their irreconcilability and their interaction may be described as 'writing conversationally', then it may still be possible to aver that 'the epistemological conversation of this text is as the everyday conversation of social life'.

CONVERSATION AND ANTHROPOLOGICAL ACCOUNTS

Conversation as focus, theme and image is no stranger to anthropological representation. Thus, we can easily accept, even expect, conversation between informants in the anthropological text; oratory, disputation, curing and cursing might all elicit precise reportage of the verbal and other expression and exchange in the field (R. Paine, A. P. Cohen, J. Favret-Saada). Similarly, we have come to accept, even expect, conversation between informant and anthropologist to be recounted; as the anthropologist enters into relations in the field, verbal and other, so that field takes shape for her, is indeed shaped by her interactions (J. Briggs, A. James, V. Crapanzano). Likewise, the anthropological text can be expected to engage in conversational exchange between the writer and his reference group; as the anthropologist makes sense of the field so his sense-making is informed by accounts he has read before, and mediated by the effect he would wish his writing to have on others (P. Rabinow, J. Clifford, A. Campbell). Finally, we now anticipate the anthropological account achieving its effect through engaging in conversation with its reader; as objective and positivistic representation is denigrated as epistemologically mistaken and morally questionable, so the reader is expected to make sense through an evocation and performance of the text (E. Bruner, S. Tyler, D. Tedlock).

What I would wish to add to this appreciation of conversation is, first, a conscious anthropological acceptance of the conversation of social life: that we use conversation as anthropological focus, theme and image because of the 'naturally occurring' importance of conversation: it goes to the heart of social exchange and cultural process. Second, I would like to add to existing anthropological usage an acceptance of the written account as itself implying conversation: conversation between systems of sense-making (Geertz), heroic stories (Austen), universes of discourse (Oakeshott), in a word, epistemes. To represent the diversity, the openendedness, the chaotic relativism that comprises cultural process is not to pretend to represent a social milieu singly, steadily and as a whole, but to engage in epistemological pluralism, to be narrationally eclectic.

Let me elaborate upon these points in turn.

CONVERSATION AS NATURALLY OCCURRING

There are two basic aspects to the proposition that conversation is an important naturally occurring feature of culture and society: epistemic diversity and epistemic interaction (cf. Rapport 1987: 141ff.).

An appreciation of naturally occurring conversation (albeit more sociological than anthropological) is nothing new in socio-cultural accounting. Symbolic interactionism (Blumer), ethnomethodology (Garfinkel) and sociology of knowledge (Berger and Luckmann) approaches all make it central to their projects. As Blumer would put it, then: if human beings act towards things on the basis of the meanings that the things have for them, and these meanings are the *sine qua non* of the social existence of things *per se*, then it is in conversation with their fellows, in the processes of interaction, that this construction of meaning takes place (Blumer 1969: 3). For Garfinkel, meanwhile, it is in conversation that the shared but implicit competency, knowledge and common-sense assumptions of culture members come into play; it is here that members do the work of artfully (if contingently and unwittingly) apprehending order and reasonableness in social life (Garfinkel 1972: 323). And again, for Berger and Luckmann, just as social reality is a precarious human construction, an ongoing everyday work in the face of entropy (and the anomie that threatens), so conversation is the most important vehicle of reality-maintenance; working away at her conversational apparatus, the individual protects and confirms the consistency of her world (Berger and Luckmann 1966: 140).

Equally, however, for each of the above theses, conversation gives onto, and can be treated in terms of, an epistemological singularity. In each case, conversation connects with (is preceded and followed by) a single social structure and a consensual culture. Through (Blumerian) symbolic interaction and mutual indication, then, a group of common objects emerges for a group of people. Such objects bear the same meaning; conversation eventuates in shared perspectives, in a high degree of consensus over what people call 'reality'. This consensus then enables group members to define and structure in common most situations in which they meet, and to act alike (Blumer 1972: 187). Meanwhile, by complying with (Garfinkelian) common background expectancies of interpretation in conversation, the stuff of everyday life gains not just an accountable and 'methodical' but also a common character. Thanks to the stable social structures underlying the processes of unconscious interpretation, cultural systems thereby replicate themselves in the form of worlds their members know in common and take for granted (Garfinkel 1964: *passim*). Finally, the conversation that (*après* Berger and Luckmann) consistently maintains a construction of reality against chaos also serves to structure subjective perceptions into a typical, intersubjective, cohesive and universal social order. This constrains what individuals experience in terms of what they can communicate, since conversation cannot but accommodate itself to the edifice of coercive categories and objective norms that is a society's language (Berger and Luckmann 1969: 66).

The proposition for the natural occurrence of epistemic diversity and epistemic interaction would posit a different character and a different end for conversation.

EPISTEMIC DIVERSITY AND EPISTEMIC INTERACTION

It is a commonplace of current anthropological reportage that today's world ('globalised', 'postmodern') is characterised by the absence of a consensual synthesising discourse, narrative or episteme and by the presence of an inexhaustible supply of them (Tyler 1986: 132). Likewise, no single locale is possessed of one local (symbolic or structural) order of things through which the world is understood and normalised: rather than an overarching ideological totalism, the locale is home to the intersection of a diversity of limited systems of meaning (Moore 1987: 730). We live, in short, in a world of 'epistemic pluralism', with individuals negotiating their ways between competing centres of philosophical gravity and the shifting balances of their power, playing off one episteme against another as different existential strategies in different contexts (Jackson 1989: 176–86).

I do not doubt the accuracy of these depictions. But how new is the condition? Has not cognitive and practical manoeuvring between a plurality of socio-historically situated epistemes ever been characteristic of individual lives? Does it not describe the local and the global in every age? I would say that it does.

Isaiah Berlin has phrased this proposition most succinctly by recalling the Kantian aphorism that 'Out of the crooked timber of humanity no straight thing was ever made' (Berlin 1990: 48). To amplify this slightly, between the supreme values, the true answers, the final ends pursued by different individuals and their diverse world-views we may expect no necessary commensurability, no final reconcilability, no true synthesis; 'great goods' can always be expected to collide, there being no determinate means of putting different 'goods' together: there is no single overarching standard or criterion available to decide between or harmonise discrete moralities. Moreover, this is so not merely in the case of the values of a succession of civilisations or nations, times and places, but also regarding contemporaneous individuals – even 'dividuals' (cf. Rapport 1993). For this reason, every social milieu can be said to be grounded in incompatibility and indeterminacy, in the 'human realities' of contradiction and ambiguity (Fernandez 1985: 750), its members in pursuit of some degree of 'disharmony of ends' (Douglas 1966: 140).

And why? Because of what every first-year anthropology student now realises: the world is culturally constructed, in social interaction, on an ongoing (*ad hoc*, contingent, conjectural, contesting, 'poetic') basis. Epistemic diversity and epistemic interaction are the natural conditions of human life because the form and content of that life are always being created anew.

Nietzsche is responsible for bringing such a realisation to modern consciousness most forcefully and polemically – and thus for philosophically undergirding the modern anthropological project of elucidating diversity (cf. Shweder 1991: 39). As Nietzsche has it, being the joint product of ineffable matter and human interpretation, there is no objective truth about the world, and it possesses no independent character: the world can be interpreted equally well in vastly different and deeply incompatible ways, its 'facts' being constructed not discovered. This being the case, there could never be a 'complete' theory or final interpretation of the world or anything else, merely an array of succeeding (conversing) perspectives: 'no meaning ... but countless meanings'; every interpretation, every 'fact', simply one version among many (Nietzsche 1968: no. 481). The world is to be thought of as a kind of artwork or literary text, requiring reading and interpretation in order to be mastered, understood, made livable. And each reading and interpretation translates into a different mooted set of practices and mode of life, each adding to the complexity and multifariousness of the indeterminate object that is 'the world'.

Possibly it is the literariness and artistry of the above depiction – Nietzsche's 'aestheticism' – which has obscured the truth (the 'truth') of this image of epistemic diversity until recently: why anthropologists have posited this diversity and interaction as a postmodern characteristic, part-and-parcel of a 'creolising' (Hannerz), 'hybridising' (Bhabha), 'compressing' (Paine), 'synchronising' (Tambiah) world, rather than an endemic feature of social life. After all, in the literary and the arty was to be risked the uncritical and impressible (the feminine); only by expunging things 'poetic' and 'figurative' could anthropology hope to eschew the 'fictional', the 'mythical' and 'fantastic', the 'intuitive' and 'subjective', the 'metaphysical' and 'evaluational', and so reach the rationality (and 'masculinity') of an ostensive scientific appreciation of society (cf. White 1976: 25; see also Layton, Chapter 8 of this volume). With the 'literary turn' in anthropology, however, this latter rhetoric has been deconstructed and the value of Nietzschean aestheticism in the depiction of society promulgated (cf. Rapport 1994: *passim*). There has also been a recognition that to eschew the endemic diversity of cultural construction in one's account – the 'maze of interaction'; rich in content, varied, many-sided, lively and subtle (Feyerabend 1975: 17–18) – may make for neatness, system, clarity and the contentment of order, but only under the aegis of some totalising dogma and at the expense of a totalitarian depiction (Louch 1966: 239).

NARRATIONAL ECLECTICISM

If the conversation of epistemes is and always has been the natural condition of social life, then how is it to be adequately represented in anthropology? How to resist the temptation, as Herzfeld (1993: 184) puts it, to reduce social experience to single models? Borrowing from Feyerabend, by being epistemologically 'opportunistic' (1975: 18); from Bohr, by insisting on epistemological 'complementarity' (Claxton 1979: 415); from Simmel, by refusing epistemological resolution or 'closure' (1971: xii). Beginning alike from the intrinsic complexity and diversity of social life, these methodological commentators meet alike in the insistence that no theory or episteme or narrative that the social commentator might import would cover all the 'facts' that are alive and being exchanged in a social milieu. Any attempt to force social life into one or other perspective ends in tautology and serves only to destroy the 'reality' under study. To adopt an eclecticism of narrational style, however, is to free one's account from an obsessional Aristotelian combat between battling singularities. And only in such eclecticism – locating human behaviour in more than one frame of reference at once; locating such (often mutually exclusive) frames of reference in conversation with one another – can one escape the notion that, ultimately, epistemic diversity can and should be 'resolved' in terms of a finite limit of possibility (society; structure) or an ultimately determining and integrating code (God; grammar).

If in modern physics, eclecticism has reached renown as a means of dealing with the mutual exclusivity of theories positing the nature of electrons as particles and as waves – as isolated material entities or as perturbations in a continuous field – then the direct corollary of this in anthropology might concern the dispute between theories of meaning. Is meaning a function of (isolated) individual intention at a particular moment, and an act that can wilfully alter or subvert any collective system that grounds it? Or is meaning a (continuous) collective fact, deriving from culturally determined codes and textual mechanisms that transcend particular volition? Narrational eclecticism would allow for such mutual exclusions (as well as others one could name – subject versus object, instance versus category, performance versus competence, event versus structure) and more plural oppositions (functionalism versus symbolic interactionism versus Marxism versus structuralism versus postmodernism) to appear within the same text. Indeed, narrational eclecticism would insist that this was the case: that the text was constructed out of a conversation between different epistemic realities.

THE ANTHROPOLOGICAL ACCOUNT

In her representation of contemporary Chagga social life (Moore 1987: *passim*) – 500,000 people living on the slopes of Mount Kilimanjaro – and cognizant of the 'fact' that the events of that life were not coherent instantiations of shared, pre-existing structures (normative, conventional, grammatical) so much as revelations of multiplicity and indeterminacy, of contestation and change, Sally Falk Moore insists that the 'event' of her text should not be characterised or informed by any single mode of knowing or interpreting. She chooses, therefore, to construct her anthropological narrative around the analysis of three 'chopped-off anecdotes' which were recounted to her (concerning the transfer of land), and to process (to converse) between and among their overlapping themes: the meaning of good and evil; the competition over a scarce resource; the contested powers and weaknesses of church and state. What the conversation of her text elucidates is that 'like a sunburst', the anecdotes can be seen to lead in all directions. They are shot through with ambiguity, with 'a contiguity of contraries'. Each anecdote carries concomitantly antithetical messages; each theme is open to contradictory interpretations; each statement made by their protagonists, or by her, their reporter, could be shown to have kinds of 'self-subversive anti-statements' attached to it. At the very least, in their detailed exposition of interlocked social-organisational frameworks, of rich systems of symbolic categories, and of multiple modes of production and class distinctions, the anecdotes offer simultaneous grist to the explanatory mills of functionalism, *structuralisme* and Marxism. But, by the same token, any attempt at a totalising truth-claim by any one such explanatory ideology can be easily deconstructed. As Chagga attachment to any single or consistent order and ordering of things is fragmentary and intermittent, so must be the anthropologist's attitude to any one episteme. The anecdotes reveal a multiplicity of epistemes, in creative combination, in terms of which Moore, like the Chagga, can continuously construct the social world as meaningful and as new.

In Moore's work can be found resonances of Amos Oz's attempts to give voice to 'the fiery collection of arguments', 'the screaming assembly of some five million prophets and prime ministers' that is modern Israel (1992; and cf. Marx 1980: 15–25). *In the Land of Israel* (1983), for example, represents a conversational journey which Oz undertakes between a few of the worlds that Israelis make for themselves. Included in Oz's figure of five million Israelis are of course Israeli Arabs, Bedouin and Druze. Leaving aside such conventional sources of epistemic diversity, however – not to mention that of the Palestinians – let me introduce here some of my fieldwork among (American) Jewish immigrants to Israel. To write conversationally about my own ethnographic experiences might be an account something like the following.

Mitzpe Ramon is a town in the Negev desert, lying roughly a third of the way along the desert road from Beer Sheva in the north to Eilat on Israel's southern tip. Set up by government agency in the mid-1950s, Mitzpe Ramon can still be described as a new-town, with pretensions to being a development town. Development, however, has been slow because, although the government provided the infrastructure of a town – apartment blocks and detached 'villas', an industrial zone, schools, clinics, visitors' centre, local government offices and shopping centre – Mitzpe Ramon was not (at least until the recent Russian-Jewish influx into Israel) a popular place to live. Even with government incentives in the form of monetary subsidies (on rent, bus tickets, tax, haulage) the town remained distant from other centres of population, unconnected from the (few) surrounding longer-established kibbutzim and army bases, and, after the opening of a newer road to Eilat, removed from transient custom. In the late 1980s, then, some thirty-five years after its founding, the town still had the feel of a frontier post (if not a ghost town). With accommodation for 6,000 it had fewer than 2,000 residents. Surrounded by the derelict shells of factory-units, unleased shops and empty apart-ments, its inhabitants scratched a living from government-sponsored programmes, from intermittent tourists, pensions and savings.

Making Mitzpe Ramon into a home, therefore, deciding that Mitzpe

Ramon would be where one would live, called for repeated if not continuous effort: justifying one's decision to come and to remain; coming to terms with one's relations with government bureaucracies; turning one's few fellow-residents into 'neighbours'. And, making this 'professional' voice into a 'personal' one (Hockey and James 1993: 4), let me list some (twenty-five) of the ways I encountered people making the place their home when, in 1989, I rented a flat from the government housing agency, moved in, and entered into interaction with local inhabitants. I was a new immigrant, open to meeting other new immigrants, English-speakers, neighbours, and anyone who would engage in conversation with me as I walked the streets, shopped and attended social gatherings:

1. Rachel: Are you an English-speaker? [as I walk past in the street carrying a Hebrew–English dictionary]. Oh, you're English; I'm American. I've been here five months – although I'm just back from the States.

2. Shmuel: There's no charge [as he comes to my flat from downstairs and provides me with a new porcelain fuse]. That's what being a neighbour means.

3. Alex: I heard somebody was moving in next door, but then I didn't see anybody for ages [as we meet on the stairs]. Will you be living here now? All the time? Will you be here on Saturday? [The day, that is, when public transport stops, when people visit their families, and when those left in Mitzpe are fewer still.]

4. Baruch: Did you get the gas fixed up in your flat? Mine's lovely now [and he takes me inside]. I don't quite know how or why, Nigel, but I'm very happy here. And like all mystical experiences, I know I shouldn't look too closely at it or it'll disappear!

5. Rachel: I didn't realise you needed a job to legally move into here [she explains during a coffee-break in Hebrew class]. Anyway, they invented one for me as an official ceramist at the Field School. I was brought here by this organisation that tries to get businesses to come to Mitzpe and then matches them up with people here: needs and skills.

6. Rachel: Have you heard the latest news? I haven't for two or three days [as we drink coffee in my flat]. What's happening with the US? . . . I guess few people will have the mental energy to live in a place like this. (And in a country of four million people, there aren't gonna be the numbers; they'll wanna be by everyone else.) But it was like the road I had to go to make me complete.

7. Sandra: We've been here four months. We spent three years in Netanya but the rents were getting exorbitant. And we far prefer the weather down here. Less hot and humid. . . . Someone in the Beer Sheva AACI told me there was an anthropologist coming here to live – the Association of Americans and Canadians in Israel. I'm going to set one

up here: liaise with the city, organise local activities. Somehow me and Irwin have got the job. So I'll be contacting you! [Hebrew class finishes and we part].

8. Jane: Do you live here? [as we meet at the bus stop]. Oh. Those blocks are where everyone begins in Mitzpe!

9. Sandra: I'm interested in knowing which natural desert plants and animals are edible, and how to prepare them [as we begin our Hebrew class]. I'd like to teach that sort of preparation: a sort of survival course.

10. Sandra: You can complain countless times to the Housing Agency and get nowhere. But we have to show them that we won't put up with just anything. [We meet in the bank queue.]

11. Rachel: This Jewishness is something in me, Nigel. And it makes something similar between all the different types in Israel: genetically alike, or the same circuiting in the head, which causes similar behaviour and reactions here.

12. Miriam: Just ask Dina at the felafel kiosk and she'll order whatever newspaper you want – like, the easy Hebrew one.

13. Alex: My parents live in Rehovot. Sometimes I visit them every week or fortnight. Then maybe not for months. [We have lunch in my flat.] I really like Mitzpe: the peace, the quiet, [laughing] no social life! First I came when I was in the army, at the Ramon base. Everyone else hated the place; Mitzpe was a joke to them. I was known as the only one on the base who liked the area and wanted to stay on afterwards by choice! . . . But I may have to leave soon when my engineering course finishes. Unless I can get a job at the astronomical observatory. That would be great!

14. Rachel: I'm off to get my unemployment pay: I feel a bit hypocritical about doing it.

15. Morris: We've already brought ten people down here with us. We'd like to start an English-speaking community of retired people.

16. Morris: We are on the Mitzpe cable TV system: 30 shekels per month for video films and BBC stuff which a man here puts out from 6 a.m. to 1 or 2 a.m. [as we watch colour TV in his villa].

17. Rachel: My shipment from the States arrived here from Haifa port, so I'm feeling more at home seeing my furniture about the apartment.

18. Rachel: There's a meeting next week to see about AACI activities in Mitzpe. I want a culture centre for poetry and art and gatherings, and getting energy. And the AACI could organise it. [We meet as she walks her dog around town.] If it really took off, I could imagine buying a villa here.

19. Morris: There's an AACI meeting on Saturday evening after *shabbat*. Please try to come, Nigel [as we meet in the supermarket]. We need to decide what kind of activities we'd want here. . . . If Rachel wants a poetry centre, etc., then we can nominate her as Head of Culture!

20. David: Meet Eugene, Nigel! We knew each other in Beer Sheva. [We

shake hands at the AACI gathering.] I was looking for somewhere to live in the Negev, and I'd already given up on Mitzpe ('cos of the bureaucracy) when Eugene came and said he'd found us a house. So next day we went to Jerusalem and sat outside the Housing Minister's office till we saw him and got permission to live here.

21. Alex: I'm not a Russian; there are no Russians here. Rachel may be still an American because she's just arrived. But I left Russia when I was 18 and I've been here ten years. My experiences are all Israeli experiences.

22. Rachel: Alex and I could put our political discussions to music. We know exactly where we converge and diverge. It's always the same.

23. Alex: The place has really changed in two years. Now there's really a circle of nice people developing. Two years ago I was about alone.

24. Dan: I've been collecting cactuses in this experimental area by the university in Beer Sheva to plant in my garden [as we meet on the bus home].

25. Rachel: What would I do if I didn't have you to talk to, Nigel? I've been very depressed. I'm still depressed but less so. . . . I'm gonna start a job gardening in the mornings. 'Cos the man I've taken up with is Head of Gardens.

The list, of course, is endless. People never stop 'making Mitzpe into their home' – it is a continuous practice – and there is nothing said or done that cannot be reckoned as in some way representing symbolic grist to the mill of home-making. Moreover, the possible orderings of the above, the interpretation of order it contains and the ways of interpreting them, are multiple. At present, the list reflects the actual words I recorded in my field journal and the chronological order of my recording them. Such listing, needless to say, already represents an interpretation, a fiction – my composition, excerption and juxtaposition.

To go further in such interpretation might be to point up a range of overlapping strategies of home-making between different speakers and/ or speech-acts:

- the seeking out of fellow old-language (English) speakers as the basis of new social relations in Mitzpe (excerpt numbers 1, 7, 15).
- the linking in of one's experiences in Mitzpe to different levels of prior experience – in Israel, in the West, in the world – so that under the conceptual aegis of 'being here', there is a continuing logic to one's life (4, 6, 11, 21).
- the boasting and sharing of knowledge about ways of dealing with local services and town infrastructure (10, 12, 14, 20).
- the expression of a complex array of emotional reactions to one's circumstances and self, all of which Mitzpe is backdrop to, mediatory to, or party to (6, 14, 17, 25).

- the placing of one's life in Mitzpe within a time-frame that seamlessly and 'naturally' links past to future (3, 7, 13, 25).

One might also go further in interpretation by pointing up how home-making strategies develop and change as speakers get to know Mitzpe and one another better:

- from recounting the serendipity that brought one to live in Mitzpe (4, 5, 20) to imagining the future developments in Mitzpe that one would have been instrumental in bringing about (9, 15, 18, 19).
- from a personal journey phrased in terms of residence in different parts of the globe or at least Israel (1, 7, 20) to journeying between residences within Mitzpe itself (8, 18).
- from the blandness of initial conversational openings (redundant, clichéd, formulaic: 1, 2, 10) to the subtleties and ironies of routine relations where even dispute can be harmonic (18, 21, 22).

One could also develop the interpretation by pointing up how home-making strategies (of the same or different speakers) are inconsistent, incompatible or paradoxical in relation to one another:

- from recognising or claiming a pioneer status for oneself in Mitzpe that inevitably cuts oneself off from the community of Israel (6, 13) to looking forward to a time when there is an Israeli community in Mitzpe (15, 18).
- from bemoaning the bureaucratic convolutions (threatening or only perversely facilitating) that preceded one's reaching Mitzpe (5, 20) to conceiving of one's establishment in Mitzpe in terms of the workings of a bureaucracy, and even becoming its functionary (7, 18, 19).
- from conceiving of one's journey to Mitzpe in terms of a new beginning or kind of life for oneself (6, 7, 13, 21) to routinising that life in terms of the skills, activities and practices with which one furnished oneself before (5, 9, 15, 17).

One could also focus on how the home-making strategies are of very different types, whose interrelations may be both polar and scalar:

- individualistic, imagining one's home in Mitzpe as centred on oneself (13, 17, 24) versus collectivistic, imagining oneself at home in a group (15, 19, 22, 23, 25).
- independent, knowing oneself to be the engineer of one's fate in Mitzpe (21, 24) versus dependent, recognising the guiding hand of others in one's finding a niche and a home (5, 20).
- from affective, seeing one's home in emotional, mental or mystical ways (11, 22) to materialistic, recognising one's home in terms of its objects and Mitzpe's physical landmarks (8, 12, 16) to both at once (2, 4, 6, 11, 13, 25).

In fact I would wish to have all these things said about conversational home-making in Mitzpe Ramon – and more: How the strategies could be seen as having an ethnic component (to speak to the social world in Israel and beyond as conceived of in terms of the politicisation of cultural identity), and a gender and a status and an age component, as well as a combination of these. How the strategies could be seen to resonate with a *structuraliste* analysis (with an elucidation of symbolic binarisms – desert/town, mystical/rational, Jewish/gentile, spontaneous/institutional, developmental/bureaucratic – in terms of which the utterances constitute a ritual text), or a Marxian analysis, or a functionalist or a psychoanalytic one, or a combination of these. How, as well as strategies of signification, I might have focused on overlapping tonalities in the above, or speakers' individualities, or perlocutionary intent, or the type of home that Mitzpe Ramon is envisaged as becoming and the outcome of its thus being signified. How the 'conversation' of these juxtaposed voices may variously translate as power-contestation, self-fulfilment, belonging or miscommunication.

What I would not wish to say is that there is a single or coherent or common-denominatory social structure that underlies the Mitzpe milieu (that explains, grounds, contextualises and determines the above attempts at home-making). Nor, indeed, would I wish to say that these attempts demand a single or coherent or common-denominatory mode of interpretation, including the interpretation that they are all about home-making, or all about any one thing at all. All that can be done is to *provide a text that represents the conversation of social life as it is (diversely) lived in individual interactions.* Further, as metaphoric representation of this, one can *offer a text that converses with itself in such different voices that any one voice acts to call into question the possible completeness of any other,* thus evoking in the reader, as in the writer, manifold interpretations: the sense of an 'incomplete project' (James 1993: 234).

EDIFYING ANTHROPOLOGY: NO ENDING

Richard Rorty has drawn a distinction between two kinds of account of social reality (1980: 357–72). One he calls 'systematic', and one 'edifying'; (Mannheim once spoke of 'systematising' and 'experimenting' to similar effect (1952: 48)). The systematic account is characterised by objectivity; the end-point is a system of monologic explanation, argument and agreement that will possess universal commensurability (so that everyone can be acculturated and conform to its language of fact and function). The institutionalisation of such an account is expected, if not to last for all eternity, at least to provide the foundations of future progress. By contrast, the edifying account is distrustful of the notion of essences and dubious about claims that reality can now accurately, holistically, singularly, disinterestedly, be explained and described. For there is ineluctably the contingency and diversity of the extant (the 'contradictions' and the 'discordancy' (Mannheim)), the situated interests of existing epistemes, and there is always the poetry of the new. Diversity and newness will always escape the bounds of ultimate commensuration between human practices. In the face of an essentialist enquiry, then, the edifying account maintains a conversation between different ways of being in the world; as reality is multiple so its realistic representation might eschew any singular, authoritative framing. In the face of systematic arguments and tradition, therefore, it offers aphorisms, satires, parodies; it esteems the continuous metamorphoses of metaphor and poetry. Clearly, both the elucidation of the conversation of social life and the representation of conversation in the account of social life that I have been arguing for in this chapter would make of anthropology an edifying pursuit.

But then, for Rorty, the edifying account not only deals in conversation as subject-matter and style, it also causes conversation to continue. In reading and then writing about the artwork of social life, it composes another chapter within it; it adds to the array of epistemic construction and interaction. Through epistemic juxtaposition and *bricolage* it goes beyond what it describes as presently existing to write something new. This Rorty describes as a transfiguring process: always opening the present to the potentialities of the new, while never surrendering commitment to conversation *per se*.

Indeed, 'transfiguration' is the edifying credo: ever to find different, fruitful ways of speaking and conversing, so as to transcend the present in new possibilities of self and society. For, by providing new writings of reality, there can always flourish an epistemic diversity and interaction, offering new ways of describing ourselves and new possibilities for thinking about our experience. Hence, an edifying account posits rewriting as the most important thing to be done, also the most dignified. It continues to secure a representation of human beings not as singular and limited epistemic objects so much as their own plural and limitless subjects.

In an edifying anthropology, finally, is to be found an estimation that the reductive process of representation may be overcome if one admits no ending. 'Wisdom', Rorty concludes (1980: 378), is the ability to 'sustain a conversation' between epistemes, while

> [T]o look for commensuration rather than simply continued conversation ... is to attempt escape from humanity.

REFERENCES

Berger, P. and T. Luckmann (1966) *The Social Construction of Reality*, New York: Doubleday.

—— (1969) 'Sociology of Religion and Sociology of Knowledge', in R. Robertson (ed.), *The Sociology of Religion*, Harmondsworth: Penguin.

Berlin, I. (1990) *The Crooked Timber of Humanity*, London: Murray.

Blumer, H. (1969) *Symbolic Interactionism*, Englewood Cliffs: Prentice-Hall.

—— (1972) 'Society as Symbolic Interaction', in A. Rose (ed.), *Human Behaviour and Social Processes*, London: Routledge & Kegan Paul.

Claxton, G. (1979) 'Individual Relativity: The Model of Man in Modern Physics', *Bulletin of the British Psychological Society*, 32: 414–18.

Douglas, M. (1966) *Purity and Danger*, London: Routledge & Kegan Paul.

Fernandez, J. (1985) 'Macrothought', *American Ethnologist* 12 (4): 749–57.

Feyerabend, P. (1975) *Against Method*, London: New Left Books.

Garfinkel, H. (1964) 'Studies in the Routine Grounds of Everyday Activity', *Social Problems*, 11: 225–50.

—— (1972) 'Remarks on Ethnomethodology', in J. Gumperz and D. Hymes (eds), *Directions in Sociolinguistics*, New York: Holt-Rinehart-Winston.

Geertz, C. (1973) *The Interpretation of Cultures*, London: Hutchinson.

—— (1983) *Local Knowledge*, New York: Basic Books.

Handler, R. and D. Segal (1990) *Jane Austen and the Fiction of Culture*, Tucson: Arizona University Press.

Herzfeld, M. (1993) *The Social Production of Indifference*, Chicago: University of Chicago Press.

Hockey, J. and A. James (1993) *Growing Up and Growing Old*, London: Sage.

Jackson, M. (1989) *Paths Toward a Clearing*, Bloomington: Indiana University Press.

James, A. (1993) *Childhood Identities*, Edinburgh: Edinburgh University Press.

Louch, A. R. (1966) *Explanation and Human Action*, Berkeley: University of California Press.

MacIntyre, A. (1981) *After Virtue*, London: Duckworth.

Mannheim, K. (1952) *Ideology and Utopia*, London: Routledge & Kegan Paul.

Marx, E. (1980) 'On the Anthropological Study of Nations', in E. Marx (ed.), *A Composite Portrait of Israel*, London: Academic Press.

Moore, S. (1987) 'Explaining the Present: Theoretical Dilemmas in Processual Ethnography', *American Ethnologist*, 14 (4): 727–36.

Nietzsche, F. (1968) *The Will to Power*, New York: Random House.

Oakeshott, M. (1962) *Rationalism in Politics and Other Essays*, London: Methuen.

Oz, A. (1983) *In the Land of Israel*, London: Fontana.

—— (1992) 'Israeli Literature.' The Raymond Williams Lecture, Hay-on-Wye Book Festival.

Rapport, N. J. (1987) *Talking Violence: An Anthropological Interpretation of Conversation in the City*, St John's: ISER Books, Memorial University of Newfoundland.

—— (1993) *Diverse World-Views in an English Village*, Edinburgh: Edinburgh University Press.

—— (1994) *The Prose and the Passion: Anthropology, Literature and the Writing of E. M. Forster*, Manchester: Manchester University Press.

Rorty, R. (1980) *Philosophy and the Mirror of Nature*, Princeton: Princeton University Press.

Shweder, R. (1991) *Thinking Through Cultures*, Cambridge, MA: Harvard University Press.

Simmel, G. (1971) *On Individuality and Social Forms*, Chicago: University of Chicago Press.

Tyler, S. (1986) 'Post-modern Ethnography: From Document of the Occult to Occult Document', in G. Marcus and J. Clifford (eds), *Writing Culture*, Berkeley: University of California Press.

White, H. (1976) 'The Fictions of Factual Representation', in A. Fletcher (ed.), *The Literature of Fact*, New York: Columbia University Press.

Chapter 12

Who is representing whom?
Gardens, theme parks and the anthropologist in Japan

Joy Hendry

INTRODUCTION

Within a day's return journey from Tokyo, and much lauded by the international tourist brochures, lies the historical, religious and aesthetically stunning site of Nikko. Set amongst the first truly spectacular mountain ranges after the monotony of the Kanto Plain, this collection of shrines and temples displays the ultimate in Japanese architectural achievement, inspired since the eighth century by the natural beauty of their surroundings. Here is the epitome of the oft-expressed Japanese feeling of oneness between culture and nature, where the vision of the designers and the skills of the craftsmen meld with the awe-inspiring creations of the gods. As the poster advocates, in introducing foreign visitors to a Japanese expression of deep appreciation, 'Don't say *kekko* (splendid) until you've seen Nikko.'

Many Japanese, if asked to name a single site to sum up their culture, to speak to the outside world of their people, would undoubtedly choose Nikko. It is accessible enough to be visited for the shortish period of hours or days usually available to visitors, and it includes many of the aspects of art, history and religion that Japanese people would feel best expressed their world view. It is also within easy reach of hot springs where humans can commune physically with the natural resources Japan has to offer. There is logically, therefore, a splendid, comfortable train which regularly leaves central Tokyo for the destination, and which carries an English-speaking hostess to take care of foreign guests.

This same train, with only a small diversion, carries passengers to another tourist spot, although this time the tourists are more usually Japanese. From Kinugawa Onsen, a hot-spring resort at which passengers alight, buses run frequently along to two late twentieth-century attractions. One of these is a reconstructed historical Japanese village, where Westernised Japanese citizens can step nostalgically back into the period when Japan was closed to the outside world; the other is a collection of 102 'world-famous' buildings, each constructed as a 'faithful replica' on a scale of 1/25 of the original site. 'As if you were Gulliver', the brochure reads, 'come and see this unique intelligent theme park . . . and experience 5000 years of history.'

The Pyramids are there, as is the World Trade Center. The Colosseum and the Parthenon lead on to the Leaning Tower of Pisa and the Duomo of Milan. The Great Wall of China is on show, as is the Taj Mahal. The Tower of London is another feature, as are Buckingham Palace, Big Ben, the Houses of Parliament, and a variety of other European castles and palaces. The Vatican Basilica of St Peter is carefully depicted, as are Nôtre Dame, Westminster Abbey and the Eiffel Tower. For some reason, Dover Castle has been selected for display, as has the only marginally earlier twelfth-century Norwegian church of Borgund. There is nothing from Africa or Australia, though the New York street scenes, and the scale model of Narita International Airport and other famous Tokyo architectural sites show evidence that the designers did not preclude twentieth-century achievements.

In the last part of the display there is actually a large number of Japanese shrines and temples, together with Japanese country scenes, and a running railway system leads back to twentieth-century Tokyo, so that the visitor is left with no doubt about Japan's important place in this museum of architectural development. Indeed, what seems at first to be a wonderful expression of the 'internationalisation' that Japan has for the last few years been firmly espousing, peters out somewhat towards the end. My disappointment was further compounded by the unappetising cosmopolitan snacks available in the coffee shop, and the total lack of a telephone that could be used to make international calls. These are readily available in most towns and cities in Japan, but the staff in the office at this so-called 'World Square' were not even aware, until I informed them, that I could make an international telephone call, collect, from their own office phones.

This park is clearly not designed for the foreign visitor. The English-speaking hostess sticks with the main-line train to Nikko, and there is only a smattering of English in evidence amongst the staff of the Tobu transport systems in the World Square area. There are also few signs written in English, and the names and explanations of the world sites are depicted in Japanese, even to the extent of transliterating the Western-language titles into the Japanese *katakana* script. Whereas pamphlets and brochures for Nikko are readily available in English, French and a number of other languages, the only English on the Tobu World Square 'Guide-book' is evidently there to add an international flavour to it.

REPRESENTATION OR APPROPRIATION

Here we have two examples of 'representation' to consider. The first is ostensibly a case of self-representation, the second less clearly so. Both examples turn the tables on the worries of the anthropologist about representing 'the other' (see Knight, Chapter 9 of this volume). In this case, the anthropologist has become 'the other', both as part of a potential audience, and as part of the culture being represented. It therefore offers an opportunity to react and analyse the representations from an unusual point of view. There is clearly the point of view of 'the represented', but in this case 'the represented' is examining the material in the context of a much wider knowledge of Japanese forms of representation.

In this chapter, I examine the two cases presented above in the context of a prior study of Japanese gardens, which itself drew on much previous work in Japan on a variety of subjects, always involving some degree of presentation or representation. I will argue that my unease at Tobu World Square is parallel to the unease (and worse) experienced by indigenous people when they find their culture has been not only represented, but *appropriated* by members of another culture for their own purposes. The extent to which this *appropriation* is amusing, irritating or downright insulting is undoubtedly related to the power differential between the peoples concerned, and it will change as this differential adjusts, but I will argue that there is also a time factor involved.

In the case of Nikko, much of what is described as Japanese culture clearly originated in China or Korea, or came via the mainland from further afield. The Buddhist temples may still be compared with Buddhist edifices elsewhere, and detailed descriptions of them may make reference to the influential factors. The early Shinto influence is less often related to possible sources in Taoism or Korean shamanism, which predate historical record in Japan, only a little older than the origins of Nikko in the eighth century, and the extant collection of buildings is clearly chosen to represent *Japanese culture.* If appropriated long enough ago, cultural influence becomes a source of pride in one's heritage, as a Chinese or Korean may experience on a visit to Nikko.

We may accuse the Japanese creators of Tobu World Square of *appropriating* foreign culture for their own purposes, but we would be less likely to cast such aspersions at the artists and craftsmen who created Nikko long ago. In the next few pages, I examine some other examples of parks and gardens in Japan to try and establish just what is being represented and why, and then return to see how these findings may shed light on the plight of the anthropologist representing the people with whom he or she has worked. I conclude by suggesting that anthropologists have a valuable role to play in this world of cultural appropriation.

GARDENS AS PRECURSORS TO THE THEME PARK

I have recently argued that sites such as Nikko National Park and Tobu World Square may be interpreted in some of the same ways as Japanese gardens (Hendry 1997), and in this section I consider why this should be so and what such parallels may tell us about forms of representation. We are concerned with quite subtle and sophisticated means of representation, which go way beyond the 'linear, academic form of writing' so much questioned in the 'Writing Culture' debate. They are, like other forms, open to a variety of interpretations, but the earliest documents to make mention of *niwa*, the word still used for 'garden', date back to the seventh century when it was used to describe a place purified for the worship of the gods (Bring and Wayembergh 1981: 145; Hayakawa 1973: 27). In the intervening centuries there have been many influences and developments, but the garden always seems to be in the business of representing something else.[1]

The famous Zen gardens of Japan are an excellent example. At one level they are designed to depict a three-dimensional version of a kind of drawing of a natural scene. Stones and pebbles replace ink as the medium, gathered in such a way that they may depict, quite without water, streams, falls and oceans, as well as mountains and rocky coasts more akin to their original shape. Amongst the stones, some small trees and bushes may be planted to represent the green elements of the scenery, but these are not essential, and some of the most famous gardens have little more than moss to relieve the grey hues of the rock and pebble.

At another level, elements of these gardens may also stand for mythical isles and mountains, such as Mt Hôrai and Mt Sumeru, as well as symbolic beings, typically a turtle and a crane. These beasts themselves stand for something else. Together they are often used as symbols of longevity, but in the Daisen-in garden in Kyoto, the former is said to represent the depths to which the human spirit can sink, since it seeks the bottom of the ocean, and the latter the heights to which the human spirit can soar (Daisen-in n.d.). Mt Hôrai, in the middle, thus represents a union of heaven and earth, joy and disappointment, which are said to comprise human experience.

Other Zen gardens are much less explicit about what they are representing, and the observer is left to contemplate and wonder at the deep thoughts of the garden designer who created it. A huge dry-stone waterfall at the so-called Moss Garden in Kyoto, created in the fourteenth century by the priest Muso Sôseki, is said by one commentator to 'express the passion that raged in the heart of a great man who ... lived in a Japan torn by civil strife ... and filled with suffering and insecurity' (Hayakawa 1973: 64). Other commentators have very different interpretations of this famous stone garden, and the more mysterious the meaning, the more appealing a Zen garden seems to be.

At yet another level, Zen gardens stand for Japanese gardens in general, and these have been used as symbols of Japanese culture. The use of a simple stone/pebble arrangement to stand for the deepest human thoughts is seen in a Japanese view as a high form of cultural achievement.[2] In an earlier period, Buddhist gardens were said to be designed to represent the Jôdô Buddhist paradise and, in this respect, Japanese gardens have been compared with the gardens of Europe, which sought to depict a paradise to come (Comito 1978: xi). In Japan they were also continuing older traditions where a lake, with islands, is a form, apparently of Chinese or Korean origin, said to have developed from a Chinese emperor's efforts to lure the gods to his palace by creating a representation of their mythical isles (Keswick 1986: 35–40; Kuck 1968: 39–43).

These isles had floated in and out of view as sailors tried to reach them, it was said, and, in Japan too, the deities were thought to inhabit inaccessible and dangerous places whose reconstructions might offer a safer site for communication. Where mountains were worshipped, for example, a shrine would be built at a suitable distance, although a smaller inner shrine is often also to be found further up into the mountain. In this case the inner shrine or *miya* is known as the *okumiya*, where the term *oku* stands for a kind of inner depth, also used to talk of the inside, private part of a house, or the deep interior of a forest. Creating a sense of *oku* is said to be an important aspect of making a garden in Japan, and it has been argued that the garden is a way of taming the outside, perhaps dangerous natural world into an inside, culturally acceptable form (Kalland 1992; Hendry 1997).

The 'natural' world is virtually inseparable from the supernatural in a Japanese view, so it is a short step to see a garden as bringing greater accessibility to the stunning scenery that lies beyond easy encounter. The modern *tsuboniwa*,[3] a tiny creation which may be fitted into the most constrained house or apartment, follows the same principles. Very often hidden from the outside world, the garden nevertheless *represents* the great outside in a safe, enclosed form. A series of rocks may depict a mighty mountain range, a dash of pebbles a roaring waterfall, and a small carefully distorted tree may suggest the wind continually pulling the branches in a particular direction. The owners of the garden may sit in the relative comfort of their own home, imagining a visit out into the rugged beauty of the Japanese wild, a visit which if made in reality could be a frightening experience requiring a good deal of time and preparation.

This fear associated with the outside in a Japanese view is an interesting phenomenon which underpins much of the argument of this chapter, though it need not detain us here for long since it is well documented elsewhere, and it is also undoubtedly a recognisable characteristic of many world views. In the Japanese case, it is part of the general socialisation of a child to make a clear distinction between the inside and the outside, and the concomitant safety and security of the former and possible dangers of the latter. The distinction between inside and outside is a major organisational feature of Japanese social life, recently analysed with great theoretical rigour as the important focus for understanding much-contested themes of self and society, hierarchy and authority, conflict, and the uniqueness of the Japanese people (Bachnik and Quinn 1994).

In practice, the boundaries of inside and outside are constantly shifting. They start for the child in the home and then move gradually further and further out through neighbourhood, kindergarten, school and, eventually, the workplace, though in any situation communication will proceed on the basis of relative shared insideness. Spatially, certain areas may be rendered relatively inside through the means of enclosure and domestication, and this I argue is what is happening in the creation of a garden, whether it be part of a home, a shrine or a temple. In each case, the representation of the outside world allows a 'taming' of it, to use Kalland's term, or 'wrapping' of it, to use my own (Hendry 1993, 1994, 1997) and makes possible communication with natural and supernatural phenomena held to dwell out in the wilder beyond.

These natural and supernatural phenomena may themselves spell danger. In a land where earthquakes and volcanic eruptions are not uncommon, and yearly typhoons bring flood and wind damage, it is hardly surprising that people would harbour a healthy respect for the forces of nature. The supernatural beings that form part of this outside 'natural' world are also often of ambiguous status. In general, if they are treated well, they will respond with benevolence, and much religious ritual is predicated on this assumption. Explanations of misfortune are very often sought, here as elsewhere, in a breach of good treatment, and solutions sought in offerings and ritual. The avoidance of such a breach is thought preferable, however, and much of Japanese social life, as well as attention to the supernatural, is based on this principle.

REPRESENTATIONS OF THE WORLD IN JAPAN

These same principles come into play in dealing with foreigners, of course, and it is my contention that theme parks such as Tobu World Square may be seen as serving a taming purpose parallel to that described above for gardens. During Japan's first encounter with Europeans in the sixteenth century, the outsiders were literally known as 'wild' barbarians (*yabanjin*), and their inevitable association with the outside *vis-à-vis* Japan implies a need to tame or wrap them for local consumption. There is an overlap between foreigners or strangers and gods in Japanese folklore – they share ambiguous qualities of benevolence and danger, for one thing, and spirits have a habit of appearing in the guise of a stranger.[4] Gardens help people come to terms with outsiders, spiritual or corporal, and representations of the outside world offer an opportunity for the same benefit.

In the last few years an abundance of foreign-country theme parks have opened in Japan, alongside an official policy of 'internationalisation'. An early example was Disneyland, which is loved by its Japanese visitors, and Tobu World Square is one of the more recent ones. In the cool north of Japan a 'Canadian World' opened in 1990 featuring the home of Anne of Green Gables and the largest lavender field in the country. In the warmer south, 'Parque España' opened in 1994, advertising specifically 'the Spanish experience without going to Spain'. A compact version of Italy is apparently to be found in the mountains of Nagano, a Russian village in Niigata (Pitman 1994: 3), and a community near Kyoto has even purchased the Danish pavilion from the 1992 EXPO in Seville to authenticate a Scandinavian touch to their community (Knight 1993).

One of the first of these nation theme parks, which has recently been rebuilt, was Hollanda Mura, a Dutch village in Kyushu, reminiscent of Deshima, the island settlement off Nagasaki which was the site of foreign, mostly Dutch, homes during the period of more than 200 years when Japan was closed to the outside world. The new 'Haus ten Bosch' sports full-size replicas of real Dutch buildings, including windmills, and several museums of Dutch art and culture.[5] Dutch students studying Japanese are invited to stay there during their year abroad, and they may be seen on the streets, hobbling about in clogs, or serving Dutch drinks and food in the bars and restaurants to supplement their allowance. An historical museum depicts Japan's past relations with the outside world, notably with the Dutch at Deshima. This island was the point of communication when Japan was closed, now Haus ten Bosch represents international encounter in a symbolic way as well.

On another island, tucked away in the Seto Inland Sea, the theme is ancient and modern Greece. Blessed with an almost Mediterranean climate, this sheltered spot had for long been well known for the production of rice noodles, but in 1973 an entrepreneur hotelier, native of the island, decided to develop another line. In these years of increasing confidence, after the defeat and destruction of the Second World War, it was appropriate to look towards peace in the world, and he decided to take advantage of the mild climate to grow a park of olive trees, denoting the ancient symbol of the olive branch. A series of international visitors have been invited to plant them, the first two being installed by the Secretary General of the United Nations and the Greek Ambassador to Japan (Hatziyannaki 1994: 54).

A replica of an ancient Greek temple was also constructed, with marble from Greece and an eternal flame carried from the original Olympic one in Athens. With a Shinto shrine inside it, this Temple of Peace serves as the focus for an annual festival, when local people dress in Greek robes and crowns of laurel and read translations of works by Homer, Herodotus and other ancient Greeks who wrote on the subject of peace. In the mid-1980s this island was discovered by a visiting Greek environmentalist who was impressed by the 'Greek spirit in Japan' and instigated a twinning arrangement with the Greek island of Milos. Various visits and exchanges have followed, a museum has been installed, and construction is underway for a cultural centre with its own theatre (ibid.).

A huge project has been designed for this island, and within the next ten years it is envisaged that there will be a complete Greek village and a 'Dolphinland' to boost the current one million Japanese tourists into a much larger international clientele. The millionaire who designed the peace park is still alive, though now in his nineties, and his original vision of peace and communication between cultures is admired by the Greek journalist who wrote of this island in *Olympic Airways Inflight Magazine* (ibid.). She also argues that while 'the West is having difficulty becoming liberated from its aesthetic and cultural prejudices', modern Japanese are better able to 'recognise values in cultures which are foreign to their own and adapt them in their own way' (ibid.: 55–6).

A less uncompromisingly positive attitude was adopted by the British journalist, Hugo Gurdon, who wrote the text in an issue of the *Weekend Daily Telegraph* of a full front page devoted to British Hills, a Japanese educational foundation's attempt to bring an authentic slice of Britain to within an hour of Tokyo (Gurdon 1994). He describes the imported reproduction British buildings, representing periods from the twelfth to the nineteenth century, and the imported British characters such as a butler fictitiously named 'Stanbury', and a publican named Bill Brown. He reports that one can not only study English, but receive tuition in a variety of British customs such as how to remove a fish bone from your mouth at an Ambassador's banquet, and how to cook gingerbread and lemon tarts in Mrs Beeton's Kitchen (ibid.). He finds the whole endeavour so deadly earnest, however, that he describes it as 'a dazzling but unintentional send-up – a rib-cracking, tear-jerking and gobsmacking pastiche' (Gurdon 1994: 1).

PURPOSE AND REACTION

This last section examines in more detail the role played by representation in some of these cases and, where available, considers the reactions of the represented. Disneyland is clearly concerned more with play and enjoyment than with representing accurately the historical, exotic and imaginary themes it calls upon to create its rides, although from the start it has employed American and other foreign helpers to add an exotic air to the parades.[6] There is also a kind of missionary zeal about the international theme of a shared Small World, and there is undoubtedly some degree of ideological fervour behind the more overt economic aims of the enterprise.

Tobu World Square, on the other hand, though still clearly an economic enterprise, makes a point of emphasising the accuracy with which the scale models of the world-famous buildings have been created, and there are no rides for the visitors. Instead, one may buy a 'play card' and cause small figures to carry out various activities to be scrutinised by the visitor. A cast of 140,000 tiny men, women and children will sing and dance, drive vehicles, and generally go about their lives in a way which is no doubt held to be an accurate representation of life in the various locations depicted. A little bit of historical data is presented in front of each building, which is also carefully dated on a Gregorian calendrical system not necessarily used to depict Japanese history.

British Hills has been created to play an educative role. This is not to negate the economic factor, for Japanese 'educational foundations' are notorious for their profit-oriented objectives.[7] It appears also to strive for authenticity, going to great lengths to consult and employ British 'experts', even if these disagree amongst themselves about their role. According to Gurdon, many of the Japanese pupils understand very little of the lectures they are given, but they can at least absorb the atmosphere.

The Greek-inspired development of the island of Shodoshima, on the other hand, turned to ideology to back up the economic side. By 1973, Japan had begun to regain self-confidence after the shock of defeat in their efforts to establish a greater empire and the first experience in their history of occupation by an alien people. The theme of peace was a powerful one to employ, and the classical Greek associations were far enough from recent international encounters and their own tarnished mythology to provide a suitable model to employ, both at home and, eventually, on an international scale. Later developments on this island have pursued the more recent theme of 'internationalisation' with their twinning arrangements, museum and so forth.

Haus ten Bosch, on the other hand, represents real Japanese history. The infiltration of knowledge from Europe was not insignificant during the period when Japan was officially closed, and if the Dutch were diplomatic enough to continue informal relations when the country was formally sealed, they would also seem an appropriate people to lead a new era of international goodwill as Japanese relations with Europe grow warm again. This community is a theme park, with an educative role and a certain authenticity ensured by its association with an excellent European university, but it is also a place for fun and enjoyment. The original village has apparently been made into a park for children, and the contemporary one sports plenty of leisure activity.

Holders of the various nationalities represented have clearly found ways to exploit the Japanese interest, whether merely in employment, or in the academic pursuits of the Dutch. The reactions of journalists are interesting too. The Greeks have had a lot longer to get used to people representing them and their illustrious past than the British have, and the sanguine reaction probably reflects this, but Gurdon does conclude on a cynical note. Commenting on the lack of agreement he discerns amongst the British employees at British Hills about how their country should be represented anyway, he concedes that the Japanese educational foundation has perhaps purchased a more depressingly accurate version of Britain than it bargained for – 'a confused and defensive little territory where a glorious past contends with a mundane present' (ibid.).

We can still laugh, however, as most who read Gurdon's piece no doubt did, and this was also the reaction of the mostly British audience of the Japanese Garden Society meeting in Cheshire when they were told about the English touches that have been chosen for a new park being constructed in Japan at the site of one of the three most famous, and earliest, public gardens, *Kairakuen* at Mito. This park will apparently include a 'grotto', a 'secret garden', an 'aromatic garden' and a 'traditional English water mill' (personal communication from the designer). It seemed ironic that a group of people who were gathered to learn about representing Japan in their own gardens should laugh when they were presented with a case of the opposite process.

APPROPRIATION AND POWER

In this last example we may well wonder, however, whether the British people gathered were in fact representing Japan in their gardens at all. As I have argued elsewhere, they liked the gardens for their aesthetic value,[8] rather than for their particular connection with Japan. They have in fact *appropriated* a cultural form for their own benefit, just as their forebears did in the nineteenth century, and it is such *appropriation* that may be the upsetting aspect of so-called representations. The British and other colonists brought various souvenirs, or trophies, back from their travels and displayed them in illustrious places like country houses and the British Museum. These are some of the representations to which their original owners object – partly because they have been appropriated by the British for their own purposes; aesthetic, educative, cultural, and so forth.

In a situation where the anthropologist is clearly in a position of economic superiority, and historical associations of inequality are invoked by the relationship between the represented and their protagonists, political and ethical issues may certainly seem important. In representations between peoples on a more equal footing, things may take on a different hue. D. P. Martinez has discussed the visual representations on the television screen of Britain in Japan, and Japan in Britain (Martinez, forthcoming). In both cases, there is much fun and merrymaking as well as serious documentary about the other, and this, I think, is a measure of relative equality and mutual respect, albeit tinged with an element of xenophobia.

For a British viewer to watch and enjoy a Japanese quiz show making fun of British people expresses a degree of sophistication that would not be possible, or even acceptable in these days of political correctness, between a pair of nations in a postcolonial situation. Similarly, Japanese people can see the funny side of the Clive James show in which they are depicted humorously. In Japan the roles of relative wealth and power are reversed in comparison with the position of anthropologists in the Third World, so that the ethnographer is often the one seeking indulgence from the informant in the exchange of gifts and services (Okely and Calloway 1992: 170–1; cf. Caplan 1994).

Furthermore, unlike the situation in other Pacific communities of Austronesia, and parts of the postcolonial world, many Japanese welcome anthropological interest in their culture. My informants are usually extremely kind and cooperative, providing that I regale them with tales of 'abroad', and they rarely express indignation about being the objects of study.[9] Indeed, as many writers have recently pointed out, the Japanese people seem almost obsessed with interest in themselves (Yoshino 1992 summarises the literature) and Japanese anthropologist Aoki Tamotsu recently bemoaned the fact that foreign anthropologists don't play a more active role in interpreting Japan accurately to the outside world. 'I am not calling on anthropologists ... to be apologists for this country', he writes, 'but we need their voices to balance shallow revisionist arguments that portray Japan as exceptional, "different" from the rest of the international community' (Aoki 1994: 5).

Aoki cites Ruth Benedict as the only anthropologist to have done this successfully to date, and this, he argues, accounts for the continuing popularity of her book, *The Chrysanthemum and the Sword* (Benedict 1954), which has apparently sold 350,000 copies in English and over a million in Japanese translation (Aoki 1994: 4–5) since it came out in 1946. He explains her outstanding achievements in terms of her exceptional cultural relativism, 'her consistently balanced contrast between America and Japan' (ibid.: 5). Aoki agrees with Geertz's assessment of the book as being about America as much as about Japan, and this he admires, quoting from *Works and Lives* that 'what started out as a familiar sort of attempt to unriddle oriental mysteries ends up, only too successfully, as a deconstruction ... of occidental clarities. At the close, it is ... us that we wonder about' (ibid.: 5, quoting Geertz 1989: 121).

Aoki's positive citation of Benedict's work is interesting in view of the mixed reaction it has engendered over the years. Immediately after the Second World War it was criticised in Japan for apparently placing her in an inferior position *vis-à-vis* the United States, although I found little substance for these allegations in a recent rereading (Hendry 1997). Some of this impression may well have been due to the poor translation of the word 'guilt' into Japanese, but it may also have been the aggrieved reaction of a defeated people to the alarmingly accurate insights of one of their conquerors. Aoki writes now from a position of relative power, and he is perhaps able to see things more dispassionately.

To return, then, to anthropological representation, may we not apply the same argument? Anthropologists strive for accuracy in their studies, and they gather material by consulting their informants, but are they writing for them, or for their colleagues in academia? Their colleagues are, after all, the ones who share a knowledge of past work and theory, and some of the classic examples have almost been totally divorced from the people they 'represent'. Recent studies of the Trobriand Islanders are interesting, as are studies of the Nuer and the Azande, but even if different, they hardly negate the earlier work, now firmly appropriated as *anthropology*.

The local anthropologist, Tamotsu Aoki, likes the work of Ruth Benedict because he feels that it depicts as much about America as it does about Japan. He feels that this is a true case of cultural relativism, and he evidently does not feel appropriated, as others seem to do. Foreign anthropologists working in Japan are usually immediately put into contact with local anthropologists, and although some of these do not feel enough respect is accorded to their work (Aoki 1994: 6), others have written of the importance of cooperation (Yoshida 1987: 21–3). Perhaps mutual respect and cooperation between anthropologists would create a truly mature situation in which representation would lose much of its political, ethical and even satirical component.

NOTES

1 For further detail of these representations, and a more complete list of references in English, see Hendry (1997). The analysis is necessarily truncated in this chapter.
2 Josiah Condor expressed this view nicely in one of the earliest descriptions in English of Japanese gardens, when he wrote, 'A landscape garden in Japan is more than a simple representation of natural views, it is at the same time, a poetical conception' (Condor 1964: 8).
3 A *tsubo* is literally about 36 square feet, although the term *tsuboniwa* is used to describe a small courtyard garden, much as in English one may describe the size of a garden as comparable with a postage stamp. It is typically enclosed within a house plot so that it is only visible from within the house.
4 The anthropologist Yoshida Teigo (1981) has written on this subject, and I have followed up some of his ideas (Hendry 1988).

5 Information about this community was provided by staff of the Centre for Japanese Studies at Leiden University who visit while their second-year students are studying there each year. I am particularly indebted to Erica de Poorter and Wim Boot.
6 In a collection of papers which examine the way Western phenomena have been adopted and adapted in Japan's consumer society (Tobin 1992), Mary Yoko Brannen argues that the Japanese owners of Tokyo Disneyland wanted and believe they have an exact copy of the American version. She discusses the Japanese modifications in their cultural context.
7 Britain in the hills as an *educational* endeavour is a little reminiscent of the role of department stores in the late nineteenth century, when their economic function was supplemented by a need to educate potential customers in the use of the often Western goods they were selling. According to Millie Creighton (1992), this role has continued into more recent times, when it has been combined also with entertainment so that she has coined the expression *edutainment* to describe these activities.
8 I examined the last example in some detail at the decennial ASA meeting, and it is scheduled to appear, together with Lola Martinez's (forthcoming) paper on television programmes, in Morphy and Banks, *Rethinking Visual Anthropology*.
9 The one exception to this general rule formed the subject matter of a paper in the ASA volume on Anthropology and Autobiography (Hendry 1992).

REFERENCES

Aoki, T. (1994) 'Anthropology and Japan: Attempts at Writing Culture', *Japan Foundation Newsletter*, 22 (3): 1–6.
Bachnik, J. M. and C. J. Quinn, Jr (eds) (1994) *Situated Meaning: Inside and Outside in Japanese Self, Society and Language*, Princeton, NJ: Princeton University Press.
Benedict, R. (1954) *The Chrysanthemum and the Sword*, Tokyo: Tuttle.
Brannen, M. Y. (1992) ' "Bwana Mickey": Constructing Cultural Consumption at Tokyo Disneyland', in J. J. Tobin (ed.), *Remade in Japan: Everyday Life and Consumer Taste in a Changing Society*, New Haven and London: Yale University Press.
Bring, M. and J. Wayembergh (1981) *Japanese Gardens: Design and Meaning*, New York: McGraw-Hill.
Caplan, P. (1994) 'Distanciation or Identification: What Difference Does it Make?' *Critique of Anthropology*, 14 (2): 99–115.
Comito, T. (1978) *The Idea of the Garden in the Renaissance*, New Brunswick, NJ: Rutgers University Press.
Condor, J. (1964) *Landscape Gardening in Japan*, New York: Dover Publications.
Creighton, M. (1992), 'The Depâto: Merchandising the West while Selling Japaneseness', in J. J. Tobin (ed.), *Remade in Japan: Everyday Life and Consumer Taste in a Changing Society*, New Haven and London: Yale University Press.
Daisen-in (n.d.) Created by Sôbisha to commemorate the 450th anniversary of Daisen-in, Kyoto: Daisen-in.
Geertz, C. (1989) *Works and Lives: The Anthropologist as Author*, Cambridge: Polity Press.
Gurdon, H. (1994) 'If You Can't Get to England, Don't Worry, We've had it Delivered', *The Weekend Daily Telegraph*, 26 November, p. 1.
Hatziyannaki, A. (1994) 'Part of Greece . . . in Japan', *Olympic Airways Inflight Magazine*, March 1994.

Hayakawa, M. (1973) *The Garden Art of Japan*, New York: Weatherhill and Tokyo: Heibonsha.

Hendry, J. (1988) '*Sutorenja toshite no minzokushi-gakusha – Nihon no tsutsumi bunka wo megutte* (The Ethnographer as Stranger: The Pros and Cons of receiving Gift-Wrapped Japan)', Yoshida Teigo and Hitoshi Miyake (eds), *Kosumosu to Shakai* (*Cosmos and Society*), Tokyo: Keio Tsushin.

—— (1992) 'The Paradox of Friendship in the Field: Analysis of a Long-term Anglo-Japanese Relationship', in J. Okely and H. Callaway (eds), *Anthropology and Autobiography*, London: Routledge.

—— (1993) *Wrapping Culture: Politeness, Presentation and Power in Japan and Other Societies*, Oxford: Clarendon Press.

—— (1994) 'Gardens and the Wrapping of Space in Japan: Some Benefits of a Balinese Insight', *Journal of the Anthropological Society of Oxford*, 25 (1): 11–19.

—— (1996) 'The Chrysanthemum Continues to Flower: Ruth Benedict and Some Perils of Popular Anthropology', in J. MacClancy and C. McDonaugh (eds), *Popularizing Anthropology*, London: Routledge.

—— (1997), 'Nature Tamed: Gardens as a Microcosm of Japan's View of the World', in Pamela Asquith and Arne Kalland (eds), *Japanese Images of Nature*, London: Curzon Press.

Kalland, A. (1992) 'Culture in Japanese Nature', in O. Bruun and A. Kalland (eds), *Asian Perceptions of Nature*, Nordic Proceedings in Asian Studies No. 3, Copenhagen: Nordic Institute for Asian Studies.

Keswick, M. (1986) *The Chinese Garden*, London: Academy Editions.

Knight, J. (1993) 'Rural *Kokusaika*? Foreign Motifs and Village Revival in Japan', *Japan Forum*, 5 (2): 203–16.

Kokuritsu, Kōen KyōKai (1981) *Nihon no Fukei (Shizen Kôen 50 shûnen kinen)*, Tokyo: Gyosei Ltd.

Kuck, L. (1968) *The World of the Japanese Garden: From Chinese Origins to Modern Landscape Art*, New York and Tokyo: Walker/Weatherhill.

Martinez, D. P. (forthcoming) 'Burlesquing Knowledge: Japanese Quiz Shows and Models of Knowledge', in Marcus Banks and Howard Morphy (eds), *Rethinking Visual Anthropology*, New Haven: Yale University Press.

Okely, J. and H. Callaway (eds) (1992) *Anthropology and Autobiography*, London: Routledge.

Pitman, J. (1994), 'Touring the World without Leaving Home', *The European: élan*, no. 224: 3.

Tachibana-no-Toshitsuna (1976) (trans. of eleventh-century ms.), *Sakuteiki* (trans. by Shigemaru Shimoyama), Tokyo: Toshikeikaku Kenkyûjo (Town and City Planners, Inc.).

Tobin, J. J. (ed.) (1992) *Remade in Japan: Everyday Life and Consumer Taste in a Changing Society*, New Haven and London: Yale University Press.

Yoshida, T. (1981) 'The Stranger as God: The Place of the Outsider in Japanese Folk Religion', *Ethnology*, 20 (2): 87–99.

—— (1987) 'Is Japan a Secular Society? – A Report on the Third Japan Anthropology Workshop Conference', *Japan Foundation Newsletter*, 15 (1): 21–3.

Yoshino, K. (1992) *Cultural Nationalism in Contemporary Japan*, London: Routledge.

Chapter 13

Representing identity

Angela Cheater and Ngapare Hopa

INTRODUCTION

It is extremely difficult to represent individual identity fully and accurately, because it is fluid, situational and fundamentally political. Complex relationships link individuals to the various categories and groups with which they are affiliated and from which they draw the components of their specific identities. Thus, the historicity of what social scientists have previously called 'culture' is contested (Touraine 1977). Furthermore, states both construct this historicity and attribute categorical identity to individuals. This chapter considers the role of the state in constructing identity, an approach shared by Gladney (1991) and Gell (1994).

Since the 1960s ethnogenesis (the ongoing creation of ethnicity) has been recognised by anthropologists (as well as by political activists involved in this process) as a political strategy in disputes over resources. Cohen (1969) argued that 'retribalisation' (the earlier term for ethnogenesis) is about protecting control over resources, and prefigured the later 'invention of tradition'. The temptation in older states, however, is to deny the political nature of ethnogenetic processes among indigenous minorities. For example, 'first nations' such as Saami, Amer-Indians, Maori have been responsible for shattering their colonists' construction of indigenous assimilation into undifferentiated democracies. These processes threaten the majoritarian assumptions of political integration in such states. However, Norton (1993) sees recently reaffirmed Maori identity as a construction of discourse, not politics; his account privileges the theoretical interpretations of outsiders (Hanson 1989; Keesing 1989; Linnekin 1990, 1992) over the detailed empirical accounts of elite insider intellectuals involved in this process (Greenland 1991; Jackson 1989; Walker 1990, 1994). We argue that this emphasis is misleading.

MAORI AND THE STATE

At the outset we question the nature of that identity known inter-nationally as 'Maori'. First, 'Maori' ethnicity is a colonial product, blanketing internal divisions among indigenous people themselves. It dates very precisely from the first week of February 1840 (Walker 1990: 94), when the missionaries drafting and translating the Treaty of Waitangi on behalf of Lieutenant Governor Hobson used 'Maori' (then meaning 'ordinary folk') in preference to 'New Zealanders' (as they had been known for 200 years) to refer to the country's indigenous inhabitants (Sharp 1990: 50). This latter designation was appropriated by colonial settlers, themselves later constructed as 'Pakeha' by the country's indigenous inhabitants.

Since 1840, therefore, the construction of Maori ethnicity has depended very heavily on the state, reflected in the special relationship which all seventy-plus Maori tribes[1] claim to the ambiguous Crown as their co-signatory to the Treaty of Waitangi. Although the British Crown was past coloniser and retains (through the Privy Council and the Governor-General) ultimate symbolic control of the (Pakeha) New Zealand state, by 1881 it had abandoned responsibility for its own Treaty of Waitangi (Orange 1987: 202). The New Zealand state now claims postcolonial status and seeks to remove the residual symbols of its former settler dependency, but rather oddly New Zealanders still refer to their state as 'the Crown'.

A second question relates to the processes involved in self-identifi-cation. Maori identity no longer has a rural base, since the urbanisation rate (80 per cent) does not differentiate Maori from other New Zealan-ders. In the 1991 census, 511,278 New Zealanders (15.2 per cent of the total) identified themselves as having some Maori ancestry, of whom 323,493 (63 per cent) claimed *only* Maori ethnicity.[2] In 1994, however, only 137,000[3] chose registration on the Maori voters' roll. This discrepancy is part of an ongoing trend. In 1975, the census rules were changed to permit ethnic self-identification and the Waitangi Tribunal[4] was estab-lished; substantial assets were subsequently transferred from the state to Maori. By 1991 the Maori proportion in the total population had nearly doubled, despite a net annual reproduction rate of 1.2 per cent. Simul-taneously, the proportion of Maori-roll voters in the total ethnic category fell steadily. In accordance with precolonial choice of political allegiance, most self-identified Maori wish to keep open their future identity options in national politics. Even at the level of national aggregates, then, collec-tive as well as individual Maori ethnicity is revealed as differentiated and situational, responding to state influences.

A third problem lies in the clear financial involvement of the state in the construction of Maoridom, particularly of 'tribes' (*iwi*) (Cheater 1994: 57-8). For example, the state has subsidised the Maori Ethnological

Research Board, urban *marae* (land set aside for ceremonial use) and the *kohanga reo* or 'language nests' for young children. In addition it has established the Maori Arts and Crafts Institute, the Waitangi Tribunal, the Maori Language Commission, tribal authority structures, various ephemeral statutory structures such as the Iwi Transition Agency, welfare services and Maori-language instruction in state schools. Finally, the role of *kaumatua* (tribal elders) was established within state bureaucracies.

In direct response to these processes of Maori identity construction by the state, oppositional pan-Maori political organisations emerged. The *kingitanga* (King Movement) started in 1853 and elected a Maori king – the Waikato chief Te Wherowhero – in 1858. Intertribal conferences were held at Auckland and Waitangi in the 1860s and 1880s, and the *kotahitanga* (Maori Parliament) was founded in the early 1890s (Orange 1987: 142, 192, 195, 224). Alternative parliaments, like syncretic religious movements of a political nature, signalled active attempts by Maori to recapture control of the production of their historicity from the rapidly developing state. However, these soon faded away to be replaced, over the past two decades, by land marches and occupations of territory over which owner-ship is disputed.

Before examining in detail contemporary conflicting representations of Maori identity arising from *iwi* and national politics, it is important to note that nearly 30 per cent of all self-identified urbanised Maori – many of whom probably do not speak the Maori language – cannot, or will not, identify with any *iwi* (tribe) or *hapu* (lineage). Given that state policy insists on devolving resources to *iwi*, people without *iwi* identity will therefore be excluded from access to the benefits of such resources, despite their self-identification as 'Maori'. Already, as an increasing number of Waitangi Tribunal claims are settled, and resources 'returned' to 'Maori' in the form of Tribal Trust Boards, these Trust Boards are compiling lists of member beneficiaries. The reconstruction of *iwi* by the state thus denies any resource-based meaning to self-representation as 'Maori' *without* effective tribal identity, even when a significant minority of Maori is detribalised. Clearly, therefore, in the Maori renaissance, 'cultural constructions of identity' have arisen from, or in opposition to, state action. This undermines Norton's (1993: 742) suggestion that identity emerges out of the generation of oppositional identities involved in the 'dialogue' of intergroup conflict, the invention of tradition, and the objec-tification of culture. Even oppositional intertribal identities have been fostered, wittingly or unwittingly, by state policy.

The state exerts a critical influence over *internal iwi* politics through its restoration of tribal resource bases. Although 335 claims before the Tri-bunal have not yet been determined,[5] the New Zealand state, which has unilaterally defined the extent of its own culpability for colonial aggression, wants final settlement of all resource claims quickly. Within the state's 'fiscal envelope', worth NZ$1 billion payable over the next decade, *iwi* are expected to negotiate their respective outstanding claims. The fiscal and date (1997) limits for final claims to the Waitangi Tribunal suggest that the state intends to cap Maori ethnogenesis by cutting its resource flow. This question of resources therefore frames the relationship between 'elite' negotiators and ordinary Maori people as a series of contests within the arena of national and tribal Maori politics. As the following examples show, the question of identity lies at the core of these contests: who decides who is Maori? What does 'being Maori' represent?

MAORI AND THE LAND

Maori expect, and their activists demand, the recognition of rights guaranteed them under Article 2 of the Treaty of Waitangi: the 'full exclusive and undisturbed possession of their Lands and Estates Fisheries and other Properties'. Maori assert that these rights, hinging on sovereign control (*rangatiratanga*), were never voluntarily relinquished but were instead gradually appropriated by the state (Jackson 1989; Walker 1990). Attempts to recover them have fuelled historical protests which continue through to the present. These have been complicated by the conflict in meaning between *rangatiratanga*, as conveyed in the Maori version of the Treaty of Waitangi, and the neologism, *kawanatanga*, used to translate British sovereignty from the English version (Kelsey 1990: 91–2).

Self-identification with the land is crucial to Maori identity – *tangata whenua* means 'people of the land' – but the state intervened early in indigenous land rights. It claimed a pre-emptive right to all unused Maori land through the Treaty of Waitangi (Orange 1987: 42), and later waged war against Maori owners reluctant to sell. Thus, by 1900, through conquest and confiscation, the new state had converted over 90 per cent of the country's land from indigenous to settler (including state) ownership (Walker 1990: 139). In particular, the confiscated (*raupatu*) land has been an issue of burning political importance to Maori ever since the land wars of 1845–72 (Belich 1986), and was inextricably interwoven into their identity construction in colonial times. We briefly examine one example of this integration of land loss into contemporary Maori identity. In the example below we can see how land loss has become entangled with attempts at reparation made within the national 'fiscal envelope'.

In the northwestern quadrant of the North Island, known as Waikato, most tribes regard themselves as descended from those founders of Maori society who arrived in the Tainui *waka* (canoe).[6] Maori identity in the Waikato is, however, ambiguous. The two options are either a putatively *descent-based waka* identity as 'Tainui', also glossed as an *iwi* identity; or a *locality- and descent-based iwi* identity as 'Waikato'. These two options are further complicated by the fact that 'Tainui' itself is a recently constructed identity: last century, *the* local identity was unambiguously 'Waikato'. 'Tainui' has only developed since 1946, when it was formally defined by the state[7] as comprising the thirty-three *hapu* (then understood as sub-tribes) of Waikato who had suffered confiscation of their lands in 1863. Tainui's institutionalised identity therefore dates from the establishment in 1947 of the Tainui Maori Trust Board (TMTB), to represent these *hapu*. The TMTB's founding goals included supporting and funding the *kingitanga* (king movement) and holding its *mana* 'until Tainui was united as a tribe'.[8]

Which *iwi* identity option ('Waikato', 'Tainui', or a hyphenated combination of the two) any individual in the Waikato region chooses is influenced by that person's view of, and relationship to, the *kingitanga* (king movement) as part of 'Tainui' rather than 'Waikato' institution-building and identity construction. Within the local Maori politics of the Waikato, it is inadvisable to express oneself, even implicitly, as being against the *kingitanga* as, in late 1994, the TMTB proposed that active support for the *kingitanga* be one criterion for its disbursement of financial benefits to *raupatu marae*. Although Tainui's claim to 1.2 million acres[9] has yielded smaller returns than many other land claims, what is important here is the state's view of this claim as a model for the settlement of others within the 'fiscal envelope'. Whether this claim has actually been dealt with satisfactorily remains to be seen. It was seemingly 'settled' by the 1946 Act, but unsatisfied members of younger generations have repeatedly succeeded in prising open apparently solid 'settlements' for renegotiation, not only in the Waikato.

Part of the Tainui *raupatu* 'settlement' involved a relatively small amount of land gifted in 1853 to the Anglican church to establish Maori schools, by an individual. But his heirs, as well as the five *hapu* in whose territory this land falls,[10] were effectively prevented from pursuing their specific claims to this land because the state, represented by the Minister of Lands, wished to hand these lands 'back to where they belong, with Tainui'.[11] 'Tainui' here did *not* mean the five *hapu* referred to above who had originally donated this land, nor even the thirty-three who had later suffered confiscation. Instead, the state willingly acceded to the TMTB's proposals to vest ownership of this and other returned land in the *kingitanga's* deceased founder[12] and to create three 'custodian trustees' from the royal lineage (including the Maori Queen) to supervise the TMTB as 'managing trustee' of the Potatau Te Wherowhero Trust. These trustees would disburse funds for educational purposes to those who registered as beneficiaries with the TMTB.

Through their recent *raupatu* claim and its compromise, Tainui's very astute negotiators therefore simultaneously strengthened, both symbolically and institutionally, their unvoiced claims to *iwi* and (for the *kingitanga*) pan-Maori identity. Although these claims were only implicitly

part of Tainui's discourse, with state collaboration they nonetheless succeeded. This was at the expense of the legitimate stakeholders in the land
who were clearly identified with specific *hapu*. Thus, these stakeholders
were placed in the difficult position of knowing that, if they were to
appeal the court's decision successfully, ownership of the land at issue
would revert to the state. If they defended their own *hapu* interests, they
ran the risk of being accused of acting against their own *iwi* and against
wider 'Maori' interests in generic reparation from the state. Their legal
case was good, but they had been politically worsted with respect to their
own interests and specific land-based identities. Nonetheless, they decided
as a matter of principle to defend their identity in further legal action
despite minimum cost estimates of NZ$25,000 and the state's attempts to
void any such action in the settlement legislation.

Clearly, over time, state and *kingitanga* have been moving closer to
one another in their mutual support, notwithstanding the *kingitanga's*
traditional rejection of state authority. Their mutual collaboration has
yielded state legitimation of ostensibly autonomous institutions and *kingitanga*/Tainui legitimation of biculturalism. The political worry for some is
that this alliance of interest may have affected specific sub-tribal identities
and effectively mystified ordinary Waikato Maori concerning their long-
term interests in restored assets.

MAORI IDENTITY AND RESOURCES

Our second example of the problem of making representations of Maori
identity centres on the question of resources. In the early 1980s, the
New Zealand Labour Party simultaneously developed two potentially
conflicting policies, involving the Treaty of Waitangi and the restructuring
of the New Zealand economy.[13] Economic restructuring saw the very
broad rights of Article 2 of the Treaty redefined as 'principles' rather han
rights (Kelsey 1990: 92–3). The corporate privatisation of state trading
operations and fisheries particularly affected Maori and their resource
claims under the Treaty (Kelsey 1990), with the result that the ensuing
contest over resources came to include litigation between the state and
Maori claimants of pan-tribal as well as *iwi*- and *hapu*-specific identities.

For example, corporatisation of state-owned assets threatened Maori
claims to a range of resources they wanted returned and therefore
affected Maori efforts to reconstitute their ethnicity on a resource base.
While the 1987 State-Owned Enterprise Act protected land claims already
lodged (depending on the Waitangi Tribunal's final recommendations
regarding specific claims), there was no protection for new claims or for
others still gestating. Furthermore, given the length of the Tribunal hearings and the speed at which corporatisation was taking place, there was
no guarantee that the resources at issue would even be in the possession

of a state-owned enterprise by the time potential future claims were formulated. Information and Crown maps on what lands were to be allocated to state-owned enterprises were unavailable since the state had not prepared them; and where there *was* information, *iwi* access to it was deliberately denied (Kelsey 1990: 86–7). Moreover, the Act covered only land, not coal, forests, rivers or lake beds, which would generate further disputes. The newly formed corporations were ignorant of the existing protections for Maori claims in their governing Act. Clearly, corporatisation created new problems for the claim process.

In response to these problems the pan-Maori, state-established New Zealand Maori Council (NZMC)[14] expressed concern that the resource interests of many smaller *iwi* remained vulnerable, and that the existing protection of claims was inadequate under the State-Owned Enterprise Act. On their behalf, therefore, in 1987 the Council applied to the High Court for an injunction preventing transfer of any assets subject to claims before the Waitangi Tribunal. The adjudication of this injunction upheld the sovereignty of the New Zealand Parliament, reiterating that the Treaty of Waitangi and its principles would not be legally enforceable unless incorporated by statute into domestic law. The practical outcome of the case was a judicial request for the Crown and Maori to cooperate in establishing a system for addressing Maori concerns. No tangible assets were gained by Maori and the Crown remained in control. However, Treaty 'principles' guided the agreement that any Crown lands sold by state-owned enterprises would be reacquired and returned to Maori ownership if this was recommended by the Waitangi Tribunal. For other resources – state-owned Forestcorp trees or Coalcorp coal – the position was unclear. Thus the NZMC intervention collectively secured some new protection for land claims, reinforcing the centrality of land within Maori identity-construction processes.

A FISHY STORY?

Perhaps the most controversial of all resource issues has been the privatisation of the fishing industry, paralleling the corporatisation battle. Indeed, fish were already on the table during the litigation and resolution of corporatisation issues: the major Maori actors were frequently stretched between the two (Kelsey 1990: 99). Although the state accommodated some Maori rights within the fishing industry, it retained ultimate control over the resource and its future use. By conferring the status of 'Maori negotiator' on individuals who were merely litigants in or observers of the claim process, the state precluded 'other potential claimants entering the debates and complicating the field' and, to some degree, detached the negotiators from their *iwi* bases (Walker 1994: 15). Elevated within the power structure of the state, these negotiators were pejoratively described by fellow-Maori as the 'brown cabinet' (Walker 1994).

Maori had dominated the New Zealand fishing industry well into the nineteenth century, until they were driven out by their colonisers, who later constructed indigenous fishing rights so that they were limited to recreational and ceremonial needs. By 1983, industrial overfishing and a failure to conserve the resource persuaded the state to create a Fishing Industry Board. However, Maori were not consulted. In 1986 this Board defined quota management areas and total allowable catches for different species. Quotas were individually transferable private property rights to catch and sell a certain tonnage of fish. Holders of quotas could use them themselves, or sell or lease them to others. This system effectively privatised the fisheries and ignored the Maori argument that, under the Treaty of Waitangi, New Zealand fisheries were solely owned by Maori.

Five tribes in the far North Island, with a long precolonial involvement in commercial fishing, whose 'Muriwhenua'[15] claim was made before the Waitangi Tribunal, feared that issuing quotas would remove fisheries from Crown control. The Tribunal therefore urgently requested the government not to allocate quotas until the claim had been considered. This request was ignored, but an interim report characterised individually transferable quotas as contrary to the principles of the Treaty, noting that there should be negotiations with the tribes concerned for the commercial right to fish their waters (Kelsey 1990: 114). In 1987 a claim to this effect was lodged in the High Court jointly by the New Zealand Maori Council,[16] the Tainui Maori Trust Board, Ngai Tahu[17] and the five 'Muriwhenua' tribes. The court ruled in favour of the claimants and advised the government to negotiate with its *iwi* partners for the use of their resource.

In keeping with the court's reiteration of the legal status of Maori and the Crown as treaty partners, and with Article 2 guarantees of *rangatiratanga*, the Maori negotiators claimed 100 per cent of the fisheries, but conceded a willingness to share 50 per cent with their treaty partner. However, this put identity at issue in that it resulted in dissension among the Maori negotiators themselves, concerned as they were to protect their individual tribal interests as much as their collective 'Maori' interests.

Over the next few months, numerous proposals sought to diminish the agreed 50 per cent Maori share. Perhaps as a defence against such proposals, the Minister of Maori Affairs commissioned a development strategy for Maori commercial fishing, which was produced by the University of Waikato's Centre for Maori Studies and Research. They recommended that Maori fishing quotas should be controlled and administered by a corporate Maori structure rather than be fragmented by distribution to *iwi*. The aim was to open the commercial fisheries to Maori participation with a strong, corporate, capital base, a move which conflicted with state determination not to deliver complete control over the fishing industry to Maori. Such a corporate structure would balance pan-Maori *rangatiratanga* against guardianship of local-level fishing interests. A fully commercial, profit-oriented company would allow for the representation of both state and regional Maori interests on its Board, while creating a network of *iwi* fishing enterprises. Regional offices would allow for representation of lower-level Maori interests through negotiation with canoe-based tribes and confederations.

Eventually, the 1989 Maori Fisheries Act delivered levels of control that fell far short of Maori expectations, even when considering localised fishing resources. Instead, the Act provided for a pan-tribal 'Maori' settlement through a two-tier structure, the Maori Fisheries Commission (MFC) and its commercial wing (Walker 1994: 15). A much-diminished quota (10 per cent) was allocated, the full acquisition of which would take four years, and the Act pre-empted independent action by *iwi* resentful over their loss of autonomy and exclusion from the decision-making process. However, in 1992 an opportunity to expand Maori fish quotas arose when an industrial fishing company, Sealords, came onto the market for NZ$375 million. MFC negotiators struck a deal with the state, which put up NZ$150 million to finance Maori in the purchase of half of Sealords; joint-venture partners bought the other half. The conditions of this arrangement required Maori to relinquish their claim to all fisheries; to surrender the protection of their existing fishing rights; and to accept a fixed 20 per cent of quota on all new species. The deal also brought Maori into partnership with private-sector capital, a new relationship also developing in other sectors.

This deal was not, however, without its critics. The cleavage between coastal and inland tribes over offshore fishing rights was a specific feature of the dispute, with coastal *iwi* arguing for limited distribution against inland tribes wanting a share. *Iwi* concerned about employment opportunities in the fishing industry were unhappy about being 'consulted' only after the agreement had been reached, and were not convinced, as one negotiator alleged, that it was 'the only deal in town' (Walker 1994: 16). The issues were not satisfactorily debated: tribal representatives were not briefed before being called to Parliament in September 1992 to sign the Deed of Settlement; some attended thinking it was just another meeting on fish, and were then expected to read a 26-page document and comprehend its economic and political implications before signing on behalf of their *hapu* or *iwi*; others refused to sign because they did not have a mandate to do so (Walker 1994: 17).

Some *iwi* later took their complaints to the Waitangi Tribunal, the High Court and the Court of Appeal. Here, for the first time, the negotiators from the MFC were questioned about their mandate and asked to specify whose interests they really represented (Walker 1992: 1). The Deed of Settlement signatures show numerous anomalies, reflecting carelessness, imprecision and haste, but its most invidious feature was the elimination of *iwi* rights to make any further claims on fisheries for commercial purposes. It also contained the seed of the 1994 'fiscal envelope':

> Maori recognise that the Crown has fiscal constraints and that this settlement will necessarily restrict the Crown's ability to meet from any fund which the Crown establishes as part of the Crown's overall settlement framework, the settlement of other claims arising from the Treaty of Waitangi.
>
> (New Zealand Government 1992: 22)

Thus, the haste to get the Deed signed, the failure of government and negotiators to ensure that the issues were properly debated on *marae* around the country, and the elimination of the right to claim under the Treaty, drew an angry and bitter response. Thirteen dissenting tribes sought a High Court injunction against the Deed.[18] At the court hearing concerns were aired about 'Maori' leadership and decision-making; the consultation process (or lack of it); types of leaders, their means of appointment and their mandates; and who particular leaders were actually representing when they signed the Deed. Technical questions were also raised: is there a difference of meaning between the Maori word *hapu* and the English word *tribe* in the Treaty texts? Is *hapu* a tribe or a sub-tribe? Should leaders of *iwi* (recently institutionalised by the state) or *hapu* (legitimated by the Treaty) represent their people? The deal was opposed by six Maori Members of Parliament, and a National Maori Congress representative enjoined the United Nations to investigate this violation of indigenous rights by the government of New Zealand (Walker 1994: 19). This confusion over ethnic identity was acknowledged by the chairman of the National Maori Congress[19] who, in 1993, cautioned that these issues would haunt the state well into the future.

The conflict over Sealords between the members of the 'brown cabinet' and *iwi* thus illuminates the complexities, tensions and dynamics involved in the (re)construction of both collective 'Maori' and specific *iwi* identities. It also highlights the influential role of the government, which clearly manipulated these processes in accordance with its own agenda by recognising specific leaders on the basis of its own particular statutory definitions.

THE FISCAL ENVELOPE: A FINAL SOLUTION?

On 8 December 1994 the state released three booklets entitled *Crown Proposals for the Settlement of Treaty of Waitangi Claims*, which confirmed previous rumours about state intentions to finalise settlement of all outstanding Maori resource claims within a limit of NZ$1 billion. Maori opposition to the 'fiscal envelope' focused on the 1995 commemoration of the signing of the Treaty of Waitangi, which, in its Maori version, preserved the sovereign decision-making of New Zealand's indigenous people. As we have shown, however, the Treaty is increasingly threatened as a future platform from which to assert a separate, resource-based Maori identity. Activists so disrupted these ritual proceedings, insulting state officials and raising the *kotahitanga* flag to displace the New Zealand Navy Ensign of the Governor-General, that officials and overseas diplomats left the *marae* and the evening events were cancelled. The media sensationalised the outrage and the embarrassment of the Prime Minister, state officials (some Maori), invited guests and local Maori hosts. While the protesters were condemned[20] for failing to observe common courtesies and *marae* protocol, a broader perspective might focus on the differing representations of Maori identity offered by Television New Zealand,[21] radical activists, Maori elders and war veterans.[22] The activists merely repeated the annual protests of a decade earlier, including the 1984 march under the *kotahitanga* banner (Walker 1990: 234–6). At the root of their protest was the issue of sovereignty, *rangatiratanga*, as well as that of identity.

By mid-September 1994, before the official release of the state's proposals on 8 December, the Minister of Maori Affairs had left no doubt about the Crown's assimilationist intentions: to determine Treaty settlements and render them non-negotiable; to limit the amount of money available for settlement; to ensure that settlements would be full and final; to retain ownership of natural resources (land, fisheries, forests); to provide services to Maori in the same way as to all New Zealanders without regard to specific Maori rights; to determine procedures (including a 'deed of mandate') for tribal representation on Treaty claims; and, finally, to remove the term 'Maori' from the law books (*Te Kawariki* October 1994, p. 1; January 1995, p. 2).

Pre-release opposition to the fiscal envelope came from various Maori groups and organisations, including young members of *ad hoc* interest groupings marginalised and disenfranchised by tribal elders, as well as older members of conservative Maori organisations, such as the Federation of Maori Authorities.

With the release of the state's proposals, the momentum of protest increased and, prompted by the requests of *iwi* seeking his advice, Sir Hepi Te Heuheu, paramount chief of Tuwharetoa, publicly wrote to the Prime Minister,[23] stating that he had 'no option but to reject the total policy framework contained in the *Crown Proposals for the Settlement of Treaty of Waitangi Claims*'; and that

> [t]he unilateral diminution by the Government of the fundamental constitutional significance of Article Two of the Treaty of Waitangi is

neither justifiable nor acceptable. I believe that policies which minimise or avoid Article Two will not provide constructive or enduring options.

Early in 1995, a meeting called by Sir Hepi to discuss the fiscal envelope proposals unanimously rejected these proposals and demanded an 'immediate halt to the disposal through sale or other means, of all assets and resources held directly or indirectly by the Crown and/or public authorities over which Maori have claimed an interest or are likely to claim an interest' (Tuwharetoa Maori Trust Board 1995). Except for a few individuals, some of whom have opposed its past actions, the Tainui Maori Trust Board, representing Waikato, was conspicuously absent. From Waikato, on the state's settlement proposals, there was silence, because, on 21 December 1994, the TMTB had signed a Heads of Agreement with the Crown for the settlement of its *raupatu* land claim, effectively (including an escalation clause) within 'fiscal envelope' parameters. An attempt by a youth group to have the assembly of tribes condemn the TMTB's actions was lost. Affirmation for Tainui's stance came from Ngapuhi and Te Arawa, both linked genealogically to the *kingitanga*. While rejecting the Crown's proposals, their representatives acknowledged the right of Tainui to make its own decisions without interference, thus wittingly or unwittingly confirming the autonomous nature of tribal politics historically through to the present. While other tribes have pursued their claims through the Waitangi Tribunal, the TMTB has, since the 1980s, recurrently sought to negotiate directly with the state on behalf of *iwi*. Its strategy has tried simultaneously to create an independent Tainui (rather than Waikato) *iwi* identity within a collective 'Maori' identity, but clearly its *iwi* identity-construction takes precedence.

CONCLUSIONS

In this chapter we have tried to link state policy and action to issues of identity and its representation at both tribal and pan-Maori levels, and to identify externally generated opportunities for, and constraints on, Maori ethnogenesis in self-proclaimed postcolonial New Zealand. The evidence we have examined here is as much legal and political as anthropological, but is of core importance to all three disciplines in understanding ethnogenesis at the different levels of *hapu*, *iwi*, and Maoridom as a whole. As the state has rigidified *iwi* through tribal trust boards, *iwi* may threaten to eliminate *hapu*. Modern political processes may thus finally destroy the core fluidity of power alignments in Maori political traditions, without overall unity being achieved.

In summary, we are disturbed by anthropological representations of identity which favour the oversimplification that ethnic identity is an innocent sociological outcome of non-threatening discourse set in contexts in which social, economic and political factors are equally weighted. For the actors themselves, 'representation' is often double-edged, as when representation of identity connotes, mutually and implicitly, political representation. When those driving the process of identity-construction define their activity as a long-term 'struggle without end' (Walker 1990) and, like postmodernists, are 'grimly serious about their self-representations' (Lee and Ackerman 1994: 43), these emic claims should not be diluted by etic 'objectivity'. In this chapter we have treated seriously political actors' representations of their own actions, being acutely aware that our interpretations, as others, may enter the political process to their detriment. In the real world of contested representations of identity as a political process, real people are harassed,[24] suffer threats to their employment and personal security, nearly bankrupt themselves on litigation over their claims to rights and resources and may die in defence of identity claims. Emic accounts are, of course, themselves part of these political processes and, as such, partisan by omission or commission, but even as partisan discourse, they self-identify as political in intent. Discourse is a very small part of a broader political reality to those living it; and we have tried to show that its major importance lies in the hegemonic discourse of statutory definitions.

NOTES

1 Although only half this number ever signed the Treaty!
2 1991 *Census*, NZ Maori Population and Dwellings, table 31.
3 A 32 per cent (33,000) increase on the previous figure of 104,000.
4 The Waitangi Tribunal investigates claims from Maori tribes and lineages to natural resources (land, water, minerals, fish, lake beds, forests, usufructuary rights impaired by industrial pollution) which, although protected under the Treaty of Waitangi, were later taken from Maori by various illegal means. The Tribunal also makes recommendations to the state regarding return of, or recompense for, these lost resources. Initially limited to recent appropriations, in the mid 1980s the Tribunal's remit was extended back to 1840, resulting in hundreds of currently backlogged claims. The New Zealand government has recently signalled its intention to disallow new claims after 1997 and to settle all existing claims which may be validated by the Tribunal within the limitations of the 'fiscal envelope'.
5 Only 96 (22 per cent) of the 431 claims registered since the inception of the Tribunal in 1975 have been adjudicated (*Te Manutukutuku* 1994, 29: 2).
6 There have been recent assertions of independent *hapu* identity that reject historical incorporation in the Tainui *waka* and claim pre-Tainui origins.
7 In the Waikato Maniapoto Claim Settlement Act.
8 Evidence of Shane Ringa Solomon to the Maori Land Court hearing at Turangawaewae on 17 March 1993, transcript p. 25.
9 The figure of 1.2 million is always quoted by the TMTB, despite its public acknowledgement that 312,262 acres (26 per cent of the original total) were returned to Maori ownership twenty years after a 1920s commission of enquiry had upheld the Waikato claim (Orange 1987: 237) and four decades before

the *raupatu* claim was lodged with the Waitangi Tribunal (Special Supplement to *Kia Hiwa Ra*, September 1994, p. 1).

10 These five *hapu* had earlier claims to this land, but do not appear to have objected to its donation for educational purposes.

11 Statement to the Maori Land Court hearing held at Turangawaewae, 17 March 1993, transcript p. 6.

12 Precedent came from the vesting, in October 1975, of title to the Royal Graveyard in Potatau Te Wherowhero.

13 'Rogernomics', named after the Labour Minister of Finance Sir Roger Douglas, restructured the state sector by separating policy, regulatory and trading roles. The state withdrew from welfare-oriented subsidies to service and production enterprises.

14 Following a 1961 state-sponsored conference of leading Maori citizens, the New Zealand Maori Council was created by the state as a permanent consultative body, comprising delegates from District Maori Councils.

15 This claim focused on customary fishing rights, but covered traditional fishing grounds within a 25-mile offshore zone hundreds of kilometres in length, thus requiring the regulation of industrial fishing in this huge coastal area (Orange 1987: 253).

16 Which, after the ruling, received from the state NZ$1.5 million *ex gratia* as a sign of good faith (Kelsey 1990: 113).

17 The major South Island tribe, with a massive stake in offshore fishing.

18 Te Runanga o Wharekauri Rekohu Inc vs. Attorney-General 1992, Court of Appeal 297/92 (November).

19 The National Maori Congress was formed in 1989 as a forum for tribes to discuss issues of relevance to Maori social, cultural and economic advancement. This voluntary association of roughly 50 *iwi* is funded by levies on the participants and attempts to present a unified 'Maori' voice to the state. Alone among Maori organisations, it has an independent, populist mandate without supporting legislation.

20 As by the press: *New Zealand Herald* 7 February 1995; *Waikato Times* 7 and 8 February 1995.

21 In June 1995, TVNZ publicly apologised for its representations of one fisheries negotiator's status.

22 Addressing a special ceremony at Rotorua the day after Waitangi, in honour of Maori veterans of the two world wars, Lt-Col Sir Charles Bennett DSO claimed that equity, justice and partnership had been swept away in the state's proposals for settling Maori grievances, leaving the remaining members of the Maori Battalion to pose several questions to themselves: did they go overseas for the wrong reasons? Have Maori been conned by the fiscal envelope of 1995? If the events of Waitangi Day 1995 had been transposed to the 1939 era, would they have volunteered? (*NZ Herald* 8 February 1995).

23 17 December 1994.

24 Pare Hopa, a former member of the Waitangi Tribunal, on behalf of her Waikato *hapu* (Ngati Wairere), has been involved in personalised disputes with the Tainui Maori Trust Board over returned resources and interpretive issues.

REFERENCES

Belich, J. (1986) *The New Zealand Wars*, Auckland: Penguin.

Binney, J. (1990) 'Kawanatanga and Rangatiratanga 1840–1860', in J. Binney, J. Bassett and E. Olssen (eds), *The People and the Land / Te Tangata me te Whenua: An Illustrated History of New Zealand 1820–1920*, Auckland: Allen & Unwin/Wellington: Port Nicholson Press.

Centre for Maori Studies and Research (1987) *Kaimoana, Kaiawa, Kairoto, Maori Fishing Rights: The Tainui Perspective*, Hamilton: University of Waikato, Centre for Maori Studies and Research.

Cheater, A. P. (1994) 'Contextualising Cultural Policy in Post-colonial States: Zimbabwe and New Zealand', *Culture and Policy*, 6 (1): 45–67.

Cohen, A. (1969) *Custom and Politics in Urban Africa*, London: Routledge & Kegan Paul.

Cox, L. (1993) *Kotahitanga – The Search for Maori Unity*, Oxford: Oxford University Press.

Gell, S. M. S. (1994) 'Legality and Ethnicity', *Critique of Anthropology*, 14 (4): 355–92.

Gladney, D. C. (1991) *Muslim Chinese: Ethnic Nationalism in the People's Republic*, Cambridge, MA and London: Harvard University Press for Council on East Asian Studies. (Harvard East Asian Monographs No. 149.)

Greenland, H. (1991) 'Maori Ethnicity as Ideology', in P. Spoonley, D. Pearson and C. Macpherson (eds), *Nga Take: Ethnic Relations and Racism in Aotearoa / New Zealand*, Palmerston North: Dunmore Press.

Hanson, A. (1989) 'The Making of the Maori: Cultural Invention and its Logic', *American Anthropologist*, 91: 890–902.

Jackson, M. (1989) 'The Crown, the Treaty, and the Usurpation of Maori Rights.' Paper presented to Conference on Human Rights in the Pacific and Asia. Wellington.

Keesing, R. (1989) 'Creating the Past: Custom and Identity in the Contemporary Pacific', *Contemporary Pacific*, 1: 19–42.

Kelsey, J. (1990) *A Question of Honour? Labour and the Treaty, 1984–1989*, Wellington: Allen & Unwin.

Lee, R. L. M. and S. E. Ackerman (1994) 'Farewell to Ethnography?' *Critique of Anthropology*, 14 (4): 339–54.

Linnekin, J. (1990) 'The Politics of Culture in the Pacific', in J. Linnekin and L. Poyer (eds), *Cultural Identity and Ethnicity in the Pacific*, Honolulu: University of Hawaii Press.

—— (1992) 'On the Theory and Politics of Cultural Construction in the Pacific', *Oceania*, 62: 249–63.

Minister of Maori Affairs (1988) *Partnership Response: Policy Statement / Te Urupare Rangapu: Te Rarangi Kaupapa*, Wellington: Ministry of Maori Affairs.

New Zealand Court of Appeal (1987) *The Treaty of Waitangi in the Court of Appeal: The Full Judgment of the Court in the NZMC's Case'*, Wellington: Government Printer.

—— (1992) *Te Runanga o Wharekauri Rekohu Inc vs Attorney-General (297/92)*, Wellington: Government Printer.

New Zealand Government (1991) *Census*, Wellington: Department of Statistics.

—— (1992) *Her Majesty the Queen and Maori Deed of Settlement (Sealords)*, Wellington: Government Printer.

—— (1994) *Crown Proposals for the Settlement of Treaty of Waitangi Claims*, Wellington: Te Puni Kokiri.

New Zealand Maori Congress (1985) *Submission of the NZMC on the Fisheries Amendment Bill*, Wellington: New Zealand Maori Congress.

New Zealand Maori Land Court Waikato–Maniapoto Maori Land District (1992) *Hearing* 23 December (*Application by the Minister of Lands to Vest Crown Land in Potatau te Wherowhero*) at Wings Conference Centre, Hamilton.

—— (1993) *Hearing* 17 March at Turangawaewae, Ngaruawahia.

Norton, R. (1993) 'Culture and Identity in the South Pacific: A Comparative Analysis', *Man* (ns) 28 (4): 741–59.

Orange, C. (1987) *The Treaty of Waitangi*, Wellington: Bridget Williams Books.

Sharp, A. (1990) *Justice and the Maori*, Auckland: Oxford University Press.

Sykes, A. (1994) *The Fiscal Envelope – The Generation Gap* (Video). Auckland: Faculty of Education, University of Auckland.

Touraine, A. (1977) *The Self-Production of Society*, Chicago and London: University of Chicago Press.

Tuwharetoa Maori Trust Board (1995) *Hirangi Resolutions*, Turangi: Tuwharetoa Maori Trust Board.

Waitangi Tribunal Division (1988) *Muriwhenua Report: WAI 22*, Wellington: Department of Justice, Waitangi Tribunal Division.

—— (1994) *Te Manutukutuku* (Newsletter), no. 29, Wellington: Department of Justice, Waitangi Tribunal Division.

Walker, R. (1987) *Nga Tau Tohetohe*, Auckland: Penguin.

—— (1990) *Ka Whawhai Tonu Matou / Struggle Without End*, Auckland: Penguin.

—— (1992) *Nga Toka Tu Moana – Maori Leadership and Decision-Making*, Wellington: Te Puni Kokiri.

—— (1994) 'Maori Leadership.' Paper presented at Hui Whakapumau / Maori Development Conference, Palmerston North, Massey University.

Chapter 14

Some political consequences of theories of Gypsy ethnicity

The place of the intellectual

Judith Okely

Representation by the intellectual or academic of ethnic ideologies could be interpreted in a purely scholastic fashion where a chronology of different theories might remain largely unread by the groups themselves. The complexity emerges when it is recognised that ideas have consequences beyond the scholar, both in the larger dominant society and for ethnic groups or minorities. There are historically specific factors which affect the emergence and influence of some ideas as opposed to others. The ideas do not spring from the intellectual as isolate. In addition, while the theories of individual intellectuals may be fully embraced, they may also be ignored, thoroughly distorted or only partially understood.

The question as to whether ideas in themselves bring change or ensure continuity can be situated in an old debate within Marxism. The now generally discredited and reductionist position of economism claimed that ideas merely reflected the mode of production. The 1970s Marxist interpretation of the role of ideas in history (via Althusser and Gramsci) rejects the notion that ideas are mere epiphenoma, but instead may reflect, and in turn affect or overdetermine, the infrastructure. Gramsci (1971) gave special place to the role of the intellectual, while Althusser (1971) emphasised the importance of pedagogy and its ideology as part of the state apparatus.

I start from the theoretical assumption that the power of some ideas as opposed to others depends on the historic moment that gave the context for those ideas to flourish. But in turn those ideas, as crystallised by academics and intellectuals, have the potential to affect history. There are additional complexities in the analysis. It cannot be presumed that intellectuals even in an established position as academics inevitably act as the state's or 'dominant group's "deputies" exercising the subaltern functions of social hegemony and political government' (Gramsci 1971: 12). Gramsci is convincingly sceptical of 'that social utopia by which the intellectuals think of themselves as "independent", autonomous, endowed with a character of their own' (ibid.: 8). Nevertheless, I contend that intellectuals and even the most ensconced academics are in a position to present ideas that are inconsistent with and potentially subversive to the currently identifiable policies and ideology associated with either Gramsci's 'civil' or 'political' society (ibid.: 12).

I suggest several broad possibilities in considering the influence of ideas and intellectuals. Some may overlap:

1 Anonymised and generalised

First, there is what can be identified as the generalised and impersonal scholarly influence of ideas and concepts in history. Here the notions have become largely detached from the original writers and theorists. My examples in this chapter include diffusionism and the association of a pristine culture and 'root' language with a single geographical place of origin for all subsequent language users.

2 Named influence within an academic specialism and possibly beyond

In contrast to Foucault's thesis that the individual author counts for little, Said (1978: 23–4) has been concerned with the dialectic between named texts and a complex collective formation. In this spirit, I am concerned with linking individual intellectuals and texts with ideas about ethnicity, and the changing position of an ethnic group.

This second category is where the intellectual's named and referenced text has influence with a specialist readership. The ideas may be utterly plausible within the specific disciplines. If written in an accessible language, the text can reach a wider readership. Some aspects may also be expedient for a specific ethnic group's construction of an ideology at that historical moment, while other aspects may be ignored. Alternatively, the ideas may be absorbed much later. Selectivity can similarly be found in the use to which the text is put by the state's majority representatives.

3 Named but unintended influence

This concerns the influence of the intellectual's ideas in entirely unintended, and possibly distorted contexts. The reading and use of the text may have the opposite effect to that imagined by the originator. Here the postmodernist's 'death of the author' and her/his intentions have relevance. Usually the context is beyond the academic discipline and yet where the texts give authority precisely because they are individually named. The ideas may prove unexpectedly convenient for another group which the intellectual had not directly addressed, for example, in this case New Age Travellers.

4 Policy adviser

A further category of influence is where an intellectual or academic acts as policy researcher or even political adviser. Broadly, the policy adviser is obliged to address the dominant decision-makers within pre-set and often limited procedures. The interpretation of his or her ideas may end up in a different form.

It is this category of influence that is most vulnerable to the immediately recognised interests of Gramsci's 'political' society, especially in Britain. In the 1960s and 1970s, there was an established practice in government of consultation with intellectuals or 'the great and the good'. My example of the Gypsies in this chapter records varied non-governmental consultations during policy formulations. The historical context has now changed. In the 1980s and 1990s, Royal Commissions have almost disappeared. The great and the good are bypassed, and almost three decades of liberal policies towards the Gypsies have been completely reversed.

5 Activist

The intellectual may have influence as an activist. Ideally, the intellectual should be in a position to combine both theory and practice. At the same time, the activist-intellectual draws on special skills as a knowledge base for action. The activist might attempt to effect change by extra-parliamentary means. Some individuals are charismatic initiators. Here the mass media can be exploitable. Again, the historical and cultural context is relevant. Whereas in England, if not Britain, the intellectual has a somewhat subdued and even denigrated position in the power structure, in France there has existed a huge respect for intellectuals beyond the academic portals (Gramsci 1971: 18; Sartre 1978).

6 The intellectual as insider or outsider

The ethnic identity of the intellectual is very relevant. Gramsci's rather flexible notion of the organic intellectual is most appropriate (1971). For the intellectual, whether as academic specialist, author, policy adviser or activist, membership of an ethnic group is cultural capital in a struggle of representation. Intellectuals as members of an ethnic group can be found in each of the categories 2 to 5 or all simultaneously. Outsider intellectuals, sympathetic or antagonistic to the ethnic group, have varying influence in the representation of ethnicity. There are also representations by individuals claiming fictive membership of the ethnic group (Liégeois 1976).

I shall examine the range of possible influences and positions for the intellectual in relation to the ideological and political representations of a relatively powerless minority, the Gypsies. Ideologies of Gypsy ethnicity have shifted, intersected or conflicted according to the historical moment. I draw mainly on my multifaceted experience of being involved with Gypsies, non-Gypsy interventions and anthropological research during a period of twenty-five years. The selective readings of my own texts by others and their influences form part of the ethnography of this chapter.

THEORIES OF ORIGIN: DEPERSONALISED OR INDIVIDUALLY AUTHORED

In the light of the first and second categories of influence, I shall consider the more general effects of non-specific social theories upon the group. Elsewhere (Okely 1983, 1984), I have outlined how the Gypsies were first recorded as 'Egyptians' in Britain in 1505 and under other labels in Europe.

By the nineteenth century, etymologists and scholars had begun to document Romany or 'Gypsy' dialects and 'languages'. Close connections were made to a pre AD 1000 Sanskrit. These findings were then combined with diffusionist theories of culture. The Gypsies provided a perfect case study: all similarities among such groups were explained by migration from India; the Aryan cradle. It suited the Indianists to privilege a linear migratory explanation for some linguistic elements, but not for the European vocabularies and languages found among Gypsies. These theories have remained influential without regard for competing theories from the social sciences. Named authors are less frequently referred to. Speculative theories have become hardened 'facts'.

There are powerful attractions in these origin myths. This is less an Orientalism (Said 1978) but more an 'Orientalisation' of Occidentals. It is paradoxical that the Gypsies became acceptable to some only if they could be reified as 'the other' from outside the West. This reification has had some disabling consequences for those so classified, although sometimes exoticism has been perceived as a form of romantic approval. Ideologies of Indian 'race' have been used to single out an acceptable or extinct mythical few. In this, non-Gypsy intellectuals and 'gentlemen scholars' have had influence (Okely 1983).

A counter-theory to Indianism can be seen as an example of the second and third categories of influence respectively. As sceptical anthropologist, in my monograph *The Traveller-Gypsies* (1983) and in 1984, I questioned the single Indian origin and linear migration as sufficient explanation for the Gypsies' first 'appearance' in Europe. I suggested that it is no coincidence that their visibility emerged with the collapse of feudalism, when a multiplicity of persons was thrown into the market place. Whereas such theories have been absorbed seemingly without huge controversy within the discipline of social anthropology, they have either been ignored by a genre of gypsiologists or mistakenly interpreted as an ideological de(con)struction of an ethnic group. Alternatively, my counter-theory has been welcomed by Scottish, Irish (Okely 1994) and New Age Traveller representatives.

During my years of fieldwork among Gypsies in England, Indian ancestry was never claimed nor ever a subject of discussion. Gypsies would sometimes with genuine intellectual curiosity ask me, as an academic expert, where they had come from. The discussions addressed broad philosophical questions.

One evening, several Travellers in my trailer asked me where human beings had come from. When I outlined the Indian origin theory for the Gypsies, one Gypsy woman poked fun at her husband: 'You little Indian you!' She was more likely to be adding a cultural layer of cowboys and American Indians than the subcontinent to the joke.

FICTIVE REPRESENTATIVES AND ACTIVISTS

Although intellectuals may be non-literate, in the case of Gypsies there are still relatively few examples of individual ethnic members of the group who are identified as literate intellectuals. A major reason is the Gypsies' history as a non-literate people. So the Gypsies' direct access to ideas emanating from academic texts may be even more distorted than that of a literate population. The other major explanation is the stigma attached to Gypsy ancestry among those individuals who have chosen to work and live in a mainly non-Gypsy ambiance. There are, however, historical moments when it is relatively safe or even advantageous to acknowledge Gypsy descent and identity. This has occurred since the 1970s in the West and in the 1990s in Eastern Europe (Beck 1993).

In the 1970s, during my early and main fieldwork, there were very few Gypsy political representatives, let alone literate intellectuals in Britain who operated in non-Gypsy (gorgio) political circles. (Gorgio is the pejorative label given by Gypsies to non-Gypsies.) The Gypsies in Britain in any case do not recognise 'leaders', although they see the utility in relevant circumstances of intermediaries and negotiators with gorgio authorities (Okely 1983). However, there was for a while the curious phenomenon of one or two gorgio intellectual-activists who assumed fictive Gypsy ethnic identity and ancestry. Alleged membership of the group was used both to give authenticity to their writing and to their political participation on behalf of Gypsies.

Here is an example of the fictive member as activist and intellectual, (categories 5 and 6). After the 1960 Caravan Sites Act in England and Wales, local authorities had closed many Gypsy-run camp sites. Wherever Gypsies or Travellers moved, they were faced with greater visibility and increased evictions. Gratton Puxon, a gorgio of middle-class English background, who had made the acquaintance of Gypsies when travelling abroad, became a leading activist. He encouraged non-violent resistance to evictions and informed the press in advance. At its inception in the late 1960s, he became the Secretary of the Gypsy Council, which included both Gypsy and gorgio officers. Both the Gypsy Council and Puxon himself captured media attention and made evictions more controversial. In the public gorgio imagination Puxon was often seen to be the sole Gypsy representative of Gypsies. Yet in my fieldwork I found that some Gypsies had no idea of his existence. Others were very ambivalent about his tactics, as Travellers became vulnerable to more punitive fines, imprisonment and greater visibility to the police. One said, 'It's all very well these gorgios laying themselves in front of the motors, but in the end it's us who are left on the side of the road to pay the fines.'

The Gypsy Council was recognised in negotiations with central government, which hitherto had responded almost exclusively to representations from anti-Gypsy housedwellers and local councils. Eventually, the mixed blessing of the 1968 Caravan Sites Act was passed. This obliged local authorities to provide sites in return for draconian powers to remove remaining Gypsies from 'designated' localities.

When Puxon was abroad, the Department of the Environment persuaded the Gypsy Council, with all the accompanying publicity, to validate the first set of designations. On his return, Puxon repudiated this strategy, but the political momentum had been lost. He and another gorgio, a linguist with a doctoral thesis on the dialects of Eastern European Gypsies, published an outstanding documentation of the centuries of persecution and Nazi genocide of the Gypsies (Kenrick and Puxon 1972). More speculatively, the authors reiterated the belief in a linear Indian origin and ended with a utopian claim:

> The present ground-swell within the Gypsy world will amount soon to a revolution. . . . The message has penetrated, particularly to a restless youth, that we are in an epoch of racial turmoil and resurgent nationalism. It is clear to Roms today . . . that though the first *Blacks* in Europe, they are the last to raise their standard and seek emancipation.
>
> (Ibid.: 210, 214)

In the 1995 amended version, all such rhetoric has been erased from the text.

A textual validation of Puxon as Gypsy 'leader' exists in the sociologist Thomas Acton's doctoral monograph (1974). While it contains excellent historical accounts of Gypsies and state policies, when the author considered the 1960s there was an attempt in the text to influence subsequent events by inflating the role of the gorgio individual as Gypsy leader of a massed international organisation (Acton personal communication). At least one review in a social science journal accepted these claims uncritically.

Puxon appeared on television wearing a kerchief, the folklorist's insignia of a 'real' Gypsy, talking of 'my people'. The Gypsies I encountered who knew him always described him as a gorgio. Certainly, the mass media presented him as a Gypsy, and in this my co-authors and I were asked to cooperate. A gorgio associate of Puxon, and the publisher's reader for the jointly authored *Gypsies and Government Policy in England* (Adams *et al.* 1975) requested, unsuccessfully, that we redescribe Puxon as a Gypsy. As the privately educated public-school son of an estate agent, he had no Gypsy kinship links, except that he had recently married a Gypsy from Yugoslavia. To have called him a Gypsy would have been consistent neither with the Gypsies' own criteria nor with those of the larger society, although it was politically expedient with gorgio officials. Puxon was always more successful, and indeed brilliant, as an intermediary in relation to the dominant society than as an indigenous leader seeking recognition by Gypsies and Travellers. In any case, since the 1980s, he has severed links with the Gypsies and is currently described as having 'returned to full-time journalism' (Kenrick and Puxon 1995: frontispiece).

TERRITORIAL NATIONALISM

In the 1960s and 1970s, the pro-Gypsy gorgio activists, like the Gypsies before and after, tried out by hit-and-miss tactics, different identities and strategies. Inspired by the Black Power movement and the anti-colonial independence struggles of the 1970s, there was considerable talk, mainly among gorgio activists, of Gypsy 'nationalism' (Kenrick and Puxon 1972; Acton 1974). There was ambiguity as to whether or not this nationalism also embraced a separate territory and nation-state (Acton 1974: 233–4), especially since Gypsies have an economy which is interdependent with that of sedentary non-Gypsies. A number of gorgios and Gypsy media figureheads, including Puxon, argued for a Gypsy homeland called Romanestan. Given the relative silence on the subject among the mass of Gypsies, this was in effect the ethnocentric imposition of a sedentarist model upon a traditionally nomadic people. Neither another slice of Palestine nor India were suggested, but instead Macedonia. Brian Raywid, a gorgio who had shared life on the road with Gypsies (1964, 1966), wrote to me in the early 1980s with considerable foresight:

> I see no point myself in even the mythical concept of a Gypsy state. It would destroy Gypsies. And the location 'chosen' (how kind of visionary gorgios to do this on behalf of Gypsies) is Macedonia, a federated province of Yugoslavia and with a mix of volatile nationalities, not least the Albanians. One wonders that the surface of the moon wasn't suggested as more practical and hospitable.

> (Personal communication 1983)

He later recalled how there were discussions among the English gorgio associates as to which of them should be the first president or prime minister of this Macedonian Romanestan utopia.

Another political strategy was the World Romani-Congress which has proved useful in the long run with UNESCO, but at the inception was imbued with nationalist trappings. Here loosely formed organisations came together under the label in 1971 (with Puxon as Secretary) for a meeting in London, followed by a festival on Hampstead Heath. Puxon, as recorded by Acton, 'freely adapted the words of Stokeley Carmichael, to say "to raise the standard of Rom nationalism is like suddenly shouting a secret in a crowded room"' (1974: 235). The Gypsies were presented with a national anthem and flag. However, the French Gypsy novelist, Mateo Maximoff, expressed the opinion that Gypsies neither wanted nor needed a nation-state. The problem was subsequently resolved by Puxon 'and other west European militants [sic]' suggesting that 'we must create Romanestan – in our hearts' (ibid.: 234). Acton, the non-Gypsy sociologist, has recently expressed a more pronounced scepticism concerning Romanestan (Acton and Gheorghe 1993: 13), but does not acknowledge that gorgio 'leaders' or 'militants' were some of the major instigators of the notion of a homeland. The majority of the Gypsies were never convinced, even in the loosest sense. Acton's own research tacitly confirmed this at the height of the alleged revolutionary movement: 'The thousand and more heads of families who paid their subscriptions to the Gypsy Council are not nationalists' (1974: 235).

Writing to me in 1993, a decade after his earlier scepticism, Brian Raywid commented,

> At least one point, however, seems to have become more rather than less relevant. That is my reference to Macedonia. Between about 1968 and the early 1980s there existed a utopian idea in certain quarters that Macedonia should become a Gypsy state. ... Even when the idea was first mooted it seemed to me a recipe for disaster, given the obvious facts, clear even then, as to the unsuitability of a Gypsy state and the unsuitability of Macedonia anyway. To save face, those who once propagated this idea, now claim that they never meant it literally.

The curiosity is that gorgio intellectuals and activists with academic credentials should have been the major instigators of this political fantasy imposed upon 'their' othered peoples. The Gypsies rarely responded to the symbolism of flags and national anthems, while an ideology of nationalism remained ungrounded in any material reality, let alone any desire for a homeland. Mercifully for Macedonia, and doubtless the Gypsies, the representation of Gypsy nationalism as a demand for a Gypsy nation-state failed to make headway. In the 1990s, Gypsies in Macedonia, like many in Romania, initiated a strategy used centuries earlier, by recording themselves as 'Egyptians' in census returns, thus claiming minority rights, but through a *non-Indian* origin.

Sometimes the gorgio fictive leaders seemed to be playing a game of schoolboy tin soldiers, with near colonialist delusions of grandeur. Already in 1965, Puxon, an Englishman among Travellers in Ireland, was referring to 'My people, the families on the road and their friends in the settled community'. Describing himself as 'Enemy Number One', he wrote: 'we have been fighting as the rebels distinctly outside the "Establishment"'. Changes in his (unarmed) strategies were metamorphosed as a 'cease-fire' (Acton 1974: 158). Consistent with their masculinist models of a social movement or even of an ethnic group, both Puxon and Acton envisaged only males as Gypsy political representatives and mediators (Acton 1974: 159, 235), despite the emergent women's liberation movement. The long-established political role of Gypsy women (Okely 1975a, 1996) was androcentrically kept off the revolutionary agenda. Since the 1990s, throughout Europe the political visibility and initiatives of Gypsy women have been more satisfactorily acknowledged.

However, in the 1970s the gorgio model for Gypsy resistance was not only masculinist but also fantasised as guerrilla warfare. For example, I was rebuked by a gorgio 'pro-Gypsy nationalist' for being part of 'the Establishment' because I was not 'taking machine guns down to a Gypsy camp'. My response was that the Gypsies were too politically sophisticated to need a naive young gorgio woman's advice. Moreover, the Gypsies had evolved their own means of resistance which were less counter-productive than those that had brought about the tragic massacre of the Black Panthers. So I lost my chance of becoming the Patty Hearst of anthropology.

GYPSIES IN DISPUTE WITH FICTIVE REPRESENTATIVES

In another example of the construction of Gypsy nationalism by wannabe Gypsies or non-Gypsy activists, the Gypsies elected to take charge of their own representation in the media and in opposition to that of gorgio representatives. In the mid-1970s, Puxon and the Gypsy Council obtained a slot on the BBC TV community action programme, *Open Door*. On a Gypsy site, a raised dais was created on the back of a lorry on which stood various 'leaders' including Puxon and Vanko Rouda, a Belgian-based Gypsy-gorgio (Liégeois 1976: 158). Speeches were made from the lorry which was foregrounded by a small crowd of Gypsies visible only as spectator silhouettes. The self-styled dignitaries presented each other with silver horseshoes for 'services to the Gypsies'. Then a 'Gypsy National Anthem' was distributed on printed handouts to the crowd below, which included gorgio social workers and supporters. The latter, who were largely the only people who could read, led the uneven singing. If the anthem had indeed been of significance to the Gypsies, they would have sung it from memory.

This scene was watched by Gypsy representatives, also filmed live in a studio. After the camp ceremony, Tommy Doherty, an Irish Traveller, declared to camera that the BBC had been 'conned'. He and other Gypsies walked out, leaving only a gorgio gypsiologist behind. As in 1971, the Gypsies rejected the ceremonial trappings of phantom nationalism.

INTERNATIONALISM AND RIGHTS AS A MINORITY

With a change in political ideology in the 1980s and even more so in the 1990s, it became more politically expedient for the Gypsies to argue for ethnic minority status with accompanying international human rights. The link with the UN was another of the earlier strategies. In this case, it met with relative success. Whereas this had depended on recognition by the larger international gorgio organisation, the nationalist strategies depended on a unilateral and impracticable consolidation among Gypsies.

Thus the ideology of ethnicity and minority rights has proved more effective both among Gypsies and non-Gypsy organisations than that of Gypsy nationalism. The United Nations and to some extent the EU, are useful bodies to be appealed to over the heads of specific national governments. But the way in which ethnicity has been defined and legitimated, doubtless through previous academic influences, has repercussions for the groups concerned. Here ethnic minority recognition would still appear to rest on a unilinear foreign migration, and one that privileges an original territory. So, again the Indian origin has political mileage. The nineteenth-century theories of race, conflated with place, retain their hold in the dominant ideologies of states. Indigenous, European ancestry is not seen as a politically useful route to recognition of the Gypsies' autonomous rights. This foreclosing of multiple histories by a geographical 'othering' simultaneously downgrades the identity and potential rights of those travelling groups who neither claim nor are granted foreign ancestry.

THE THEORY OF SELF-ASCRIPTION

An alternative route to ethnic status had been provided by Barth (1969), whose notion of 'self-ascription' was useful not only on an individual level but also as a way of considering what the Gypsies *themselves* chose as significant markers for group membership. Barth's text offered a route to combining outsider and insider perspectives. This was a succinct way out of having to define an ethnic group by external and fixed 'traits', including geographical origin. Hitherto, the etymologists and linguists had mainly defined 'real' Gypsies by the extent to which they were said to use a form of Romani language. These scholars and others also conflated biological notions of race with arbitrary classifications of physiognomy and even 'behaviour' (Okely 1975b).

Although Barth has been criticised for concentrating on the boundaries rather than what they contained, in the 1970s I moved beyond the suggestion that self-ascription was a free-floating individualistic decision, but saw that instead it could include the content, or whatever the group itself ascribed as significant for their identity, culture or practice (see Cheater and Hopa, Chapter 13 of this volume). Among one of the 'primary' principles which Barth implicitly seemed to suggest that groups might themselves use for inclusion and exclusion was that of descent. Rehfisch, who had made the first anthropological field study of Gypsies in Scotland and in Britain (1958), had suggested that a Gypsy could claim membership if he or she had at least one Gypsy parent. Here the principle of descent operated in a flexible manner.

POLICY ADVISER AND EXPERT

The discussion of Barth's text and concepts introduces an example of the fourth category in which the academic may be called upon as policy adviser. Depending on the nature of that advice and the political climate, the academic, intellectual and/or representative member may influence government policy. As with the case of the charismatic activist, the conditions have to be ripe both for the intellectual to be consulted and for that knowledge to be heeded. The very term 'expert witness' is hegemonically loaded. In the centres of power it carries with it the notion of detached knowledge and political neutrality. It also presumes that other lay people, including ordinary members of an ethnic group, are not themselves expert witnesses.

In the policy-oriented project of the 1970s in which I was initially involved, I was able to use some of Barth's suggestions to argue for the recognition of Gypsies as an ethnic group (Okely 1975b). Unlike so many other minorities, they could not appeal to a recent, distant place of origin as a marker. Neither could they call themselves 'black' and then be in a position to use the Race Relations Act (*pace* Kenrick and Puxon 1972). The publication of our book (Adams, Okely *et al.* 1975) proved opportune for the independent government consultant, John Cripps (1976). It showed not only the Gypsies' identity as an ethnic group, but also the viability of their flexible economy.

Under a Labour government and still in a post-1960s semi-liberal climate, there was a greater openness towards minorities. The Cripps inquiry, initiated by the government, interviewed Gypsy representatives and supporters nationwide. Whereas the 1968 Caravan Sites Act had carried the covert assumption that Gypsies should be sedentarised and assimilated by means of official site provision, by contrast, the ensuing report unequivocally recognised the Gypsies' rights to remain nomadic. A key sentence was: 'The Secretaries of State now have no wish to deny the gypsies [sic] a nomadic existence' (1976: 7). Moreover, their identity as an ethnic group was recognised. Cripps introduced the concept of 'self-ascription' as a means of getting round all the muddles of who was a 'real' Gypsy. Much of the report was a flattering plagiarisation of our book, but with a general acknowledgement in the frontispiece. However, in accord with the unscholarly style of government and journalistic texts, there was neither a bibliography nor a system of referencing, with the result that due credit was not given to Barth – an example of the first category of influence where specific theorists are no longer named.

Despite the academic and other contributions to the 1970s policy, the non-assimilationist stance was reversed by the Conservative government in the 1990s. The Criminal Justice Act of 1994 abolished mandatory official site provision and any special planning consideration for Gypsy private sites. The long-term aim is unequivocally the settlement and housing of Gypsies. All the suggestions of Cripps, others' academic research sympathetic to Gypsies and Gypsy delegations have been passed over. Thus the intellectual's influence on ideologies of ethnicity in the state policy sphere are often fragile, dependent on hegemonic approval.

RACE RELATIONS LEGISLATION AND THE ACADEMIC AS EXPERT WITNESS

In some instances, the social scientist may be called upon as expert witness, either to defend or to challenge discrimination. Consistent with category 4, in this case the intellectual's expertise is institutionalised in the law of the dominant society. Although the Cripps Report could be seen as a positive influence, the Gypsies remained vulnerable to racist discrimination, so long as there was no court ruling defining them as an ethnic group. Hitherto, a Gypsy had been defined as a person of 'no fixed abode', so could not complain about discrimination under the 1976 Race Relations Act. In 1988, a letter was forwarded to me from the Oxford Institute of Social Anthropology. Some local solicitors were trying to defend an Irish Working Men's Club which had refused entry to some Travellers. They sought an expert witness:

> the Plaintiff must establish that he was treated less favourably than others on racial grounds or by virtue of his racial grouping. The plaintiff, ... attempts to claim the protection of the Act on the basis of his ethnic origin, saying that a Gypsy or Traveller is a member of an ethnic group. ... You will appreciate that the Expert we are seeking would be one who could give evidence to the effect that 'Travellers' or Gypsies are not member [sic] of a racial or ethnic group.
>
> (Ferguson Bricknell & Co. 1988)

The letter assumes that anthropologists are the experts on 'racial grouping' and that they might be relied upon to testify *against* a member of a minority claiming discrimination. Needless to say, I did not follow up the matter. It was not possible to trace the complainant and offer my services instead to him. Later, I discovered that the parties settled out of court and that one Traveller emerged several thousand pounds richer and that a fellow anthropologist Sinéad ni Shuineer, had acted as expert witness on *his* behalf.

An example of category 3, where the influence of the intellectual's theories is unintended and entirely distorted, occurred that same year in London. In a prosecution of a pub that had displayed a 'No Travellers' sign, I heard to my horror that the defence had quoted, without consultation, lines of my 1983 monograph. The extracts referred to my critique of a purely biological or 'racial' model for an ethnic group. The judge was fixated on the biological model for a racial group. After an appeal, the unchallenged verdict was that Gypsies, but not Travellers, were an ethnic group. In some gorgio gypsiologist circles it was claimed that my questioning of a single Indian origin had invited discrimination, because the Gypsies could not be defined by foreignness.

In 1993, I was asked to act as 'expert witness' in a case in Scotland, where a Traveller complained of racial discrimination after being refused a drink in an hotel. I was asked by the Commission for Racial Equality to prove that Scottish Travellers are an ethnic group (Okely 1984, 1994). Again, Barth's 'self-ascription' and 'principle of descent' were relevant. Given that traditionally neither the Scottish and Irish Travellers, nor gorgio gypsiologists have presented an Indian origin for these groups, any international claims to ethnic recognition for all Gypsies on such grounds would have worked against them. The Traveller understandably settled out of court. Regrettably, the chance to establish a precedent was lost.

INSIDER GYPSY INTELLECTUALS AND ACTIVISTS AS REPRESENTATIVES

The following examples fit with my fifth and sixth categories of influence outlined above; the intellectual as member of, and activist for, the ethnic group. These Gypsy intellectuals also illustrate the different available ideological positions in relation to the mythical or apparently empirically proven historical origin of the Gypsies. Given the privileging of exoticism in gorgio discourse and institutions, the Gypsies 'Indian' origin(s) continue to be debated as part of their mythical charter of authenticity. Two of these Gypsy academics emerged during the 1980s in Europe and the US. The third, a Scottish Traveller, became prominent in the early 1990s.

Ian Hancock, now a linguistics professor at the University of Texas, is also a political activist. He has tirelessly drawn attention to anti-Gypsy legislation and media misrepresentation. *The Pariah Syndrome* (1987) is his overview of the history of Gypsies. Trained at the School of Oriental and African Studies, London, as a linguist rather than as a social scientist, he is deeply influenced by the diffusionist and etymological theories of non-Gypsies, which authenticate the Gypsies as Indian migrants.

Until recently, Hancock was the United States representative for the International Romani Union at UNESCO. The recognition of Gypsies' rights within certain UN organisations, including UNESCO, has been achieved in part because of the declared Indian origin of the Rom or Gypsies throughout the West. Ian Hancock's presence as a forthright and brilliant speaker at international academic or political conferences has a powerful influence on his audiences' perceptions and encourages their granting of ideological space for Gypsies as a persecuted group with valid claims to human rights.

Nicolae Gheorghe, formerly vice president of the International Romani Union, is a Romanian sociologist at the University of Bucharest. As with a number of Gypsies in Eastern Europe, it was for a long time safer for him to pass as a non-Gypsy. Since 1989, some academics have felt encouraged to reveal their Gypsy connections (Beck 1993). In Romania, there are, in contrast to Gypsies in Britain, a number of literate Gypsies with greater access to textually constructed ideologies.

Gheorghe collaborated in research and publication with the American anthropologist Sam Beck and, in contrast to Hancock, suggested an indigenous origin for a group of Romanian Gypsies (Beck and Gheorghe 1981: 19). Subsequently, at a seminar in 1993, and with tongue in cheek, he described with approval how one or two Romanian Gypsy 'kings' have, in the 1990s, made well-publicised trips to India, their 'homeland'. These kings were welcomed by high-ranking Indian officials, so further validating their non-European, exotic status. Gheorghe, with a social scientist's scrutiny, presented these developments as powerfully symbolic and to be exploited, regardless of his or others' scepticism (Liégeois 1976).

By contrast, Hancock described his own visit to India as eliciting feelings that he belonged there. He said that he knew, in some deep mystical sense, that that was where his Gypsy ancestors came from. The description of his experience was part of his 1990 plenary address at an international conference at the University of Leiden. It was offered as proof of the migratory theory which has become part of the ideological construction of Gypsies for some Gypsies and gorgios in the West.

No one is in a position to deny another person's experience of specific emotions and inner knowledge. Hancock's public identity as Gypsy brings an additional experiential dimension to an academic debate. It forecloses any alternative theory about the historical origins of Gypsies. His belief becomes a social fact, as Gheorghe would recognise, and may influence both gorgio and Gypsy ethnic ideologies.

The third example of a Gypsy intellectual is Willie Reid, a Scottish Traveller who attended Stirling University. In 1993 he and other Travellers formed a political organisation for Scottish Travellers. At the first meeting, they decided to incorporate the label 'Gypsy' as well as Traveller in the title. One of the main reasons for this was the apparent need to differentiate themselves from New Age Travellers. Reid declared: 'We've been robbed of the word Traveller by the New Age Travellers.' The label 'Traveller' used by outsiders had previously been used in contrast to the then-stigmatised 'Tinker'. There was also a feeling that the adoption of the label 'Gypsy' meant less ambiguity in recognition as 'an ethnic group'. This latter phrase has now entered common parlance. In the 1970s I never heard it in the field, but more significantly never among the few Gypsies who moved in public gorgio political circles. Again this is an example of the first category of influence above.

Gorgio gypsiologist discourse has not bestowed Indian origin upon Scottish and Irish Travellers (Okely 1994). Reid presents a novel critique of those who have presented varying origins for Scottish Travellers, highlighting the mixed blessings of the Scottish folk revivalists who stumbled on the Travellers in the 1960s. Traveller songs, stories and dances were recorded but then appropriated by the gorgio Scottish Nationalists and folklorists who looked for remnants of the

> 'pre-Christian era' ... 'high Celtic Society' ... the 'neolithic period', 'fallen Cairds' and ... 'ancient Ossianic hero-tales' among the Travellers. ... Gypsies/Travellers ... were more than willing to clad themselves in tartan and play the part. ... All this ... presented a very unfair ... and distorted image.
>
> Travellers were seen 'as noble savages ... whose culture and lifestyle was static.
>
> (Reid 1993: 5)

Neatly balancing an insider's view with that of gorgio scholars, Reid rejects the suggestion that Travellers are the custodians of an exclusively Scottish culture. He argues that such folklore belongs to the Gypsy/Traveller community, which transcends Scotland's national boundaries.

At an ESRC workshop in 1993, Reid hinted of his own acceptance of the theory that an independent ethnic group could only be explained by migration from another locality, rather than by self-recruitment and continuing self-generation. He found himself in disagreement with an English Gypsy and representative of the Gypsy Council, who reiterated the theory that English Gypsies came from abroad, whereas Scottish Gypsies were mainly descendants of existing local groups. 'If Scottish Travellers were only indigenous groups', Reid asked the English Gypsy, 'why did they want to be distinctive?' The English Gypsy had contested that his group had always 'married among themselves', whereas Scottish Travellers had often married outsiders. Reid replied that Scottish Travellers tended to marry cousins. Here was another criterion for authenticity or difference based on extent of group endogamy. Formerly, this debate would have been conducted among gorgio scholars using the language of race, blood and purity.

There were mainly gorgios; some academics, community workers, students and part-time scholars at this workshop. But the dialogue between these two men was a mark of changed times. Two Travellers who had read gorgio texts about their groups, now as self-ascribed members, were using outsiders' theories, but trying them out in terms of their own identities and the wider political context within which Travellers have to survive. The interplay between historical, scholarly theory and the personal involvement of the two discussants had a dramatic intensity that could not be compared with, say, a discussion between individuals from a literate tradition.

OUTSIDER INTELLECTUALS AND THEORIES IN CONFLICT

The encounters at the same workshop seemed at first to be relatively benign. During a lull in the evening social, a New Age Traveller was supporting my alternative thesis that the Gypsies and Travellers could as well have been generated from within as from without. He agreed with the collapse of feudalism thesis and what he called my primarily political and economic explanatory theories. It seemed that such theories could be interpreted as a textual guide to the construction of the New Age Travellers' own 'ethnicity'. I said that I was extremely interested as to whether the New Age Travellers could themselves form a self-reproducing group, i.e. if the offspring of such Travellers were to prefer and choose partners from the current group, which at present consists of self-selected random persons, without a principle of descent. He stared dramatically: 'I can tell you it's already happened.' This was extremely exciting because the emergence of the New Age Travellers could be a late twentieth-century version of the Gypsies' consolidation in earlier European history. The economic consequences of Thatcherism had contributed towards an alternative form of resistance among alienated and disaffected individuals who had taken to the road and exploited solidarity. Here, nearly twenty-five years on from my first fieldwork, I found myself in dialogue with a new form of Traveller and a budding intellectual representative of his loosely aligned group. He had 'left the road' in order to study and take a degree. Just as he was saying to me: 'That's a cracker of a book, yours!', a prominent gorgio supporter of the Indian, 'racial', and 'black' origin of Gypsies came up and gestured towards some Bosnian Gypsy refugees whom he had urged to come along and 'entertain' us that evening with accordion, song and dance.

'Indianist': Well, Judith, they speak the language. Did they pick that up by chance?

Anthropologist: I don't deny the language, like many others, has some Indo-European connections. I question whether those who use Romani dialects can all be said to be descendants of Indians.

'Indianist': How did the language get there then?

Anthropologist: Along the trade and pilgrim routes. There was continuous movement back and forth.

'Indianist': You think they just blacked up their faces and then some went back to China!

Anthropologist: If you're talking about their dark hair, eyes and skin, there are people of the same phenotype in the Mediterranean and parts of Eastern Europe. One of the Bosnian Gypsies said his wife was a gorgio. I doubt she has blonde hair, paler skin or blue eyes.

The irate gorgio walked away, then returned at speed: 'Every time I read your book I want to *burn* it!'

I was taken aback that my attempt to dismantle a potentially racist ideology should have provoked such a reaction. If it had come from an insider Gypsy, I would have felt obliged to think in even more careful ways about the implications of publishing my critique of Indianism, just as I have respected confidentiality on individual details (Okely 1987). However, those Gypsies who have read my work, including Hancock, Gheorghe and Reid, have reacted positively while, as in most intellectual debates, expressing disagreements on some matters. The insider Gypsy intellectuals see me as a resource and I am happy to be in a position to reciprocate something of what I have gained from Gypsies.

The extreme emotional investment that the gorgio scholar above had in Indianism was combined with an archaic and selective view of Gypsy culture as a whole, for his Orientalist interest in Gypsies hardly extended to their contemporary way of life and beliefs.[1] The Bosnian Gypsies, when asked by him to play some music for the assembled seminar participants, declined because at least one of them was in public mourning for his recently deceased father (cf. Okely 1983, ch. 12, for mourning rituals). They delicately avoided embarrassing him by claiming they had 'forgotten' to bring their instruments. Still not getting the message, the gorgio went and found an accordion. The Gypsies told him somewhat unconvincingly that they didn't know how to play that model. Later, the Bosnian Gypsies asked an Irish anthropologist why they had been invited for the evening. Not being professional musicians, they had not understood their function as exotic entertainers. Hitherto, in Yugoslavia, they hadn't experienced the phenomenon of a gaggle of gypsiologists interested in their 'culture'.

These Bosnian Gypsies were a poignant example of the adjustments Gypsies have to make according to the historical moment and transformations in the wider context. Their desperate escape to Britain coincided with changes in their identity, not only in relation to new types of gorgios who privileged different forms of ethnicity, but also among themselves. One man explained to me in French that the group assembled that evening contained 'Serbs', 'Muslims' and 'Croats'. They were all intermarried, and, like the Bosnians in general, had hitherto not been obliged to reify differences (cf. Bringa 1994). Exile had not undermined their identity as Gypsies, but they would have to experiment with new labels.

Later that evening an English Gypsy drew my attention to the gorgio Indianist, who was teaching the Gypsy a scholastic form of Romani: 'He says you've written that there's no such people as Gypsies!' The Gypsy had not read my book ('I never read') so he was relying on the gorgio's misreading. Here is an example of my third category where a text is distorted beyond the author's control. I explained I did not think that the emphasis on Indian origin was the way to identify all Gypsies. What happened to the Irish and Scottish Travellers and other groups like the Sinti and Yeniche who never claimed nor were assigned a foreign origin? It seemed questionable to set up criteria that downgraded or excluded groups who also believed themselves to be Gypsies. He smiled and said in any case the Irish were not Gypsies, nor even 'real Travellers'. 'So and So' in the International Romani Union wanted them out. I rather mischievously pointed out that the Indianist thought that he, the English Gypsy, was also less 'real' than the Bosnians because he had fair hair and blue eyes. The Indianist was then challenged on this and did not deny his privileging of the Eastern Europeans. I left them to continue the debate.

While the questioning of the mono Indian origin for all Gypsies may be intellectually plausible for social scientists, I recognise that the Gypsies themselves may pick and choose – including from gorgio intellectuals – what they see as politically expedient. However, it is puzzling as to why the work of the gorgio anthropologist should be seen as a near-inflammatory threat to gorgio intellectuals and gypsiologists. There is psychic as well as political capital in Orientalism. Over the years, no new evidence has emerged to modify my scepticism towards the Indianist line. Meanwhile, the Indianist linguistic discourse is hegemonically extended.

In the wider political and historical context, which the academy inhabits, the intellectual's influence is beyond individual control. The text can be appreciatively absorbed, misrepresented or provide powerful legitimacy. The Gypsies may be largely written about by gorgios, but they have to be acquainted with the dominant society's ideologies and plans for them. They adapt and distort accordingly. If a specific ideological mood has changed, the Gypsies know this. The exotic images enhanced in popular gorgio ideological representations have helped to create, enhance or racialise Gypsy ethnicity. The social scientist may feel compelled to analyse and deconstruct them. Whether or not the appeal of such representations can be dismantled by theoretical scrutiny is another matter. As critics of Hobsbawm and Ranger (1983) have suggested, it is insufficient to expose people's traditions as recent, invented and therefore false consciousness if the circumstances in which they are generated are not also considered. The anthropologist intellectual can neither choose nor predict what aspects of ethnic ideology a group may need or desire.

At the same time, there are arrogances and dangers in acting as a fictive leader of an ethnic group. Instead, there are more transparent political opportunities for alliance, support or action and individual testimony by outsiders. There are also pedagogical and political possibilities in texts. Puxon and Kenrick's extensively amended (1972) and newly titled volume *Gypsies under the Swastika* (1995) confirms their more grounded and long-lasting contribution as intellectuals. The book evinces less speculation than its predecessor. They have meticulously documented the much-neglected Gypsy Holocaust. One former office holder in Gypsy organisations has relinquished any lingering claims as fictive leader and foreteller of the Gypsies' 'Destiny' (Puxon and Kenrick 1972).

Intellectual and academic writing may influence a subsequent generation, the majority of whom are non-Gypsies who may later acquire hegemonic powers. Some will be Gypsies. Although texts cannot suit every political contingency for vulnerable minorities, their range in critical content has potential for good. Texts can subvert received, racist and repressive representations, and more besides.

NOTE

1 This man simultaneously worked for the Gypsies as an intermediary in asylum disputes.

REFERENCES

Acton, T. (1974) *Gypsy Politics and Social Change*, London: Routledge & Kegan Paul.
Acton, T. and N. Gheorghe (1993) 'Political Factors Affecting the Presentation of Romani Identity.' Paper presented at ESRC Seminar on Romani Studies, University of Greenwich. (In press: University of Hertfordshire Press.)
Adams, B., J. Okely, D. Morgan and D. Smith (1975) *Gypsies and Government Policy in England*, London: Heinemann Educational Books.
Althusser, L. (1971) 'Ideology and the Ideological State Apparatuses', in *Lenin and Other Essays* (trans by B. Brewster); New York: Monthly Review Press.
Barth, F. (1969) 'Introduction', in *Ethnic Groups and Boundaries*, London: Allen & Unwin.
Beck, S. (1993) 'Racism and the Formation of a Romani Ethnic Leader', in G. Marcus (ed.), *Perilous States: Conversations on Culture, Politics, and Nation*, Chicago: University of Chicago Press.
Beck, S. and N. Gheorghe (1981) 'From Slavery to Coinhabiting Nationality: The

Political Economy of Romanian Gypsies.' Paper presented at Symposium on the Social Anthropology of Europe, IUAES, Intercongress, Amsterdam.
Bringa, T. (1994) *We Are all Neighbours*. Granada film.
Cripps, J. (1976) *Accommodation for Gypsies*, London: HMSO.
Gramsci, A. (1971) *Selections from the Prison Notebooks* (ed. and trans. by Q. Hoare and G. Nowell Smith), London: Lawrence & Wishart.
Hancock, I. (1987) *The Pariah Syndrome*, Ann Arbor, MI: Karoma Publishers.
Hobsbawm, E. and T. Ranger (eds) (1983) *The Invention of Tradition*, Cambridge: Cambridge University Press.
Kenrick, D. and G. Puxon (1972) *The Destiny of Europe's Gypsies*, London: Heinemann.
—— (1995) *Gypsies under the Swastika*, Hatfield: University of Hertfordshire Press.
Liégeois, J. P. (1976) *Mutation Tsigane*, Brussels: Complexe.
Okely, J. (1975a) 'Gypsy Women: Models in Conflict', in S. Ardener (ed.) *Perceiving Women*, London: Malaby.
—— (1975b) 'Gypsy Identity', in B. Adams *et al.* (eds) *Gypsies and Government Policy in England*, London: Heinemann Educational Books.
—— (1983) *The Traveller-Gypsies*, Cambridge: Cambridge University Press.
—— (1984) 'Ethnic Identity and Place of Origin: The Traveller-Gypsies in Britain', in H. Vermeulen and J. Boissevain (eds), *Ethnic Challenge: The Politics of Ethnicity in Europe*, Göttingen: Edition Herodot, Forum 8.
—— (1987) 'Fieldwork up the M1', in A. Jackson (ed.), *Anthropology at Home*, London: Tavistock.
—— (1994) 'An Anthropological Perspective on Irish Travellers', in M. McCann, S. O' Siochain and J. Ruane (eds), *Irish Travellers: Culture and Ethnicity*, Belfast: Institute of Irish Studies.
—— (1996) *Own or Other Culture*, London: Routledge.
Raywid, B. (1964) 'On the Road with Londonside Gypsies', *Journal of the Gypsy Lore Society*, 1–2.
—— (1966) 'Reminiscences of Life on the Road', *Journal of the Gypsy Lore Society*, 3–4.
Rehfisch, F. (1958) 'Tinkers of Perthshire and Aberdeenshire.' Unpublished thesis, School of Scottish Studies, Edinburgh.
Reid, W. (1993) 'Scottish Gypsies/Travellers and the Folklorists.' Paper presented at ESRC Romani Studies Seminar, University of Greenwich. (In press: University of Hertfordshire Press.)
Said, E. (1978) *Orientalism*, London: Penguin.
Sartre, J. P. (1978) *Sartre by Sartre*. Film transcript (trans. by R. Seaver), New York: Urizen Books.

Chapter 15

Appropriate anthropology and the risky inspiration of 'Capability' Brown

Representations of what, by whom, and to what end?

Sandra Wallman

For present purposes, two essential features of representations are key. One is that they simplify the reality they represent; the other is that any meaning imputed to them will be socially constructed. This said, we should note that representations are of many kinds. One social psychologist emphasises a distinction between *collective* representations, which 'assume a homogeneous and closed group and [the] degree of group coercion... intrinsic to Durkheim's theory', from *social* representations, which are 'interactive processes' which come 'closer to the idea of exchange' (Moscovici 1987: 516). A similar distinction is implicit in anthropological concern with the fixity or flexibility of the representations that we borrow from our respondents and (or?) visualise at our desks. How far is this interpretation consistent across situation and interest group? Will it hold through time? In each case, what is the scope for negotiating meaning; for concealing or revealing the fact that changes of the context which decides that meaning have occurred; and for communicating it undistorted across cultural or professional divides?

In every case representations are about simplification for the sake of communication. Especially where the idea to be conveyed is strange therefore – as it often is when we set out to visualise or to foster change of any kind – it behoves an intending communicator to start the negotiation with an image that her intended audience already knows. '[T]he unfamiliar must be transformed into the familiar. Recognisable metaphors must be found to communicate new ideas' (ibid.).

I

The main aim of this chapter is to sketch and defend the parameters of an applied anthropology appropriate to this pre-millennial, postmodern era. I use the term *appropriate anthropology* to represent a new gloss on application. It signals changes in three components of the profession's quiver that have always been especially vital to those who set out as practitioners in the real world. The crucial tools are *context* because it is inevitably other-things-happening that govern the meaning and outcome of events; *capacity*, because individuals and social systems can be pro-active, adapting to and influencing events as much as they react to them; and *communication*, to the extent that the findings of research have no value unless and until they are conveyed to a designated audience.

The word 'applied' in any case needs refining. It is both too abstract and too narrow to convey the range of things done in its name. It is also loaded with meanings – maybe now obsolete, but for some still an excuse to look down on or away from anything that smacks of deliberate rele-vance. By simple analogy with other subjects – mathematics, economics, physics – we should be talking about a branch of the discipline that applies mainstream theory to the solution of practical problems, whether the problem in focus is grandly posed – development, health, gender, race relations – or very specific: 'What are/will be the social effects of/ impediments to building *that* road through *this* territory?' The subject's findings have been useful at both levels. But although, unique among the disciplines, we talk of applying 'the perspectives' rather than the theories of anthropology, it has not been our habit to reflect on them aloud, or to communicate what they are.

Two reasons for this inexplicitness suggest themselves. The first, running firmly against the grain of this chapter, is the simple conceit that only professional anthropologists can grasp or need to grasp the complexities of social context and human agency. The second inheres in our research methodology and bears on the way data are represented. It is that models of any sort tend to be evaluated in terms of tidiness as much as explana-tory value: tidiness is, after all, easier to assess and to convey. Since no real situation can be tidy in this sense, any model must be an abstraction of it. In 'pure' or 'academic' research endeavours it is appropriate to concentrate on very few of its dimensions, tidily selected for the purpose at hand and at some chosen distance from the data, and to set the many other things happening aside.

But if the problem is defined at ground level and the aim is, say, to understand/predict/support the treatment decisions a woman makes when her child is sick, then the very untidiness of ordinary life is key. No single 'theory' will have the necessary *practical* relevance, and a kind of analytic eclecticism offers the best chance of being useful (Barnett and Blaikie 1994; Wallman 1977: 3–5; 1996). Paradoxically, in circumstances requiring application on the ground, the unifying framework needs to be pitched at the distance of generality – of 'perspective' only – so that 'all' the relevant other-things-happening can be taken into the frame.

However unworthy or worthy the reasoning, the effect either way has been that the perspectives of anthropology were only rarely conveyed outside the discipline. The point here is that political-economic develop-ment at large has begun to challenge the appropriateness of our traditional performance script and to complicate research practice. The changes are ubiquitous, even global; I am concerned only with their effect on each of the profession's core issues. *Context* has become more difficult to define since the 'wholes' that focus the holism of our perspective are not as clearly bounded as they were, or as we used to picture them. Our bluff has been called on *capacity* now that the one-time 'objects' of ethnography increasingly must be recognised as active subjects in the analysis as well as the management of their own lives. And *communication* is complicated by the fact that the range of people interested in, if not actually paying for, our understandings now extends far outside the discipline, and it includes a good number who are ignorant of or confused by its assumptions.

The new emphasis amounts to changing the way we represent our subjects and our subject matter, both to ourselves and to people outside the discipline. It is not therefore by chance that three caveats to the question of representation are demonstrated in these pages. They are standard pieces of practical anthropological reasoning, no more (and no less!) than common-sense statements, but (so?) rarely spelt out. Here, however, for reasons that will emerge, it is important to be explicit. Thus: (1) Representations, models and pictures suit different purposes and are cast at different levels of abstraction; (2) the meaning(s) of each of them is (are) governed by the professional and political context(s) in which it is conveyed and received; and (3) even a change of context that profoundly alters the meaning or purpose of a representation may not show in, or diminish the impact of, its visualised form.

Opportunities for misinterpretation abound. Some are illustrated in this cautionary tale of an effort to represent models of social change and human agency in ways appropriate to this moment, by reference to models of nature and images of landscape designed for another purpose in another time. The moral of the story is that no assumption underpinning a representation/model/image is self-evident.

II

An anthropology appropriate to the demands of work outside the academy will need representations of context and the capacity of 'others' which can readily be grasped by a non-specialist. To my knowledge the discipline has none in currency. But during the drafting of a public lecture about the differences that make a difference to people's ability to adapt to crisis change – in this case the unrelated crises of unemployment in England and the HIV/AIDS epidemic in Africa – inspiration came from the example of a man who had never set foot in any academy and had no professional reason to be concerned with the social world and its problems. I refer, as suggested in the title of this paper, to the famous eighteenth-century English gardener Lancelot Brown – known, apparently affectionately, in his time and since, as 'Capability' Brown.

There are benefits gained by taking a starting point outside social science in this way. Within the academy, a paradigm that is not the special property of any discipline is a useful medium for multidisciplinary exchange; maybe better progress can be made in a discourse that is not the exclusive claim of any one of the disciplines involved. Outside it, more people identify with the logic of gardening than of social science, and practitioners may empathise with the immediacy and efficacy of the decisions a gardener has to make. These benefits aside, however, stepping outside one's own area of competence is a risky business, and there were moments during the preparation of this chapter when I much regretted having done so. The value as well as the cost of my naivety will become clear as we continue (*pace* Gluckman and Devons 1964).

Not being much of a gardener, in the beginning I knew of Lancelot Brown only as 'the landscape designer who saw capabilities for improvement in every garden'. I was struck by the 'capability' notion, saw landscape as a metaphor for social context and knew, from the gardening books, that he was a master at conveying his vision to clients who themselves had no gardening expertise. On this basis I was persuaded of a good enough analogy with the main elements of 'appropriate anthropology' and looked for ways of adapting his ideas to its demands.

The first of them concerns *capacity*. It is that the leading questions about change should be positive. As Brown put it: What is the capability of this environment? Similarly in anthropology we must ask: What is the capacity of this social system, this community, this person to manage in normal circumstances, and to adapt when circumstances change? Sections V and VI demonstrate this perspective and suggest ways of representing the question applied to unemployment and epidemic.

The second idea, sharpened, as it happens, by the disappointing outcome of my own efforts at gardening, concerns *context*. It is that the assessment of capability depends on taking into account the whole picture, the whole garden as it is, could be, will be. Transposed into anthropology the statement becomes: social capacity cannot be properly assessed by examining items of behaviour or belief in isolation. Capacity is a function of context. It is a characteristic of whole social systems.

The third idea concerns *communication*. It cannot be imputed directly to Brown, but is exemplified by him. The lesson is that professional acumen cannot be sustained by practical skills alone. Brown of course had practical skills in abundance, but just as crucial to his success was an unusual two-pronged talent; first for visualising capability, and then for communicating the vision to prospective clients. Translating the lesson into social science, we learn that the contribution of anthropology to understanding or enhancing social capacity depends on our ability both to visualise the capability system, and to communicate that vision to others who are involved in its outcome – whether as professional or private persons.

Hadfield's *History of British Gardening* sets out the great man's career:

> Lancelot Brown was born in 1715 ... of a family in modest circumstances. He died in 1783, by then Sheriff of Huntingdon, something more than mere gardener to King George III, friend of other men of calibre. ... In the meantime he had swept away old gardens, even whole villages, and created vast new scenes to replace them. ... He influenced many ... and his manner was widely copied by professional and amateur imitators alike.
>
> ... Brown was essentially a practical man, with an eye for a certain type of landscape. After riding round an estate for a few hours, he would have visualized not only how his standardized landscape could be imposed upon the existing scene, but how it could be done at the least expense. He could see just where a trickling stream might be dammed to form an 'ample lake', or slightly modified to create a sparkling cascade. The placing of the trees was conceived in practical as well as in the aesthetic terms. The levellings and smoothings of sharp banks, the winding path, the placing of ornamental buildings, all were worked out almost to a rule. Horace Walpole said of him that 'such was the effect of his genius that he will *least* be remembered; so closely did he copy nature that his works will be mistaken for it'.
>
> (Hadfield 1985: 211–13; emphasis added)

Brown worked to a formula: everything partaking of the old art and geometry was obliterated. Gardens should provide 'a necessary escape into nature'. This was the movement against contrived gardens. In more grandiose language, it was even described as a 'Revolution against constraint'. Clearly, what was happening in the gardens of the gentry was coloured by the political context of the time. Here is Hadfield again, this time describing the 'new movement' itself:

> As the 18th century proceeds it is well to emphasize the connection of gardening with politics, and particularly with 'English liberty – that liberty of which the new gardens themselves were a sort of symbol'. [For example the] serpentine path [represented] a safety valve which had allowed the English to let off steam, while the compressing geometry and regularity of the French avenues had held down the pressure till France exploded.
>
> (Ibid.: 210)

III

Ideas about what is appropriate social research and what interventions should be built on it are just as inevitably products of their time. Of the three strands that make up the appropriate anthropology braid however, only the *capability* strand is truly modern: it reflects the political ideals that Western governments now espouse in their relations with the so-called Third World. For a number of years, in line with the wider ethos, it was fashionable for social scientific analysis to blame the world system and/or the rich for the poverty of the poor, visualising the unfortunate – in whatever sense of the word – as passive, not responsible, without capacity to take charge of their lives (see, e.g., Frank 1969; Valentine 1968; Rodney 1972).

Gradually it began to be clear both that the frame did not fit the reality very often, and that it was resented by those whose autonomy it denied. The changes of course went in parallel with political events on the wider scene, the fading of colonialism and the eclipse of Marxism having obvious effect. Anthropologists were prominent among those who expressed scepticism of the then-dominant models (as Firth 1972) and fuelled the argument for more explicit actor orientation. Among them, in the late 1970s, introducing the volume *Perceptions of Development*, I wrote:

> Those who explain development, and more important, non-development, as (only) the result of global structures of exploitation effectively take all decisions about the future out of the hands of those that may purport to champion.... They invalidate the current efforts and perceptions of any but select academicians and supranational consortia.... It is of little importance that these approaches are labelled by one or other political philosophy, but it is essential that the aspirations and opinions of people subject to the processes of development or non-development be taken seriously – however inconsistent they appear to be, and however limited their power in the political-economic market-place.
>
> (Wallman 1977: 8)

And a few years later, apparently with more confidence, in *Eight London Households*:

> Although the subjects of this book are typical inner city residents, their collective story is not a bleak tale of deprivation and disadvantage. It is not that they want for nothing: all of them work hard to make ends meet and can remember times when every day life was too much to cope with. But most of them get by well enough, and as they see it, the inner city setting offers as full a range of possibilities for a decent life as any other.
>
> (Wallman 1984: 3)

This is not sentimentality or wishful thinking at work: in even the most dire circumstances these 'best view' perspectives are entirely practical. They match the strategy of Lancelot Brown who tackled the bleakest landscape by asking himself 'What are its capabilities?' In the anthropological version of the strategy, capability is approached by a succession of common-sense questions designed to fill in the essential details of the picture, which is to say that we set out to define and map the significant context of the problem or the person or the place in focus.

IV

Again, the first assumption of this approach is that every setting has capabilities, however limited. The second point is that capability is context-specific. To assess one we need to understand the other. So what needs to be said about context? According to Webster's dictionary, context is two things. It is: '*The whole situation, background or environment relevant to some happening or personality.*' And it is '*That which comes before and after an item or event or word and gives it its meaning.*'

These definitions imply most importantly that *context is a coherent whole.* It is defined from a centre; it covers whatever is logically connected to that centre. Hidden in this is the fact that the boundaries of context are arbitrary, *ad hoc*, impermanent. They are defined by the logic of the (whole) situation, because it is only that logic which connects the [constituent] parts of a context to its centre, and which ensures the coherence of the whole. Not by coincidence, two quotes from the great gardener say the same thing: 'The whole should correspond together.' And: 'Nothing can be more truly beautiful than the bird's eye assemblage of objects' (Hadfield 1985: 183).

The second element of the dictionary definition is that *context is in process.* It is a sequence of events in time. We cannot understand the meaning of a social item or event unless we know what happened before and after it. This too is echoed by Brown's poetic judgement of a landscape: 'The view is beheld with a moving variation' (Hadfield 1985: 215).

Anthropology is distinguished from other social sciences by a package of perspectives in which the notion of context is essential. Its presence shows itself in the way we tend to 'explain' relationships or attitudes or social events by looking for their connections with other-things-happening in a defined analytic whole.

The main difficulty is that the appropriate scope of the whole system in which those other things are happening is not empirically obvious. It is not only that the boundaries of a context have to be arbitrarily drawn, it is also necessary to decide which context – or which level of context – is most relevant to making sense of the matter in hand. Given the multipurpose flexibility of the context notion and the general untidiness of ordinary life, it is easy to fail for lack of decision. How can we use context as a unit of study if we don't know what it is and where it ends? I identify very readily with the small girl who says she knows how to spell 'banana' but she doesn't know when to stop! The classic anthropological version of the dilemma was described (and illustrated!) by Ernest Gellner in the essay 'Concepts and Society' (1973). His essay is especially cogent to this discussion because it illustrates both the contextual reasoning of early anthropologists trying to redraw the representation of 'primitive others' that the political context of the time imposed on them, and the unintended consequences of their revision.

The other difficulty, mooted at the beginning of this chapter, is that analytic frames remain opaque and personal if they cannot be communicated – whether among anthropologists or between disciplines. Private visions do not qualify as science and are not useful in application. It is communication of the vision that makes it workable. Context therefore has to be explicitly defined and plainly visualised so that each of us can know which dimensions of the mess of social reality the other has in focus.

Definition of context is not difficult once both the need to bound it and the arbitrariness of the boundary have been acknowledged. But what about the need to communicate what has been visualised? How should we set about representing a multidimensional whole on a flat page? Is it possible to convey what one anthropologist/film-maker has called the 'all at once-ness' of social life, even by using film in the way she recommends (Freudenthal 1988)? The complexity stretches our professional capacity for appropriate response. Again, 'Capability' Brown provides a useful model. Just as his professional status depended on the efficient application of a systematic formula of work, so it must be with the professional credibility of anthropologists. I stress that it is 'Capability's' *approach* that is valuable. His assumptions about landscape are now largely outmoded, and in the light of today's concerns there is no reason for us to *like* what one writer has called 'the destruction that he wrought before he created' (Hadfield 1985: 213). Certainly we should not copy it. It is his ability to decide priorities, recognise capabilities, visualise outcomes that we can usefully emulate.

My point is that it is not possible to unravel the complexity of social life without making explicit analytic decisions about context. Nor is it appropriate. These days to say that 'social context counts' is only to state a well-known fact. What the 'real world' wants to know is *how* it counts? Which aspects count when? Do they count equally in every setting? What are the key elements needed to understand this piece of behaviour? To solve this problem? To ameliorate this or that crisis?

The next sections demonstrate a capability approach to these questions by sketching two items of recent work. The first is concerned to account for the responses of different areas and different kinds of individual to the crisis of job loss in Europe; the second to identify and (ultimately) to enhance community capacity to cope with the HIV/AIDS epidemic in Africa. In each case it has been necessary to make more or less arbitrary decisions:

1 to distinguish which domain or type of context is in focus at each stage of analysis;
2 to delimit its boundary so that a finite system can be visualised;
3 to define the dimensions of it most crucial to the problem in hand.

V

The first example comes from a paper published under the title 'Time, Identity and the Experience of Work' (Wallman 1990). In the terms of this discussion, it set out to account for different capacities to adapt to changes brought by unemployment. My argument was that, financial implications apart, the experience of employment or unemployment is governed by the patterns of time and identity investment that each job or no-job situation entails. The members of an occupational group are not entirely alike in any respect, and there are important comparisons to be made amongst individuals whose objective financial circumstances are similar.

I based the argument on an intuited vision of identity in industrial society being dominated by reference to three domains: local community or place; ethnic or family origin; and work (in the narrow sense of occupation or employment). It seemed to me possible that the identity strength of each depends on the identity strength of the others. If this is so, then more self-investment in work means less self-investment in the family; more localism means less consciousness of ethnicity as such; and more of either of these last two means less social or psychological dependence on the job, and maybe, by extension, less pain in the event of job bereavement or unemployment.

In every case a person will shift identity investment from one context to the other according to the capabilities and constraints of circumstance. In ideal or 'best case' circumstances, time and identity resources are diffused across the three vital domains – occupation, domestic group and local community, as sketched in Figure 15.1. If one of those domains falls away, the self which was invested in it is readily translated into another domain. When, for example, a person becomes unemployed, the time and identity previously spent on occupation can be redistributed across family or local community interests. The shift is feasible because this individual is already rooted in the other domains; and the reinvestment is safe because the other domains are sufficiently distinct from occupation to be unaffected by the job loss as such. This is the *high capability* mode.

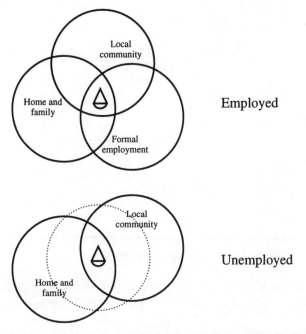

Employed

Unemployed

Figure 15.1 'High capability'. Time and identity diffused across livelihood

Figure 15.2, by contrast, visualises time and identity investment in mining, dockland and single-industry communities, and then the disaster brought about by the collapse of the industry concerned (see, classically, Jahoda *et al.* 1972). The crucial points in this case are that the occupational domain is/has been dominated by one industry; and that some combination of tradition, infrastructure and the technology of that industry has caused the three domains to be closely overlaid. In traditional docklands, for example, men who worked together lived as neighbours within walking distance of their employment, and even the social life of their wives was focused around the concerns of the docks. The effect of generations of this pattern was to tie dockers to each other by employment, locality *and* kinship – whether directly as brothers and cousins, or indirectly through the links of their wives and children – and to create a tightly bounded, locally distinct and fiercely conservative occupational group. In these circumstances, the collapse of the employment base is experienced as the destruction of community and continuity at a blow. This, in the same crisis of job loss, is the *low capability* mode.

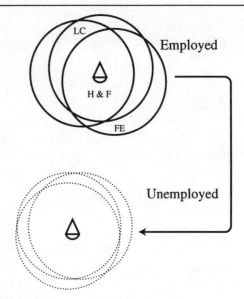

Figure 15.2 'Low capability I'. Miners, dockers, Marienthal

Figure 15.3 is an addendum which makes a similar but different point. While the last figure shows what can happen when a community is dominated by one industry, this one shows individuals monopolised by a single domain. The subtitle of the paper was a question: 'What do housewives and chief executives have in common?' My answer is that stereotypical housewives are 'only' involved in family matters, and workaholic chief executives are 'entirely' obsessed by their jobs – each at the cost of neglecting other domains. Deprived of the monopolising context – the housewife when her children grow up and leave home, the executive when illness or redundancy lays him off – each will have lost the locus of time and identity that had underpinned the sense of self.

The inference is that each of the three domains is vital to the composite identity structure of the individual. Too narrow a focus of time or self therefore creates other problems. Where overidentification with one domain occurs it is diagnosed as pathology. 'Workaholics' are, by definition, too closely identified with their employment. In popular as well as clinical expectation, therefore, they are bound to be neglecting other obligations and are probably suffering from stress – obviously a *low capability* mode. The healthy balance would seem to be a spread of identity – of time and the self – across all of livelihood so that each domain, each vital context, gets and gives its due. This, by contrast, is the *high capability* mode.

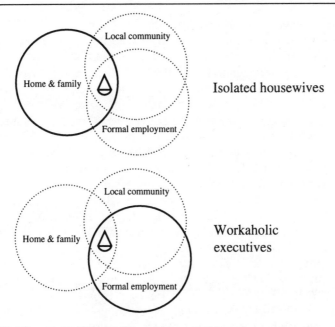

Figure 15.3 'Low capability II'. The self invested in only one domain

VI

In the employment crisis example, the domains of context in focus were defined as local community, occupation and home or family; and variations in the capability of each system to cope with unemployment were explained by the different investments of time and identity in each of them. In this second example, pursuing the same strategy in the AIDS circumstance, the untidiness of social life is sorted into four other domains, so that the system can begin to be defined, and we can hope eventually to identify the variables and interconnections that account for a higher or lower capability to deal with a disastrous epidemic. You will notice that the terms used and the shapes presented are different, but that the logic of the landscape gardener is still in force.

The images illustrating the analytic reasoning used in this case were developed in an effort to communicate appropriate anthropological perspectives to a necessarily sceptical biomedical audience at the Stockholm International AIDS Congress in 1988. Even before the conference, the medical research specialists must have been aware that a contextual inference underpins any effort to understand and control HIV disease. Implicitly at least, we all know that every estimate for the spread of HIV/AIDS, and every public education programme designed to stop it, is based on assumptions about social context. The medics were also – like the rest of us – aware that context unstructured is a chaotic mess, and that scientific comparison demands explicit definition of the items to be compared. Moreover, underlining the problems of representation discussed in Section I, their experience of social science is apt to have been limited to the extreme ends of a continuum strung between the very obvious and the totally obscure. To be capable of making a contribution in this setting therefore, a practitioner anthropologist has no choice but to make some arbitrary and explicit decisions directed towards visualising the complexity, which 'everybody' acknowledges, in a form that simplifies the point without misrepresenting the reality.

In that period, and probably only in the northern hemisphere, the most commonly visualised metaphor for AIDS was an iceberg. In those specific contexts of time and place, it could represent the fact that a large proportion of HIV infections are not only invisible, but dangerous because they are invisible. It is not clear whether the 'experts' imposed this representation on the public, or whether they simply appropriated, relabelled and fed back an image already compatible with local praxis (cf. Paine 1989, 1992). Most likely both processes were at work: all communication depends on some kind of synergy between sender's and receiver's representations, even when an exchange is flawed by misunderstanding and brings results that neither party anticipated (as in Sachs 1989).

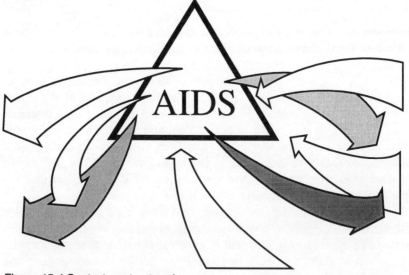

Figure 15.4 Context unstructured

Whatever the antecedent conditions of the AIDS-as-iceberg representation, I built on it by visualising the ocean around the iceberg as the context of the epidemic, with something in the water – sharks perhaps? – to stand for the social factors affecting it (Figure 15.4). I then structured the chaos of context – now readily represented by the random movement of the sharks in the water – around four kinds of concern. Each defines a domain or subset of the social whole. The four subsets are (1) national institutions and resources; (2) local organisation and social process; (3) custom and practice affecting the body; and (4) prevailing opinions and attitudes of mind (Figure 15.5). Somewhat less arbitrarily, the figure also shows a two-way relationship between social context and the AIDS pandemic. The outward arrows indicate the impact of AIDS on society, and the inward arrows the effects of society on AIDS itself. The two flows are not so readily distinguished in real life, but it makes sense to talk as if they were. Figure 15.6 visualises the outward set, to indicate that the impact of AIDS depends on the social-cultural setting in which it occurs. Figure 15.7 narrows the focus to concentrate the viewer's eye on one of the four domains designated. The point to be made is that AIDS has a general impact on social life, but will have a different (*and researchable*) specific significance in each domain. The essential reverse of the same logic could be shown just by reversing the direction of the arrow; i.e. the characteristics of the 'body' domain in a particular social-cultural setting (sexual practices, ritual practices) affect the prevalence, incidence, management, etc. of the disease.

It needs to be emphasised that these visualisings worked well with respect to communicating an anthropological approach to biomedical

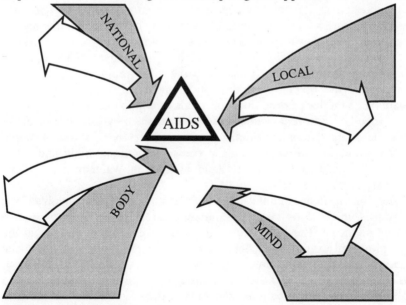

Figure 15.5 Context structured

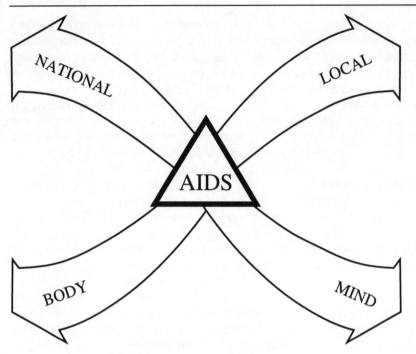

Figure 15.6 The impact of AIDS on society and culture

specialists. I am proud to say that the full set of images, with its argument, was published in the medical *Journal of Acquired Immune Deficiency Syndrome* shortly after the conference (Wallman 1988). But the second tranche of reasoning in this AIDS-related example has to narrow down to *local* and *body* domains as lead-lines into the context of the capacity of particular communities to deal with the AIDS epidemic as it affects them. Once the objective of the job in hand shifts to understanding capability at the local level, different kinds of context have to be brought into focus, and different 'whole' systems need to be visualised. In effect the iceberg image now moves off-screen, relegated to the status of simple starting point for the complicated processes of ethnographic and other kinds of enquiry in the various field areas (see Wallman *et al.* 1992; Wallman 1996).

While in the first example the principal other discipline involved was economics, in these by far the dominant interest comes from allopathic or 'bio'-medicine. The general objectives, however, are the same as in the unemployment example – to achieve a better understanding of the social landscape, to determine how and how far that landscape can adapt to crisis or rapid change and then to communicate this understanding to the other discipline and/or to non-academics with a significant interest in it. But the specific objectives of AIDS-related research are more directly interventionist. They are to enhance community and individual capacity to cope with the effects of the epidemic, and to build on local capabilities for preventing the further spread of HIV and other sexually transmitted diseases.

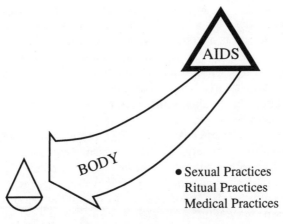

Figure 15.7 The impact of AIDS on the domain of body

The first aim is provoked by the fact that studies of coping in the face of crisis are most often focused on economic and demographic effects. Even in AIDS research there has been rather little reference to other health issues, or to questions of community identity and morale. Clearly a 'capability' study will need to document and monitor the impact of the epidemic on labour supply and economic performance at the local level, but it must also deal with the fact that the idea and fear of AIDS may themselves provoke crisis by blighting the capability the local community once had. Many studies have shown that morale is crucial to the ability to respond to new dangers and demands (Raphael 1986). In this light, any effort to help will only be capacity-enhancing if it can build up *affective* as well as economic support systems. This is only to say again that capability is context-dependent and that context has many dimensions.

Addressing the second objective – the prevention of HIV – we need to apprehend the dimensions of context that affect what health professionals define as 'risky' sex, so that more effective HIV prevention may be designed. The 'riskiness' of sex, for these purposes, increases in the following circumstances:

1 sex with many partners;
2 sex with an infected person;
3 special sexual or body practices;
4 sexual debut before maturity;
5 sexual intercourse when other STD is present.

At first sight the focus of interdisciplinary research into the prevention of any sexually transmitted disease, HIV included, might seem to be in the area narrowly defined as sexual behaviour. But apart from the special difficulties of asking questions about sex, we cannot assume that we know which aspects of life are or should be included under the 'sexual behaviour' or even the 'sexual attitudes and behaviour' rubric. In terms of STD/HIV, sexual behaviour is about body contact and physical practice. In terms of real life and prevention it is about family, local organisation, morality, cosmology, opportunity, economics, treatment options and risk assessment. Here clearly both action and the meaning of action depend on other things happening, other priorities, obligations, opportunities, expectations and worries.

The scope of *appropriate* AIDS research therefore has to be wider than sexual behaviour in general or risky sex in particular, even when the objective is to illuminate a very specific set of problems. Just as research into medical co-factors requires that HIV is examined in the full context of general health, so the understanding of sexual behaviour demands that the specifics of it are studied in their socio-cultural context. A first step in thinking or talking about it is achieved by putting the medical and social domains of context together and visualising them as a single system (Figure 15.8). Next we can proceed to identify the combinations of variables that account for a greater or lesser capability to prevent the spread of HIV.

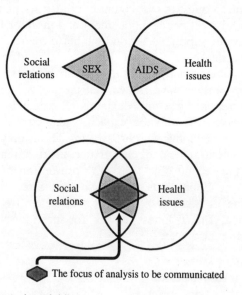

The focus of analysis to be communicated

Figure 15.8 Contexts 'overlaid'

VII

But we are stuck with the fact that social variables do not sit still; the context is always in process. Just as we begin to understand a community's capacity to cope with AIDS or unemployment or crisis change, the change in focus will itself have altered that capacity by generating institutions and attitudes to replace the ones that sustained its original form (as Barth 1966). In this sense appropriate anthropology cannot aspire to once-and-for-all answers: it is the courage to formulate questions that is the *high capability* mode for social research.

I said at the start that I proposed this chapter's title on the basis of inexpert knowledge of the work of 'Capability' Brown. At this point I want to underline two useful errors – one Brown's and one mine – that were revealed in the course of preparing the text to fit it. They are useful because, in spoiling the tidy case I had intended to present, they suggested deeper and, I think, more significant analogies. Putting a positive gloss on it, I could say that the inspiration of 'Capability' Brown goes even further in this arena than I originally supposed.

Brown's error was that, in setting out to unleash the 'natural' capability of landscapes, he imposed a stereotyped notion of 'nature' that was ultimately no more free than the 'unnatural' constraints it replaced. My error was in allowing myself to be so impressed by the practical and horticultural aspects of gardens and gardeners – about which I know little – that I originally neglected to think about the effect of social and political contexts on definitions of capability itself – a subject about which any social scientist might be expected to know a lot.

I shall finish with one cautionary comment and three rules of thumb. The cautionary comment is this: images of the natural, original or traditional forms of gardens and cultures are structured by past experience, present prejudice, and future purpose. Similarly, the dimensions of capability or capacity, like those of landscapes and social systems, are thrown into relief by contrasts which are in vogue when the selection is made. Thus the representations of 'Capability' Brown make excellent sense as reactions to the 'excesses of constraint' put upon landscape by his predecessors, and as expressions of the politics of the time. The fact that his detractors now accuse him of imposing a stereotyped view of nature on the properties of his happy clients only confirms that the contrasts in the picture have changed. It is no less true of anthropologists trying to contribute appropriately in the arena of contemporary issues. Our visions – whether defined as models, representations or images – are sharpened by contrast to other disciplines and other political climates. But if we define ourselves too narrowly in opposition to what others see and do, we are as prone to falling over backwards as was the great gardener himself. Once-and-for-all answers are not our business.

Allow me one last example: The imposition of *our* views on *them* is neither politically nor professionally acceptable in this era – whether 'we' are the employed and 'they' the unemployed, or 'we' the rich Euro-Americans and 'they' the poor Africans. Nor should it be. But we must be careful of freezing *their* views in *our* version of their traditions, of locking them into a vision that is no longer appropriate because the contexts of their lives are now significantly different. We do so out of respect for culture of course, but sometimes we forget that culture, like nature, changes.

Finally, the three rules of thumb: *One*: Accept that single-stranded explanations can only tell a very partial story. Unemployment is not only about money; HIV is not only about sex. Whatever the item in focus, it is only made intelligible in the context of other things happening around it. *Two*: Assess the system's capabilities in tandem with its limitations. Resist the temptation to deny one and exaggerate the other. It is true *both* that people blighted by unemployment or epidemic have choices to make, *and* that context determines the options available and sensible at the time. And *three*: Learn to live with the limits to professional capability. Social systems are constantly in process and yet may take ages to change. Because they are complex we are not able to visualise the best outcome in detail, and we cannot be confident that it will be wholly appropriate when it occurs.

In these respects 'Capability' Brown had an edge on the rest of us. He was confident that he could visualise the effect of his work, and – more fortunate still – given his field, he had better reason than we do to expect that the outcome of his effort would be beautiful.

REFERENCES

Barnett, A. and P. Blaikie (1994) 'On Ignoring the Wider Picture: AIDS Research and the Jobbing Social Scientist', in D. Booth (ed.), *Rethinking Social Development*, Harlow: Longman Scientific and Technical.

Barth, F. (1966) *Models of Social Organisation*, Royal Anthropological Institute Occasional Papers No. 23, London.

Firth, R. (1972) *The Sceptical Anthropologist? Social Anthropology and Marxist Views on Society*, Proceedings of the British Academy, LVIII, London: Oxford University Press.

Frank, A. G. (1969) *Latin America: Underdevelopment or Revolution?* New York: Monthly Review Press.

Freudenthal, S. (1988) 'What to Tell and How to Show it: Issues in Anthropological Filmmaking', in J. R. Rollwagen (ed.), *Anthropological Filmmaking*, Chur: Harwood Academic Publishers.

Gellner, E. (1973) 'Concepts and Society', in I. C. Jarvie and J. Agassi (eds), *Cause and Meaning in the Social Sciences*, London: Routledge & Kegan Paul.

Gluckman, M. (ed.) (1964) *Closed Systems and Open Minds: The Limits of Naivety in Social Anthropology*, Edinburgh: Oliver Boyd.

Hadfield, M. (1985) *A History of British Gardening*, Harmondsworth: Penguin.

Jahoda, M., P. L. Lazarsfeld and H. Zeisel (1972) *Marienthal: The Sociography of an Unemployed Community*, London: Tavistock.

Moscovici, S. (1987) 'Answers and Questions', *Journal of the Theory of Social Behaviour*, 17 (4): 513–29.

Paine, R. (1989) 'Making the Invisible "Visible": Coming to Terms with Chernobyl and its Experts, a Saami Illustration', *International Journal of Moral and Social Studies*, 4 (2): 39–62.

—— (1992) ' "Chernobyl" Reaches Norway: The Accident, Science, and the Threat to Cultural Knowledge', *Journal of Public Understanding of Science*, 1: 261–80.

Raphael, B. (1986) *When Disaster Strikes*, New York: Basic Books.

Rodney, W. (1972) *How Europe Underdeveloped Africa*, London: Bogle-l'Ouverture.

Sachs, L. (1989) 'Misunderstanding as Therapy: Doctors, Patients and Medicine in a Rural Clinic in Sri Lanka', *Culture, Medicine & Psychiatry*, 13: 335–49.

Valentine, C. (1968) *The Culture of Poverty: Critique and Counter Proposals*, Chicago: University of Chicago Press.

Wallman, S. (1977) 'Introduction', in S. Wallman (ed.), *Perceptions of Development*, Cambridge: Cambridge University Press.

—— (1984) *Eight London Households*, London: Tavistock.

—— (1988) 'Sex and Death: The AIDS Crisis in Social and Cultural Context', *Journal of Acquired Immune Deficiency Syndromes (AIDS)*, 1: 571–8.

—— (1990) 'Time, Identity and the Experience of Work', in F. Bovenkerk *et al.* (eds), *Wetenschap en Partijdigheid*, Assen: Van Gorcum.

—— (with K. Kalumba, I. Krantz, and L. Sachs (1992) 'Plan for Field Research in Rural Zambia', *Community Capacity to Prevent, Manage and Survive HIV/AIDS*, Working Paper No. 1, Stockholm/Hull/Lusaka: IHCAR, Karolinska Institute.

—— (1996) *Kampala Women Getting By: Wellbeing in the Time of AIDS*, London: James Currey/ Ohio University Press/Fountain Publishers/ EAEP.

Name index

Subject index

Aboriginal land claims 7, 122–41
accountability 6, 161
action, ethnographic writing and
    culture in 16, 24–6, 32
Africa: Congo 46; HIV/AIDS 246, 247,
    252, 255–61, 262
agency 6, 16, 20, 108, 110
AIDS, in Africa 246, 247, 252, 255–61,
    262
Alawa 7, 122–41
alterity, anthropology and 5, 34–48
ambiguity, in anthropological account
    184
Amer-Indians 208
American Anthropological
    Association 87
ancestors, Alawa 122, 129, 132–4,
    138–40
anthropological account see
    ethnographic writing
anthropologist: as expert 67n4, 123,
    233–6; as part of self-representation
    in Japan 144, 146, 147–8, 156–7, 158
applied anthropology 3, 12–13; for
    postmodern era 244–62
appropriation 7, 13; cultural 7, 196,
    203–5
Association for Scottish Ethnography
    98n1
Association of Social Anthropologists,
    conference (1984) 34
Australian landscape 7, 122–41
authorial style 3, 10–11
authority 1, 5–6, 14, 31–2, 161
auto-anthropology (Strathern) 161–2,
    171
auto-ethnography 94
Azande witchcraft 71, 128

Banjar 19
biculturalism 213
Borneo 18–21, 27–30, 31, 32
Bosnian Gypsies 239–40, 241
boundary-making 97

capacity 244–62
caste 9, 103–19
Celts 92, 93
ceremony see ritual practice
Chagga 184–5
Christianity, as first modernist project
    36–8
collective representation 8–10, 244;
    family 54
colonialism 249; and anthropology 36;
    Australia 122, 123, 130, 137; Gypsy
    fictive leaders 232; India 103–19; and
    Maori identity 8, 209, 215
communication 244–62; failure of
    26–7, 32
conception affiliation, N. Australia
    136–7
conflict management 19
Congo 46
context 244–62
conversation, culture and
    representation as 11, 89, 177–91
Cripps enquiry into Gypsies 234, 235
crofting, Scotland 92–3, 96
cross-cultural storytelling (Tsing) 28
cross-cultural translation see
    translation
cultural appropriation, Japan 7, 196,
    203–5
cultural fundamentalism (Stolcke) 88
cultural process, conversation as 177–9,
    180–1

SOAS LIBRARY